Minority Faiths
AND THE
American Protestant Mainstream

Minority Faiths
AND THE
American Protestant Mainstream

Edited by

JONATHAN D. SARNA

UNIVERSITY OF ILLINOIS PRESS
Urbana and Chicago

The publisher gratefully acknowledges the contribution provided
by The Pew Charitable Trusts.

© 1998 by the Board of Trustees of the University of Illinois
Manufactured in the United States of America
1   2   3   4   5   C   P   5   4   3   2   1

This book is printed on acid-free paper.

Library of Congress Cataloging-in-Publication Data

Minority faiths and the American Protestant mainstream / edited by
Jonathan D. Sarna.
    p.   cm.
Includes bibliographical references and index.
ISBN 0-252-02293-9 (alk. paper). — ISBN 0-252-06647-2 (pbk. : alk. paper)
    1. Protestant churches—United States—Influence. 2. United States—Religion.
3. Christian sects—United States. 4. Religious pluralism—United States.
I. Sarna, Jonathan D.
BR516.5.M56   1998
200'.937—dc21   97-4617
                                                               CIP

To my in-laws, James S. and Elinor G. A. Langer,
with admiration and love

Contents

Acknowledgments

This volume seeks to broaden understanding of American religion by exploring how minority faiths confronted, often in diverse and creative ways, the multitudinous challenges posed to them by the American Protestant mainstream. Minority faiths appear all too often in the literature only as victims of history, acted upon by the majority. Here they emerge as historical actors in their own right, operating within a comparative—and competitive—religious setting.

The Pew Charitable Trusts sponsored this project as part of its Religion Program, then under the able direction of Joel A. Carpenter. Pew's generous and enthusiastic support made possible what proved to be an extraordinary scholarly collaboration. It was my good fortune, in planning and executing this project, to be able to work with a research team that included Edwin Gaustad, David O'Brien, and, for a time, Albert Raboteau. I learned much from interacting with these generous scholars and greatly appreciated their guidance. William R. Hutchison also joined us for one of our meetings and provided sage counsel as well as invaluable insights.

Institutionally, the Lown School of Near Eastern and Judaic Studies at Brandeis University, where I teach, cooperated on this project with the Department of History of the College of the Holy Cross, the home institution of David O'Brien. Both schools benefited from this partnership, which has now been cemented through the establishment of linked Kraft-Hiatt professorships at both institutions. Brandeis's strength in American Jewish history and Holy Cross's in American Catholic history made this project a particularly fertile ground for collaborative endeavor. Our contributors and research team met on both campuses, and we are grateful to the many individuals who worked hard to make the long, arduous meetings a success.

The contributors to this volume deserve special thanks for their willingness to move beyond their fields of expertise and for agreeing to revise their chapters, sometimes several times over. All of the contributors read and commented upon earlier drafts of each chapter, and drafts of the whole volume were subsequently reviewed by the research team and by outside readers. My friend and collaborator in other projects, Ellen Smith, curator of the American Jewish Historical Society, offered a particularly searching critique of our penultimate draft, and the present volume is infinitely better for her efforts. Two readers for the University of Illinois Press also made significant suggestions that redounded to our benefit. As always, I thank my wife, Ruth Langer, and my children, Aaron and Leah Sarna, for their forbearance.

Minority Faiths
AND THE
American Protestant Mainstream

The Interplay of Minority and Majority in American Religion

JONATHAN D. SARNA

Sometime in 1903 or 1904 the great Talmudic scholar Rabbi Jacob David Willowski of Slutsk (1845–1913), then serving a brief and contentious term as chief rabbi of Chicago, took time from his studies to write, in Hebrew, a lengthy disquisition on the state of Judaism in America. "Jews were exiled to the United States, a land blessed with prosperity," he began. "Here they prospered and won respect from the people. But the ways and customs of this land militate against the observance of the laws of the Torah and the Jewish way of life." First and foremost, he complained, the state requires young Jews to attend public school with non-Jewish children, "boys and girls together." A young person who "spends most of his days in the public school," he warned, "learns the ways of the gentiles and becomes estranged from Judaism." He also condemned the "difficulty of observing the holy Sabbath" in America; the "absolute idolatry" of "keeping Sunday as the day of Sabbath rest"; the widespread violations of Jewish dietary laws (kashrut) and marital laws; and even the "great evil" caused by "freedom of the press," which permitted "wicked men" to establish periodicals that vilified God, Torah, and religious scholars, all with impunity. In the end, he offered a suggestion based upon what he had learned from Jews' Catholic neighbors in Chicago. He urged Jews to establish Jewish schools where Jewish boys could learn Torah as well as secular subjects. "The Poles who came to this country did this," he observed, "establishing schools in their churches to prevent the corruption of their faith. Why," he wondered, "should we not do the same for our children?"[1]

Willowski's jeremiad points to significant issues in American religious history that merit close attention. First, his concern was for the survival of his own minority faith in the face of overwhelming majority pressure to assimilate. American Judaism, he understood, did not operate in its own little world, cut off from the Protestant mainstream; it was instead in constant and ongoing tension with "the ways and customs of this land" that threatened its continuity. As for American religion, it appears from his account to be dynamic and contentious, a battle-ground of clashing cultures and minority faiths struggling to maintain their separateness in a "land blessed with prosperity." Assimilation and accommodation, central themes to historians of American religion, were anathema to Willowski. He emphasized resistance to the main-stream instead.

Second, Willowski's comments underscore the significance of edu-cation as a focal point of religious and cultural contention. Defenders of the faith worried, and not without reason, that public schools would imbue their children with the values of the mainstream, leading them to become "estranged" from their parents and cultural heritage. At a time when the majority of Americans (including most Jews) celebrat-ed public schools as vehicles for imbuing children with "American values," minorities, akin to Willowski, posed disturbing questions con-cerning the compatability of nonsectarian public education with the goal of minority faith preservation.

Finally, Willowski's disquisition demonstrates that even those most resistant to cultural domination recognized that they were not swim-ming all alone against the tide. They saw themselves, instead, as part of a community of "religious outsiders" and understood that they had much to gain from observing those swimming beside them who shared parallel goals. Just as Polish-Catholic parochial schools captured Rabbi Willowski's imagination, so too in many other cases members of mi-nority faiths selectively borrowed survival strategies learned from their neighbors. The desire "to prevent the corruption of their faith" was a goal that even those who disagreed mightily with one another could all rally around.

This dynamic relationship between minority outsiders and majori-ty insiders features all too rarely in the historiography of American religion. Early historians of American religion, such as Robert Baird, whose *Religion in America* appeared in 1843, were so stridently Prot-estant in orientation that non-Protestants barely intruded into their histories at all. Later scholars broadened their definition of American religion, but the history and development of American Protestantism continued to dominate their narratives. Indeed, the "Protestant synthe-sis" reigned supreme for much of the twentieth century. As late as 1972, Sydney Ahlstrom was still complaining that "the overwhelming con-cern" among the "new generation" of American religious historians, his contemporaries, "continued to be the rise and development of the Protestant tradition."[2] Non-Protestants, when they appeared at all, figured either as objects of history, missionized and influenced by the

Protestant majority, or alone in short chapters that isolated them from the main story of American religion, to which they formed something of a sideshow.

More recently, as R. Laurence Moore has observed, historians of American religion have begun to pay closer attention "to the persistence of sectarian feelings, to the apparent permanence of division, to the everlasting ability of strange, new religions to attract a following."[3] Catherine Albanese has stressed "the manyness of religions in America" beginning even before the colonial period with "Original Manyness: Native American Traditions."[4] Robert N. Bellah and Frederick E. Greenspahn's volume on "interreligious hostility in America" probed tensions between Jews and Christians, Protestants and Catholics, liberals and conservatives, and established churches and emerging ones.[5] Finally, in a widely noticed book, Moore himself argued that religious outsiders—he focused on Mormons, Catholics, Jews, Christian Scientists, millennialists, Protestant fundamentalists, and black Protestants—"have been an indispensably dynamic force in American religious history," giving "energy to church life and substance to the claim that Americans are the most religious people on the face of the earth."[6]

These and related studies since the 1970s have broadened the canvas of American religion, teaching us much and illuminating some of the multitudinous ways that minority faiths (like minority groups generally) have contributed to American life. But they paid scant attention to the theme that has dominated minority faith history in the United States, a theme that was, and remains, central to the religious experience of millions of Americans. That theme is the dynamic encounter between minority outsiders and majority insiders in American religion; the tensions, both individual and denominational, between pressures to conform to the religious patterns of the mainstream; and countervailing pressures, applied by individuals such as Rabbi Willowski, to resist them and remain apart.

The word *encounter*—familiar to students of Native American and immigrant history—underscores the importance of treating minority group members as historical actors in their own right rather than just as victims of history acted upon by the majority.[7] Instead of looking again at prejudicial attitudes that scores of works have already documented, we need to examine the broader relationship between America's minority and majority faiths. How, for example, did minority faiths respond to majority challenges? How did they succeed, socially, politically, and culturally, in maintaining their outsider status, passing it on to their children, and even in converting others from inside to outside? How, in time, did they transform America itself? Much of the drama of American religious history unfolds through the answers to questions like these. Minority-majority encounters represent a source of contention and pain, to be sure, yet also, as the chapters in this volume demonstrate, a stimulus for wondrous creativity.

The chapters that follow describe scenes from this great and continuing drama. The focus is on a critical period in the history of American religion, roughly from 1860 to 1920. The population more than tripled during these years, from 31.4 million to 106 million, and Americans spread out across the length and breadth of the country, filling in the frontier. Immigrants—almost thirty million of them—contributed heavily to both of these trends, and many immigrants, including Catholics, Jews, Mennonites, and Eastern Orthodox, adhered to faiths palpably different from those of the Protestant mainstream. Minority faiths that originated on the American scene likewise captured growing numbers of adherents at this time, including Mormonism, African American churches, and Christian Science. Meanwhile, the denominational families that constituted the Protestant mainstream—Congregationalists, Episcopalians, Presbyterians, Baptists, Methodists (white divisions only), and later the Disciples of Christ and many Lutherans—were losing ground. Although accurate statistics are hard to come by, William R. Hutchison estimates that these denominations, once home to the majority of Americans, represented by the early years of the twentieth century only "a minority of the population."[8] The America that this erstwhile majority had known was rapidly changing, becoming ever more religiously and ethnicly pluralistic; by 1920 the old dream of forging a Protestant America was effectively dead. Mainstream Protestants continued, nevertheless, to constitute the establishment in American religion, filling positions of power and authority and exercising enormous influence in public life.

In addition to this establishment, the dramatis personae of this study include Jews, Catholics, Mormons, members of African American churches, and Protestant immigrants. Some of the most significant minority-majority interactions in American religious history involved these players. To do full justice to minority faiths, of course, our cast should have been a great deal larger. "By the beginning of the twentieth century," J. Gordon Melton reports, "some two hundred different religious bodies representing sixteen different denominational families" could be found in the United States.[9] Native American, Asian, Eastern Orthodox, Islamic, Adventist, Christian Science, spiritualist, and many additional American religious communities experienced encounters with the Protestant mainstream and developed strategies for preserving separate identities under its shadow. How closely their experiences paralleled those of the faiths considered here remains to be determined. Still, the accounts in this volume represent, at the very least, significant case studies—reflecting if not the full range of responses to mainstream Protestant challenges then certainly a wide range.

The first half of this book focuses on the survival strategies of America's largest and best-known minority faiths. Each chapter illumines the others, for strategies employed by one faith turn out to apply much more widely and parallels abound. Benny Kraut makes this clear in an analysis of "Jewish Survival in Protestant America." Observing that Jews ("the quintessential survivalists of world history") have more historical experience in being a minority than any other American faith, he uncovers "four broad strategies of survival" that have shaped Jewish communal relationships with the Protestant mainstream and promoted Jewish religious preservation: migration and mobility, development of a communal infrastructure, selective adaptation, and communal defense. Not even one of these strategies, he admits, is "inherently Jewish. . . . other groups . . . adopted some or all of them within their own experiences." Indeed, each of the minority faiths portrayed in this volume has employed at least one of these strategies to advantage; several, over the course of their history, have used all four.

Catholics, by far the largest religious minority in the United States, focused primarily on the issue of adaptation. That proved controversial. "By 1800," Jay Dolan observes in "Catholicism and American Culture," "it was clear that Catholics in the United States were supporting two different and competing understandings of Roman Catholicism. One encouraged the idea of the adaptation of religion to the American cultural environment; the other sought to transplant intact to the United States the European model of Catholicism." Supporters of both strategies considered theirs the key to developing and strengthening Catholicism in the United States. In one sense, the Catholic debate is a local variant on an enduring problem within Christendom that H. Richard Niebuhr characterized in *Christ and Culture* (1951) as "the double wrestle of the church with its Lord and with the cultural society with which it lives."[10] But the debate also reflects more than this, for it represents a fundamental tension—between accommodation and resistance, between absorption and retention, and between assimilation and identity—that is characteristic of all groups that seek simultaneously to be part of and yet apart from the dominant culture. The enduring Catholic struggle that Dolan portrays thus has its counterpart in the history of every American minority faith. Each in its own way struggles with the painful need to draw boundaries that both include and exclude.

The three remaining chapters in Part 1 focus on the strategies that

Kraut characterized as migration, mobility, and the development of a communal infrastructure. Mormons, Protestant immigrants, and African Americans, in different ways and for different reasons, sought to preserve their faiths and cultures by moving and living apart from the mainstream. Reprising a classic religious pattern, they set forth into the wilderness in search of a Promised Land, an enclave. They hoped to find refuge from persecution and the security to follow the dictates of their faith without being encumbered.

Mormons offer a prime example. Unlike so many other American religious minorities, they did not start out as religious outsiders, nor were they ethnically distinct. To the contrary, Mormonism emerged in the early nineteenth century from the ranks of religious insiders caught up in the wave of religious enthusiasm that swept through western New York state. Some incipient Latter-day Saints, Jan Shipps shows in "Mormonism and the American Religious Mainstream," actually "had difficulty in differentiating themselves from other Christians operating in the field at the same time." Even where they were "different," she argues, they were not yet wholly "other." Yet partly through their own actions and partly through those of their oppressors, Mormons soon metamorphosed into a religious minority; they became outsiders. They moved west, departing U.S. territory to escape religious persecution; they developed a cohesive community in Deseret; and they adopted distinctive practices, such as polygamy, that dramatically distinguished them from their neighbors. These strategies effectively secured Mormonism's survival and fueled its growth. In the Mormon case, self-segregation, migration, and the development of a communal infrastructure not only separated the faith from the mainstream but also made possible Mormonism's development into a major American religion.

By contrast, the Protestant immigrant denominations examined by James D. Bratt in "Protestant Immigrants and the Protestant Mainstream" proceeded in the opposite direction. These Mennonite, Missouri Synod Lutheran (German), and Christian Reformed (Dutch Calvinist) immigrants began as religious outsiders. Before emigrating from Europe they had defined themselves as standing spiritually and physically apart from the mainstream and faced persecution. They came to America seeking refuge, and like so many other religiously persecuted immigrants arrived in the New World determined to maintain their minority faith intact. They lived apart, creating their own "tribal" enclave communities "with a complete set of social, religious and educational institutions and an all-absorbing meaning system," and in their churches they resisted both the English language and modernity. Their survival strategy was to insulate themselves from the mainstream as much as possible. What makes their experience distinctive, Bratt shows, is that assimilation into the mainstream would for them, as Protestants, have been easy. Indeed, they faced considerable pressure to conform, particularly during World War I, and selectively they did accommodate. But akin in some ways to the Jews, they also resisted this pressure. Like many adherents of minority faiths, they feared that "becoming an insider would be so easy, yet so costly."

African Americans, of course, did not have it so easy. Race determined their minority status; vanishing into the Protestant mainstream was not an option. But migration certainly was. Some blacks heeded calls to "return" to Africa, others moved across the country to the American West in the hope of achieving a state of their own, still others in the twentieth century moved east into industrializing cities. In parallel, a spiritual migration took place. Thousands of African Americans, beginning in the nineteenth century, moved out of white-dominated denominations and joined black churches. In "Exodus Piety," David Wills explains that all of these migrations resonated with the biblical theme of Exodus. They carried with them the hope for freedom. Wills's exploration of "exodus piety" among African Americans parallels, in many respects, the experiences of Mormons and Protestant immigrants. In all three cases, the strategy for survival entailed physical separation from the mainstream and was suffused with biblical and Zion-oriented metaphors. But, as he points out, there was a critical difference: the "African American's relation to the land was in its origins an involuntary one . . . exodus piety was a way of embracing the land, but only as a stranger."

The second half of this volume moves beyond strategies for survival to explore arenas of conflict, areas where minority and majority faiths struggled, competed, and clashed. Students of American religious history have often sought to avoid such divisive subjects, preferring to focus on questions pertaining to one faith alone or on the beliefs, practices, influences, and changes that many shared. Even Moore's work on religious outsiders, which did highlight conflict, was organized denominationally. Here, however, chapters focus on issues that actually formed the substance of confrontations between minority faiths and the American Protestant mainstream, beginning with the Bible.

The Bible might at first glance seem like a strange place to begin, for standard accounts consider it to have been an important unifying factor in American religion. That, Mark Noll indicates in "The Bible, Minority Faiths, and the American Protestant Mainstream," is only half right. Although the Bible did indeed serve as "a central defining ele-

ment of the mainstream national culture through at least the two generations after the Civil War," mainstream Protestant understanding of
the Bible, rooted in the 1611 Authorized English translation known as
the King James Version, also proved discordantly divisive. Catholics
and Jews opposed the King James Version as sectarian; they preferred
translations of their own. Other minority faiths also produced their own
translations, and in some cases supplementary scriptures and independent interpretations as well. The aim in each case, Noll explains, was
"to establish or preserve a community's own scriptural identity over
against the biblicism of mainstream Protestantism." Arguments over
the text, translation, and interpretation of Scripture challenged the
religious authority of the mainstream. Through these challenges, America's minority faiths carved out "space for themselves in an environment dominated by the mainstream Bible."

    Disputes over the interpretation of Scripture also formed part of a
broader "competition for souls" among America's minority and majority faiths. Whether or not they enlisted legions of missionaries in their
cause, all religious groups were subject to missionary challenges. Church-
state separation effectively created a "free market" in religion in the
United States: missionaries and counter-missionaries enjoyed full freedom to operate. The Protestant mainstream took full advantage of this
freedom, concerned not just with producing religious conversions but
also, as R. Scott Appleby makes clear in "Missions and the Making of
Americans," with Americanization. Here interreligious conflict was at
its most raw, with mainstream and minority faiths both thrusting and
parrying, missionizing and counteracting missionaries. One result, parallel in some ways to what Noll found in his study of the Bible, was an
effort by religious outsiders to carve out space for themselves by strengthening their "enclave cultures" and huddling together. Faced with external pressures to convert, some minority faiths turned inward, redoubling
their efforts to meet the social and spiritual needs of their own people.

    Public schools served as yet another arena of conflict between ma-
jority and minority faiths. Described by one student as "the primary
bearer of a new civic faith, closely related to liberal Protestantism,"
public schools, like missions, frequently linked Protestantization and
Americanization.[11] The schools' religious character, objectives, and
curricula became, as a result, regular subjects of interreligious contention. The more profound challenge faced by adherents of minority
faiths, however, was the common school ideal itself, the belief that state-
sponsored schools should promote common attitudes, loyalties, and
values. Could the twin goals of minority faith preservation and public
education be reconciled? Could parents pass distinctive religious values, tenets, and culture on to children within an educational system that

promoted cultural homogenization? As a practical matter, Virginia Lieson Brereton reminds us in "Education and Minority Religions," conditions varied from place to place, and complexities abounded. In some cases, local communities developed informal arrangements that took account of students' differing religious sensitivities within public schools. Elsewhere, such defenders of the faith as Rabbi Willowski deemed public schools of any sort antithetical to minority faith survival and supported parochial schools instead. These tensions—between unity and diversity, insiders and outsiders, and majority rule and minority rights—have convulsed American education and American religion for much of the nation's history. At the deepest level they reflect tensions endemic to the American experience as a whole.

The final arbiter of these tensions has always been the Supreme Court. Difficult questions that pit one or more minority faiths against the Protestant mainstream have often ended at the Court's bar, and, as Robert Handy shows in "Minority-Majority Confrontations, Church-State Patterns, and the U.S. Supreme Court," the Court's position has changed. In the late nineteenth century, its membership was entirely Protestant, and its rulings tended to support mainstream Protestant Christianity against minority challenges. "This is a Christian nation," Justice David J. Brewer declared for the Court in 1892. Protestants, he felt, enjoyed special status in society. By contrast, Mormons seeking the right to plural marriage, Catholics seeking state aid for parochial schools, and Jews seeking to observe their Sabbath on Saturday instead of Sunday all found themselves isolated; both the government and the courts were against them. By the second quarter of the twentieth century, the period immediately following this book's primary focus, both the Court's membership and American society as a whole were much more pluralistic. In 1925 Catholics (with support from other minority faiths) won an important legal victory known as the Magna Charta of parochial schools; the case, *Pierce v. Society of Sisters,* guaranteed parochial and private schools the right to exist. Fifteen years later, an even more important case, *Cantwell v. Connecticut,* strengthened the hand of minority faiths still further. In a unanimous decision, the Court overturned the conviction of two Jehovah's Witnesses arrested while evangelizing and soliciting funds for their religious movement, and for the first time it applied the strict Constitutional guarantees of religious freedom to the states under provisions of the Fourteenth Amendment. Weighing the rights of an unpopular minority faith against those of the majority, the Court, defying precedent, ruled squarely for the minority. As a result, minority faiths were greatly emboldened, and after World War I a flood tide of new litigation ensued that led to historic decisions that strengthened the rights of minority faiths even more.

Side by side with this immensely important Constitutional struggle, a parallel ideological struggle took place. Minority faiths and the Protestant mainstream "engaged in a complex pattern of contests and negotiations" that ultimately redefined American national identity. As James H. Moorhead recounts in "God's Right Arm?" minority faiths recast national symbols formerly "cloaked in Protestant language and overlaid with notions of Anglo-Saxon superiority" in ways that affirmed "their own visions of American destiny—visions in which they as much as white Protestants" were included. The result, following a period of great interreligious conflict in the 1920s, was what Robert Handy has called "the Second Disestablishment," the Protestant loss of a commanding role in American culture.[12] By the end of World War II, a more inclusive and pluralistic understanding of American national identity had emerged. Popularized in a 1955 best-seller, it was summed up in the famous three words of Will Herberg's title: *Protestant, Catholic, Jew.*[13]

Rabbi Willowski would have been astonished by this development, and so would many of the other faithful featured in this book. Concerned with minority group survival and confrontation with the Protestant mainstream, they scarcely imagined that one day they might be perceived as part of the mainstream. Yet even as America's spiritual focus broadened to embrace religions once relegated to the periphery, a new group of religious outsiders emerged, particularly in the wake of immigration law changes enacted in 1965. Indeed, the recent encounters of Islam, Buddhism, Hinduism, the Unification Church, and many other contemporary religious outsiders with today's Judeo-Christian mainstream suggest intriguing parallels to the experiences of groups portrayed in this book. Survival strategies, arenas of conflict, pressures to conform to religious patterns of the mainstream, countervailing pressures to resist them and remain apart, Supreme Court battles, and efforts to recast national symbols to make them more religiously inclusive—all remain relevant subjects today. The chapters that follow thus illumine central themes both in the history of American religion and the ongoing story of American social change.

 Notes

1. J. D. Willowski, *Sefer Nimukei Ridvaz* (Chicago: 1904), unpaginated introduction [in Hebrew]; on Willowski, see Abraham J. Karp, "The Ridwas, Rabbi Jacob David Wilowsky 1845–1913," in *Perspectives on Jews and Judaism: Essays in Honor of Wolfe Kelman*, ed. Arthur A. Chiel (New York: The

Rabbinical Assembly, 1978), 215–37, which partially translates this text, and Aaron Rothkoff, "The American Sojourns of Ridbaz: Religious Problems within the Immigrant Community," *American Jewish Historical Quarterly* 57 (June 1968): 557–72.

2. Sydney E. Ahlstrom, *A Religious History of the American People* (New Haven: Yale University Press, 1972), 10.

3. R. Laurence Moore, *Religious Outsiders and the Making of Americans* (New York: Oxford University Press, 1986), 20.

4. Catherine L. Albanese, *America: Religions and Religion,* 2d ed. (Belmont, Calif.: Wadsworth, 1992), 21, 24.

5. Robert N. Bellah and Frederick E. Greenspahn, *Uncivil Religion: Interreligious Hostility in America* (New York: Crossroad, 1987).

6. Moore, *Religious Outsiders and the Making of Americans,* 21, 208.

7. Thomas A. Tweed, *The American Encounter with Buddhism, 1844–1912* (Bloomington: Indiana University Press, 1992), employs this terminology. His study, however, seeks to show how much "dissenters" shared "with those in mainline Protestantism and Victorian culture" (xxi). Here, by contrast, we stress cultural resistance and religious confrontations.

8. William R. Hutchison, *Between the Times: The Travail of the Protestant Establishment in America, 1900–1960* (New York: Cambridge University Press, 1989), 4, 304.

9. J. Gordon Melton, ed., *The Encyclopedia of American Religions* (Tarrytown: Triumph Books, 1991), 1:xxxix.

10. H. Richard Niebuhr, *Christ and Culture* (New York: Harper and Row, 1951), xi.

11. Charles Leslie Glenn, Jr., *The Myth of the Common School* (Amherst: University of Massachusetts Press, 1988), 146.

12. Robert T. Handy, *A Christian America: Protestant Hopes and Historical Realities,* 2d ed. (New York: Oxford University Press, 1984), 159–84.

13. Will Herberg, *Protestant, Catholic, Jew: An Essay in American Religious Sociology* (Garden City: Doubleday, 1955).

PART I

Strategies for Survival

ONE

Jewish Survival in Protestant America

Benny Kraut

Jewish survival is a miracle with historical causes.
—Israel Friedlander[1]

Among all the distinctive American ethnic, racial, and religious groups, Jews stand out as having the longest and most successful historical record of surviving cultural interactions and confrontations with host societies while living as a minority in their midst. Indeed, it would be both fair and accurate to portray them as the quintessential survivalists of world history.[2]

Historically, Jewish survival was rooted first and foremost in the will to endure as Jews on both an individual and communal level. Regardless of the discrete challenges posed by either hostile or tolerant societies in which they dwelled, Jews actively promoted group self-preservation and pursued those courses of action they deemed necessary for communal cohesion and continuity.[3] They devised and throughout their history consistently implemented four broad strategies of survival that shaped their community's relationship to the majority culture and assumed responsibility for and jurisdiction over essential Jewish needs.

1. *Geographic mobility and relocation.* Either in reaction to utterly untenable societal circumstances that rendered Jewish life impossible or attracted by the promise of better socioeconomic and religious conditions elsewhere, Jews migrated and immigrated to new regions in order to perpetuate Jewish existence.

2. *Erection of Jewish communal infrastructures.* Wherever Jews transplanted themselves, they established religiocultural institutions and organizations that made possible the transmission of Jewish traditions, values, and patterns of behavior that reinforced social cohesion, mutual aid, and a sense of ethnic community.

3. *Assessment of and adaptation to the host environment: acculturation in open societies.* Living as a minority required that Jews take stock

of and adjust to the specific set of physical and cultural challenges to group survival that they faced in each society. The distinctive character of the surrounding environment—whether politically moderate or repressive, culturally open or closed, socially and ethnically homogeneous or heterogeneous, economically advanced or backward, religiously fervent or quiescent—determined the extent and nature of Jewish interaction with it, contributed to the agenda of internal communal concerns, and precipitated differentiated patterns of Jewish-Gentile social and cultural interchange. In comparatively more open and pluralistic societies, or societies that exhibited such tendencies, Jewish adjustment expressed itself in diverse forms of acculturation.

4. *Jewish defense.* Jewish communities and their leaders responded to assaults against their cultural character, economic livelihood, and physical existence. The nature of their reaction—political lobbying with rulers, pleading, bribery, economic leveraging, religious and intellectual polemics, and even armed resistance—was clearly dictated by the character of the threats or actions taken against them. The varied tactics of defense did not often dispel slanders, nor did they prevent tragedy when the majority condoned or deliberately initiated acts of violence, as history has all too often demonstrated. Nevertheless, Jews invoked measures of communal self-defense as a means of group survival.

These four are not inherently Jewish strategies; other groups have adopted some or all of them. But they are fundamental and paradigmatic to the Jewish historical experience, which has afforded Jews, living as a minority under the sovereignty of Western and Eastern civilizations for two millennia, abundant opportunities to apply them.

America, a more recent host society for a minority Jewish population, presented another such opportunity, and Jews used the same strategic approaches to advance group survival in the New World. This is particularly the case between the end of the Civil War and the onset of World War I (1865–1915), an extraordinary period in American Jewish life, when, in many respects, the most intense and creative American Jewish wrestling over issues of group continuity took place. Those fifty years witnessed a tidal wave of European Jewish immigration to America; a remarkable upbuilding of Jewish organizations, institutions, and communities; a strikingly rich assortment of models of American Jewish acculturation, complete with ideological justifications for them; and approaches to Jewish defense tailored to the particular American historical setting.[4] By resorting to the same four historical survival strategies, American Jewry replicated the principles and processes of group maintenance that had sustained Jewish existence for centuries. But the application of these four survival strategies to an American society exceptional in world history engendered a singular Jewry unique in Jewish history.[5]

The Strategy of Relocation: Immigration to America

Toward the end of the eighteenth century and during the course of the nineteenth, the historic Jewish self-understanding that had bolstered the Jews' will to survive as a group apart was severely tested in Europe. Until that time, most Jews believed themselves to be God's specially chosen nation, ordained with a religious mission to live as a people apart in a unique religiocultural lifestyle. They believed that their lives testified to the reality of the one true God, who would ultimately redeem them in messianic times and return them to the ancestral, promised land of Israel. These core national self-perceptions undergirded Jewish group identity, reinforced Jews' sense of a shared common past, and helped forge the far-flung Jewish communities around the world into an international community that transcended spatial and temporal boundaries.

But now, in Central and Western Europe, the cultural and sociopolitical framework of Jewish life was being reshaped, and eventually shattered, by repercussions of new intellectual and political trends that threatened to undermine traditional Jewish self-understanding. Enlightenment ideals, with their rational and scientific critique of the sacred texts and theological beliefs of revealed religions, aroused some Jews to question the validity of their inherited religion. Compounding this challenge, newly emerging nation-states, in the wake of the demise of the feudal order, seemed to promise their Jews political emancipation and legal equality contingent on their thoroughgoing social, cultural, and religious "improvement."

The allure of this promise found many Jews expecting to become accepted as equals by the majority and initiating what they considered to be the requisite changes in Jewish social mien, religious behavior, and national loyalties. Anticipating material gain, social ease, and the opportunity for broadened cultural horizons, some began reforming Judaism, propounding modernized expressions of religious identity, beliefs, and ritual practice more in consonance with the temper of the times. They redefined Jews solely in religious terms, repudiated Jewish nationality and all pretensions of returning to Zion, and avowed primary national allegiance to the state in which they lived. But by mid-century, political and social equality for Jews was still not forthcoming, while continuous discriminatory legislation, especially in southern Germanic states, curtailed natural family growth and retarded Jewish economic livelihood, igniting widespread Jewish disillusionment.

In contrast, the radically different social milieu of Eastern Europe, with its autocratic regimes, backward societies, and massive numbers of Jews in dire poverty restricted to the Russian Pale of Settlement, provided no hope for emancipation. Permitting and even encouraging that anti-Jewish feelings be vented in physical violence, czarist Russia by the last decades of the nineteenth century provoked some Jews to pursue more extreme measures to improve their plight. A good number discarded their Jewish identity and joined revolutionary movements dedicated to the overthrow of despotic czarist regimes and to the creation of an ideal society yet to be born. Still others conceived of the solution to the problem of Jewish existence in Eastern Europe in ideologically innovative secular, national, and cultural redefinitions of the Jewish collective, spearheading the rise of new movements such as secular Zionism, Jewish socialism, and cultural autonomism, each of which claimed to have discovered the solution to the "Jewish Question" in the East.[6]

Nineteenth-century European sociopolitical forces and intellectual currents, therefore, caused enormous ferment in Jewish life and presented no idle threat to Jewish survival. Although the majority of Jews perhaps still clung to Jewish tradition and sought to perpetuate communal affairs and ideals as they knew them, many in both Central and Eastern Europe questioned traditional Jewish self-conceptions and assumptions about the value, purpose, and character of Jewish group distinctiveness. Struggling painfully with the problems of both physical survival and the culturally wrenching task of harmonizing the imperatives of the Jewish past with the social realities of the present, increasing numbers of European Jews in the course of the nineteenth century concluded that the battle for survival in Europe was too dangerous and precarious, and ultimately futile, especially in light of a reportedly more attractive, although risky, alternative overseas.

And so, emulating a historic Jewish example of group behavior under stress, many Jews relocated to a new region, joining the millions of other Europeans who crossed the Atlantic to the United States. Jewish immigration to America, consequently, must be understood as a survival strategy of European Jews, who transferred their grappling with the issue of continued Jewish existence from the Old World to the New.[7] In the process, the immigrants transformed a tiny, insignificant American Jewish community into a burgeoning new center of Jewish life.

Between 1825 and 1880, 150,000 to 175,000 European Jews, three-quarters of them of German national or cultural background, impatient with the slow and incomplete process of political emancipation and the persistent socioeconomic limitations imposed on them by their home states, arrived on American shores. From an infinitesimal community of 4,000 in 1825, the American Jewish population increased steadily, reaching 50,000 in 1840, 150,000 in 1860, and 250,000 by 1880. But these numbers pale in comparison to those that followed. Fleeing the forced segregation, economic strangulation, and government-sanctioned pogroms of repressive regimes, between 1880 and 1920 more than 2.1 million Jews, primarily from Russia and Russian-Poland, immigrated, constituting almost one-third of all East European Jewry. Owing to the constant stream of this particular immigrant wave (between 1880 and 1910, German Jewish immigration was relatively minuscule), the population of American Jews by 1914 climbed to 3.5 million and represented approximately 3 percent of the total American population.[8]

The immigration of European Jews to America between 1865 and 1915 effectively resolved concerns about physical safety and economic opportunity. But it did not shield Jews from the same stresses of modernization and secularization that had begun to alter and, for some, erode Jewish identification in Europe. Having brought with them traditional loyalties as well as an array of new fully or partially developed Jewish self-conceptions, European Jews once again confronted the preeminent existential dilemma agitating Jews in the modern age, only in the more hospitable American setting: Could the historic Jewish will to survive apart, which had nourished minority life in diaspora communities for two millennia, be sustained? If so, how would it be best achieved?

The Strategy of Immigrant Community-Building

Unlike such affirmed assimilationists as House of Rothschild agent, banker, and politician August Belmont, who came to America to detach himself from Jewish ties, the preponderance of immigrant European Jews ventured to the United States to live as Jews, not to disappear. Fostering group survival, therefore, was a priority goal for them. Their instinctive, initial efforts to achieve it saw them establish communal infrastructures across the country to reinforce Jewish religious and ethnic separatism within American culture and etch the boundaries of distinctive Jewish social space and sacred time.

Community-building did not spring from any rational, preconceived, centrally coordinated program for Jewish survival, nor was it an elite phenomenon. On the contrary, originally it reflected the reflex reaction of Jewish laypeople who did what had to be done to care for themselves and their families and who resorted to the same institutions and patterns of association they had known in Europe. In Central and Eastern Europe, religious and ethnic bonds had been translated into organizational activity and highly structured communal entities, such as *gemeinden* in Germanic lands and *kehillot* in Russia and Poland. It was natural, therefore, for immigrants to transfer familiar social institutions, cultural values, religious customs, and the ambience of home regions to their new environment to provide sociopsychological support in the wake of the disorienting immigrant experience.

Consequently, although Jewish immigrants spread out across America, the two-thirds of them who lived in the Northeast by 1915 clustered residentially and established urban Jewish neighborhoods and ethnic communities. This was true for German Jews in the Gilded Age and certainly was the case with the appearance of dense urban ghettoes of East European Jews in New York, Philadelphia, Boston, Baltimore, Cleveland, and Chicago.

Jewish neighborhoods featured a wide range of Jewish institutions. Jews created ethnic synagogues and one-room *shtiblech* (prayer rooms) that resonated with the nuanced liturgical styles of their native regions. They held on to them as long as possible, contributing to the panoply of ethnic congregations of German, Bohemian, Silesian, Hungarian, Slovakian, Russian, and Polish origin that persisted into the first decades of the twentieth century. Jews also founded cemetery associations and a veritable multitude of fraternal, social, welfare, cultural, and educational organizations, including immigrant aid associations, free loan societies, sick funds, hospitals, orphan asylums, literary societies, Jewish schools, social clubs, newspapers, and philanthropic agencies. East European Jews in the early twentieth century recreated a vibrant and powerful Jewish labor movement that constituted a Jewish subsociety with its own brand of secular Jewish identification, an abiding commitment to mutual assistance among members, and progressive political and economic platforms.[9]

Organized self-help to foster social cohesion and group survival, therefore, was the first principle of immigrant Jewish associationalism. No other American group organized itself so conspicuously or as comprehensively; no other group of similar size and resources established as intricate a network of communal agencies to advance its cause. One suggestive statistic at the beginning of the period succinctly underscores and foreshadows this recurring Jewish impulse for organized self-help: In 1860, when New York Jews constituted only 5 percent of the city's population, the number of their social and welfare institutions equaled the total number of all comparable non-Jewish agencies. By the Civil

War's end, with only a very small increase in Jewish population, the number of such Jewish organizations exceeded corresponding non-Jewish ones.[10]

Community-building was not synonymous with communal unity or uniformity. Between the Civil War and World War I the American Jewish community was institutionally fragmented. The large number of immigrant organizations and institutions, ever replenished by newly formed associations of more recent arrivals, certainly contributed to this condition. But what significantly exacerbated communal discord in virtually every American city was the perception and reality of deep-seated, inter-ethnic rivalry between Jews from Germanic lands and those from Russia and Poland. Indeed, the American Jewish community was twice-born in this era; German Jewish institutions, established and flourishing by the 1880s, were mostly paralleled and duplicated by East European Jews seeking to take care of themselves.

To cite but a handful of representative examples, Mount Sinai, the German Jewish hospital in New York, soon found its counterpart in the East European Beth Israel, which, among other things, offered its patients kosher food. The national German Jewish fraternal organization, B'nai B'rith, catering mostly to middle-class German Jews by the 1880s and resistant to the inclusion of East European Jews in its membership, was more than offset by the East European lodges such as Kesher Shel Barzel and the more than two thousand East European *landsmanshaftn* (voluntary ethnic and social welfare associations based on shared European regions) that had proliferated by 1915.[11] The Hebrew Union College (1875), seminary for Reform rabbis who until the early 1890s were essentially of Central and West European origins, was soon matched by the religiously traditional Jewish Theological Seminary (1887 and again, 1902) and the more yeshiva-oriented Rabbi Isaac Elchanan Theological Seminary (1915), both of which in this era served more traditional and Orthodox East Europeans.

Clearly, the sheer magnitude of the numbers of East European immigrants precluded German Jewish agencies from directly absorbing them into their preexistent social service and cultural networks. But institutional duplication had much deeper historical roots: Both groups of Jews carried over from Europe not only their distinctive cultural predispositions, religious proclivities, and subethnic social characteristics but also a mutual disdain and disregard that had originated in Europe and continued to manifest itself. Tensions between the two ethnic Jewries, moreover, were heightened in America because of the salient fact of most German Jews having settled in large numbers in the United States before the mass immigration of East Europeans and at a time when the country still courted prospective immigrants. Hence, they successfully adjusted to America earlier, occupied positions of leadership and communal authority, and considered their particular patterns of Americanization normative for all Jews.

The mass arrival of Russian and Polish Jews, however, not only supplanted the Germans numerically, but jeopardized their carefully cultivated American social standing, communal hegemony, and status as self-appointed Jewish spokesmen to the gentile community. Landing at a time of mounting American resentment against foreigners, therefore, the Yiddish-speaking East Europeans frequently encountered a patronizing noblesse oblige attitude from the German Jews, who typically assumed a patron-client stance toward the newcomers. Resentful, East Europeans followed their own group survival instincts, erecting their own communal organizations and institutions to serve their needs.[12]

To be sure, external threats and crises tended to foster inter-Jewish communication and cooperation, however temporary, that overcame even pronounced inter-ethnic divisions. The grand Jewish communal stewards of the day—Louis Marshall, Jacob Schiff, and Oscar and Nathan Straus, to cite but a few—undertook unparalleled political and fiscal initiatives on behalf of persecuted Jews in Russia and then assisted them—not always motivated by selfless altruism—educationally, culturally, and economically upon their relocation in America. Nevertheless, the abiding institutional and cultural inter-ethnic competition lingered on, arguably until at least the mid-twentieth century; by 1915 there was not one united, homogeneous, national Jewish community, but rather two broad, independent, and fractious even if interactive American Jewish subethnic communities.[13]

Adjustment to America: The Strategy of Acculturation

Following the initial period of resettlement and the overcoming of immediate socioeconomic and communal exigencies, immigrant European Jews between 1865 and 1915 proceeded to do what all previous peripatetic Jews had done: They took stock of their new environment, gradually determined the appropriate spheres of interaction with their host society, and assessed the opportunities and challenges to Jewish survival that it presented. In doing so, Jews experienced firsthand the clash between two equally compelling national visions vying to determine the character of the American nation and its cultural and political norms: an inclusivist view that conceived of America as an open, neutral civic society, grounded in democratic freedom, the separation of church and state, and de facto ethnic pluralism; and an exclusivist conception that denied cultural pluralism and took for granted that America was and ought to be a culturally homogeneous Protestant society dominated by the spirit of an evangelical Protestant temper.[14] This battle over the nature of America and the precise relationship of Protestantism to American civic culture decisively influenced Jewish group adjustment to American society; Jews perforce had to navigate between the two positions and the concrete social implications that emanated from each as they transformed America from a temporary haven to a permanent home and puzzled out new American and Jewish identities.

On the one hand, Jews came to appreciate wholeheartedly the *novum* that America represented in Jewish history. The first nation in world history to grant them unconditional political liberty and religious freedom, the United States, Jews believed, proffered a national polity that genuinely embraced them. Understandably, they gravitated to and positively reveled in the inclusivist national ideal. Moreover, they found America particularly congenial because of the pervasive biblical character of American culture.[15] The initial organizing myths of American society, rooted in Puritan and Protestant biblicism passed down culturally from the colonial period through the nineteenth century, ensured that generations of Jews could point to the prevailing Jewish scriptural tone, language, and concepts undergirding the nation from its inception; through the Bible, they found a direct link between themselves and the country's forebears and asserted a common American and Jewish patrimony.

Not surprisingly, therefore, popular Jewish lore glorified an inclusivist America in grandiose, almost mythic, terms, starkly differentiating its receptivity to Jews from the abhorrent European attitudes, a contrast that became ever more polarized at century's close with the eruption of racist nationalism in Central and Western Europe and pogroms in the East. To transplanted American Jews, Old World Europe became the bogeyman for New World America, its paradigmatic and despised oppression antithetical, in the Jewish imagination, to America's beloved archetypal freedom.[16] And they recognized that American freedoms and opportunities constituted a profound boon to Jewish survival. Unlike their experiences in Europe, Jews in America were free to live most anywhere, take up most any occupation, and create whatever religious, social, and communal institutions they wanted. They were not legally circumscribed in behavior, nor did they need to conform to self-definitions imposed by others.

But extensive freedom cut both ways, and it unleashed countervailing forces in Jewish life that some communal leaders feared would endanger American Jewish existence. The new Americans quickly became acquainted with the social and structural byproducts of constitutionally guaranteed political and religious freedom. Because formally appointed religious or communal hierarchies dictating behavior could not exist, all communal and cultural associations were voluntary; free market competition, therefore, governed all forms of social affiliation, not merely the capitalist economy.[17] In America, Jews learned, one was not required to identify as a Jew; one voluntarily chose to do so in whatever manner pleased the individual. And not all choices Jews made between 1865 and 1915 promoted group survival.[18]

Religiously lax, Jewishly alienated, and otherwise assimilating descendants of German and East European immigrants, attracted by the socially leveling pull of American culture, sapped communal strength, as did such Jewish founders of universal religious movements as Felix Adler (Ethical Culture) and Rabbi Charles Fleischer (Boston Sunday Commons).[19] This fifty-year period, however, also saw the consequences of an array of choices *in the name of Jewish survival* that not only reflected varied patterns of Jewish sociocultural adjustment to America but also weakened the community and generated much internal discord: caustic debates between proponents of secular modes of identification such as Zionism and socialism and advocates of Jewish religious identification; bitter intra-religious polemics among competing visions of Judaism, augmenting the already rife subethnic quarrels; perpetual lay-rabbinic flare-ups over control of communal and religious institutions; and embittered conflicts over strategies of Jewish defense and the desirability of ethnic politics.[20]

Learning how to contend with American culture, therefore, was a daunting task for immigrant Jews. The very features of American society they grew to cherish also proved potentially hazardous to group cohesion and continuity; as Maurice Fishberg, an anthropologist, mused in 1907, "The Jews are . . . paying a high price for their liberty and equality—self-effacement."[21] The challenge confronting American Jews, therefore, was how to espouse Americanism and its liberal political ideals, how to embrace and be embraced by the American national collective yet maintain Jewish group boundaries and validate the abiding worthwhileness of group distinctiveness and separatism.

The preeminent, although not exclusive, strategic response to this dilemma expressed itself, as in prior Jewish experiences with open societies, in the social dynamic of acculturation. To be sure, on one level Jewish acculturation constituted an unconscious organic social process, as many immigrants and their children over time very naturally found their cultural and religious sensibilities changing. But the multivalent forms of acculturation also reflected the deliberate strategy pursued diligently by those who thought they could preserve group coherence by minimizing the perceived disjunctions between the Jewish minority and the American majority. By aggressively Americanizing Jewish culture and by underlining the commonality of American Jews with other Americans, they hoped to illustrate to themselves and the host society how profoundly American they and their culture could become while still affirming Jewish loyalties. The animating drive was the yearning to belong and to be acknowledged as belonging to America. Despite being neither Protestant nor Anglo-Saxon, despite constituting only a tiny fraction of the total American population, Jews sought recognition as cultural insiders in America and wished to ensure that their group differences did not render them "other" in the American nation.[22]

SOCIAL AND INSTITUTIONAL ACCULTURATION

Acculturating Jews consciously adopted American and American Protestant social trends, institutional patterns, cultural values, and intellectual orientations, adapting many into the warp and woof of daily life. Like their neighbors, they too celebrated Thanksgiving and national holidays such as July 4 and held special synagogue prayer services when national fast days were declared. They incorporated the national heroes intimately associated with the formulation of American freedoms—such as Washington, Jefferson, and Lincoln—into the pantheon of Jewish heroes, granting them quasi-biblical status.[23] More significantly, they found repeated ways of meshing Americana with Judaica and integrating American cultural symbols and events into traditional Jewish practices. A particularly salient example occurred in April 1889, when the centennial of George Washington's inauguration fell on Passover, granting Jews the opportunity to recall and celebrate simultaneously the two most glorious occasions of Jewish freedom in history—ancient biblical freedom from Egyptian slavery on the one hand and contemporary American religious and political liberty on the other. In New York, every Jew who bought ten pounds of matzo was given a free picture of Washington, and the city's Orthodox chief rabbi, Jacob Joseph, composed a prayer to be read in all synagogues under his charge. Across the country, synagogues were decorated with red, white, and blue bunting, while at the Passover Seder itself many Jews sang not only traditional songs pertaining to the biblical Jewish liberation but also "The Star Spangled Banner" and "America," which were later inserted into an American Passover Haggada issued during World War I.[24]

In the acculturation process, venerable Old World Jewish institutions were Americanized. Synagogues and temples, in varying degrees, not only incorporated more English into their services but also rewrote constitutions and reconfigured their governance structure to comply with the rhetoric of American democratic principles.[25] The traditional Jewish burial society, the *hevra kadisha,* its status and sanctity eroded when crass materialism invaded its precincts, ultimately was supplanted for most Jews by American Jewish funeral homes.[26] Even the recreated traditional yeshiva of East European Jews in New York, in the wake of student pressure, introduced secular studies into its curriculum.[27] But perhaps the most profound experiment to wed American ideals to traditional Jewish institutions took place in New York City when Rabbi Judah Magnes led an effort to create a communal *kehilla* (an autonomous, self-governing communal structure interweaving and supervising a network of educational, religious, and social institutions) that sought to centralize Jewish communal authority, transcend subethnic, religious, and ideological divisions, and base its polity in principles of American voluntarism and democracy. The New York *kehilla* was an Americanized version of a historic Jewish communal framework, which, despite its shortcomings and brief existence (1908–22), served as an instructive model of ethnic community-building in American society.[28]

Jewish emulation of specifically Protestant values and practices was reflected in a variety of ways. Some Jews, although not with the same fervor as fellow Protestants, expressed anti-Catholic sentiments, as if sharing the Protestant majority's bigotry better integrated them into America.[29] Far more illustrative and widespread, however, were other instances of Jewish appropriation of Protestant cultural practices. Like the Protestants, Jewish children flocked to the public schools, and by the 1870s most Jewish all-day private and communal schools had closed, unable to compete with the free, better equipped public institutions. Later-arriving East European Jewish children came to share German Jewish assumptions about the almost sacred value of nonsectarian and nonreligious public education, its Protestant biases, however blatant and offensive, notwithstanding.[30] Even long-lived, traditional Jewish organizations were recast in Protestant style. By the turn of the century, Jews, like their Protestant counterparts, also tried to professionalize their welfare services and introduced the Protestant value of scientific study of institutional procedures to maximize benefit into their own philanthropic and social service agencies.[31] American synagogues, especially Reform temples, were Protestantized in liturgical style and worship service, and the position of rabbi was gradually transformed from that of a Jewish legal expositor and religious edu-

cator to that of preacher, pastor, administrator, and professional leader of prayers.[32]

Jewish adaptation to America and the Protestant majority precipitated historically new Jewish institutions and activities as well. The
Christian Sunday school was exemplar to the Jewish Sunday school and
Talmud Torah; Protestant tract and bible societies and circuit preaching were imitated by like-minded Jewish versions; YM-YWCAs were
imitated by YM-YWHAs; the Protestant Social Gospel stimulated Jewish variations; the Chautauqua Society triggered Rabbi Henry Berko-
witz's efforts to publicize Judaism through his Jewish Chautauqua Society; Christian lodges and social clubs, which frequently spurned
Jewish members, sparked the creation of Jewish lodges, such as B'nai
B'rith, as well as upper-class Jewish clubs like New York's Harmonie;
Episcopalian, Methodist, and Presbyterian publication societies were
models for the revived Jewish Publication Society; middle-class Protestant women and their public actions set examples for Jewish wom-
en, especially for those of upper-class German Jewish extraction, who
also channeled their energy into sisterhood auxiliaries, social reform,
benevolent and educational enterprises, and eventually the National
Council for Jewish Women; Protestant clerical unions were paradigms
for rabbinic unions, and Protestant lobbying on behalf of particular
religious and moral interests, such as Christian temperance and the
Sunday Sabbath, was paralleled by Jews of the Jewish Sabbath Alliance
lobbying public officials against Sunday Blue Laws, claiming that they
diminished Sabbath observance in the Jewish community.[33]

RELIGIOUS ACCULTURATION

Social and institutional acculturation was complemented and indeed
nurtured by the process of religious acculturation and the Americanization of Judaism. Between 1865 and 1915, American Jews, like Catholics, confronted a fundamental religious dilemma—preserving religious authority and sanction for a historical religious tradition in a land
whose leitmotif is personal freedom and sustaining—or, if necessary,
reinterpreting and amending—inherited religious texts, ideas, and practices in a manner compelling to modern and American sensibilities. In
meeting the challenge, most Jews retaining religious identification responded with various degrees of religious acculturation, but they differed markedly over the inviolate essentials of Jewish thought and practice as well as the parameters of permissible religious and theological
change.

The impulse to religious reform comprised the most far-reaching
illustration of religious acculturation. Reform Judaism was the first

religious movement in America to establish a national institutional base
and denominational consciousness. Although early signs of Reform can
be traced to Charleston, South Carolina, in the 1820s, as well as to
other local synagogue developments during the 1840s and 1850s,
American Reform Judaism began flourishing in the two decades following the Civil War because of the indefatigable efforts of such leaders as Rabbi Isaac M. Wise; the grass-roots desire of upwardly mobile
German Jewish laymen demanding a less foreign style of Judaism; and
the arrival in midcentury of European Reform leaders and thinkers such
as Samuel Hirsch, David Einhorn, Samuel Adler, Bernhard Felsenthal,
Kaufmann Kohler, and Solomon Sonneschein, among others, who gave
intellectual direction to the movement. By the end of the 1870s Reform
Judaism had captured the religious allegiance of the majority of American Jews, and, had the subsequent mass immigration of Eastern European Jews not taken place, Isaac M. Wise's triumphal proclamation
that Reform Judaism was "the American phase of [world historic] Judaism" might well have proven prophetic.[34]

It is evident from Reform publications, liturgical revisions, newspapers, sermons, major rabbinical conferences (in Philadelphia in 1869
and Pittsburgh in 1885), and the annual meetings of the Central Conference of American Rabbis after 1890 that the essential principles of
American Reform were European in origin. Save for a social justice
motif that began to have meaningful impact on the movement only after
1900, American Reform Judaism devised no new theology or ideology. Like its European antecedents, American Reform upheld ethical
monotheism as the core belief of Judaism; allied Judaism to reason,
science, progress, Enlightenment philosophy, and evolution; rejected
allegedly antiquated rituals and the commanding authority of biblical
and rabbinic Judaism; repudiated Jewish national identity and messianic aspirations linked to a return to Zion and the rebuilding of the
temple; defined Jews as a non-national religious community; and
affirmed a universal religious mission to propagate ethical monotheism in the world.[35]

But American culture most assuredly stamped the Reform movement
with explicit and far-reaching Americanist traits. Reform temples so
aped Protestant churches that by the end of the century it was sometimes difficult to differentiate some of the former from the latter. The
prayer service included mixed seating, extensive portions of the liturgy in English, meditations with bowed heads, the sermon as spiritual
focal point, the removal of distinctive Jewish garb such as prayer shawls
and head coverings, and new customs such as confirmation. More radical temples instituted Sunday services as the main weekday worship

assembly, at first to deal with synagogue absenteeism but also to align Judaism's day of rest with common American practice.[36]

Indeed, the American environment essentially shaped Reform's dual American Jewish identity, ultimately undergirding its affirmation of the concordance between Judaism and Americanism. Reform Judaism's interpretation and legitimation of Jewish separatism solely on religious grounds conformed perfectly with the regnant Protestant model of the congregational polity serving as the basis of distinctive group association. The Protestant majority accepted religious divisions within the American polity; Reformers, therefore, had no trouble conceiving of themselves as Americans in the same fashion that they perceived Protestants defining themselves as Americans. "Inside his synagogue, he must be the Jew," Reform Rabbi Joseph Krauskopf exclaimed, "[but] outside [he must be] the American, as indistinguishable from others as Baptists and Presbyterians are indistinguishable from each other outside their respective churches."[37]

Even more boldly, dozens of Reform leaders such as Wise, Kohler, Samuel Hirsch, and Solomon Schindler as well as elite Jewish communal officials within the Reform orbit, for example, Louis Marshall and Jacob Schiff, interpreted the meaning of America in Jewish religious terms and the meaning of Judaism in American ideals. They read liberal American political ideals back into biblical Judaism while portraying the latter as the inspiration and source for these same values and ideas. Sharing with America a common biblical heritage, the Judaism and prophetic ideals of Ancient Israel were not only congruent with American principles, Isaac M. Wise proclaimed, but also the prototype of American democracy.[38] Moses promulgated the virtues of liberty and democracy, Wise averred, and therefore his religious revolution represented one pole of the democratic ideal; the American Revolution was the other. The American Constitution was nothing other than "Mosaism in action." In the view of Oscar S. Straus, lawyer, politician, diplomat, and, as secretary of commerce and labor in the Theodore Roosevelt administration, the first Jew to serve in an American cabinet, the ancient Hebrew Commonwealth was the political model for the American Republic.[39]

Against the background of the Reformers' repudiation of Jewish nationality and national rebirth, this equation of Jewish religious ideals with American political ones found them, paradoxically but understandably, translating American nationalism into a virtual Jewish religious principle. America was the new Jewish Zion, demanding fealty and tugging at Jewish heartstrings. In addition, Reformers meshed their conception of the universal Jewish religious mission to humanity with the widely presumed American political mission to disseminate republican democracy to the world; hence, Reformers were not averse to approve of what some would designate American imperialism in the Spanish-American War at the end of the century.[40]

The logic of Reform ideology also contained implicit assumptions about preferred Jewish social attitudes, which Reformers tried to shape into communal policy. For the most part, Reform Jews adopted the melting pot social image of America at the turn of the century and also favored by the American Protestant establishment, which galvanized their efforts to transform the East European immigrants into Americans as quickly as possible. The preponderance of Reformers, with important exceptions, vigorously denounced Zionism as an untenable Jewish ideology inimical to the American Jewish cultural synthesis. They also condemned what now would be called ethnic politics, rejecting Jewish political clubs and the idea of a Jewish vote based purely on Jewish interests, and were therefore decidedly uncomfortable with the unabashed ethnic politics of immigrants in urban wards.[41] That the behavior of the old-guard communal stewards such as Marshall and Schiff contradicted their own rhetoric—both quite clearly engaged in Jewish ethnic politics—did not diminish the persistence and force of their anti-ethnic discourse.[42] Moreover, given the conception of Jews as solely a religious community, even Jewish philanthropy—perceived at times by Gentiles as a separatist, and hence unnecessary, group endeavor—was justified by Jews in this circle not on the basis of filial ethnic fraternity but rather on religious principles couched in universal biblical terms in order to deflect outsider criticism of excessive, "un-American" Jewish clannishness.[43]

Reform Judaism's model of religious acculturation, substantially redefining Judaism and projecting an ideological symbiosis of soul between Judaism and Americanism, effectively wrenched traditional Jewish ideas from their biblical and religious context and superimposed them onto a different American reality. But this image of the utter congruency between American political and Jewish religious ideals, of Jews being the originators and bearers of cherished and paradigmatic American values, provided Reformers with an empowering rhetoric to delineate themselves as quintessential Americans, insiders par excellence.

Proponents of traditional Judaism also acculturated and Americanized their patterns of religious behavior. But they dissented vigorously from extreme Reform measures even as they struggled to specify what changes could and should be made in the practices and beliefs of the tradition. Unlike Reform Jews, however, traditionalists in the fifty-year period under consideration did not overhaul Jewish theology, divorce

Jewish nationality from religion, or renounce Jewish national or ethnic kinship. They did not feel constrained to revolutionize Judaism for
the sake of social and cultural reconciliation with America. Instead, they
adopted American rhetoric of religious freedom and equality and the
separation of church and state as justifications supporting traditional
religious practice: Religious liberty, they contended, afforded Jews the
opportunity to practice their religious culture fully and therefore was
a blessing. As impassioned as any Reformers, traditional Jews asserted the total compatibility between Judaism and Americanism. Orthodox Rabbi Bernard Drachman, a native American trained in Germany, professed a "harmonious combination of Orthodox Judaism and
Americanism," while East European Rabbi Bernard Revel exclaimed
at the laying of the cornerstone of the Rabbinical College of America
(later renamed Yeshiva University) in 1915, "I see no conflict, no in-
consistency between Americanism and Judaism."[44]

To some degree, before and at the onset of the influx of the East
European immigration, the coherence and solidarity of the traditionalist orientation in Judaism was attained less by the clarity and uniformity of its religious position and more by its anti-Reform stance. A
broad range of traditional religionists joined forces to excoriate a Reform Judaism that, in their view, had run amok. Thus, in 1886 and
1887, in the wake of the radical eight-point plank promulgated at the
Reform Rabbinical Conference in Pittsburgh in 1885, Orthodox spiritual leaders Drachman and Sabato Morais, together with moderate
reformers Benjamin Szold, Alexander Kohut, and Marcus Jastrow,
established the Jewish Theological Seminary Association as an alternative to Reform's Hebrew Union College in Cincinnati. They tried to
fashion a school dedicated to the training of traditional rabbis and
teachers and the "promotion in America of the knowledge and practice of historical Judaism." Lacking funds, students, and charismatic
leadership, however, the seminary failed, only to be revived in 1902 and
funded mostly by leaders of the German Jewish establishment who
hoped it would produce Americanized, English-speaking rabbis to serve
Orthodox East European immigrants.[45]

By the third decade of the twentieth century the seminary had become the central institution of a gradually evolving, peculiarly American, Conservative Jewish religious movement, its intellectually elite
rabbinic graduates finding a constituency among upwardly mobile,
acculturating East European Jews and the middle-of-the-road synagogues they were creating—far more traditional than Reform temples
and more American in style and tone than most immigrant congregations.[46] But the early history of the seminary testifies to the inchoate-

ness of the traditional Jewish religious camp until that time and to the looseness of its boundaries and nebulousness of its religiocultural self-definition. Although seminary faculty Israel Friedlander carved out a coherent ideological perspective for Conservative Judaism distinct from Orthodoxy in the early years of the twentieth century, his intellectual precision was more the exception than the rule. Internal splits among traditional religionists were frequently rooted as much in class distinctions as in profound quarrels over religious ideology and practice.[47] Still, because it favored secular learning and applied some scientific methodology to the study of some classical Jewish texts, the seminary's Orthodoxy was disputed by a segment of immigrant traditionalists. But for all intents and purposes, until World War I the seminary was an Orthodox institution in theology and commitment to religious practice, and some of its faculty and students—even Friedlander himself—organized institutions that ultimately became mainstays of the Orthodox community.

Gradually, however, the East European immigrants precipitated a more refined demarcation of religious positions within traditional Judaism by intensifying the debate over the degree of acculturation that could be sanctioned by the tradition. Were local and regional European customs still mandatory in America? Could English be incorporated into the prayer service, and, if so, how much? Was the divider separating men and women in the traditional synagogue still necessary? Were extra precautionary stringencies in the dietary laws still to be followed? Was Yiddish necessary for the survival of traditional Jewish religious culture? Could scrupulously pious Jews send their children to public schools? These and a myriad of other questions required answers, and the responses that emerged revealed a spectrum of religious attitudes within traditional Judaism, which nevertheless seemed to coalesce into three broad religious tendencies: a nascent conservative movement on the left; acculturating, accommodationist Orthodox Jews in the center; and culturally resisting Orthodox Jews on the right.[48] Each represented a different point of equilibrium for traditionalists' encounters with American society. The boundaries among the tendencies in the early decades of the twentieth century, however, were often blurred and certainly permeable; some traditionalists identified with both the Orthodox right and center, even as others felt more at home in the newly forming Conservative synagogues.[49]

Orthodox Jewish leaders applauding American freedom and the merit of religious acculturation circumscribed the process within constraints the Reformers had long rejected. The parallels in their approach with that of the Rev. Isaac Leeser, an antebellum traditionalist leader, are instructive. In his day, Leeser, a Philadelphian, permitted the adoption of American Protestant forms to enhance the content of Judaism. Hence, he delivered English sermons, promoted the Jewish Sunday school, and inaugurated the first Jewish Publication Society to propagate Jewish knowledge after the fashion of Protestant tract and Bible societies.

Subsequent generations of Orthodox Jews employed similar tactics. With East European Jews fleeing to public schools, Orthodox communal leaders supported Talmud Torah schools that offered supplementary Jewish education on Monday through Thursday afternoons and Sunday mornings. They were also open to new pedagogic techniques in those schools, sermons in English rather than Yiddish, and more elaborate Sabbath afternoon services for those who felt compelled to work on Saturdays. Drachman's disciples at the Jewish Theological Seminary organized the Jewish Endeavor Society, which established dignified young people's prayer services with English sermons to try to win back the religiously indifferent.[50] In 1912 Israel Friedlander, together with Mordecai Kaplan, a seminary student and future founder of the Reconstructionist movement in Judaism, initiated the Young Israel synagogue movement, which featured social events such as dances and boat rides under synagogue auspices and subsequently became a long-standing institutional pillar of the acculturating Orthodox Jewish community.[51] Rabbi Herbert Goldstein of New York's Institutional Synagogue of Harlem added a full range of social activities to his congregational programming, including dance classes, gym activities, and library and artistic events, in an effort to put second-generation East European Jews at ease with Orthodox Judaism.[52]

On an institutional level, therefore, acculturating Orthodox Judaism accepted certain American cultural conventions, broadening the concept of what the synagogue could become and opening it to new avenues of American social and recreational interaction. But traditional theological beliefs, ritual practices, and the inherited liturgy were essentially unchanged, even if many Orthodox laymen ultimately designed their own religious compromises in personal religious behavior.

In contrast to acculturating Orthodox Jews, other traditionalists self-consciously resisted acculturation and sought to restrict the impact of American society while they replicated not only East European Orthodoxy in America but also the style in which it was conveyed. Advocates of this religiocultural posture organized one-room heder schools that offered traditional Jewish education in Yiddish, and they established the first yeshiva, Etz Chaim (1886). The rabbis, educators, and laymen among them argued for the primacy of Yiddish as a prerequisite for the future of Orthodox Judaism, as did earlier German Reform leaders such as David Einhorn and Samuel Hirsch, who had insisted on the indispensability of German for authentic Reform Judaism.

Proponents of this Orthodoxy viewed acculturation not as a strategy for survival but as the stimulus for religious attrition and group dissolution. To them, American culture represented a grave threat to Jewish survival, and they endorsed a social distancing from its influence and the re-creation of European-style rabbinic authority as the best defenses against its inroads. But the authority of individual Orthodox rabbis was significantly diluted in America, and all attempts to reestablish a centralized communal rabbinical authority and unify Orthodoxy foundered. The brief tenures of Rabbis Jacob Joseph and David Willowski, appointed chief rabbis of New York and Chicago, respectively, ended in failure, bitter frustration, and even communal chaos.[53] The American environment of religious freedom and voluntarism, in which any individual could assume ritual roles without proper rabbinic accreditation, was simply not conducive to the institutionalization of a hierarchical chain of rabbinic command.

To be sure, Orthodox resistors of American culture had solid achievements about which to boast. Opposed to the Union of Orthodox Congregations established in 1898 by acculturated Orthodox Jews—many of whom associated with the Jewish Theological Seminary, rendering both their Orthodoxy and institutional initiatives suspect—they founded their own rabbinic organization in 1902: Agudat ha-Rabbanim.[54] Its goals were to safeguard religious, particularly Sabbath, observance; control and supervise the kosher meat industry; encourage traditional yeshiva learning; and generally support fellow Jews resisting the enticing blandishments of their new environment. In 1904 the organization distributed a circular discrediting rabbinic graduates of the Jewish Theological Seminary, and in 1914 it prohibited Orthodox congregations from affiliating with the new seminary-inspired synagogue federation, the United Synagogue of America (1913). Although the actions of the Agudat ha-Rabbanim earned some communal support, the organization by World War I had failed to fulfill its objectives on any large scale, and it did not nurture its brand of Judaism among second-generation Jews. The Americanizing accommodationist impulse was simply too strong. Only since World War II, particularly from the 1960s to the present, has the ideology of more right-wing, separatist Orthodoxy made significant gains.

By 1915 the strategy of religious acculturation had won out among religiously identifying Jews, and the acculturation process found them on a religious continuum: Reformers on the left, Orthodox resistors

on the right, and culturally accommodationist Orthodox and embry-
onic Conservative Jews in the middle. From one perspective, all the
groups formulated some brand of American Jewish religious synthesis. Even Agudat ha-Rabbanim, which desisted as best it could from
American culture, appropriated some American societal forms, such as
the rabbinic union, to support its particular agenda.[55] But they differed
fundamentally over the legitimate scope of religious acculturation, and
one group's legitimate American Jewish religious synthesis was another's heresy or religious myopia. Hence, the invectives hurled by leaders of the various religious movements and orientations at each other
typically concentrated on invalidating the others' American Jewish
religious acculturation as inauthentic or inappropriate. In the eyes of
the interlocutors, the others' brands of American Judaism either violated historic definitions of Jews and Judaism or were anachronistically
Jewish and insufficiently modern and American. Between 1865 and
1915, therefore, religion was both a ground for working out the details of Jewish acculturation in America and an enduring source of
communal disunity and friction in American Jewish life. These internecine controversies over religious authenticity, within and across the
Jewish religious movements, continue to the present day.[56]

THE ACCULTURATION OF JEWISH NATIONALITY

However much they opposed each other's definition of Judaism, Reform and Orthodox Jews concurred that religion was the primary factor distinguishing the American Jewish collective, and—save the smaller
group of Orthodox resistors—they agreed that religious acculturation,
within the limits outlined by each movement, was a desirable strategy
fostering Jewish survival. But by the close of the nineteenth century,
and into the early decades of the twentieth, Jewish self-understanding
and introspective assessment of the factors that would sustain American Jewry were broadened radically. Mounting European anti-Semitism, the rise of secular Jewish national and international movements,
increasing anti-Jewish fervor in the United States, and the flood of East
European immigrants who established urban ghettoes evincing a vibrant, ethnically rich, Yiddish culture as well as potent labor and socialist ideologies led some Jewish leaders and thinkers to realize that
the conceptualization of world Jewry in religious terms and of American Jews as but one religious community among others within one
united American nationality did not fit the new historical circumstances.
Religious justifications for Jewish separatism within an American identity were either supplemented or supplanted by alternate models of
American Jewish acculturation and predicated on a different Jewish self-

understanding: that the physical bond of Jewish nationality (or race or peoplehood, both words were used interchangeably during the period to denote the physical dimension of the Jewish group) constituted the preeminent pole of Jewish group cohesion and identity, not religion.[57]

This recognition united under its banner both secular and religious Jews, including such important voices within Reform Judaism as Richard Gottheil, Bernhard Felsenthal, and Stephen Wise, who came to reject Reform's anti-nationalist Jewish posture and gravitated to various modes of Zionist expression.[58] On one hand, secularists like the Zionists and socialists, for example, dismissed the necessity of religion and posited group boundaries to inhere in the Jews' common descent, history, culture, class, or purported national destiny. Religionists, on the other hand, still assuming religion to be a vital ingredient in Jewish identification (the degree of importance separated Jewish Theological Seminary President Solomon Schechter from Reform-ordained Judah Magnes and both from social theorist Horace Kallen), emphasized that Judaism was a product of the people and espoused the primacy of Jewish peoplehood. Indeed, this stress on the national substratum of the Jewish religion led to broadened, new definitions of Judaism.[59] Anticipating Mordecai Kaplan's later avowal that Judaism was an "evolving religious civilization," for example, Bernhard Felsenthal, a Reformer and Zionist, in 1901 asserted that Judaism is not equivalent to the Jewish religion but rather is "the sum of all ethnological characteristics which have their roots in the distinctively Jewish national spirit."[60] At the very least, both secular and religious nationalists could agree with Magnes that the "tie that connects Jew to Jew, that makes every Jew wherever he may be or whatever may be the type of his mind a member of the Jewish community, has as its basis a national or, at all events, a racial [meant in the sense of the contemporary usage of ethnic] element."[61]

Affirming Jewish national loyalties, however, left Jews groping for a way to reconcile ethnic kinship with American national identity. The Protestant congregational model of group religious associationalism was not suitable for Jews professing Jewish nationality and had to be replaced with another. But with what? In response, two daring models of Jewish national acculturation were advanced. One Americanized Jewish nationalism, while the other reconfigured Americanism so that Jewish national separatism and cultural identity were warranted on American grounds.

In 1913 Louis Brandeis, a prominent Boston attorney and future Supreme Court justice, assumed the leadership of the American Zionist movement, which until that time had been weak with few signs of better prospects ahead. Ironically, this thoroughly acculturated Jew, until 1907 at the outer margins of the Jewish community, American-ized the most visibly separatist form of Jewish national identity, rein-terpreting Zionism philosophically, existentially, and organizationally in accordance with the American Progressive ethos. Brandeis identified the Jewish national cultural renaissance with Jeffersonian liberalism and Wilsonian progressivism. He conceived of Zionist pioneers working the land of Israel as latter-day New England Pilgrims and romanticized Palestinian Jewish colonies as recreations of early American colonial communities.

By linking Zionists to American Pilgrims, Brandeis integrated him-self and all Zionist supporters into the American national mythic iden-tity. Instead of a separatist American Judaism interpreted analogically to American Protestant biblical roots, a distinctive Jewish nationality was made consonant with American nationhood and a movement of Jewish national rebirth equated with American patriotism and liberal reform. Brandeis's American transfiguration of Zionism, meshing Jew-ish and American national aspirations, electrified American Jews and transformed the rather moribund national Zionist organization into a mass-membership association. It reconciled conceptually the two na-tional identities and allegiances that many Jews felt deeply but, up to that point, could not comfortably defend.[62]

The other model of Jewish national acculturation within American-ism, both historically prior to and simultaneous with that of Brandeis, was located in the ideology of American Jewish cultural Zionists. Cul-tural Zionism was at once both a sociocultural movement bearing a coherent, although by no means uniform, ideology and an acculturat-ing tactic for American Jewish survival. Its advocates, such as Solomon Schechter, Judah Magnes, Mordecai Kaplan, Israel Friedlander, and Horace Kallen, differed on the centrality and meaning of religion, the viability of European Jewish life, and the policies of political Zionism. Nevertheless, they did reach consensus on other critical ideas that con-stituted the core beliefs of the cultural Zionist ideal: the indivisibility of Jewish nationality from Jewish religion; the necessity of seeking Jew-ish cultural inspiration from Jewish Palestine; and the expectation that cultural Zionism would contribute to Jewish national, cultural, and spiritual renewal in America, promote self-reliance, attract the young and hence unite the generations, and heal the religious and cultural fragmentation of Jewish life.[63]

But in advancing cultural Zionism as a movement of Jewish renew-al its proponents also reconceptualized America, projecting a new ideo-logical conception of the nation grounded in the reality of Jewish na-

tional-cultural separatism. Friedlander, Magnes, and Kallen contended that Jewish nationalist self-perceptions were entirely appropriate
within the American polity because the ideal cultural model of the
country was neither de Crèvecoeur's image of America as a nation in
which "all nations are melted into a new race of men" nor Israel Zangwill's depiction of America as "God's crucible, the Great Melting Pot
where all races of Europe are melting and reforming," but rather
America as a democracy and republic of nationalities rooted in cultural pluralism.[64]

Kallen's articulation of cultural pluralism in 1915 and 1924 is more
widely cited by the secondary literature on the subject, but both Friedlander and Magnes to some degree anticipated his vision.[65] In a 1907
address entitled "The Problem of Judaism in America," Friedlander
asserted that a culturally plural ideal of America was consistent with
the putative "true" Anglo-Saxon American spirit. "The idea of liberty
as evolved by the Anglo-Saxon . . . signifies liberty of conscience, the
full untrammeled development of the soul as well as the body," he
observed, and "the true American spirit understands and respects the
traditions and associations of other nationalities, and on its vast area
numerous races live peaceably together, equally devoted to the interests of the land."[66]

Even more pointed, "A Republic of Nationalities," Judah Magnes's
February 1909 sermon at New York's Temple Emanu-El, argued that
preserving immigrant national and cultural identities was not only
pragmatically useful because it mitigated immigrant disorientation but
also culturally normative within the American polity. Although individuals could be members only of one political nation at one time,
Magnes claimed, they could concurrently affirm multiple nationalities;
hence Americanization did not demand the abandonment of nationality. Explicitly repudiating Zangwill's metaphor in his play The Melting Pot (1908), Magnes proclaimed, "America is not the melting pot.
It is not the Moloch demanding the sacrifice of national individuality.
America is the land conceived in liberty and dedicated to the principle
that all men are created free and equal. And a national soul is as pre-
cious and God-given as is the individual soul."[67]

This image of a culturally pluralist American republic of nationalities was invoked also by socialists, Yiddishists, and secular Zionists who
conjured up the identical model—so reminiscent of the multinational
political realities of their native East European regions—and used it to
bolster their own national ideologies and brand of American Jewish
ethnic politics. Thus, Chaim Zhitlovsky, a writer, orator, and Yiddish
socialist, held up as his democratic ideal an America as exemplar of

"nationalities living in peace and cooperative harmony," a "United States of United Peoples" benefiting from the rich diversity of its distinctive national groups.[68] Similarly, Zionist leader Louis Lipsky wrote in 1909 that "America is the meeting-place of the nations of the world. . . . In order to occupy a place in the America where the races of Europe meet, the Jew as a self-respecting citizen, must claim that he is a Jew by nationality. If he does not do that he is an *American* citizen with a blemish."[69]

This Jewish reconceptualization of America underscores the reciprocal nature of the dynamic of Jewish acculturation. America clearly had a profound impact on its Jews. They, in turn, were not merely passive beneficiaries of the historically "Judaic" elements of American culture or of the particularly favorable set of national circumstances and socioeconomic opportunities the country offered them. Rather, they themselves were active agents in defining America. Jews not only self-consciously desired to contribute to the country, and clearly did so, they not only made American culture and nationality their own, but they also felt free to participate in the molding of that culture and nationality and to help determine American self-understanding of its national character and ideals. The fact that a Jewish minority could even think of participating in that process and that a host society was structured in such a way as to enable them to do so is unique in Jewish history. That, together with the novel patterns of acculturation that arose, differentiated American Jews diachronically and synchronically from Jews in other times and other places and signifies the unique nature of the American Jewish experience.

The Strategy of Defense

American Jewish acculturation patterns were built on assumptions of an inclusivist societal model fully compatible with both Jewish cultural distinctiveness and American insider status. But these presumptions were resisted by antithetical exclusivist trends in American culture, rooted in Protestant triumphalism and secular bigotry, which jeopardized Jewish standing as American equals and portrayed Jews as outsiders.[70] To be sure, America was not Europe but neither was it yet the "promised land" fulfilled. As with other host societies, therefore, Jews in America devised strategies of communal defense to contend appropriately with the challenges posed by the specific American context. They defended their group's sense of place in and vision of America, dissented from any definition of America as a Christian nation, and fought in various ways the patterns of prejudice to which they were subject.[71]

The most omnipresent problem that American Jews encountered was
the varied forms of discrimination arising from the obfuscation of
church-state lines in American society, as mainstream Protestants tried
to shape the country in their religious image. Although many Protestant leaders sought with legislative and judicial measures to have America constitutionally declared a Christian (that is, Protestant) country,
most supported the political ideal of church-state separation. Through
a host of social causes and voluntary organizations, however, they also
strove tenaciously to sculpt an American civic and moral culture governed by Protestant cultural styles and moral tastes enshrined in public law.

Jews experienced the effects of Protestant triumphalism in one of two
ways: either as a byproduct of Protestant self-affirmation, in which
Protestant actions were not directed at Jews but still left them feeling
unfairly victimized, or in direct attacks explicitly targeting them as the
objects of Protestant attention and scorn. Examples of the former included Sunday Blue Laws upholding the Christian Sabbath as the national day of rest, ruled constitutional by the Supreme Court in 1896
and 1900; political initiatives of the Christian temperance movement
and Sabbath observance campaign fortified by Protestant zeal, which
attempted to translate Protestant morality into American common law;
Bible readings from the King James Bible, the reading of the Lord's
Prayer, and the singing of Protestant hymns in American public schools;
christological references in official presidential and state government
Thanksgiving and national Fast Day proclamations; attempts by the
National Reform Association to amend the Constitution and declare
America a Christian nation; judicial assertions by several Supreme
Court justices that America is indeed a Christian nation; and the draft-
ing of international treaties, such as those between the United States
and Switzerland (1857) and China (1858), whose documentary language protected the rights of American Christians in these lands, implicitly excluding protection to American non-Christians.

Protestant initiatives specifically aimed at Jews included missionary
drives from the second decade of the nineteenth century to at least the
middle decades of the twentieth. Missionary activities intensified in
specific historical circumstances, and the arrival of the East European
Jews sparked renewed efforts that especially targeted children in ghettoes. Mainstream Protestant bodies such as the Episcopalians and Presbyterians justified these endeavors not merely on religious grounds but
also with the rationalization that they were necessary for the immigrants' Americanization.[72] Too, determined to retain their self-perceived
social standing and cultural hegemony, members of the Protestant in-

tellectual elite such as Henry Adams, David Starr Jordan, and Charles
B. Davenport contributed significantly to the xenophobic nativism,
Anglo-Saxon conformism, and secular racism of the anti-immigration
movement that gathered much force in the late nineteenth century.
Although such sentiments were not focused exclusively against Jews,
East European Jews nevertheless bore much of the brunt of the attacks.
Leading Protestant clerics and academicians—R. Heber Newton, Wash-
ington Gladden, Robert Collyer, and W. H. P. Faunce, for example—
advanced unsavory public perceptions of Jews as clannish, unpatriotic, avaricious, and fomenters of race pride.[73] These pronouncements
frequently carried an ominous threat of Jewish exclusion from the
American polity, as in a bold declaration in 1909 by the Rev. Frederick Lynch, pastor of Brooklyn's Pilgrim Church, that "one cannot be a
Jew [except in religion] and a real American at the same time."[74]

Protestant disdain for exotic, alien East European Jews was inter-
woven with Protestant disdain for Judaism. Few Protestant ministers
and intellectuals had any genuine appreciation for the Jewish religion
on its own merits, and Protestant evangelicals and liberals of all stripes
were united in trivializing Judaism as debased and superseded by (Protestant) Christianity. While Dwight Moody, for example, reiterated the
deicide charge against Jews at revivalist meetings, while Protestant-
tinged Populist rhetoric often linked the Jews to the devil, more liberal Protestants such as Lyman Abbot scored Judaic legalism as well as
Jewish ethnicity and nationalist particularism and repeated standard
Christian supersessionist theology: "Judaism is Christianity in the bud;
Christianity is Judaism in the flower."[75]

To be sure, American Protestantism did show Jews a more positive
side, expressing admiration, collegiality, and even friendship for them,
if not for Judaism. The Protestant press in editorials and news stories
sometimes lauded Jewish virtues of thrift, close family bonds, philanthropy, and moral probity.[76] On occasion, Jews were welcomed into
Protestant Masonic fraternities, and individual ministers, especially
Unitarians, enjoyed cordial relations with their Reform Jewish rabbinic
peers, exchanging pulpits and newspaper subscriptions and joining
petitions denouncing European anti-Semitism.[77] The liberal Protestant
Free Religious Association invited Jews to participate and to sit on its
board, while organizers of the World Parliament of Religions made sure
that Judaism was represented.[78] These Protestant overtures, however,
could not compensate for the moments of bitter frustration Jews experienced in the face of hostile Protestant anti-Jewish sentiments, particularly evident in the national debates over European immigration.
Liberal Reform Jews such as Kaufmann Kohler and Emil G. Hirsch,

proponents of interfaith interaction and understanding, expected the most from the Protestant world and were among the most disappointed in the face of deliberate or inadvertent Protestant prejudice.[79] However much they and their colleagues worked to refute it, however much Jews tried to actualize the inclusivist model of America, at the turn of the twentieth century many came to the regretful conclusion that, fundamentally, America was a Christian (that is, Protestant) nation.[80]

Complementing Protestant antagonism was widespread secular anti-Jewish bigotry and socioeconomic discrimination expressed in sundry ways: denial of bank credit, negatively slanted Dun and Bradstreet reports, exclusion from public places such as hotels and beaches, job discrimination, and defamation of character through pejorative appellations of Jews as Shylocks and arsonists. The Panic of 1873 and the great depression of 1893–97 certainly fanned the flames of impassioned secular socioeconomic animus against Jews, which in the wake of mass East European immigration was profoundly augmented by rising nativist and Populist rhetoric marking foreign Jews as the enemy. Although the distinctions between religious and secular motivations for anti-Jewish fervor could sometimes be clearly drawn yet at other times remain ambiguous, Jews consistently were more inclined to ascribe all manifestations of anti-Jewish malice to the impetus of religious prejudice.[81]

For most of the nineteenth century Jews reacted to perceived church-state violations with the demand for parity and did not invoke Jefferson's "wall of separation" idea until the end of the nineteenth century and the opening decades of the twentieth, when widespread Protestantization of American culture and the intensity of societal anti-Semitism suggested that approach as being more fruitful for safeguarding Jewish rights. The tactics Jews used on church-state issues varied. For example, they petitioned governors and members of Congress against insensitive and unfair Christian proclamations, protested through the press and the lobbying of communal leaders against the provisions of American treaties with foreign governments that discriminated against them, fought in court over the repeal of Sunday Blue Laws or the lack of Jewish exemptions from them, lobbied against Bible readings and Christian hymns in public schools, boycotted public schools on Christmas, and joined with the religiously radical Free Religious Association and the secular National Liberal League to defeat proposed Christian amendments to the Constitution.[82]

In defending their interests against the intrusive Protestantization of civic life, Jews consistently invoked the pluralist, inclusivist model of America. The country was not founded on Christianity nor was its society Christian, Louis Marshall chided Supreme Court Associate

Justice David J. Brewer, and to affirm the Christian character of the nation was, in fact, deviant, un-American behavior.[83] Marshall's declaration exemplified but an extreme example of the common practice of Jews when combating Protestant coloration of supposedly religiously neutral institutions and social practices: framing Jewish arguments in liberal American rhetoric, identifying their cause with "true" American values, and projecting parochial group concerns as universal American problems. Thus, arguing against laws forcing them to close their businesses on Sunday, Jews contended that religious compulsion was of no religious value and infringed on their liberty of conscience and hence on both grounds was patently un-American. Contesting King James Bible readings in public schools, the Central Conference of American Rabbis Committee on Church and State in 1906 criticized the sectarian nature of the texts, which, it held, could never be impartial; hence, the argument went, such Bible readings obstructed American democracy rather than fostered it, as Protestants maintained, and should be discontinued.

The implicit anti-Judaism of mainstream Protestantism was rebutted by Jewish religious leaders with their own version of Jewish triumphalism. The axiomatic belief of Protestant liberals that their religion represented the religion of humanity was disputed by rabbis, who staked the identical claim for Judaism. Protestant assertions that "Judaism is germinal Christianity; Christianity is fructified Judaism" were rebuffed with Jewish proclamations that whatever is true in Christianity is Jewish in origin—and whatever is not Jewish is not true.[84] Protestant missionizing, which implicitly assaulted the integrity of Jewish life even as it underscored embarrassing, painful realities of Jewish religious laxity and indifference, social alienation, and educational inadequacies, ironically strengthened the Jewish community. Inevitably, missionary actions that exploited areas of Jewish weakness and tried to win over susceptible Jews such as the poor and the orphaned prompted leaders to initiate new institutions and programs—orphanages, Jewish hospitals, and after-school youth activities—that improved the vulnerable areas of Jewish social, religious, and cultural life the missionaries had uncovered.[85]

As to secular prejudices, Jews, by their associational patterns, considerably neutralized—although did not defeat—the persistent socioeconomic discriminations they encountered. Denied admission into Christian fraternal organizations and social clubs, they established their own; denied credit from banks or unfairly receiving poor credit ratings from Dun and Bradstreet reports, German and East European Jews created their own internal Jewish credit system that linked American

Jews to each other and, some, to European relatives and friends. Rejected by American trade unions, which also opposed the immigration of foreign workers, East European Jews initiated their own. By 1914 the 104 Jewish unions associated with the United Hebrew Trades, which had a total membership of more than one-quarter of a million, was unafraid of using political pressure and the vote to advance Jewish causes.[86] The shunning of Jews, in effect, contributed to the evolution of a distinctive economic subcommunity among both the German and East European Jews, which in the long run reinforced Jewish economic independence as well as political consciousness and, eventually, leverage.[87]

Attacks against the Jewish character precipitated multiple Jewish reactions. Jews boycotted the newspapers and literary materials whose caricatures vilified them. Jewish papers and communal spokesmen rebutted public images depicting Jews as materialistic, ethnocentric Shylocks and glorified reputed Jewish virtues, such as excellent family relations, industriousness, and responsible citizenship. Against charges of tribalism and clannishness, Jews contended that their actions on behalf of other beleaguered Jews represented the finest expression of the American value of self-help, while slurs against immigrant Jews were met with Jewish polemics and serious scholarly studies demonstrating speedy immigrant absorption and adjustment to the country and predicting their vast potential economic and cultural contribution to society.[88] At the same time, ever-vigilant of what others thought of them, Jews took pains to change whatever behavior threatened to shame the community. Jewish leaders were particularly sensitive to Jewish crime, white slavery, and prostitution and labored, unsuccessfully, to put an end to them. Some German Jewish efforts to hasten the Americanization of East Europeans, therefore, could also be construed to be part of Jewish self-policing, as the former set up settlement houses for the latter, as well as technical institutes to wean them from the needle trades, and established a variety of agencies to remove them to the interior of the United States and away from congested urban ghettoes.[89]

A favorite tactic Jews employed to deflect anti-Jewish stereotypes or calumnies was education. Rooted in the liberal premise that rational ideas logically presented could overcome prejudice, communal leaders were preoccupied with the pedagogic mission of teaching Gentiles the positive virtues of Jews and Judaism, affirming Jewish patriotism, and informing America of the major contributions Jews had made to the country. Invariably, therefore, the educational initiatives intended for important internal reasons had an apologetic, public relations agenda

as well. Examples abound. The Jewish Publication Society was rees-
tablished in 1888 to produce books to educate Jews and also to improve communal relations by advancing appealing images of Jews as
human beings and patriots, intimately connected with American society. The annual *American Jewish Year Book*, first published by the Jewish Publication Society in 1899—and modeled after Protestant and
Catholic yearbooks—hoped to alert not only Jews but also non-Jews
to the considerable Jewish achievements during the year.[90] The editors
of the twelve-volume *Jewish Encyclopedia* quite consciously assumed
that the scholarly material about Jews and Judaism that they published
would refute false accusations, decrease anti-Semitism, and enhance the
favorable understanding of the Jewish faith.[91] Founded in 1892, the
American Jewish Historical Society assumed both a scholarly and communal agenda, but the former was adjunct to the latter. Collecting and
publishing material on American Jews, it was hoped, would not only
create and preserve an objective historical record but also disseminate
knowledge of Jewish centrality to the American story, thus reducing
anti-Jewish hatred and benefiting Jewish welfare. Hence, in 1892 and
on the occasion of the four-hundredth anniversary of Columbus's voyage to the Americas, Oscar S. Straus, the society's first president and
himself the author of the earlier filiopietistic *The Origin of the Republican Form of Government in the United Sates of America,* enlisted
Mayer Kayserling, a European historian, to write a history of the discovery of the New World illustrating the instrumental role Jews had
played in America's history from its earliest days. The apologetic tone
of some of this material is seen in bold relief in Simon Wolf's massive
The American Jew as Patriot, Soldier, and Citizen (1895), which responded to an accusation that Jews did not fight loyally for the Union
in the Civil War with a comprehensive list of Jewish patriots who had
fought in all American wars.[92]

All Jewish defense tactics—education, political and legislative lobbying, court challenges, public propaganda, and equating Jewish aspirations with American convictions—were used in the community's
most concentrated public battles against the persecution of Jews abroad,
particularly in Europe. Ironically, the need to stand up on their behalf
served essential American Jewish survivalist purposes, furnishing many
Jews with a minimalist raison d'être for group solidarity; uniting, however transiently, the disparate elements of the community; and confer-
ring—or reinforcing—the privileged status of communal leadership on
those actively engaged in these endeavors.[93] Specific local and regional crises of European Jews sparked the creation of the first American

Jewish defense organizations, the Board of Delegates of American Israelites (1859), the American Jewish Committee (1906), and the American Jewish Joint Distribution Committee (1914), all of which in their respective ways initially sought to alleviate the distress of foreign Jews. Indeed, only after their inception did the former two organizations recognize the need to focus on Jewish domestic issues as well. And although the tactics of American Jewish defense on behalf of foreign Jews did not frequently succeed in steering American political policies in their favor, they did produce a few notable triumphs, such as the successful American Jewish Committee campaign that led to the abrogation in 1912 of the Russian-American Treaty of 1832 to punish Russia for its treatment of its Jews.

The logic of defending Jews abroad inevitably compelled American Jews to realize, despite some initial misgivings on the part of the German Jewish establishment, that Jewish emigration had to be supported and even recommended. Previously settled East European Jews were willing to be aggressive, even confrontational, in efforts to maintain American open doors to their fellow Jews. The communal stewards of the elite American Jewish Committee, on the other hand, resorted to the defense tactics of public education as well as to legislative and judicial activism suffused with American inclusivist rhetoric in the effort to foil the evolving American policy of immigrant restrictionism. In their mind, this movement united Protestant religious animus with secular enmity and was particularly dangerous. Max J. Kohler, for example, champion of Jewish rights, ardent foe of American anti-Semitism, and expert in immigration law, devoted much of his legal career to the defense of all minorities against anti-immigration forces between 1907 and 1917. The son of Kaufmann Kohler, a native German Reform Jewish theologian and president of Hebrew Union College, Max Kohler consistently placed himself on the high ground of American liberty and liberality in his court briefs and public writing on the subject. Adopting Jefferson's adage "shall oppressed humanity find no asylum on this globe" as his motto, he assailed congressional legislators and government leaders for undermining cherished American traditions by denying immigrants due process, judicial review, and appeal, and resolutely challenged America to live up to its own best ideals. That his efforts and those of others failed to prevent the promulgation of the 1917 immigration law and its literacy test detracts neither from his high-minded idealism nor obscures the American rhetoric advanced on behalf of Jewish and other immigrants seeking entry into the United States.[94]

Conclusion

Did the application of the four Jewish survival strategies between 1865 and 1915 succeed in their goals? The answer must be nuanced and equivocal although weighted in the affirmative. On the one hand, the strategies of building communal infrastructures and acculturation did not preclude communal fragmentation, ideological cleavage, and religious divisions, which not only drained communal energies but also later undermined American Jewish advocacy on behalf of European Jews suffering under Nazi oppression. Nor did they prevent the loss to the Jewish community of untold tens of thousands of immigrants as well as second- and third-generation Jews, who, attracted to American culture and finding religious or ethnic Judaism irrelevant or redundant, lost the will to survive as Jews and assimilated outright into the general population. The strategy of Jewish defense did not really mitigate domestic expressions of anti-Semitism, which only intensified during the 1920s and 1930s, nor prevent the lynching of Leo Frank in 1915. Moreover, Jews failed by World War I to thwart the implicit anti-Judaism of mainstream Protestantism and convince its adherents that America was not a Christian country, ideas that only very slowly began to dawn on select numbers of Protestants during the 1920s and 1930s.[95]

On the other hand, European Jews who had relocated to America were spared much of the travail of nineteenth-century European Jewish life, not to speak of the atrocities European Jews experienced from World War I through the Holocaust. Had more of them immigrated earlier and been given the chance to do so after 1921, fewer would have been murdered later. Too, the communal organizations and infrastructures that were established did produce institutionally rich and variegated Jewish religious movements and ethnic communities that gave coherence and sustenance to Jewish life and successfully nurtured historic traditions of Jewish culture and self-help while planting new models of American Jewish living. Most Jews still retained the will to survive as Jews and acted upon that impulse. And although hostility against Jews and their cognizance of it contributed immeasurably to their group identity and will to survive as Jews, the strategies of community-building and the multiple modes of acculturation and Jewish defense provided the means by which to make Jewish continuity a reality.

Beyond 1915, the tenacity of the Jewish ideological reconceptualization of America bore fruit. By 1915 Jewish advocacy of the ideals of cultural pluralism and the strict interpretation of church-state separation, both of which reinforced Jewish equality in America, had made no significant headway in American culture. But the currents of subsequent twentieth-century American history soon transformed Jewish perceptions of America into reality. The cultural hegemony of the Protestant establishment waned by midcentury, and by the 1960s cultural pluralism replaced the melting pot as the primary metaphor of the ideal American polity; church-state separation was increasingly understood in terms of the wall of separation, so much so that by the 1980s some complained that the "naked public square" was not what the Founding Fathers had in mind.[96] Whether resorting to the image of a Judeo-Christian basis for American civilization, to the metaphor of a triple melting pot, or to the ideology of cultural pluralism, in the course of the twentieth century the tiny minority of American Jews had established the fact that their separate Jewish existence could cohere with American culture.[97] To this point at least, America has proven another viable center for historic Jewish survival.[98]

Notes

I thank my friends and colleagues Steven Bowman, David Goldenberg, and Michael Satlow for their helpful comments and express my special gratitude to Barbara Selya, managing editor of the Hebrew Union College Press, for her sound editorial judgments.

1. See citation quoted in Baila Shargel, *Practical Dreamer: Israel Friedlander and the Shaping of American Judaism* (New York: Jewish Theological Seminary of America, 1985), 113.

2. Useful one-volume histories of the Jews are Haim Hillel Ben-Sasson, *A History of the Jewish People* (Cambridge: Harvard University Press, 1976), and Robert M. Seltzer, *Jewish People, Jewish Thought: The Jewish Experience in History* (New York: Macmillan, 1980). For a brief analysis of the diverse contemporary sociological discussions about future survival, see the text and notes of Nathan Glazer, "American Jewry or American Judaism," in *American Pluralism and the Jewish Community,* ed. Seymour Martin Lipset (New Brunswick: Transaction Publishers, 1990), 31–41; see also Marshall Sklare, "American Jewry: The Ever-Dying People," *Midstream* 22 (1976): 17–27; and Henry L. Feingold, "American Jewish History and American Jewish Survival," *American Jewish History* 71 (1982): 421–31.

3. This essay probes Jewish this-worldly initiatives to ensure group survival and takes no position on the theological/metaphysical claim invoked by traditional Jews that cites biblical covenantal promises and Jewish fidelity to divine imperatives as the self-evident explanations for ultimate Jewish historic continuity. But even traditionalists would have to concede that Jews "did something" to perpetuate the Jewish people in order to fulfill God's master plan,

and that something is the subject under discussion. For a nuanced interpretation of the scope and limitations of Jewish power in autonomous diaspora communities, see David Biale, *Power and Powerlessness in Jewish History* (New York: Schocken Books, 1986).

4. Useful broad syntheses of American Jewish history for this period include Naomi W. Cohen, *Encounter with Emancipation: The German Jews in the United States, 1830–1914* (Philadelphia: Jewish Publication Society of America, 1984); Hasia R. Diner, *A Time for Gathering: The Second Migration, 1820–1880* (Baltimore: Johns Hopkins University Press, 1992); Gerald Sorin, *A Time for Building: The Third Migration, 1880–1920* (Baltimore: John Hopkins University Press, 1992); Arthur A. Goren, *The American Jews* (Cambridge: Harvard University Press, 1982); and Howard M. Sachar, *A History of the Jews in America* (New York: Knopf, 1992).

5. On the uniqueness of American Jewry, see Benny Kraut, "What Is American about American Jewish History and Judaism? A Methodological Inquiry," in *What Is American about the American Jewish Experience?* ed. Marc A. Raphael (Williamsburg: The College of William and Mary, 1993). The literature claiming exceptional status for American Jewish life relative to the rest of Jewish history is substantial. See, for example, Ben Halpern, *The American Jew: A Zionist Analysis* (New York: Theodor Herzl Foundation, 1956); Abraham J. Karp, "What's American about American Jewish History: The Religious Scene," *American Jewish Historical Quarterly* 52 (1963): 283–94; Martin A. Cohen, "Structuring American Jewish History," *American Jewish Historical Quarterly* 57 (1967): 137–52; Jonathan D. Sarna, ed., *The American Jewish Experience* (New York: Holmes and Meier, 1986), xiii–xix; Naomi W. Cohen, *Essential Papers on Jewish-Christian Relations in the United States* (New York: New York University Press, 1990), 4–5; Seymour Martin Lipset, "A Unique People in an Exceptional Country," in *American Pluralism and the Jewish Community*, ed. Lipset, 3–30; Shmuel Eisenstadt, "The American Jewish Experience and American Pluralism: A Comparative Perspective," in *American Pluralism and the Jewish Community*, ed. Lipset, 43–52; Stephen J. Whitfield, "American Jews: Their Story Continues," in *The American Jewish Experience*, ed. Sarna, 284–93; and Henry Feingold, "The American Component of Jewish Identity," in *Jewish Identity in America*, ed. David Gordis and Yoav Ben-Horin (Los Angeles: Susan and David Wilstein Institute of Jewish Policy Studies, 1991), 69–80. For a more circumscribed comparative analysis contrasting American Jewry with German Jewry, see Michael A. Meyer, *The German Jews: Some Perspectives on Their History* (Syracuse: Syracuse University Press, 1991), 1–16.

6. For a broad overview of modern European Jewish history, see Howard M. Sachar, *The Course of Modern Jewish History* (New York: Dell Publishing, 1977).

7. Lucy Dawidowicz, "A Century of Jewish History, 1881–1981: The View from America," *American Jewish Year Book* 82 (1982): 3–101, esp. 4–5.

8. See Lloyd P. Gartner, "Immigration and the Formation of American Jewry, 1840–1925," *Journal of World History* 11 (1968): 297–312; and Lloyd

P. Gartner, "Jewish Migrants en Route from Europe to North America," in *The Jews of North America*, ed. Moses Rischin (Detroit: Wayne State University Press, 1987), 25–43. For more detailed material on German Jewish immigration, see Cohen, *Encountering Emcipation* and *Essential Papers*, and Diner, *A Time for Gathering*, as well as the collected essays of Rudolf Glanz in *Studies in Judaica Americana* (New York: Ktav Publishing House, 1970). On East European immigration, see Samuel Joseph, *Jewish Immigration to the United States, 1881–1910* (New York, 1914; repr. New York: Arno Press, 1969), and Simon Kuznets, "Immigration of Russian Jews to the United States: Background and Structure," *Perspectives in American History* 9 (1975): 35–124. Abraham Karp puts the figure of German Jewish immigrants between 1880 and 1910 at only 20,400; see his *Haven and Home: A History of the Jews in America* (New York: Schocken Books, 1985), 113. Against this view, however, see Avraham Barkai, "German-Jewish Migrations in the Nineteenth Century, 1830–1910," *Leo Baeck Institute Year Book* 30 (1985): 301–18.

9. On the German Jews' institutional life, see Cohen, *Encounter with Emancipation*, passim; for similar accounts of Eastern European Jews, see Karp, *Haven and Home*, 90ff, 158ff. On East European socialists and radicals, see Gerald Sorin, *The Prophetic Minority: American Jewish Immigrant Radicals, 1880–1920* (Bloomington: Indiana University Press, 1985).

10. See Nathan Kaganoff, "The Jewish *Landsmanshaftn* in New York City in the Period Preceding World War I," *American Jewish History* 76 (1986): 58; see also Nathan Kaganoff, "Organized Jewish Welfare Activity in New York City, 1848–1860," *American Jewish Historical Quarterly* 56 (1966): 27–61.

11. On *landsmanshaftn,* see the issue of *American Jewish History* 76 (1986) dedicated to that topic, especially the articles by Daniel Soyer, Hannah Kliger, Susan Milamed, and Shelly Tenenbaum; see also Michael R. Weisser, *A Brotherhood of Memory: Jewish* Landsmansaftn *in the New World* (New York: Basic Books, 1985).

12. The friction and ambivalent relationships between German and East European Jews is a fundamental theme in American Jewish history and the subject of voluminous studies. See Cohen, *Encounter with Emancipation,* passim; Sachar, *A History of Jews in America,* passim; see also Moses Rischin, "Germans versus Russians," in Rischin, *The Promised City* (Cambridge: Harvard University Press, 1962); Robert Rockaway, "Ethnic Conflict in an Urban Environment: The German and Russian Jew in Detroit, 1881–1914," *American Jewish Historical Quarterly* 60 (1970): 133–52; and Charles Wyszkowski, *A Community in Conflict: American Jewry during the Great European Immigration* (Lanham: University Press of America, 1991).

13. A case can be made that there were more subcommunities, if one takes into account the religious divisions, Jewish labor movement, and other ideological cleavages that found broad social appeal. Nevertheless, this categorization has much merit because many of the religious, social, economic, and ideological fissures of the community were rooted in the deep national or eth-

nic split between the Germans and the Russians. Jacob R. Marcus argues that one can speak of the "American" Jew only after 1921, when the passage of the immigrant quota law cut off mass Jewish immigration and rendered the fusion of one American ethnic Jewry inevitable. See Marcus, "Periodization of American Jewish History," *Publications of the American Jewish Historical Society* 47 (1958): 125–33, and "Background for the History of American Jewry," in *The American Jew: A Reappraisal,* ed. Oscar I. Janowsky (Philadelphia: Jewish Publication Society of America, 1964), 1–25, esp. 16–22.

14. Robert T. Handy's work on this tension is particularly insightful: see *A Christian America: Protestant Hopes and Historical Realities,* 2d ed. (New York: Oxford University Press, 1984), and *Undermined Establishment: Church-State Relations in America, 1880–1920* (Princeton: Princeton University Press, 1991). A helpful synthesis of Jewish interactions with Protestant America is in Egal Feldman, *Dual Destinies: The Jewish Encounter with Protestant America* (Urbana: University of Illinois Press, 1990).

15. See, for example, on this theme, James Davison Hunter, *Culture Wars: The Struggle to Define America* (New York: Basic Books, 1991), 71. An example of a contemporary Jew's insistence on the pervasive impact of the Hebrew Bible on America is Abraham I. Katsh, *The Biblical Heritage of American Democracy* (New York: Ktav Publishing House, 1977).

16. East European press accounts referred to America as the *goldene medinah* (golden land), and some Jews, such as Isaac Mayer Wise, claimed to have been inflamed with the American spirit while still in Europe. See Sefton D. Temkin, *Isaac Mayer Wise: Shaping American Judaism* (New York: Oxford University Press, 1992), 1.

17. On the tactics of selling religion in the marketplace, see R. Laurence Moore, *Selling God: American Religion in the Marketplace of Culture* (New York: Oxford University Press, 1994).

18. Representative voices from across the religious spectrum expressed grave concern over the future of Judaism in America. See Jonathan D. Sarna, *People Walk on Their Heads: Moses Weinberger's Jews and Judaism in New York* (New York: Holmes and Meier, 1982) for a caustic Orthodox criticism of American Jewish lifestyle. In 1906 Solomon Schechter lamented that America is the "Galut [exile] of Judaism, . . . of the Jewish soul," cited in Jerold S. Auerbach, *Rabbis and Lawyers: The Journey from Torah to Constitution* (Bloomington: Indiana University Press, 1990), 105. Israel Friedlander complained that the more prosperous Jews become, the more defenseless their Judaism; see "The Problem of Judaism in America," in Friedlander, *Past and Present: Selected Essays* (New York: Burning Bush Press, 1961), 168. Reform Jews worried as well; Rabbi I. S. Moses commented in 1885 that the "future of Judaism in this country looks gloomy in the extreme," cited in Kerry M. Olitzky, "Sundays at Chicago Sinai Congregation: Paradigm for a Movement," *American Jewish History* 74 (1985): 362. Rabbi Charles Levi in 1909 mused that perhaps it was time to worry about making American Jews more Jewish rather than more American, which had been the prior all-consuming concern.

On this, see Leon A. Jick, "The Reform Synagogue," in *The American Synagogue: A Sanctuary Transformed*, ed. Jack Wertheimer (New York: Cambridge University Press, 1987), 95.

19. On Felix Adler and his impact on American Jews, see Benny Kraut, *From Reform Judaism to Ethical Culture: The Religious Evolution of Felix Adler* (Cincinnati: Hebrew Union College Press, 1979); on Fleischer, see Arthur Mann, ed., *Growth and Achievement: Temple Israel, 1854–1954* (New York: Riverside Press, 1954).

20. Examples of struggles for institutional control can be found in Benny Kraut, "A Unitarian Rabbi? The Case of Solomon Sonneschein," in *Jewish Apostasy in the Modern World*, ed. Todd M. Endelman (New York: Holmes and Meier, 1987), 272–308; and Jonathan D. Sarna, *JPS: The Americanization of Jewish Culture* (Philadelphia: Jewish Publication Society of America, 1989), 17–24, esp. 22.

21. Cited in Cohen, *Encounter with Emancipation*, 172.

22. Although one group of Orthodox Jews quite deliberately cultivated outsider status for the sake of Jewish self-preservation as they understood it, that was not the norm. I differ with the interpretation of R. Laurence Moore in *Religious Outsiders and the Making of Americans* (New York: Oxford University Press, 1986), 72–101.

23. Benny Kraut, "The Ambivalent Relations of American Reform Judaism with Unitarian in the Last Third of the Nineteenth Century," *Journal of Ecumenical Studies* 23 (1986): 58–68, esp. n24.

24. A full account of the events that transpired that spring can be found in the article by David Geffen in *The American Israelite*, March 24, 1994, B-5, B-25.

25. Daniel J. Elazar, Jonathan D. Sarna, and Rela G. Monson, eds., *A Double Bond: The Constitutional Documents of American Jewry* (Lanham: University Press of America, 1992), esp. Sarna, "What Is American about the Constitutional Documents of American Jewry?" 35–56, and sample synagogue constitutions, 148–90.

26. Arthur A. Goren, *Saints and Sinners: The Underside of American Jewish History* (Cincinnati: American Jewish Archives, 1988), 1–28, esp. 12–21; see also Goren, "Traditional Institutions Transplanted: The *Hevra Kadisha* in Europe and America," in *The Jews of North America*, ed. Rischin, 62–78.

27. On secular studies introduced into the Rabbi Isaac Elchanan Theological Seminary, see Gilbert Klaperman, "Yeshiva University: Seventy-Five Years in Retrospect," *American Jewish Historical Quarterly* 54 (1964): 19.

28. On Magnes's *kehilla*, see Arthur A. Goren, *New York Jews and the Quest for Community: The Kehilla Experiment, 1908–1922* (New York: Columbia University Press, 1970); on Magnes, see Goren, *Dissenter in Zion: From the Writings of Judah L. Magnes* (Cambridge: Harvard University Press, 1982). Refer as well to a fine collection of essays dedicated to Magnes in *Like All the Nations? The Life and Legacy of Judah L. Magnes*, ed. William M. Brinner and Moses Rischin (Albany: SUNY Press, 1987).

29. Feldman, *Dual Destinies*, 117.

30. Lloyd P. Gartner, "'Temples of Liberty Unpolluted': American Jews and Public Schools, 1840–1875," in *Bicentennial Festschrift for Jacob R. Marcus,* ed. Bertram W. Korn (New York: Ktav Publishing House, 1976), 157–89; Moshe Davis, *The Emergence of Conservative Judaism: The Historical School in Nineteenth Century America* (Philadelphia: Jewish Publication Society of America, 1962), 34–64; Hyman B. Grinstein, "In the Course of the Nineteenth Century," and Meir Ben-Horin, "From the Turn of the Century to the Late Thirties," both in *A History of Jewish Education in America,* ed. Judah Pilch (New York: National Curriculum Research Institute of the American Association for Jewish Education, 1969); Goren, *New York Jews and the Quest for Community,* 110–33; Stephan F. Brumberg, *Going to America, Going to School* (New York: Praeger Publishers, 1986); Shlomit Yahalom, "American Judaism and the Question of Separation Between Church and State," Ph.D. diss. [in Hebrew], Hebrew University, 1981 13, 24.

31. Goren, *New York Jews and the Quest for Community,* 16–17; see also Alan Silverstein, *Alternatives to Assimilation: The Response of Reform Judaism to American Culture, 1840–1939* (Hanover: University Press of New England, 1994), esp. Part 3, "1900–1930: American Corporate Culture."

32. Feldman, *Dual Destinies,* passim; Lance J. Sussman, "Isaac Leeser and the Protestantization of American Judaism," *American Jewish Archives* 38 (1986): 1–21; Wertheimer, ed., *The American Synagogue,* passim; Jacob R. Marcus and Abraham Peck, eds., *The American Rabbinate: A Century of Continuity and Change* (New York: Ktav Publishing House, 1985), passim; Daniel J. Elazar, "The Development of the American Synagogue," *Modern Judaism* 4 (1984): 255–74.

33. For the YM-YWHAs, see Cohen, *Encounter with Emancipation,* 53; see also Benjamin Rabinowitz, "The Young Men's Hebrew Associations," *Publications of the American Jewish Historical Society* 37 (1947): 221–326. For Judiasm and the Social Gospel, see Feldman, *Dual Destinies,* 133–38; and Martin P. Biefield, Jr., "The Americanization of Reform Judaism: Joseph Krauskopf: A Case Study," in *When Philadelphia Was the Capital of Jewish America,* ed. Murray Friedman (Philadelphia: Balch Institute Press, 1993), 162–71. For the Jewish Chautauqua Society, see Malcolm H. Stern, "National Leaders of Their Time: Philadelphia's Reform Rabbis," in *Jewish Life in Philadelphia 1830–1940,* ed. Murray Friedman (Philadelphia: Institute for the Study of Human Issues, 1983), 185–94. For Jewish lodges and clubs, see Cohen, *Encounter with Emancipation,* 51–52; and Deborah Dash Moore, *B'nai B'rith and the Challenge of Ethnic Leadership* (Albany: SUNY Press, 1981). On the Jewish Publication Society, see Sarna, *JPS,* 17–20. For women's organizations, see Nancy B. Sinkoff, "Educating for 'Proper' Jewish Womanhood: A Case Study in Domesticity and Vocational Training, 1897–1926," *American Jewish History* 77 (1988): 572–600; Beth Wenger, "Jewish Women and Voluntarism," *American Jewish History* 79 (1989): 16–36; Faith Rogow, *Gone to Another Meeting: The National Council of Jewish Women, 1893–1993* (Tuscaloosa: University of Alabama Press, 1993); and Pamela S. Nadell, "A Land of Opportunities: Jewish Women Encounter America," in *What Is Amer-*

ican about the American Jewish Experience? ed. Raphael, 73–90. See also Benjamin Kline Hunnicutt, "The Jewish Sabbath Movement in the Early Twentieth Century, *American Jewish History* 69 (1979): 196–225.

34. On American Reform Judaism, see the relevant chapters of Michael A. Meyer, *Response to Modernity: A History of the Reform Movement in Judaism* (Detroit: Wayne State University Press, 1995); see, too, Leon A. Jick, *The Americanization of the Synagogue* (Lanham: University Press of New England, 1976); Jick, "The Reform Synagogue," 85–110; and David Polish, "The Changing and the Constant in the Reform Rabbinate," in *The American Rabbinate,* ed. Marcus and Peck.

35. Kraut, *From Reform Judaism to Ethical Culture,* passim; Meyer, *Response to Modernity,* passim. For differing interpretations of the rationale and meaning of the Pittsburgh Platform, see Jonathan D. Sarna, "New Light on the Pittsburgh Platform of 1885," *American Jewish History* 76 (1987): 358–68; Sefton D. Temkin, "The Pittsburgh Platform: A Centenary Assessment," *Journal of Reform Judaism* 32 (1985): 362–67; and the essays in *The Changing World of Reform Judaism: The Pittsburgh Platform in Retrospect,* ed. Walter Jacob (Pittsburgh: Rodef Shalom Congregation, 1985).

36. On the evolution and controversies surrounding mixed seating, see Jonathan D. Sarna, "The Debate over Mixed Seating in the American Synagogue," in *The American Synagogue,* ed. Wertheimer. On the Sunday Sabbath issue, see Stuart E. Rosenberg, "The *Jewish Tidings* and the Sunday Service Question," *Publications of the American Jewish Historical Society* 42 (1953): 371–85; Kraut, *From Reform Judaism to Ethical Culture,* 114–18; and Kerry M. Olitzky, "The Sunday-Sabbath Movement in American Reform Judaism: Strategy or Evolution?" *American Jewish Archives* 34 (1982): 75–88, and "Sundays at Chicago Sinai Congregation," 356–68.

37. A good study of the theme of concordance is David Strassler, "The Changing Definitions of the 'Jewish People' Concept in the Religious-Social Thought of American Reform Judaism during the Period of the Mass Immigration from East Europe, 1880–1914," Ph.D. diss., Hebrew University, 1980 (Krauskopf quotation on 192). See, too, Cohen, *Encounter with Emancipation,* ch. 4. For a trenchant analysis of this concordance as but sham and delusion, see Auerbach, *Rabbis and Lawyers.*

38. See Wise's comments in *The American Israelite* as cited in Temkin, *Isaac Mayer Wise,* 94.

39. Oscar S. Straus, *The Origin of Republican Form of Government in the United States of America* (New York: G. P. Putnam's Sons, 1885); see also Naomi W. Cohen, *A Dual Heritage* (Philadelphia: Jewish Publication Society of America, 1969), ch. 14.

40. On Reform Judaism and Zionism in this period, see Strassler, "The Changing Definitions of the 'Jewish People' Concept," passim; Cohen, *Encounter with Emancipation,* 285–86, 290–97; Melvin I. Urofsky, *American Zionism from Herzl to the Holocaust* (Garden City: Anchor Press, 1975), passim; Meyer, *Response to Modernity,* 293–462, passim; and Michael A. Meyer, "American Reform Judaism and Zionism: Early Efforts at Ideological Rap-

prochement," *Studies in Zionism* 7 (1983): 49–64. On Spanish-American War and Reform acceptance of the self-perceived American mission, see Strassler, "The Changing Definitions of the 'Jewish People' Concept," 54ff.

41. Cohen, *Encounter with Emancipation,* 129ff; Goren, *New York Jews and the Quest for Community,* 220–21; Sachar, *A History of Jews in America,* 155ff; see also Lawrence H. Fuchs, *The Political Behavior of American Jews* (Glencoe: Free Press, 1956), 59–60, 124ff.

42. Sachar, *A History of Jews in America,* 215–38; Cohen, *Encounter with Emancipation,* 238ff; David Dalin, "Louis Marshall, the Jewish Vote, and the Republican Party," *Journal of Political Studies Review* 4 (1992): 55–84.

43. See 1906 comments of Julian Mack, president of the National Conference of Jewish Charities, defending separate Jewish charities in these terms, cited by Timothy Smith, "Biblical Ideals in American Christian and Jewish Philanthropy, 1880–1920," *American Jewish History* 74 (1984): 17.

44. Drachman citation in Jeffrey S. Gurock, "Resistors and Accommodators: Varieties of Orthodox Rabbis in America, 1886–1983," in *The American Rabbinate,* ed. Marcus and Peck, 18. On Drachman, see Jeffrey S. Gurock, "From Exception to Role Model: Bernard Drachman and the Evolution of Jewish Religious Life in America, 1880–1920," *American Jewish History* 76 (1987): 456–84. Revel quote in Gilbert Klaperman, *The Story of Yeshiva University, the First Jewish University in America* (New York: Macmillan, 1969), 242. On Revel, see Aaron Rakeffet-Rothkoff, *Bernard Revel, Builder of American Jewish Orthodoxy* (Philadelphia: Jewish Publication Society of America, 1972).

45. On the history and origins of the conservative movement, see Davis, *Emergence of Conservative Judaism;* Robert E. Fierstein, *A Different Spirit: The Jewish Theological Seminary of America, 1886–1902* (New York: Jewish Theological Seminary of America, 1990); and Robbert E. Fierstein, "Sabato Morais and the Founding of the Jewish Theological Seminary," in *When Philadelphia Was the Capital of Jewish America,* ed. Friedman, 75–91.

46. Marshall Sklare, *An American Religious Movement: Conservative Judaism* (Lanham: University Press of America, 1985), passim; Deborah Dash Moore, *At Home in America: Second Generation New York Jews* (New York: Columbia University Press, 1981), esp. 123–48.

47. On Friedlander's conscious articulation of a religious position he identified as clear and distinctly different from both Reform and Orthodoxy, see Shargel, *Practical Dreamer,* 103–19; see also Charles Liebman, "Studying Orthodox Judaism: A Review Essay," *American Jewish History* 80 (1991): 415–23, esp. 417.

48. The relevant articles here are Gurock, "Resistors and Accommodators"; Gurock, "From Exception to Role Model"; and Jeffrey S. Gurock, "A Generation Unaccounted for in *American Judaism," American Jewish History* 77 (1987): 247–59.

49. See Gurock, "Resistors and Accommodators," 30–35, for accounts of such rabbis as Philip Hillel Klein and Moses Z. Margolies, both powerful figures in the more right-wing or culturally resisting organization Agudat ha-

Rabbanim, who nonetheless participated in Magnes's *kehilla* and were willing to work with modern Orthodox Jews. See, too, Philip Rosen, "Orthodox Institution Builder, Rabbi Bernard Lewis Levinthal," in *When Philadelphia Was the Capital of Jewish America*, ed. Friedman, 126–45.

50. Gurock, "From Exception to Role Model," 476ff; Jeffrey S. Gurock, "Jewish Endeavor Society," in *Jewish American Voluntary Organizations*, ed. Michael N. Dobkowski (New York: Columbia University Press, 1986), 228–31.

51. Gurock, "From Exception to Role Model," 482; Abraham J. Karp, "Overview: The Synagogue in America: A Historical Typology," in *The American Synagogue*, ed. Wertheimer, 19; Charles S. Liebman, "Orthodoxy in American Jewish Life," *American Jewish Year Book* 66 (1965): 21–98, passim.

52. Jeffrey S. Gurock, *When Harlem Was Jewish, 1870–1930* (New York: Columbia University Press, 1979), 193–208.

53. Abraham J. Karp, "New York Chooses a Chief Rabbi," in *The Jewish Experience in America: Selected Studies from the Publications of the American Jewish Historical Society*, ed. Abraham J. Karp (Waltham: American Jewish Historical Society, 1969), 4:125–84; see also Aaron Rothkoff, "The American Sojourns of the Ridbaz: Religious Problems within the Immigrant Community," *American Jewish Historical Quarterly* 57 (1968): 557–72; and Ira Robinson, "The First Hassidic Rabbis in North America," *American Jewish Archives* 44 (1992): 501–15.

54. On Agudat ha-Rabbanim, see Gurock, "Resistors and Accommodators," 21–37; for a parallel of Orthodox resistance to and accommodation with America with that of socialist radicals, see Jeffrey S. Gurock, "Change to Survive: The Common Experience of Two Transplanted Jewish Identities in America," in *What Is American about the American Jewish Experience?* ed. Raphael, 54–72.

55. Gurock, "From Exception to Role Model," 468.

56. Jack Wertheimer, *A People Divided: Judaism in Contemporary America* (New York: American Jewish Historical Society, 1993).

57. Cohen, *Encounter with Emancipation*, 272–73; see also Strassler, "The Changing Definitions of the 'Jewish People' Concept," passim, on the internal Jewish discussion over the appropriate group self-designation ("Jew," "Hebrew," or "Israelite") and the nuances each conveyed.

58. Meyer, "American Reform Judaism and Zionism"; Cohen, *Encounter with Emancipation*, 295–98; Strassler, "The Changing Definitions of the 'Jewish People' Concept," chs. 4–8; Karp, *Haven and Home*, 364–69; Melvin I. Urofsky, *A Voice That Spoke for Justice: The Life and Times of Stephen S. Wise* (Albany: SUNY Press, 1982); "The Influence of Zionism on the American Jewish Community: An Assessment by Israeli and American Historians," *American Jewish History* 75 (1985): 130–83; Evyatar Friesel, "American Zionism and American Jewry: An Ideological and Communal Encounter," *American Jewish Archives* 40 (1988): 5–23. See, too, the articles on American Zionism in *American Jewish History* 69 (1979), especially that by Ben Halpern: "The Americanization of Zionism, 1880–1930," 15–33.

59. Deborah Dash Moore, "A New American Judaism," in *Like All the Nations?* ed. Brinner and Rischin, 41–55.

60. Cited in Karp, *Haven and Home,* 354; see also Polish, "The Changing and the Constant in the Reform Rabbinate," 195.

61. Cited in Strassler, "The Changing Definitions of the 'Jewish People' Concept," 230.

62. On Brandeis, see Auerbach, *Rabbis and Lawyers,* 123–49; Melvin I. Urofsky, *Louis D. Brandeis and the Progressive Tradition* (Boston: Little, Brown, 1981); Philippa Strum, *Louis D. Brandeis: Justice for the People* (Cambridge: Harvard University Press, 1984); Allon Gal, *Brandeis of Boston* (Cambridge: Harvard University Press, 1980); Ben Halpern, *A Clash of Heroes: Brandies, Weizmann, and American Zionism* (New York: Oxford University Press, 1987); and Evyatar Friesel, "Brandeis' Role in American Zionism Historically Reconsidered," *American Jewish History* 69 (1979): 15–33.

63. On cultural Zionism, see Goren, *New York Jews and the Quest for Community,* passim; Karp, *Haven and Home,* 364–71; Shargel, *Practical Dreamer,* passim; Evyatar Friesel, "Magnes: Zionism in Judaism," in *Like All the Nations?* ed. Brinner and Rischin, 69–81.

64. Karp, *Haven and Home,* 362.

65. Horace M. Kallen, "Democracy versus the Melting Pot: A Study of American Nationality," *Nation,* Feb. 18, 1915, 190–94, and Feb. 25, 1915, 217–220; Horace M. Kallen, *Culture and Democracy in the United States: Studies in the Group Psychology of the American Peoples* (New York: Boni and Liveright, 1924); Milton R. Konvitz, ed., *The Legacy of Horace M. Kallen* (Cranbury: Fairleigh Dickinson University Press, 1987); John Higham, *Send These to Me: Jews and Other Immigrants in Urban America* (New York: Atheneum, 1975), 196–230, esp. 203–10.

66. Israel Friedlander, "The Problem of Judaism in America," in *Past and Present,* 159–84; on Friedlander, see Shargel, *Practical Dreamer,* passim.

67. For Magnes generally, see Goren, *New York Jews and the Quest for Community,* passim, esp. 47–49, where the citation appears, and Goren, ed., *Dissenter in Zion,* passim. See also Friesel, "Magnes," 75ff.

68. Cited in Moore, "A New American Judaism," 49; see also Karp, *Haven and Home,* 366–67.

69. Cited in Moore, "A New American Judaism," 49, emphasis added.

70. See Handy, *A Christian America,* and *Undermined Establishment,* passim, as well as Feldman, *Dual Destinies,* esp. 108–61; see also Morton Borden, *Jews, Turks, and Infidels* (Chapel Hill: University of North Carolina Press, 1984). On anti-Semitism, see David A. Gerber, ed., *Anti-Semitism in American History* (Urbana: University of Illinois Press, 1986), particularly the editor's introductory essay; Leonard Dinnerstein, *Antisemitism in America* (New York: Oxford University Press, 1994); Leonard Dinnerstein, ed., *Uneasy at Home: Antisemitism and the American Jewish Experience* (New York: Columbia University Press, 1987); Michael N. Dobkowski, *The Tarnished Dream: The Basis of American Anti-Semitism* (Westport: Greenwood Press, 1979); and Jonathan D. Sarna, "American Anti-Semitism," in *History and Hate: The*

Dimensions of Anti-Semitism, ed. David Berger (Philadelphia: Jewish Publication Society of America, 1986), 115–28.

71. Benny Kraut, "The Dissent of American Judaism from American Religion," *Shofar* 7 (1989): 1–12.

72. On missions to the Jews, see "Missions and the Making of Americans: Religious Competition for Souls and Citizens" by Scott Appleby in this volume. See, too, David Max Eichhorn, *Evangelizing the American Jew* (Middle Village: Jonathan David Publishers, 1978); Benny Kraut, "Towards the Establishment of the National Conference of Christians and Jews: The Tenuous Road to Religious Goodwill in the 1920s," *American Jewish History* 77 (1988): 388–412; and Benny Kraut, "A Wary Collaboration: Jews, Catholics, and the Protestant Goodwill Movement," in *Between the Times: The Travail of the Protestant Establishment in America, 1900–1960,* ed. William R. Hutchison (New York: Cambridge University Press, 1989), 193–230, esp. 207–10.

73. Feldman, *Dual Destinies,* 139–49, esp. 143–45; see also Robert Andrew Everett, "Judaism in Nineteenth-Century American Transcendentalist and Liberal Protestant Thought," *Journal of Ecumenical Studies* 20 (1983): 396–413.

74. Goren, *New York Jews and the Quest for Community,* 48–49n18, 264.

75. Cited in Feldman, *Dual Destinies,* 143; see also Benny Kraut, "Francis E. Abbot: Perceptions of a Nineteenth Century Religious Radical on Jews and Judaism," in *Studies in the American Jewish Experience,* ed. Jacob R. Marcus and Abraham Peck (Cincinnati: American Jewish Archives, 1981), 90–113; Kraut, "The Ambivalent Relations of American Reform Judaism with Unitarianism," 58–68.

76. For examples, see Louise Mayo, *Ambivalent Image: Nineteenth Century America's Perception of the Jew* (Rutherford: Farleigh Dickinson University Press, 1988), passim.

77. Tony Fels, "Religious Assimilation: Jews and Freemasonry in Gilded-Age San Francisco," *American Jewish History* 74 (1985): 369–403; Benny Kraut, "Judaism Triumphant: Isaac Mayer Wise on Unitarianism and Liberal Christianity," *AJS Review* 7–8 (1982–83): 179ff; see also Kraut, "A Unitarian Rabbi?" 272–308.

78. Kraut, "Francis E. Abbot," 95–96; Kraut, "Judaism Triumphant," 194–202; Egal Feldman, "American Ecumenism: Chicago's World's Parliament of Religions of 1893," *Journal of Church and State* 9 (1967): 180–99; Rebecca Trachtenberg Alpert, "Jewish Participation at the World's Parliament of Religions, 1893," in *Jewish Civilization: Essays and Studies,* ed. Ronald A. Brauner (Philadelphia: Reconstructionist Rabbinical College, 1979), 1:111–21.

79. On Kohler, see Karla Goldman, "The Ambivalence of Reform Judaism: Kaufmann Kohler and the Ideal Jewish Woman," *American Jewish History* 79 (1990): 495–96; for a sampling of Hirsch's attitude, see Kraut, "Francis E. Abbot," 106.

80. Not that many Jews could (or cared to) distinguish among the Protestant denominations. Even German Jews, not to speak of the later arriving East Europeans, were not sensitive to the nuances of Protestant social and theological divisions.

81. For depictions of these phenomena, see Naomi W. Cohen, "Antisemitism in the Gilded Age: The Jewish View," *Jewish Social Studies* 41 (1979): 187–210; Higham, *Send These to Me;* Oscar Handlin, "American Views of the Jew at the Opening of the Twentieth Century," in *Publications of the American Jewish Historical Society* 40 (1951): 323–44; Richard Hofstadter, *The Age of Reform* (New York: Knopf, 1955), 174–91; Dobkowski, *The Tarnished Dream,* passim; John Higham, *Strangers in the Land: Patterns of American Nativism, 1860–1925* (New Brunswick: Rutgers University Press, 1988), passim; Stephen G. Mostov, "Dun and Bradstreet Reports as a Source of Jewish Economic History: Cincinnati, 1840–1875," *American Jewish History* 72 (1983): 333–53; and David A. Gerber, "Cutting Out Shylock: Elite Anti-Semitism and the Quests for Moral Order in the Mid-Nineteenth Century American Marketplace," in *Anti-Semitism in American History,* ed. Gerber, 201–32.

82. On church-state issues, see Naomi W. Cohen, *Jews in Christian America: The Pursuit of Religious Equality* (New York: Oxford University Press, 1992); Jonathan D. Sarna, *American Jews and Church-State Relations: The Search for "Equal Footing"* (New York: American Jewish Committee, 1989); and Yahalom, "American Judaism"; see also Cohen, *Encounter with Emancipation,* passim; Handy, *Undermined Establishment,* ch. 3; Borden, *Jews, Turks, and Infidels,* 58–74, 79–92, 103–11; Albert M. Friedenberg, "The Jews and the American Sunday Laws," *Publications of the American Jewish Historical Society* 11 (1903): 101–15; and Leonard Bloom, "A Successful Jewish Boycott of the New York City Public Schools," *American Jewish History* 70 (1980): 180–88.

83. Cohen, *Encounter with Emancipation,* 98–99.

84. Kraut, "Judaism Triumphant," passim; George L. Berlin, *Defending the Faith: Nineteenth-Century American Jewish Writings on Christianity and Jesus* (Albany: SUNY Press, 1989).

85. Jonathan D. Sarna, "The American Jewish Response to Nineteenth Century Christian Missions," *Journal of American History* 68 (1981): 35–51; Johathan D. Sarna, "The Impact of Nineteenth-Century Christian Missions on American Jews," in *Jewish Apostasy in the Modern World,* ed. Endelman, 232–54; Jeffrey S. Gurock, "Jewish Communal Divisiveness in Response to Christian Influences on the Lower East Side, 1900–1910," in *Jewish Apostasy in the Modern World,* ed. Endelman, 255–71.

86. Sorin, *The Prophetic Minority,* 85.

87. Diner, *A Time for Gathering,* 60–85; Fuchs, *Political Behavior of American Jews,* 124ff; Goren, *New York Jews and the Quest for Community,* 25–42; Mostov, "Dun and Bradstreet," 353; Cohen, *Encounter with Emancipation,* 330ff; Karp, *Haven and Home,* 128ff; Shelly Tenenbaum, "Immigrants and Capital: Jewish Loan Societies in the United States, 1880–1945," *American Jewish History* 76 (1986): 67–68, 71; Barry E. Supple, "A Business Elite: German-Jewish Financiers in Nineteenth Century New York," in *The American Jewish Experience,* ed. Sarna, 76.

88. Jeffrey S. Gurock, "From *Publications* to *American Jewish History:* The Journal of the American Jewish Historical Society and the Writing of American Jewish History," *American Jewish History* 81 (1993–94): 192–93.

89. Goren, *New York Jews and the Quest for Community,* 159–86; Arthur A. Goren, "Mother Rosie Hertz, the Social Evil, and the New York *Kehillah,*" *Michael: On the History of the Jews in the Diaspora* 3 (1975): 188–210; Sachar, *A History of Jews in America,* 140–73; Jenna Weissman Joselit, *Our Gang: Jewish Crime and the New York Jewish Community, 1900–1940* (Bloomington: Indiana University Press, 1983); Gary Dean Best, "Jacob Schiff's Galveston Movement: An Experiment in Immigration Deflection, 1907–1914," *American Jewish Archives* 30 (1978): 43–79; Uri D. Herscher, *Jewish Agricultural Utopias in America, 1880–1910* (Detroit: Wayne State University Press, 1981).

90. Sarna, *JPS,* 24, 70ff.

91. Shuly Rubin Schwartz, *The Emergence of Jewish Scholarship in America: The Publication of the Jewish Encyclopedia* (Cincinnati: Hebrew Union College Press, 1991).

92. Gurock, "From *Publications* to American History," 156–72.

93. Benny Kraut, "American Jewish Leaders: The Great, Greater, and Greatest," *American Jewish History* 78 (1988): 201–36.

94. Max J. Kohler, *The Immigration Question, with Particular Reference to the Jews of America* (New York: Union of American Hebrew Congregations, 1911); Cohen, *Encounter with Emancipation,* 241–46.

95. Kraut, "A Wary Collaboration"; Kraut, "Towards the Establishment of the National Conference of Christians and Jews"; Mark Silk, "Notes on the Judeo-Christian Tradition in America," *American Quarterly* 36 (1984): 65–85.

96. See the introductory and closing essays by William R. Hutchison in *Between the Times.* Richard John Neuhaus, *The Naked Public Square: Religion and Democracy in America* (Grand Rapids: W. B. Eerdmans, 1984); Stephen L. Carter, *The Culture of Disbelief: How American Law and Politics Trivialize Religious Devotion* (New York: Basic Books, 1993).

97. On the melting pot concept, see Will Herberg, *Protestant, Catholic, Jew: An Essay in American Religious Sociology* (Garden City: Doubleday, 1955).

98. Discussions, debates, and prognostications about the American Jewish future will only be more pronounced as scholars begin to publish analyses of the 1990 National Jewish Population Survey. For a preliminary digest of its findings, see Sidney Goldstein, "Profile of American Jewry: Insights from the 1990 National Jewish Population Survey," *American Jewish Year Book* 92 (1992): 77–173.

TWO

Catholicism and American Culture: Strategies for Survival

JAY P. DOLAN

The relationship between religion and American culture has fasci-
nated scholars for years. Protestants, Catholics, and Jews have grap-
pled with the issue since setting foot on the North American continent.
For Cecil Calvert, the English Catholic founder of Maryland, it was
an issue that surfaced in England even before the first wave of settlers
set sail for Maryland in 1633. To encourage Protestants to join his
Maryland adventure, he issued strict instructions to his brother Leonard, the governor of the new colony, urging that Catholic adventur-
ers practice their religion in private during the course of the journey
across the ocean lest they offend the sensibilities of the numerous Protestants sailing with them.

Once a government was established in Maryland, one of its first acts
was to pass a law in 1639 to guarantee that the "Holy Churches within this province shall have all their rights and liberties." Ten years after this legislation, the Maryland assembly passed another, more detailed law known as the Act Concerning Religion, which sought to
guarantee the toleration of differing Christian religions. Although it was
neither an eloquent statement on behalf of religious freedom nor a
radical proposal for the separation of church and state, it did represent a significant effort to adapt the Catholic European tradition regarding the relationship between church and state to a New World
environment.

Throughout the colonial era Catholics in Maryland continued to
modify their religious traditions to fit the Chesapeake situation. Giv-
en the absence of churches, their religion became centered in the home;
given the scarcity of clergy, lay people became more involved in maintaining and sustaining the Catholic tradition. Such persistent efforts represented a conscious attempt to design a strategy for the survival of
religion in a new cultural context. This was true not just for Catholics
but for Protestants and Jews as well.

Although numerous examples of the adaptation of Catholicism to American culture were present during the colonial era, a more significant place to begin an examination of that relationship is the republican era that began in the late eighteenth century (1780–1820). The American Revolution and the birth of a new nation had begun a period that historians are inclined to label the age of democracy. It was a transitional time that transformed religion in America in the same manner that it changed political life. In religion as in politics, the people's choice became determinative. People sought to gain control over their own destinies, spiritual as well as political. Heaven was democratized, and salvation became a possibility for all God's children not just the Calvinist elect. This democratic surge altered the landscape of American religion. It was the driving force behind the growth of Methodism, it gave birth to the Disciples of Christ, and it was a major reason for the popularity of Joseph Smith and the Mormons. It also shaped the organization of synagogues as Jews sought to declare their rights and privileges. The passion for democracy permeated the Catholic community as well, particularly in the government of local parishes.

The American legal system encouraged the development of the trustee form of church government, a style Catholics quickly adopted. The system endorsed four major principles of the democratic experience: the sovereignty of the people, popular elections, religious freedom, and a written constitution. In his study of trusteeism in this period, Patrick Carey has shown how the spirit of democracy surged through the Catholic community and changed how people thought about their church. In desiring to have it adapt to American culture, Catholics wanted their religion to be more in step with the times and reflect the prevailing democratic spirit.[1]

Catholics who advocated this new style of government were pushing for more than just accommodation. They had a different understanding of what the church should be. In their opinion, the monarchical tradition of European Catholicism was not suited to the United States. As one prominent Catholic layman put it, "This people never will submit to the regime in civil or ecclesiastical affairs that prevails in Europe. . . . a different order prevails in this country. . . . The extreme freedom of our civil institutions has produced a corresponding independent spirit respecting church affairs. . . . The opinion and the wishes of the people require to be consulted to a degree unknown in Europe."[2] Mathew Carey, who wrote these words, and others like him wanted the church to be more democratic and less monarchical or authoritarian; they wanted "a National American Church with liberties consonant to the spirit of government under which they live."[3] In advocating more democracy they articulated in an inchoate manner an understanding of church that was modern and democratic rather than feudal and monarchical.

Just as the spirit of democracy influenced the way Catholics thought about their church, the spirit of the Enlightenment changed the way they thought about their God. Joseph Chinnici has written extensively on this subject and in a convincing manner has documented how the Enlightenment influenced Catholic thought.[4] John Carroll, for example, the first bishop of Baltimore, was a child of the Enlightenment; he endorsed religious toleration, the separation of church and state, the personal, interior dimension of religion, and the support of benevolent causes. His was a reasonable piety rooted in natural reason but perfected by divine revelation. Mathew Carey, a prominent Irish Catholic immigrant in Philadelphia, was yet another example of the Enlightenment way of thought. Carey was a strong advocate of the "spirit of toleration" that he said "distinquishes this enlightened age." His religion had a strong personalist quality as well as a heavy dose of moralism. A humanist, he found inspiration in the classical writers and what he termed their "genuine Roman or Grecian spirit."[5] In addition, he found nurture in the ritual and sacraments of Catholicism and respected the authority of the clergy. Like many people of his time who sought "to adapt their belief in God to modern ideas," Carey integrated the doctrine of Catholicism with the demands of reason so central to Enlightenment thinking.[6] He was able to reconcile moralism and spirituality, faith and reason, and nature and the supernatural. In this manner Carey integrated his religion with the culture of the age so that his Catholicism blended with the prevalent Enlightenment culture.

It is evident that throughout the republican era some Catholics attempted to adapt their religion to the American cultural environment, which was permeated by Enlightenment thought and inspired by democratic ideals. But this was not the only strategy of adaptation Catholics adopted. Another understanding of Catholicism was prevalent in the United States, and that view eventually became the dominant model. It was a more traditional model of the church that emphasized the weakness of human nature, the prevalence of sin, and the need for the church and its clergy to help people overcome the worldly environment. It stressed the authority of the hierarchy and the subordinate role of the laity; its model of government was the medieval monarchy and not the modern republic. Historians have labeled this model of Catholicism "Tridentine Catholicism" after the Council of Trent because that sixteenth-century church council promoted the reformation of Catholicism by endorsing such a style of religion. Tridentine Catholicism was prevalent in eighteenth-century Europe, and by the middle of the nineteenth century, after a brief period when Enlightenment-inspired Catholicism had gained popularity, the model was revived and restored to prominence.

A fine exemplar of Tridentine Catholicism was Ambrose Marechal, John Carroll's successor as the archbishop of Baltimore. Born in France, Marechal joined the Sulpicians, a society of diocesan priests, and was ordained a priest in 1792 in Paris. He fled Paris because of the turmoil of the French revolution, not even taking time to celebrate his first Mass as a priest. He headed for the United States, where he worked primarily as a missionary in Pennsylvania and Maryland and also taught some courses at St. Mary's, a seminary operated by the Sulpicians in Baltimore. When the revolution cooled, he returned to France for a few years and then was sent back to Baltimore to teach again at St. Mary's. In 1817 he was appointed the archbishop of Baltimore.

As the archbishop of Baltimore, Marechal strongly opposed any efforts to promote a republican model of Catholicism. He endorsed the idea of religious liberty but wanted no part of democracy in the church. As far as he was concerned, the spirit of democracy was the reason for many of the church's problems in the new nation. Americans loved "the civil liberty which they enjoy," he wrote. As he put it, "The principle of civil liberty is paramount with them," and even the lowest magistrate is elected by the vote of the people. Such principles governed Protestant churches, and in his opinion Catholics "are exposed to the danger of admitting the same principles of ecclesiastical government." Marechal strongly opposed this tendency and sought to establish the supreme authority of the clergy and weaken the power of the lay trustee system.[7] His model of the church was very French and very monarchical. Moreover, it was the model gaining ascendency in France after the downfall of Napoleon in 1814.

Like Marechal, many other French clergy fled to the United States during the revolution, and most of them included in their cultural baggage a traditional understanding of Catholicism. Their presence was especially influential in Kentucky, where they sought to shape the piety of the people according to the French model. The French-born Stephen Badin and his Belgium-born contemporary Charles Nerinckx were pioneer priests in Kentucky. They brought their own style of Catholicism to the new nation, and any idea of adapting the traditional French style of Catholicism to the United States was totally foreign to them. They were especially noted for promoting a stern code of morality that discouraged dancing and theatergoing. Although Enlightenment Catholicism encouraged a personal and plain style of religion that stressed the positive side of human nature, toleration, and the reasonableness of religion, the moralism of Badin and Nerinckx was rooted in a negative view of human nature and the need to curb its evil tendencies. Their severity in the confessional was well known, and people complained continuously about both men. Nerinckx, for example, told people to rise at 4 A.M. and forbade them to dance; Badin would impose such penances as holding a hot coal while reciting the Our Father and the Hail Mary or digging a shallow grave and lying in it a brief time each day for a week. Although they were eccentric in their understanding of spiritual life, the priests shared a fundamentally pessimistic view of human nature characteristic of European Catholicism. Many Kentucky Catholics did not approve of that style of piety, and their resistance suggests that they were attuned to a more moderate and positive type of spirituality.[8]

Badin conducted many parish missions, the Catholic counterpart to Protestant revivals, along the Kentucky frontier, and they too promoted this understanding of Catholicism in which sin and fear were the foundation on which religion rested. These French missionaries were bringing their own style of Catholicism to the new nation, and any idea of adapting the traditional French style of Catholicism to the United States was totally foreign to them.

Kentucky was also the setting for clashes between the monarchical and republican models of Catholicism. Kentucky Catholics were known as ardent Jeffersonians and supported a republican view of government in both the civic and religious arena. The absence of clergy encouraged lay leadership, and most congregations organized themselves into religious societies and wrote republican constitutions that supported the idea of lay trustees. Badin, however, resisted what he called such "extravagant pretensions of Republicanism" and continually opposed any manifestation of lay independence. The bishop of Bardstown, Benedict Flaget, also had to deal with such independence and acknowledged that the people were indeed "good republicans."[9]

The contrast between the two opposing views of the church was captured clearly in a letter written by the French-born bishop of New Orleans to a Vatican official: "It is scarcely possible to realize how contagious even to the clergy and to men otherwise well disposed, are the principles of freedom and independence imbibed by all the pores in these United States. Hence I have always been convinced that practically all the good to be hoped for must come from the Congregations or religious Orders among which flourish strict discipline."[10] Discipline in a hierarchical church was essential, whereas independence and freedom were counterproductive to the goals of an organization based on authority and the chain of command.

By 1800 it was clear that Catholics in the United States supported two different and competing understandings of Roman Catholicism. One encouraged the idea of the adaptation of religion to the American cultural environment, and the other sought to transplant the European model intact. The dilemma facing U.S. Catholics concerned how to be both Catholic and American. The traditional understanding of Catholicism emphasized such virtues as authority and conformity, which seemingly went against the grain of the American ideals of freedom and independence; the more American, more modern understanding stressed such virtues as democracy and toleration, which appeared incompatible with the traditional Tridentine model. The tension between the two understandings had existed since the earliest days of the Maryland colony, when the Calverts, who supported an accommodationist view, did battle with Jesuit missionaries who wanted to transplant the clerical privileges they enjoyed in Europe to the Maryland frontier. Matters became more intense after the American Revolution, when a popular surge of democracy took hold in an environment greatly influenced by Enlightenment thought.

The end of the republican period coincided with the advent of large-scale immigration, and Roman Catholicism was one of the religions most affected by that development. Immigrant laity and clergy brought to the United States a European model of church that was not in harmony with the spirit of democracy. As a result, the republican style of Catholicism that surfaced during the decades following the Revolution became less popular and plausible. Catholicism became a church of immigrants, and the major challenge for much of the nineteenth century was to provide for their religious needs. The visibly immigrant nature of Catholicism intensified with each decade and raised the question of the relationship between Catholicism and American culture, an issue that would persist throughout the century of immigration from 1820 to 1920. It became especially significant during the 1850s.

The protagonist of this discussion was Orestes Brownson, a recent American convert to Catholicism and a well-known writer. In the summer and fall of 1854 Brownson published a series of controversial articles in *Brownson's Quarterly Review,* arguing that the Irish and all other immigrants "must ultimately lose their own nationality and become assimilated in general character to the Anglo-American race." The Irish resented this and accused Brownson of being anti-Irish and soft on anti-Catholic nativists.[11] He had clearly endorsed the Americanization strategy—that is, the need for Catholics to adapt to American culture—and reiterated that theme two years later at a July commencement address at St. John's College. In the address, most of which appeared in an essay Brownson published in the fall of 1856, he celebrated the American nation, "a people with a great destiny, and a destiny glorious to ourselves and beneficient to the world."[12]

The essay, "Mission of America," was in the spirit of Manifest Destiny, a popular expression and belief that celebrated the providential role and destiny the United States possessed. Brownson rejected the idea that Catholics should "separate themselves from the great current of American nationality, and . . . assume the position in political and social life of an inferior, a distinct, or an alien people, or of a foreign colony planted in the midst of a people with whom they have no sympathies." Rather, he wanted them to "take their position as free and equal American citizens, with American interests and sympathies, American sentiments and affections, and throw themselves fearlessly into the great current of American national life." For Brownson, being American meant possessing "self-reliance, energy, perseverance," what he called "the chief elements of success." Most important, he believed that the future of America rested in the hands of Catholics. "It is only through Catholicity that the country can fulfill its mission. . . . The salvation of the country and its future glory depend on Catholics." He concluded by warning that it was "the duty of all Catholic citizens . . . to be, or to make themselves, thorough-going Americans." Those who would not he considered to be "'outside barbarians' and not within the pale of the American order."[13]

It would be hard to find a more explicit endorsement of the Americanization strategy, but it was not to go unchallenged. At the end of the St. John's commencement ceremony, the archbishop of New York, John Hughes, addressed the students. As one person noted, he "harangued the graduates with completely opposing views, denying the existence of the advantages the laws of the country are said to offer Catholics, which Brownson had taken pains to emphasize; asserting further that liberty for Catholics existed only on paper, and not in fact, and exhorting them to prepare for days of oppression and persecution in the future."[14] Hughes clearly wanted Brownson to avoid any "allusion to the nationality of our Catholic brethren" and did not want him to "write or say anything calculated to represent the Catholic religion as especially adapted to the genius of the American people as such."[15]

Even though Hughes was clearly not launching an anti-American tirade, he did not agree with Brownson about the advantages that the United States held for Catholics. This was not surprising, given the wave of anti-Catholicism sweeping the country in the 1840s and 1850s. He also wanted to avoid endorsing any nationality over another. But Hughes did go further, and in a letter to Brownson he denied the convert's contention that "if the Catholic religion had been or could now be presented to the American people through mediums and under auspices more congenial with the national feelings and habits, the progress of the Church and the conversion of Protestants would have been far greater."[16]

What Hughes was saying was that Catholicism could not and should not adapt to American culture. Brownson had hinted at this in an imperfect manner, but he never developed it or explained how it would happen. The most he could say was that "grace does not destroy nature, nor change the national type of character. It purifies and elevates nature, and brings out whatever is good, noble, and strong in the national type." If Catholicism could be "adapted to the wants of the simple, the rude, the barbarian, and the savage," he said, surely it could adapt itself to the "active, energetic, self-reliant American character."[17]

The controversy between Brownson and Hughes was about more than nationality. Brownson clearly wanted Catholics to become more American, and Hughes saw this emphasis as divisive. He wanted to emphasize the Catholic dimension of the American Catholic dilemma. He was more interested in self-defense, intent on transplanting the Catholicism of the Old World to the United States and establishing an immigrant church strong enough to withstand the attacks of a nativist American society. But Brownson wanted Catholicism—"Catholicity" was the word he used—to adapt itself to the American culture. He never explained how that would take place, and within a year he had repudiated the idea, most likely in response to Hughes's strong objection.

The repudiation took place in a review Brownson had written of Isaac Hecker's *Aspirations of Nature*. He explicitly denied any "design to Americanize Catholicity" and sought to distance himself from any group (or "new school," to use Hughes's phrase) that sought to achieve this.[18] It appears evident from Brownson's strong repudiation of his earlier position and Hughes's equally strong condemnation of any attempt to "Americanize Catholicity" that both men were talking about the relationship between religion and American culture.

The "new school" to which Hughes referred was a small group of clergy and laymen in New York City who met regularly during the 1850s to discuss issues of mutual interest. Their chief concern was the relationship between American culture and Catholicism. As Hughes put it, they wanted to "show that the Catholic religion and the American Constitution would really fit each other as a key fits a lock; that without any change in regard to faith or morals, the doctrines of the Catholic church may be, so to speak, Americanized—that is represented in such a manner as to attract the attention and win the admiration of the American people."[19] The one person who would develop that theme more than anyone else was Isaac Hecker. Although not a regular member of the new school, it provided him with "the moral support and intellectual stimulation" he needed to articulate his vision of a Catholic America.[20]

Like Brownson, Hecker was a convert to Roman Catholicism; after his conversion he joined the Redemptorist order and was ordained a priest in 1849. He eventually left the Redemptorists and in 1858 founded a new order, the Paulists, officially known as the Missionary Society of St. Paul the Apostle. Hecker was enthusiastic about Manifest Destiny, as many Protestant evangelicals were. But he gave it a different twist. In his opinion, the providential destiny of America would be realized only when America became Catholic. According to Hecker, the destinies of the United States and American Catholicism were so bound together that Catholics alone would be able to guide the nation toward "its highest destinies." To achieve that goal it would be necessary for Catholics "to put aside European ways and adapt to American conditions."[21] As he put the matter in a letter to his colleagues in the Redemptorist order, "So far as it is compatible with faith and piety, I am for accepting the true American civilization, its usages and customs; leaving aside other reasons it is the only way in which Catholicity can become the religion of our people." And in a letter to a Catholic laywoman he reiterated that point and wrote, "Our faith must take root in our national characteristics."[22] "Every age has its own characteristics," he told her, and therefore the type of spirituality suitable for American Catholics must reflect the age in which they lived. What this consisted of exhibited some of Brownson's ideas, concepts also popular among many American intellectuals. These included such ideas as personal initiative, self-reliance, freedom of action, and a positive attitude toward the world. Hecker's positive regard for the world, or what he called "the age," was rooted in his belief that the divine spirit becomes more manifest as history unfolds; that is, with each passing age God becomes more present in the world through the medium of the church.

Hecker's vision of religion was so dynamic that he envisioned Catholicism transforming American society, but that could not take place until Catholicism became more American. One of his most explicit statements was a comment he made shortly before his death regarding the recent establishment of Catholic University in Washington, D.C.

"The work of the new University, " he wrote, "planted in the political center of this free and intelligent people, will tend to shape the expression of doctrines in such wise as to assimilate them to American intelligence—not to minimize but to assimilate. To develop the mind there is never need to minimize the truth; but there is great need of knowing how to assimilate the truth to different minds."[23] The statement was reminiscent of his belief that the spirituality of the people must be in tune with the age; in other words, religion, both in its doctrinal and spiritual expression, must adapt itself to the age.

Given Hecker's vision, it was clear what his strategy would be for the survival of Catholicism in the United States. Catholicism must become American, and only then will it prosper. As his epitaph phrased it, "In the union of Catholic faith and American civilization a new birth awaits them all, a future for the Church brighter than any past."[24] If it remained a foreign colony, as some of his contemporaries described the church, then it would never realize its destiny in America.

Throughout his life as a Catholic, Hecker strived to adapt his religion to the American environment. In addition to founding a new religious order that would seek to unite Catholicism and American life, he developed a new apologetic in the hope that his reasoning would influence Protestant Americans; he encouraged a new type of spirituality that emphasized sanctity in the world and not apart from it; he founded a press to distribute religious pamphlets and books; he established a periodical that would address the issues of the day; and he lectured throughout the nation hoping to gain converts to Catholicism. His was an energetic style of Catholicism that encouraged the involvement of the laity and sought sanctification in the world, not apart from it.

John Hughes was the antithesis of the American-born Hecker. An Irish-born immigrant who grew up in Ireland, a culture steeped in religious conflict and discrimination, he viewed Protestant America as a religiously hostile environment. He became a strong advocate of Catholic schools and separate institutions for the sick and dying, orphans, and delinquent children, as well as a devotional Catholicism that emphasized the role of the clergy and the need for external rituals. Hecker, by contrast, stressed the interior workings of the spirit in each individual. Although Hughes was clearly not anti-American, his model of Catholicism was the fortress community that opposed the dominant culture, not in a prophetic manner but as an adversary.

Hughes represented the majority opinion of Catholics in the nineteenth century. Throughout the era, clergy and laity worked together to establish parish communities that served the needs of immigrants. In these parishes immigrants could hear the gospel preached in their own languages, and they could sing the familiar hymns of the old country. Many parishes had elementary schools, and some even had high schools. Through these institutions each wave of immigrants passed the faith on to the next generation. The ethos that inspired the schools was the preservation of the faith; there was no question of adapting Catholicism to the American environment. The religion of the Old World was to be transplanted intact to the United States and passed on to succeeding generations. Although people could become American, their religion could not. Nevertheless, the dilemma of how to be both American and Catholic, and the tension that this created, did not go away. Others who followed Hecker sought to adapt the religion of Catholicism to the American culture, a practice that became most evident in the late nineteenth century.

The late nineteenth century was, in the words of Arthur Schlesinger, Sr., "a critical period" in the development of American religion.[25] An emerging urban and industrial nation presented formidable challenges to churches. Equally formidable were the challenges presented by developments in the intellectual realm. Darwin's theory of evolution occupied the attention of theologians for years as they sought to come to terms with the biblical account of creation and Darwin's evolutionary theory about the origins of life. A new theology that was more humanistic and ethical in focus was gaining popularity and would radically change the way people thought about religion. New theories of biblical criticism challenged the accuracy of many biblical stories; indeed, they challenged the very truthfulness of the Bible itself. New universities, more secular and less religious, became the citadels of the new learning, and for the first time in American history unbelief became as respectable as belief. Knowledge and learning had become America's icons. William Onahan, a Chicago Catholic layman, spoke for many when he underscored the necessity of education. "The age has become inspired by a passion for knowledge and is athirst for more and higher learning," he said. "This higher learning is everywhere in request, and the young man who aspires to highest rank and position must be equipped with this higher knowledge. There is room only in the lowest plane for the ignorant and the illiterate."[26]

The new intellectual environment radically transformed the religious landscape. Protestantism became more fragmented with the emergence of theological modernism and fundamentalism, and American Judaism witnessed the consolidation of the Reformed tradition and eventually underwent further division with the founding of the Conservative tradition. Even though Catholicism did not undergo the radical fragmentation experienced by Protestants and Jews, the new social and intellectual environment presented formidable challenges for Catholics in the United States. A key issue was the one Hecker had considered all his Catholic life: the relation between Catholicism and American culture. Now, however, the discussion would move beyond the idea of American culture to include the broader concept of modernity or modern culture.

Unlike earlier discussions of the relationship between Catholicism and American culture, the debate during the 1880s and 1890s was not confined to a handful of individuals. It involved leading members of the hierarchy, numerous clergy, and some lay people, and it occurred in periodicals and along the lecture circuit for a decade and more. It was as public and heated as any previous debate in American Catholic history.

The key figure in the hierarchy was John Ireland, the archbishop of St. Paul, Minnesota. Joining Ireland were John Keane, bishop of Richmond, Virginia, and later rector of Catholic University, and Denis O'Connell, rector of the North American College in Rome. Another prelate with a decidedly Americanist impulse was John L. Spalding of Peoria, Illinois, but he was not as actively involved in the discussion as the others. Cardinal James Gibbons, archbishop of Baltimore, was also a strong supporter of Ireland and the others.

The relationship between Catholicism and America was a theme John Ireland had been developing for many years. In November 1884, speaking before bishops gathered at the Third Plenary Council of Baltimore, he first gave "formal expression" to the issue that "was to dominate his thought and action for many more years to come."[27] His most developed thoughts on the issue were later presented in two other speeches, one entitled "The Mission of Catholics in America" was delivered in 1889 on the occasion of the centennial celebration of the establishment of the American hierarchy, and a second, "The Church and the Age," was given in 1893 on the anniversary of Cardinal Gibbons's episcopal consecration. In both speeches Ireland came across as American as Uncle Sam and as Catholic as the pope. He wanted to launch what he called "the new, the most glorious crusade. Church and age!" He also wanted to unite the two, making them mutually compatible and harmonious because "in both the self-same God" works so that "they pulsate alike."[28] This would first mean that Catholics would have to cast aside their foreign traits and become American. It was a theme he hammered home most energetically in discussions about the Germans. But for Ireland, more than just the question of nationality was involved.

John Ireland also believed that the religion of Catholicism had to adapt itself to American culture. As he put it, "The Church must herself be new, adapting herself in manner of life and in method of action to the conditions of the new order, thus proving herself, while ever ancient, to be ever new, as truth from heaven it is and ever must be."[29] This meant adopting new ways to present the Catholic message to American society. That involved change, and Ireland realized the challenge that posed. "The Church never changes," he said, "and yet she changes." To solve the dilemma, he like Hecker distinguished between the divine and the human, the essentials and the accidents. "The divine never changes," he wrote, "it is of Christ, the same . . . forever. But even in the divine we must distinguish between the principle and the application of the principle; the application of the principle, or its adaptation to environment, changes with the circumstances. And thus, at times, there seems to be a change when there is not change." The "Church," he said, "while jealously guarding the essentials," should be ready "to abandon the accidentals, as circumstances of time and place demand."[30]

What Ireland was trying to do in these lectures—and throughout his life—was "to justify his deep-seated conviction that the Church must initiate an over-all rapprochement with a modern culture which at some point in the past had passed her by."[31] More than ethnic identity was at issue. Ireland realized the need for the church to change and adapt to the age. In his mind it had done this in the past, and it must do it once again. But as Dennis Dease observed, "Ireland inevitably ran up against the problem of change in the Church; he knew that the Church must at times listen to the voice of the world and read the signs of the times. Yet Ireland's basic concept of the Church, like that of Brownson and Hecker, was ahistorical: he regarded the Church as transcending history and as unchanging in essence."[32] For this reason he could never fully develop his life-long belief that Catholicism must adapt to the age and the culture in which it is situated. He did not have the theological tools or methods to develop the idea in more than a general way.

Reinforcing John Ireland's crusade to unite church and age was the emergence of a Catholic middle class that also sought to adapt the Catholic way of life to American culture. Its members gave the "American Victorian values of male and female roles, home life, self-culture and education, temperance, sabbatarianism, and good citizenship . . . a Catholic form."[33] This was confirmation of the timeliness and value of Ireland's crusade.

Ireland's agenda, and that of his Americanist allies, was quite clear. They favored a more tolerant attitude toward Protestants, a more favorable attitude toward public schools, and even the possibility of some type of arrangement whereby Catholic children could be encouraged to attend public schools. Ireland also endorsed the American idea of the separation of church and state and was enthusiastic about the virtues of democracy, believing that the rest of the world should imitate the United States. He was inspired by his enthusiastic belief in progress and the idea that the present age was superior to what had gone before it.

For Ireland, the United States represented the apogee of progress. This belief in the progressive or evolutionary development of civilization was central to the Americanist point of view and provided the energy and enthusiasm necessary to sustain the crusade to unite church and age. Critics clearly recognized that fact and saw this principle as essentially hostile to the Catholic faith. In an astute, historically important article, Thomas Preston, a key aide to Archbishop Michael Corrigan of New York, the most formidable opponent of the Americanists, underscored the point emphatically: "The doctrine, that we have greater light in our age, that we better understand the truths of our revelation than the ages before us; that we have theologically taken upon ourselves the wings of human progress, is not simply an empty boast, it is a serious error." Preston warned that "there is no more dangerous disposition, if it should ever become popular, than the belief that there is an American Catholicity which is in advance of past times, which differs materially from the faith once delivered to the Church and always preserved by her, which boasts of a freedom from restrictions which bind the ages of the past."[34] It is clear from Preston's critique of the agenda of what he called an "American Catholicity" that much more was at issue in this debate than ethnic identity.

For Preston, the solution to the American Catholic dilemma was to preserve the faith intact and oppose any attempt to adapt it to the American environment. But other Catholic intellectuals were trying to do just that. This was most evident among theologians who wrote in the late nineteenth century. As Scott Appleby has argued, there was a link between the progressivism of Americanists such as Hecker and Ireland and the modernist theologians who followed them. Americanists wanted Catholicism to "adapt itself to the values of the modern American republic"; modernist theologians wanted Catholicism to adapt itself to the best that modern philosophy and science had to offer. The theologians took the desire for adaptation beyond the pragmatic, political platform of the Americanists and fashioned an ideology of theological adaptation that represented the "theological and philosophical expression of Americanism."[35] Like the Americanists, they argued that if Catholicism was to survive in the United States and in the modern world it would have to reconcile with the age. For the theologians this meant more than political, social, or cultural adaptation. It meant reconciling the ancient beliefs of Catholicism with the new learning.

The issue that most challenged the foundations of Christianity during these decades was Darwin's theory about evolution and his concept of natural selection. Among Catholics, the debate over evolution was not as prolonged and divisive as it was among Protestants. Nonetheless, it was a popular theme in the 1890s. The key person in this discussion was John Zahm. A Holy Cross priest on the faculty of the University of Notre Dame, Zahm was an accomplished scientist and educator. After he entered the evolution discussion during the 1880s he lectured widely and wrote numerous essays promoting the compatibility of science and religion. By the 1890s he had clearly endorsed the theory of evolution and was widely praised for his efforts. In 1896 he published his major work on the topic, *Evolution and Dogma*. The book was the culmination of his thinking and confirmed his reputation "as a leading Catholic apologist and educator."[36]

Zahm's endorsement of theistic evolution eventually attracted the attention of Catholic theologians in Rome and elsewhere, who viewed evolution in particular and modernity in general as hostile to religion. By 1898 opposition against Zahm had escalated to such an intense degree that church authorities in Rome condemned his book and prohibited further publication. The condemnation persuaded Zahm to abandon his efforts to reconcile theology and modern science although it was clear to him that the survival of Catholicism depended on adaptation to the modern world, specifically to modern science and the concept of evolution. In that sense he was clearly an apologist for modernity.

There were others, however, who pushed the concept further and self-consciously sought to reconcile Catholic beliefs with modern thought. The most important center for this school of thought was St. Joseph's Seminary in New York, established in 1896 and directed by priests of the Society of St. Sulpice. Following the lead of seminaries in Boston and Baltimore, which the Sulpicians also administered, St. Joseph's Seminary sought to modernize the traditional program of formation and adapt it to the American culture. This meant a modification of a stern French Sulpician tradition of seminary formation, a mentality that "often regarded as a sin against the spirit to complain of cold rooms, bad food, poor hospital treatment, long kneeling at prayers, and other violations of the rules of health and common sense."[37] Other adaptations included the encouragement of physical exercise; lectures by distinguished visiting scholars, both Protestant and Catholic; and reading rooms where students could find some of the best secular magazines and newspapers along with the usual collection of Catholic periodicals. Seminarians also attended classes at New York University and Columbia University. But the Sulpicians wanted to do more than promote physical fitness and good reading habits. The faculty at St. Joseph's sought to teach the modern approach to such ancient disciplines as history, philosophy, and theology. That meant rejection of the traditional neo-scholastic methodology and its ahistorial, classicist perspective and an endorsement of an historical, critical approach in theology. In this way they hoped to achieve a "synthesis of modern science and revealed truth."[38]

The area undergoing the most change was the study of the Bible. Propelled by the new history and its concern for data and new techniques in textual criticism, dramatic changes were occurring. A major issue concerned the authorship of the Pentateuch; another was the meaning of inspiration and inerrancy. At St. Joseph's and other Sulpician seminaries the latest advances in Bible studies became part of the curriculum, and the writings of European scholars who supported a more modern approach to the study of the Bible were made available to students.

Another important development at St. Joseph's Seminary was the founding of a journal, New York Review, in 1905 that sought to educate the American clergy in the new theology emerging in Europe. Its goal was to reconcile an ancient faith with modern thought. As one of its editors put it, the purpose of the journal was "not to abandon the old in favor of the new, but rather to interpret with becoming care and reverence the old truths in the light of the new science." What this meant, according to Appleby, was "to provide for the American Catholic church the epistemological, theological, apologetic, and ecclesiological foundations for the new worldview" that was emerging.[39]

For the theologians at St. Joseph's Seminary, the Catholic strategy for survival was clear. It had to reconcile the ancient truths of Catholicism with modern thought. Americanists such as Ireland wanted Catholicism to become more American, a general feeling that was widespread within the Catholic culture. It could mean a multitude of things—endorsing democracy, supporting the temperance crusade, or promoting patriotism, for example. The theologians pushed the Americanist agenda one step further and advocated the modernization of Catholic thought, bringing it into harmony with the advances of modern learning. Both positions generated a good deal of debate, and by the 1890s two opposing schools of thought existed among Catholics. Americanists and modernists were in the minority, however. The majority opinion did not endorse the historical, developmental method-

ology of the modernists and rejected their efforts to synthesize traditional beliefs of Catholics and modern thought. Those who opposed
any such synthesis controlled the seats of power in Rome and were able
to persuade the papacy to condemn any efforts at Americanization or
modernization.

The first such condemnation came in 1899, when Pope Leo XIII
condemned what he called "Americanism" and labeled as "reprehen-
sible" the idea that "the Church ought to adapt herself somewhat to
our advanced civilization, and relaxing her ancient rigor, show some
indulgence to modern popular theories and methods." The pope also
warned against the concept that the church in America could be "different from that which is in the rest of the world."[40] The condemnation effectively ended John Ireland's crusade to unite church and age.
But it did not end the debate about the church adapting itself to the
modern age; that continued for several years in a intellectually robust
manner as Catholic intellectuals sought to reconcile Catholicism and
modern thought. Then, in 1907, Pope Pius X condemned what he labeled modernism and published a syllabus of errors, effectively end-
ing the search for a synthesis between modern thought and traditional
Catholic belief. The ahistorical, classicist methodology of neo-scholas-
ticism continued to be the dominant theological system within Roman
Catholicism.

The consequences of that development were significant. Theologically, it meant that American Catholics could no longer, publicly at least,
seek to reconcile modern thought with traditional Catholic doctrine.
The theological strategy was to resist modernism as much as possible
and punish those intellectuals who thought differently. Pastorally, it
meant a strategy of religious separatism whereby the parish became an
island community set apart from the rest of the nation's religiously
pluralistic society. For many people the parish became a total community where all religious, social, and recreational needs were met through
a host of societies and organizations. This was especially true in parishes organized for recently arrived immigrants from Eastern and Southern Europe. But it was also the case in Irish and German parishes in
this pre-World War I era. As one woman described her parish, "Our
lives were centered around Sacred Heart church and one another."[41]
The centerpiece of the strategy was the parish school, which served as
a "culture factory" for Catholics and passed on and preserved intact
the tradition of Catholicism. Any effort to fashion a Catholicism that
was in tune with American culture was no longer encouraged. This
would hold fast through the 1920s, when 100 Percent Americanism
engulfed the church as well as the nation.

Ever since Catholics set foot on the shores of North America they have sought to adapt their religion to the new environment. This desire has always ignited a debate about what is the best strategy for survival in the new land. On one side, integationists wanted Catholicism to adapt to American culture. At virtually every important juncture in the brief history of Catholicism in the United States they have raised the issue and sought to persuade others that Catholicism must adapt. On the other side, separatists wanted to maintain the integrity of Catholicism by maintaining its traditions and resisting adaptation.

In the 1890s and early 1900s the debate took on greater significance because the issue included not just the relationship of Catholicism to American culture, or what can be called the question of group identity. It also included the relationship of Catholicism to the broader theme of modern culture, especially modern thought. Separatists won out each time and were able to fashion a religious culture that was enormously successful in meeting the needs of a predominantly immigrant people. Yet the question of adaptation would not go away. During the decades between the two world wars, especially the 1930s, Catholics once again raised the issue of adaptation. The relationship between Catholicism and American culture became the center of a vigorous debate in the late 1940s and 1950s. This debate has continued to the present day. Once again it has gone beyond the issue of the Americanization of Catholicism to include the larger theme of the stance of Catholicism toward modern thought and culture. How to be both Catholic and American still remains a dilemma for American Catholics.

Notes

1. Patrick W. Carey, *People, Priests, and Prelates: Ecclesiastical Democracy and the Tensions of Trusteeism* (Notre Dame: University of Notre Dame Press, 1987).

2. Mathew Carey, *Address to the Rt. Rev. Bishop Conwell and the Members of St. Mary's Congregation* (Philadelphia, 1821), 3–4; Mathew Carey, *Address to the Rt. Rev. the Bishop of Pennsylvania and the Members of St. Mary's Congregation, Philadelphia* (Philadelphia: n.p., 1820), 3.

3. Quoted in Patrick W. Carey, "Republicanism within American Catholicism, 1785–1860," *Journal of the Early Republic* 3 (Winter 1983): 416.

4. Joseph P. Chinnici, *Living Stones: The History and Structure of Catholic Spiritual Life in the United States* (New York: Macmillan, 1989).

5. Quoted in Edward C. Carter II, "The Political Activities of Mathew Carey, Nationalist 1760–1814," Ph.D. diss., Bryn Mawr College, 1962, 25; Diary of Mathew Carey, Dec. 1, 1824, Rare Book Room, University of Pennsylvania.

6. See James Turner, *Without God, without Creed: The Origins of Unbelief in America* (Baltimore: Johns Hopkins University Press, 1985), 35ff.

7. "Archbishop Marechal's Report to Propaganda, October 16, 1818," in *Documents of American Catholic History,* ed. John Tracy Ellis (Chicago: Henry Regnery, 1967), 1:214.

8. Clyde F. Crews, *An American Holy Land: A History of the Archdiocese of Louisville* (Wilmington: Michael Glazier, 1987), 64.

9. Crews, *An American Holy Land,* 102; Jay P. Dolan, *The American Catholic Experience: A History from Colonial Times to the Present* (New York: Doubleday, 1985), 119–20.

10. Dolan, *The American Catholic Experience,* 121.

11. Ibid., 296.

12. Orestes A. Brownson, "Mission of America," in *The Works of Orestes A. Brownson,* ed. Henry F. Brownson (Detroit: T. Nourse, 1884), 11:567.

13. Brownson, "Mission of America," 11:556–57, 576, 584.

14. Quoted in Thomas R. Ryan, *Orestes A. Brownson: A Definitive Biography* (Huntington, Ind.: Our Sunday Visitor, 1976), 534.

15. Quoted in Henry F. Brownson, *Orestes A. Brownson's Latter Life: From 1856–1876* (Detroit: H. F. Brownson, 1900), 71.

16. Brownson, *Orestes A. Brownson's Later Life,* 71–72. Hughes wrote an important essay on this topic in November 1856: "Reflections and Suggestions in Regard to What Is Called the Catholic Press in the United States," in *Complete Works of the Most Rev. John Hughes, D.D., Archbishop of New York,* ed. Lawrence Kehoe (New York: Lawrence Kehoe, 1865), 2:686–701.

17. Brownson, "Mission of America," 559.

18. David J. O'Brien, *Isaac Hecker: An American Catholic* (New York: Paulist Press, 1992), 121–23; William LeRoy Portier, "Providential Nation: An Historical-Theological Study of Isaac Hecker's Americanism," Ph.D. diss., University of St. Michael's College, Canada, 1980, 309.

19. Hughes, "Reflections and Suggestions," 688.

20. Portier, "Providential Nation," 319.

21. Quoted in Dolan, *The American Catholic Experience,* 308, and O'Brien, *Isaac Hecker,* 154.

22. Quoted in O'Brien, *Isaac Hecker,* 154, and Portier, "Providential Nation," 324.

23. Quoted in O'Brien, *Isaac Hecker,* 316.

24. Portier, "Providential Nation," 320.

25. Arthur M. Schlesinger, Sr., "A Critical Period in American Religion, 1875–1900," *Massachusetts Historical Society Proceedings* 65 (1930–32): 523–46.

26. William Onahan, "The Jesuits in Chicago," address given at the silver jubilee of St. Ignatius College, June 24, 1895, Chicago, Ill.

27. Marvin R. O'Connell, *John Ireland and the American Catholic Church* (St. Paul: Minnesota Historical Society, 1988), 193.

28. Quoted in Dolan, *The American Catholic Experience,* 309.

29. Ibid.

30. Quoted in R. Scott Appleby, *Church and Age Unite: The Modernist Impulse in American Catholicism* (Notre Dame: University of Notre Dame Press, 1992), 85, and Dennis J. Dease, "The Theological Influence of Orestes Brownson and Isaac Hecker on John Ireland's Ecclesiology," Ph.D. diss., Catholic University of America, 1978, 220.

31. Dease, "The Theological Influence," 221.

32. Ibid., 244.

33. Paul G. Robichaud, "The Resident Church: Middle Class Catholics and the Shaping of American Catholic Identity, 1889 to 1899," Ph.D. diss., University of California Los Angeles, 1989, 297.

34. Thomas S. Preston, "American Catholicity," *American Catholic Quarterly Review* 15 (April 1891): 399, 408.

35. Appleby, *Church and Age Unite*, 7–8.

36. Ibid., 36.

37. Quoted in Joseph M. White, *The Diocesan Seminary in the United States: A History from the 1780s to the Present* (Notre Dame: University of Notre Dame Press, 1989), 230.

38. Appleby, *Church and Age Unite*, 109.

39. Ibid., 109, 163.

40. Pope Leo XIII, *Testem Benevolentiae*, in *Documents of American Catholic History*, ed. Ellis, 2:539, 546.

41. Quoted in Dolan, *The American Catholic Experience*, 206.

THREE

Difference and Otherness: Mormonism and the American Religious Mainstream

JAN SHIPPS

As he had done nearly every day for more than fifty years, Mormon Church President Wilford Woodruff made an entry in his journal on September 25, 1890. Writing in a firm hand despite his eighty-three years, the prophet, seer, revelator, and fourth chief administrative officer of the Church of Jesus Christ of Latter-day Saints headquartered in Salt Lake City noted that the U.S. government had "taken a Stand & passed Laws to destroy the Latter day Saints upon the Subject of poligamy or Patriarchal order of Marriage." As a result, he wrote, he had reached a point in his life that placed him "under the necessity of acting for the Temporal Salvation of the Church."[1] Taken the previous day, the action to which he referred was the promulgation under his hand of a manifesto that simultaneously announced interdiction of the practice of plural marriage (technically, polygyny) to the Latter-day Saints and to the world.[2]

Woodruff's proclamation, usually simply referred to as the Manifesto, was a shattering blow to many of the members of the religious institution over which he presided. But circumstances left the church president with little choice. On the secular front, the Saints faced opposition to their church-led political and economic system that was serious enough to threaten the continuing existence of a distinctive Mormondom. At the same time, they faced religious hostility powerful enough to jeopardize the very existence of their church as the institutional embodiment of a peculiar people whose system of belief and practice made them unique. Woodruff's Manifesto announcing that the church would no longer sanction polygamous unions parried both the secular and the religious threats.

Because the antagonism of their opponents in both arenas had centered on plural marriage, relinquishing their unconventional marriage system allowed the Saints to get two for the price of one, as it were. They gained statehood for Utah, which allowed them to get out from under what they regarded as the tyranny of federal rule.[3] At the same time, the cessation of further practice of plural marriage checked the torrent of denigration and vilification to which the LDS community had been subjected by members, both clerical and lay, of America's mainline churches. In particular, the Manifesto blunted the often-repeated charge that polygamy turned individual Saints into sinners and made the movement barbaric.[4]

The fact that the price the Saints paid for political deliverance also led to a lessening of religious opposition to Mormonism is one indication of how tangled was the web of secular and religious motives that fueled the antagonism the Saints faced at the end of the nineteenth century. Unraveling that web completely is an impossible task. But to the extent it is feasible to do so, separating and following the various secular and religious strands of opposition to Mormonism is the best way to reconstruct the story of this peculiarly American minority faith and the American religious mainstream.

The place to start is with an appreciation of the dynamism of Mormonism that makes it distinctive, even unique. From its very beginnings the "Church of Christ" founded by Joseph Smith, Jr., and his followers in 1830 diverged from all other forms of Christianity at two crucial points. The new ecclesiastical body was led by a man its members regarded as a living prophet, and its scriptural canon included the Book of Mormon, a work the prophet said he had translated from engravings on plates of gold to which an angel had directed him. These elements set the movement apart although it was unquestionably Christian in its call for repentance and baptism by immersion. Mormonism's distinctiveness intensified dramatically as the prophet introduced new doctrines, a new form of church organization, and a new set of religious rituals. Throughout Smith's life and in several significant instances afterward, "line upon line" of new doctrine was appended to what the movement's adherents already believed.[5]

Revelations came forth during Joseph Smith's lifetime in such profusion that summary is difficult. Yet without doing too much violence to the complexity of the LDS belief system, it is possible to say that the Mormonism that existed in the late nineteenth century rested on the foundation of Christian claims that gave rise to the movement. Over that foundation were settled two discrete and autonomous overlays of theology and doctrine, revealed one after the other during Smith's prophetic career. These belief strata—or three doctrinal and theological layers—may be described as follows:

• Starting out as a somewhat idiosyncratic form of primitive Christianity, Mormonism was both restorationist and millennialist. The movement rested on dual restoration claims. One was that the true church had been absent from the earth from the time of a "Great Apostasy" at the end of the Apostolic era until its restoration in 1830. The other was that the only true and legitimate priesthood had been restored to the earth through the agency of Joseph Smith and that the newly restored church was led by members of this priesthood. Carried about the countryside by the prophet and his followers, the church's message centered on the claim that the restoration was accomplished and that the end time was rapidly approaching. With regard to this last, Mormon preachers pointed to the coming forth of the Book of Mormon as a sure sign of the nearness of the end of time.

· Two-and-a-half years after the formal organization of the church, a pivotal revelation called the prophet's father to the office of church patriarch. This calling led directly to the institution of a new ritual, the patriarchal blessing, of which an essential part is a declaration of lineage. As church members received individual patriarchal blessings, they were typically informed that their lineage extended backward to Israel through Ephraim, Benjamin, or Judah.[6] In a related development, the Saints started to make a clear distinction between the lesser priesthood of Aaron and the greater priesthood of Melchizedek, and a perception of priesthood as a privilege of lineage took hold in the LDS community. Revelation also called for the construction of a temple. Together these developments added a Hebraic dimension to Mormonism which, in time, would carry the Saints beyond the metaphorical Christian understanding of adoption into Israel to a conviction that the actual blood of Israel coursed through their veins. For the Mormons, this conviction separated humanity into two camps: those who were members of Abraham's family and those who were not. The former (Latter-day Saints and Jews) were God's chosen people; all the rest were Gentile.

· The "fulness of the Gospel" is the way Saints describe the layer of theology and doctrine added to the LDS stratified configuration in the closing years of Joseph Smith's life. This final overlay is composed of a set of tenets dealing with tiered heavens and eternal progression toward godhood plus several esoteric rituals. These include not only the celestial order of marriage, which united a man and a woman for time and eternity, but also the endowment ordinance, which bestowed power from on high on worthy Saints. In addition, ordinances of baptism and marriage by proxy were introduced into Mormonism. All of these rituals had to be performed in Mormon temples under proper priesthood authority. All peculiar to the LDS Church, they were presented to the Saints as ancient temple ordinances. For that reason, and because the revelation on celestial marriage made provision for the patriarch of a latter-day family to take wives in addition to his first one, much as Abraham, Isaac, and other ancient patriarchs had multiple wives, this set of tenets completed what the Saints came to know as yet another restoration. This made three: restoration of church and priesthood, restoration of Israel, and "the restoration of all things."

When the theological and doctrinal content of each of these layers was put in place, the Saints were impelled to act, and their actions lent substance to Mormonism's religious claims. As Mormonism's Christian base was being put into position, for example, the actions of Smith and his followers included the formal organization of the church and the sending of missionaries to preach the restored gospel and issue a warning of the impending apocalypse to all who would listen. Hearers were introduced to the Book of Mormon, which as a material reality could be "seen and hefted," and encouraged to gather to "Zion," a specific and very literal place (Jackson County, Missouri) designated by revelation as the initial site of the Second Coming.

While many believers flocked to that area, not long after the church was organized the prophet and his family moved from western New York to Kirtland, Ohio. They were joined there by many Mormons, and it was in Kirtland that the first Mormon temple was built. The 1833 calling that made Joseph Smith, Sr., patriarch to the church also came in Kirtland. Ohio, too, was the place where the Mormon prophet and his followers started to develop a program that had as its goal retaining the family, and thus patriarchy, at the center of culture.[7] Although not a strategy developed specifically for the purpose, this program countered the efforts that American colonists had made at the time of the American Revolution to loosen the bonds of society in order to allow authority to extend outward from republican government rather than downward from monarchy, efforts that continued apace.[8] The Saints did this by creating the first of what might be called LDS cultural islands, where religion, economics, politics, and other dimensions of life were thoroughly intertwined.

If the base on which the superstructure of Mormonism was built is a form of restorationist Christianity and the second level adds a strong Hebraic dimension to the faith, the uppermost layer is more esoteric. Adding unconventional doctrines, such as eternal progression toward godhood, and novel rituals, such as marriage for time and eternity, it changed Mormonism so dramatically that some of Smith's followers refused to accept the final theological and doctrinal layer as either true or binding. Holding onto the tradition as it existed before the final cryptic doctrinal and theological layer was revealed, they repudiated celestial marriage and other temple rituals.[9] But those who embraced the "fulness of the gospel" incorporated the esoteric concepts into their belief systems and set about building temples, participating in the performance of temple ordinances, and creating a society within which plural marriage could flourish.

At each stage, the actions precipitated by LDS beliefs created new and intrusive realities that were vexing to outside observers. Preaching that blazoned a brace of exclusive claims about the only true church and only legitimate priesthood asserted a hierarchy of ecclesiastical organizations that was troubling in a nation struggling with the implications of the separation of church and state. Even before the advent of plural marriage, the formation of autonomous cultural enclaves seemed both undemocratic and frightening. When polygyny was added to the mix, the Mormon reality assumed alarming, even monstrous, proportions. The Latter-day Saints appeared to non-Mormons to endanger traditional Christianity (both Protestant and Catholic), the United States of America, the democratic system, and the monogamous base of "civilized" family life.[10]

Although what the Mormons believed was private, their actions were public. Moreover, in the manner of Newton's third law, public action generates public reaction. Although LDS beliefs, especially those connected with "Smith's gold Bible," often provoked ridicule, the actions of the Saints generated reactions that sometimes exceeded the mathematical principle that "to every action there is always opposed an *equal* reaction" [emphasis added]. The explanation for this disproportionate reaction lies in the fact that Mormonism generated both secular and religious responses. But the responses were not always equally intense and not always equally hostile. At some points during the development of Mormonism, the religious response was more extended and more hostile than the secular response. At other points, the negative secular reaction to the Saints overwhelmed religious reaction. Altogether, however, the response to Mormonism throughout the nineteenth century was by and large negative and hostile. Moreover, this negativity and hostility escalated from intense competition to a full-scale crusade to destroy Mormonism, root and branch.

At an early point in its existence, Mormonism resembled other Christian denominations, especially the Disciples of Christ and to some degree the Methodists. Its fundamental religious claims contrasted with claims of other primitivist and restorationist churches (most of which likewise held that theirs was the true church) primarily in that this particular restorationist church was led by a prophet and possessed the Book of Mormon. Although its supplementary scripture's greatest significance to the faith today is that it is "another testament of Jesus Christ," in the years immediately following the organization of the church the Book of Mormon was more important as a signal of the impending opening of the millennium.[11] In this addition, in those early years the work was the prime support of Smith's status as a "choice seer," a prophet.[12]

A good case can be made for the Book of Mormon being an anti-evangelical tome, but just like the Baptists, early Mormon preachers called their hearers to repentance and challenged them to be baptized by immersion.[13] Spiritual gifts, too, especially healing, speaking in tongues, and the interpretation thereof, were much in evidence in the worship services in which members of the new church participated. Thus the truly dramatic differences between this Church of Christ and other Christian bodies were not immediately apparent.

Nevertheless, as early as 1830 it is possible to distinguish between secular and religious reaction to the Latter-day Saints. The initial secular response was a combination of ridicule of the Book of Mormon and investigative reporting designed to prove that Joseph Smith was a fraud, nothing more than a village scryer whose family had been engaged in magical pursuits and money-digging for years.[14] Religious figures, members of the clergy in particular, also published books and articles dismissing the Book of Mormon, holding that despite its claim to be an ancient text, it was a contemporary document.[15] But the initial religious response was not limited to attacking the Mormon prophet and his followers in print. Many religious leaders—preachers, ministers, and lay people—confronted the Saints directly, engaging in public debate with Mormon preachers, exhorting their own followers to ignore invitations to meet with Mormon missionaries, preaching against Mormonism as a heresy, and even disrupting Mormon meetings by burning some "evil smelling thing" in the room or making such a clatter outside that it was impossible to hear the speaker inside.[16]

Although the First Amendment disestablished the church at the federal level, some states continued to have Congregationalist and/or Presbyterian establishments for decades. By 1830, however, Methodism was unquestionably the largest Protestant denomination, and Baptists outnumbered Congregationalists and Presbyterians. At the same time, there were many areas (counties) in which Lutherans, Quakers, German Reformed, Dutch Reformed, Moravian, Mennonite, and Campbellites were predominant.[17] In addition, the sectarian polity of the Baptists and the sectarian sensibilities of the Methodists worked against the formation of a quasi-establishment, all of which means that in Mormonism's early years the Protestant mainstream was a nascent concept rather than a reality. The situation remained so unsettled that the nation was, in effect, a religious marketplace in which denominations continually jostled for members, cultural power, and moral authority.[18]

Before the advent of Mormonism, the only thing about which Protestants seemed to be in total agreement was their united opposition to Roman Catholicism. Joseph Smith and his followers provided a second common adversary, and it is likely that the united front that the nation's largest denominations mounted against this "upstart" faith was consequential in the shaping the Protestant mainstream.[19] For all that, however, religious people and religious organizations treated Mormonism in its earliest manifestation (i.e., as a restorationist form of millennialist Christianity) as a competitor in the religious marketplace not as an implacable foe. Rather than some more insistent weapon, such as the whip or sword, the instrument of choice was persuasion. The members of the church were seen as having adopted a set of doctrines and order of worship so terribly mistaken that it was heretical, but Saints were not a different order of humanity altogether.[20] They were different; they were adversaries in the search for truth, but they were not Other.

This attitude toward Smith and his followers survived for a very short period. In the mid-1830s the Saints concentrated on the Book of Mormon's promise that Joseph, the "choice seer," would be an instrument in God's hands in "bringing to pass much restoration unto the house of Israel." They believed they were seeing the prophecy in 2 Nephi 3:24 fulfilled. The prophet resided in their midst, patriarchal blessings were assuring them of their Abrahamic lineage, and the temple under construction was beginning to tower over Kirtland. Within this Ohio Mormon town, which had become an encapsulated culture set down inside the larger culture, authority rested with the prophet and the church. As things turned out, Smith and the main body of Mormons were unable to stay in the area long enough to figure prominently in regional political contests, and the internal economic system they developed seems to have had a negative impact on the financial stability of the region. That, plus ever-increasing numbers of converts flooding into the area and the completion and dedication of the temple, altered the situation, generating an increasingly hostile response to Mormonism.

Yet the most serious and most consequential reaction to the Ohio Saints was not religious but secular. As Kirtland flourished, the original settlers in the area became frightened of Mormon power and started to blame Joseph Smith and other church leaders for what was happening. As early as 1832, an Ohio mob tarred and feathered Smith and administered a brutal beating to his counselor Sidney Rigdon. These same LDS leaders became targets five years later when, in spite of their failure to obtain a state charter, the Saints established a bank that caused widespread economic distress. The confusion that ensued spawned so much stress (and apostasy) within the city and so much enmity against the Saints in the surrounding area that, for their own safety, Smith and Rigdon were forced to flee the state.[21]

In the meantime, the Mormons in Independence, the center of the Missouri "stake" in the tent of Zion, also faced a hostile reaction. Although religion was never totally absent from the bitterness shown to the Saints, Gentile opposition in Missouri was likewise mainly secular. Already alarmed by the rapid increase in the LDS population in Jackson County, the older settlers became enraged by an editorial in the Mormon newspaper assuring any free blacks who wished to join the Saints that they would be welcome in Zion. As a result, a mob of Missourians destroyed the offices of the *Evening and Morning Star,* and Saints fled from Jackson to Clay County because of threats and attacks against them by other Missourians. In Clay County, too, the animosity of their neighbors was so intense that they were asked to leave. Most of the Missouri Mormons moved to the sparsely settled northwestern part of the state. There they were soon joined by the prophet and many of the Kirtland Saints.

Understanding themselves as a restoration of ancient Israel, the Mormons again created an enclave, this time using the pattern found in Exodus 18:21–26 to organize themselves into a wilderness-based covenant community. With astonishing rapidity, thriving Mormon settlements came into being, but just as quickly non-Mormon Missourians took offense, not merely at the LDS presence but at the public statements many Saints made about God having given them the area as an inheritance. Mormons often talked of defending what was theirs by [divine] right, and in a open meeting on July 4, 1838, Sidney Rigdon— who stood next to the prophet at the head of the church—preached a sermon in which he warned Gentiles that drivings and other forms of mob violence against the Saints would no longer be tolerated. "And that mob that comes on to disturb us; it shall be between us and them a war of extermination, for we will follow them, till the last drop of their blood is spilled, or else they will have to exterminate us, for we will carry the seat of war to their own houses, and their own families, and one part or the other shall be utterly destroyed—Remember it then all Men."[22]

Given the Saints' perceptions of their situation as analogous to the wilderness experience of the Hebrews, the framework from which such rhetoric issued was undoubtedly religious. Yet the grounds on which the prophet and his followers met the non-Mormons a month later had little to do with religion. A skirmish between the Mormons and non-Mormon settlers in the area started over a civic matter: the right of Mormons in the small town of Gallatin to vote in state and county elections. Although the initial blow seems to have been struck by a Latter-day Saint reacting to being told that he was lying when he said that the Saints had the gifts of healing and speaking in tongues, the general melee that pitted Saints against the Gentiles made it clear that what was really at issue was power.

As the Gallatin fracas escalated into guerrilla warfare, gradually drawing more Mormons and larger and larger numbers of non-Mormons into pitched battles, the militia intervened. Efforts made to settle the situation came to naught, and at length the power of the state was brought to bear against the Saints. The prophet and leaders of the church were imprisoned in the jail at Liberty, and the governor issued an order that read in part, "The Mormons must be treated as enemies, and must be exterminated or driven from the State if necessary for the public good." No longer were Latter-day Saints simply different; they were adversaries whose struggle to defend what they believed God had given them subverted the state's peace and tranquility to such an extent that they had to be driven out, if necessary at the point of a gun.

To what extent non-Mormons in the nation appreciated the operations of transformation wrought within the LDS community by the combination of mobbings and drivings and the Saints' conviction that they were chosen people cannot be determined. But in the six years that followed their expulsion from Missouri it is clear that Mormonism become a national rather than an essentially local phenomenon. The nation took notice as the Saints settled in Commerce, Illinois, renamed it Nauvoo, built up a city (which for a time would be the largest in the state), and started work on a temple that would be even grander than the one in Kirtland. Nauvoo and the Mormon prophet became something of a tourist attraction, visited by a procession of journalists that included John Quincy Adams. As a consequence, the Saints, their beliefs, and their activities became an item of interest in the *New York Herald,* the *Boston Bee,* and many other newspapers. "Old Joe Smith" even made several appearances in what passed for the national press in 1840, the *Niles Register.*[23] What was published was by no means altogether favorable, written—as so much of it was—with tongue in cheek. But neither did it present Mormonism as dangerous.

Be that as it may, fear of the new thing soon developed in Illinois. The Saints had been welcomed into the state when they fled from back across the Mississippi River. But inhabitants became concerned when they realized that with increasing numbers of Mormons settled in the western part of the state, the existing balance in political power could be destroyed and the economic climate could undergo unwelcome change. A town whose people paid heed to their prophet in religious matters (when he revealed changes in the ecclesiastical hierarchy, for example) as well as secular ones (as when he directed them how to cast their ballots in the fall elections) startled citizens of the region.[24]

Their concern about what was going on in Nauvoo intensified when the sitting mayor, an adventurer named John C. Bennet, was excommunicated and forced to flee, carrying with him a discredited insider's store of information that was soon published abroad. Within the city, however, Joseph Smith took this setback in stride, becoming mayor as well as prophet, seer, revelator, and president of the church and the high priesthood. Most of his followers approved. In addition, most cheered when, as its commander-in-chief, Smith donned his new full-dress uniform and, with sword at his side, paraded the units of the city's militia, now christened the "Nauvoo Legion."

Effectively separated from the Gentile world, most of the Saints understood events in the context of Israel literally being gathered out of the world to reside under a Zionic covenant that eliminated distinctions between church and state. Outsiders saw a situation in which religion was unrighteously mixed up with politics, the economy, and, what was most frightening (and prefiguring Waco more than a century hence), the military. These dissimilar perceptions would lead to crisis. But not until dissension developed within the "kingdom on the Mississippi" after the prophet introduced eternal progression toward godhood, marriage for time and eternity, and other esoteric doctrines into Mormonism. And not until the prophet and some other Mormon leaders had started to practice plural marriage.[25]

Throughout the history of the movement, some Saints had "kicked against the traces," questioning the divine source of new revelations and complaining about the extent to which the church and its leaders controlled every aspect of Mormon life.[26] This time, however, dissent was not limited to a few Mormons. It was so widespread and reached so far into the upper echelons of leadership that it broke into the open with the publication of a newspaper, the *Nauvoo Expositor,* in whose first and only issue the prophet was accused of "trying to christianize [the] world by political schemes and intrigue."[27] The *Expositor* issue also contained an article that can be read as an acknowledgment that the "mysteries of the kingdom" included plural marriage. The prophet responded by calling the city council together, accusing the newspaper of being a civic nuisance, and asking the council to declare the press to be libelous and authorize its destruction. When it acceded to the prophet/mayor's request, members of the Nauvoo Legion wrecked the press and pied its type.

Immediately understood as an attack on freedom of the press, this action provided an opening for the non-Mormon newspaper at the county seat to characterize Joseph Smith as a tyrant and for the Saints' political adversaries to take up arms against him. As had occurred earlier in Missouri, the state government was brought into the fray. This time, however, the governor traveled with a militia escort to Hancock County where Nauvoo was located, saw to the arrest of the prophet, and undertook a personal investigation of the situation. While he was thus engaged, rogue members of the local militia descended on the jail where Smith was incarcerated and brutally murdered him.[28]

An analysis of the rhetoric used against them makes it obvious that religious prejudice figured prominently in the animosity to Mormonism in Kirtland, Missouri, and Nauvoo.[29] Even so, at crisis points in the history of the movement to that time economics, politics, and other issues ordinarily denominated as secular were the irritants that engendered such violent confrontation between the Saints and non-Mormons. For Saints who held on to Mormon doctrine and theology in all its fullness, the situation would not change dramatically after the prophet's murder.[30] Opposition to Mormons would continue because of their economics, politics, and social institutions.

But opposition would appear from another quarter as Mormonism's theological base, its claim to be the restored Christian church, was overwhelmed—at least in the perceptions of non-Mormon Christians—by its theological and doctrinal superstructure. The Saints' belief in the literal gathering of Israel and a North American Zion as a reality and their acceptance of the esoteric, but nevertheless actual, "restoration of all things" represented by the practice of plural marriage were read as signs that the Mormons were not Christian. No matter how ordinary a Mormon enclave appeared to the naked eye, it was heathen country. Where once the Saints had merely been different, in mainstream eyes those who followed Brigham Young to the intermountain West were journeying into Otherness.

Kinship connections within the group of Mormon adherents helps to explain the initial success of the movement. Intermarriage among church members and between members and converts, a common occurrence, forged new kinship ties. Moreover, by 1847, when the Saints were driven from Nauvoo, Mormonism had been in existence for seventeen years, long enough for a second generation of Saints to be a visible reminder that being Mormon meant more than belonging to a church. When all this was added to the heightened perception of themselves as Israel that persecution begot, the LDS community took on many of the characteristics of an ethnic group even before the Saints traveled through the "wilderness" to the intermountain land of promise.[31] This intensified perceptions of Mormons as Other.

Describing the troubled relationship that developed in terms of a struggle between the Mormons who went west and the federal government on the one hand and the Latter-day Saints and mainstream Protestantism on the other is an analytical strategy that imposes a clearer distinction between the secular and the religious than would have been recognized at the time. Mormons and Latter-day Saints were one and the same; they were (and are) people with either an ethnic or a membership connection to Mormonism and whose lives have both secular and religious dimensions. In like manner, at the time of the greatest conflict between the Utah Mormons and the nation, some of the very same people were leaders in both the federal government and mainstream Protestant bodies. Nearly all members of the government's executive and judicial branches were members of mainstream Protestant churches, and the overwhelming majority of *Congress* was also Protestant. Their roles in government were essentially secular. But what they said in Congress, and how they voted, made it clear that they were also religious people whose words and actions were as often animated by faith as by the practicalities of political life. Keeping the fact of this dimensional duality in mind when considering Mormons in the West is particularly important; the way religion affected politics (and politics affected religion) in Utah Territory was decisive for Mormonism in the long term and, by extension, for the dynamics of religious life in an increasingly religiously diverse nation.

After having been driven from well-established enclaves in Ohio, Missouri, and Illinois, a sizable proportion of the Mormon population left the United States in 1847. They moved west and started to settle in the Great Basin the year before the land stretching between the Rocky Mountains and the High Sierras became U.S. territory.[32] Establishing a city near the Great Salt Lake that would become the seat of a Mormon kingdom "in the tops of the mountains," the Saints attempted to join the Union in 1849. They proposed to call the area—which, among themselves, they were already calling Zion—the state of Deseret.[33] Unfortunately for them, however, the discovery of gold in California and the slavery question so complicated the issue of statehood that, as a part of the Compromise of 1850, Deseret became a U.S. territory. Brigham Young was appointed territorial governor, but Congress refused to accept the name its residents had advanced and called the area Utah instead.[34]

Disappointed, the Saints nevertheless continued with the creation of Mormon country, a realm that was at once "Utah," a U.S. territory where members of a regular religious institution that understood itself as the Church of Jesus Christ carried out the ordinary pursuits of everyday life, and "Deseret," the Kingdom of God populated by Abraham's seed, where the restoration of all things proceeded as in days of old. Moving from Utah Territory to the state of Deseret involved migrating from one mode of existence to another, but Saints, for the most part, became accustomed to making the transition. Although alternative political and economic systems were put in place in the kingdom of the Saints, most Mormons nevertheless moved easily from attendance at a public sacrament meeting in a local ward house or a church conference in a structure on Temple Square—which stood at the center of both Utah and Deseret and was therefore open to all comers—to the sacred precincts of the temples constructed in Manti, St. George, and Logan, which were exclusively reserved for worthy Saints.

But all was never tranquil in Zion after 1852, when the church announced to the world that "celestial marriage" was a part of Mormonism.[35] One reason for this is that husbands of plural wives could negotiate the divide between Utah and Deseret with reasonable ease, but women who married into plurality were permanent residents of Deseret. They could not easily enter into the life of Utah Territory because in doing so they became, in the eyes of the non-Mormon world, mistresses at best—at worst, prostitutes.[36]

Another reason the announcement of celestial marriage ended the serenity in Zion was that it directed the nation's attention to Utah. That many Mormon men were entering polygamy so outraged those who were not Mormon—members of other Christian churches as well as those who simply participated in U.S. civil society—that the Saints were regularly and viciously attacked in the religious and secular press and from the nation's pulpits. These attacks exposed the Saints to pressure from the federal government, which, by virtue of Utah's territorial status, exercised formal political authority in the area.[37] The announcement also provided the nation's Protestants with a rationale for launching a crusade against the Saints.

Historians seeking to capture the flavor of the anti-polygamy movement and the larger anti-Mormon campaign typically depend on three major sources of information: what was published in the secular press (books, periodicals, and newspapers); what occurred in government (chronicled in congressional, legislative, and court records and in the papers of members of the executive branch of the territorial and national governments); and the writings (letters, diaries, and autobiographies) of LDS men and women who suffered the campaign's consequences.[38] As a result, the manifestly religious reaction to the situation, as represented by actions of the ecclesiastical bodies that made up the nation's religious mainstream, is neglected. This is unfortunate because that is almost half the story. Distinctions, however, must be made among the various non-Mormon religious activities in Utah Territory. In some quarters no adversarial relationship developed; in others, what amounted to a state of warfare existed throughout the territorial period and beyond.

As a substantial number of non-Mormons settled in the area in the 1850s and 1860s, a priest was needed to serve Roman Catholic communicants, and many Protestants not only hungered for preaching of the word but also for congregational life.[39] An Episcopal parish was organized in Salt Lake City in 1867, and a Roman Catholic parish was organized four years later.[40] The Protestant Episcopal bishop who oversaw the work of his denomination in the Mormon kingdom was the irenic Daniel S. Tuttle, who did not believe it was his task to undermine the Mormon faith. Although the Roman Catholic press railed against the dangers posed by the LDS Church, in Utah itself Fathers Patrick Walsh and Lawrence Scanlan were content to serve the local Catholic population without trying to convert Mormons to Catholicism or warn the world at large against them.[41]

The same cannot be said for the evangelical Protestant churches. After the few more or less independent "home missionaries" who worked there in the 1850s discovered that Utah Territory was not a fertile missionary field, the churches at the center of the American religious mainstream adopted two inter-related strategies in their fight against the "Mormon Menace." They turned their attention to the young after they discovered that adult Saints (many of whom were— or whose parents had been—converts to Mormonism from evangelical Protestantism) proved extremely difficult to convert away from their new faith. And they established congregations whose ministers stood at the forefront of Protestant mainstream opposition to the Saints.

The Methodists and Presbyterians, both arriving in 1869, and Congregationalists, who arrived five years later, were joined by the Baptists (in 1881) and Lutherans (in 1882) in establishing a network of free schools (nonexistent in the territory at the time) where children of the "deluded Mormons" could receive a "true Christian education." These schools, which had teachers certified by the various denominational agencies, were open nine months a year, and they attracted large numbers of LDS students, almost none of whom turned away from Mormonism.

The several evangelical Protestant denominations who maintained schools in the area, and the Disciples of Christ as well, all organized congregations in Salt Lake City and/or Ogden, which had developed into a metropolis at the time of the building of the transcontinental railroad. Sometimes congregations were organized in both cities. Large and handsome houses of worship bearing witness to the Protestant presence in an "alien land" were also constructed. These congregations, as were the denominational schools, were supported almost entirely from contributions from denominational mission boards and private individuals outside Utah.

The leaders of these evangelical Protestant churches ministered to their local congregations, but they had an additional responsibility of equal, if not greater, importance. As ministers who served in the very heart of this "heathen land," they served as conduits for news of the "devilish" goings-on in Deseret. As guest preachers, Protestant ministers from Utah, "who were in a position to know," often filled pulpits in well-attended services in the nation's largest urban congregations, thereby informing thousands of evangelical Protestants about the heretical beliefs and "pagan practices" of the Latter-day Saints. Of greater importance, nearly all of the ministers of Utah's Protestant churches wrote anti-Mormon pamphlets, some of which gained huge circulations among Protestant ministers.[42] Thus, the Utah ministers' view of what was going on reached Protestants all across America. Listening to their local ministers preach sermons Sunday after Sunday in which Mormon leaders were demonized and Latter-day Saints characterized as dangerous to the nation's true churches and Christian homes energized the members of mainstream churches to take action against the Saints. In doing so, they attacked Mormonism's Achilles' heel, polygamy, calling it a heinous sin.

In the secular arena, polygamy was regarded as a crime. But whether as sin or crime, plural marriage became the boundary that set Saints apart from all other inhabitants of the nation's religious and secular cultures. It made them much more vulnerable than they had been when all non-Mormons knew about was the alternative political and economic systems the Saints put in place as their kingdom started to take shape on the American frontier.[43] Despite the Saints' vigorous advocacy of their right under the First Amendment to their unconventional marriage system, in less than a decade, at the urging of the nation's mainstream churches as well as non-Mormon politicians in Utah, the U.S. government started attempting to constrain the practice. Its pressure was first manifested in 1862 in a federal anti-bigamy statute (in the Morrill Act) that outlawed polygamous cohabitation. This legislation was later strengthened by the Poland Act in 1874.

The LDS Church challenged the constitutionality of the 1862 statute by setting up a test case and then arguing, first in a territorial court and later in the U.S. Supreme Court, that the Mormon defendant, George Reynolds, practiced plural marriage because he understood it to be a religious obligation.[44] Thus, the church brief argued, his marital actions were protected by the First Amendment. In the interim between the passage of the Morrill Act and a decision on its constitutionality, Mormons continued to marry into plurality, confident that obedience to the principle was a key element in the plan of salvation that God had revealed through his prophet Joseph Smith. That they could do so with relative impunity to successful prosecution was due to two legal realities: Jurors empaneled to adjudicate such cases in Utah Territory were usually Latter-day Saints who decided against the prosecution, and wives could not be forced to testify against their husbands. Subsequent legislation closed these loopholes, but they initially allowed the Saints to get around federal prohibitions against a man having more than one wife for religious reasons.[45]

The outcome of the Saints challenge to the Morrill Act's constitutionality was a definitive expression of the government's stand against polygamy, handed down by the U.S. Supreme Court in *Reynolds v. United States* in 1879.[46] In upholding the conviction of Brigham Young's private secretary, who admitted to having more than one wife, the Court concluded that chaos would ensue if "professed doctrines of religious belief" were allowed to become "superior to the law of the land." Hence it concluded that the free exercise clause of the First Amendment deprived Congress of power to legislate about "mere opinion" but left it "free to reach actions which were in violation of social duties or subversive of good order."[47] Maintaining a distinction between belief and behavior, opinion and action, the Court conceded that polygamous sects might be well ordered, but it held also that because polygamy was a corollary of patriarchy, whose natural consequence was despotism, the Morrill Act outlawing polygamy was constitutional.

In its description of polygamy as being "odious among the Northern and Western nations of Europe," the Court neglected to mention Southern and Eastern Europe, where Catholicism flourished. Was this, as Catharine Cookson suggests, an indication that the Court's decision in the Reynolds case was intended as a bulwark of Protestantism?[48]

Making such a determination is patently impossible. Yet one thing seems clear: In framing its argument so that patriarchy, a principle at the center of Mormon doctrine, was represented as suspect, or even illicit, the Court's decision created a dilemma for the Latter-day Saints. If they continued to contract plural marriages and exercise their conjugal rights within those marriages they would be breaking civil law; if they refused to enter into the "Patriarchal Order" by marrying into plurality, they would be calling the entire Mormon theological program into question. As might have been expected given the psychic and physical price they had already paid to become part of the Mormon community, a large number of Saints opted for the former. In so doing, they set the stage for an inevitable confrontation not only between Mormons and the American religious mainstream but also between religion and the secular side of society.

The reasonably benign circumstances in which plural marriage initially flourished in Deseret started to deteriorate somewhat even before Congress supported the Morrill Act with the Poland Act of 1874. Yet the practice continued unabated throughout the 1870s and, despite the ruling in the Reynolds case, into the 1880s as well. But passage of the Edmunds Act in 1882 specifically defined polygamy as action rather than opinion and extended the definition of plurality; the marriages themselves and not just their consummations were prohibited. This made convicting polygamists easier and caused the situation to become much more volatile. Volatility increased when the provisions of the 1882 bill were strengthened in 1887 by passage of the Edmunds-Tucker Act, which stipulated that the government could use virtually any means necessary to stop the practice of plural marriage. The 1887 bill, whose provisions were declared constitutional in 1889, dissolved the corporation that allowed the LDS Church to function as a legal entity, allowed for the seizure of church property, and prohibited the church's ownership of land, whether improved or unimproved. By the end of the decade, additional legislation was proposed that would have disenfranchised the Saints and removed from the electoral system the choice of persons to serve in practically every public office in Utah.

Throughout the 1880s, in what was known as the "Raid," federal marshals pursued and arrested known and even rumored polygamists in the Mormon culture region. In response, so many LDS leaders left their wives and families to fend for themselves and hid out in the mountains, or fled to Mexico and/or Canada, that all except the most critical business of the church had to be suspended. Despite their efforts to avoid discovery, capture, and prosecution, enough Mormon men were arrested, charged, tried, and imprisoned that Mormon culture almost reached a state of general collapse. For all practical purposes, what amounted to a state of war between religion and the state stretched across the Great Basin.[49]

Although President Woodruff remained in close consultation with his brethren in the leadership cadre of the church in the days and weeks before the Manifesto was released to the press, as Mormon prophet and chief LDS ecclesiastical leader he alone assumed responsibility for publicly prohibiting further official countenancing of plural marriage. And when—as was perhaps inevitable—the question arose of whether the Manifesto was merely a decision impelled by the church president's reasoned assessment of the political and legal situation, Woodruff explained that he had been shown "by vision and revelation" that temple ordinances for the living and for the redemption of the dead would both be discontinued, possibly permanently, unless Saints stopped entering plural marriages.[50] Perhaps for that reason, when the text of the Manifesto was subsequently presented to the church assembled in semiannual conference, it was sustained as revelation and, at least officially, accepted as church policy.

Statehood for Utah, which the Mormons appear to have desired above almost all else, would likely have never occurred without their relinquishing the practice of plural marriage. But Woodruff's decision to issue the Manifesto is by no means the whole story. During the 1880s the Saints disassembled the Mormon political kingdom. The LDS Peoples's Party was dismantled, and members of the church were encouraged (and sometimes directed) to become members of the Republican and Democratic parties. Virtually simultaneously, in what Leonard Arrington, the distinguished economic historian who served as LDS Church historian and head of the LDS Church Historical Department, called "the great capitulation," the church gave up its control of the kingdom's economy. It stopped the Mormon boycott of Gentile businesses and products, sold Zion's Cooperative Mercantile Institution (ZCMI) to a syndicate of Mormon businessmen and financiers, and disposed of business enterprises that formed the territory's infrastructure, including the Deseret Telegraph system and the Utah Light and Railway Company.[51] In addition to the cessation of the illegal practice of plural marriage, these actions satisfied the federal government, thus allowing Mormons and the world to come to terms. Those terms allowed the Saints to keep their temples and thus to keep the restoration of all things intact. They had to give up the practice of plurality but not the principle of celestial marriage.

Perhaps this, as much as their suspicion that the Mormons did not intend to keep their word about forbidding further plural marriages, made the evangelical Protestant church membership and clergy in Mormon country wary about what the future held. No doubt another reason for their reluctance to take the Saints at their word was that the Saints' suspension of the practice of polygamy threatened to undercut the success of Utah Protestant appeals to denominational mission boards and individuals in evangelical churches for funds to fight the Mormon peril, funds that also supported local Utah congregations. In any event, the religious response to the Manifesto and the Saints' dismantling of the kingdom certainly cannot be compared to a treaty of peace; it was less a truce than a watchful, apprehensive standoff.

Distrustful of the negotiations that led up to statehood, the members of the mainstream churches in Utah were indignant when President Benjamin Harrison issued an amnesty proclamation that pardoned all persons liable under the provisions of the various anti-polygamy measures if, since the time of the issuing of the Manifesto, they had abstained from "unlawful cohabitation."[52] Mainstream Protestants were particularly distressed that the proclamation failed to spell out whether a Mormon man simply had to have contracted no additional plural marriages since the Manifesto in order to receive amnesty or whether he was required in addition to have terminated his conjugal relations with all his wives except the first one. This ambiguity was made to order for those outside LDS culture inclined to expect the worst.

The amnesty proclamation also caused trouble within the LDS community. Although church leaders at the highest level gradually concurred in the policy forbidding new plural marriages, nearly all continued to live with the plural wives to whom they were already married in 1890. This was true in the church at every level. As welcome as it was, the ambiguous interpretation of the amnesty proclamation increased the almost inconceivable confusion precipitated by the abrupt demise of a social institution in which citizens of the kingdom had invested profound faith and extraordinary commitment. The confusion was exacerbated by the many rumors of post-Manifesto plural marriages and news that plural marriages were being solemnized outside the boundaries of the United States. Some such liaisons were openly acknowledged, lending substance to evangelical ministers' charges that the Manifesto was a sham.

Then, in 1890, in a local climate charged with confusion and suspicion, Brigham H. Roberts, a prominent member of the Mormon hier-

archy and a polygamist, was elected to Congress. His election opened
the way for the evangelical Protestant churches to mount a renewed
attack against the Saints. As a result, Roberts was not allowed to take
his seat, but the subsequent election to the U.S. Senate of Apostle Reed
Smoot had a different outcome. That election made way for the religious mainstream to refurbish all the many charges about Mormons
being deluded, pagan, and sinful. But after an incredible brouhaha and
a four-year Senate investigation, the fact that Smoot was not a polygamist worked with political reality to cause the Senate to allow him to
retain his seat, which he would keep for a quarter of a century.

Unlike passage of the Edmunds-Tucker Act and some earlier anti-
polygamy legislation that resulted from the combined pressure of
Mormonism's secular and religious opponents, the outcome of the
Smoot investigation was at base a renewal of the pact the government
made with the Saints in the 1890s. In demanding an end to the practice of plural marriage before allowing Utah to become a state when it
well knew that the territory was also Deseret, the nation recognized
that although belief generates action whose consequences government
may regulate, belief itself cannot be so regulated. This was made clear
in the government's refusal to condemn a people to outsider status for
continuing to hold to a religious principle while insisting that it not be
acted upon, which is what happened when statehood was granted to
Utah. The government's refusal to condemn an elected official for the
beliefs of his people, even if he was not acting on those beliefs (which,
finally, is what happened in the Smoot affair) reiterated the nation's
commitment to a form of religious freedom that is not absolute.

Discontinuing the practice of plural marriage did more for the Saints
than make statehood for Utah possible. As long as men married multiple wives simultaneously, LDS culture was the epitome of Otherness
in America—as surely as being Jewish or being black meant being perceived as Other. When evidence of plurality's practice disappeared, the
importance of Mormon temples increased, and the significance to the
faith of celestial marriage for time and eternity, albeit to one partner,
was enhanced. As part of this process, this tangible sign of being Mormon was turned into symbol, a development that slowly altered perceptions of LDS culture. Latter-day Saints did not cease being regarded as different, but they were not altogether Other.

Latter-day Saints continued to live in LDS enclaves for many years
following the demise of plural marriage and the achievement of statehood. This pattern persists in the lives of Saints who reside in the
American West. But things have changed dramatically. When polygamy constituted the boundary surrounding them, the Saints were effec-

tively sequestered from the world. As that boundary disappeared, it was replaced by one both permeable and unconfining. Where once Zion was in Utah (and before that Nauvoo, Far West, and Kirtland), in the twentieth century Zion is "where the people of God are."

Mormonism's confrontation with the American religious mainstream did tragic things to individual Saints and perhaps to individual evangelical Protestants. Certainly it was tragic in its production of ill-will and abhorrence for the adversary on both sides. Yet the outcome of the confrontation was by no means unrelievedly tragic. In pulling the Latter-day Saints back across the great divide from Otherness to difference, the Manifesto removed a major obstacle to Mormonism's becoming a universal church and worldwide faith.[53]

The confrontation also clarified how religious freedom does (and does not) operate in the United States. In the process of its resolution, the struggle between the Saints and the mainstream demonstrated that although the nation may, and probably always will, have some sort of religious mainstream, it does not and cannot have an establishment. Establishments impose orthodoxy, which does not—and can never—exist for long in the land of the free. People may believe what they please. As to what they do, that is another matter.

Notes

The author wishes to acknowledge with thanks the assistance rendered to her on legal issues by Sarah Barringer Gordon.

1. Susan Staker, ed., *Waiting for World's End: The Diaries of Wilford Woodruff* (Salt Lake City: Signature Books, 1993), 387. The date of this entry suggests that Woodruff's reference was to a decision of the U.S. Supreme Court in *The Late Corporation of the Church of Jesus Christ of Latter-day Saints v. United States 136:1.* This decision upheld the constitutionality of the provisions of the Edmunds-Tucker Act, which had threatened dissolution of the church as a legal corporation and seizure of its property unless the practice of plural marriage was immediately abandoned.

2. The text of the Manifesto, headed "Official Declaration," is included as "Official Declaration—1" in the Book of Mormon scripture known as the Doctrine and Covenants [hereafter cited as the D&C] of the Church of Jesus Christ of Latter-day Saints (291–92 in the 1981 edition). For circumstances surrounding Woodruff's decision to issue the Manifesto against polygamy, see Thomas G. Alexander, *Things in Heaven and Earth: The Life and Times of Wilford Woodruff, a Mormon Prophet* (Salt Lake City: Signature Books, 1991), 261–68. Without exception, historical accounts of the form of Mormonism

that took shape in the intermountain West all emphasize the importance of the Manifesto to the history of the Latter-day Saints.

3. Evidence that the Mormons regarded themselves as victims of federal tyranny is found in letters, diaries, sermons, and virtually every other form of historical record left by Latter-day Saints who lived in Utah Territory between 1850 and 1890. Indication of the virulence and intensity of this feeling may be drawn from the sermons and talks of Brigham Young and other leaders of the church between 1854 and 1886, collected in the *Journal of Discourses by Brigham Young, His Two Counselors, the Twelve Apostles, and Others,* reported by George D. Watt (Salt Lake City: Photo Lithographic Reprint, 1956), 26 vols. The following selection, drawn passim, from the index entries under "U.S. Government" provides a flavor of how this feeling was expressed: "abuses of against LDS," "anti-Mormon activities of," "blood of prophets upon," "confidence in lacking because of misrule," "corruption by wicked leaders," "dishonest condition of," "evils existing in threaten overthrow of," "graft in probable," "LDS injustices of provoke righteous anger," "LDS troubles created by," "oppressions by to meet God's retribution," "territorial rights denied by," and "wicked men in not opposed by LDS but left to Satan." It is important to note, however, that in addition to such scornful references the index contains an equal number of references to Mormon sermons and talks in which the U.S. system of government was venerated. Although some scholars interpret the latter as "window dressing," it is much more likely that the division discloses the Saints' extreme ambivalence toward the nation.

4. The most famous reference to plural marriage as barbaric comes from the 1856 platform of the Republican Party. There polygamy is yoked to slavery, and the two practices are described as "twin relics of barbarism." Abundant evidence of denigration and vilification of the Latter-day Saints by members of non-Mormon religious groups is found in religious publications. A content analysis of 30 percent of the articles in the periodicals published or sponsored by religious organizations and indexed in *Poole's Index* and *Reader's Guide* between 1860 and 1960 revealed that all except one fit into one of three negative categories, with at least half rated as extremely negative. Because these articles were part of a larger study, it is not possible to say that they were selected strictly at random, but it is safe to say that they were "more or less randomly selected."

5. "Line upon line" refers to the concept of continuing revelation. Mentioned in Isaiah 28:10 and in the Book of Mormon (2 Nephi 28:30), the promise of revelation unto the faithful, "line upon line, precept upon precept," was a part of a revelation given through Joseph Smith on August 6, 1833 (D&C, sec. 98). See James B. Allen, "Line upon Line," *The Ensign* (July 1979): 32–39.

6. The church has retained this ritual throughout its history, but patriarchal blessings are now ordinarily conferred by a stake patriarch. The calling of a presiding patriarch for the whole church, an office that was hereditary by tradition and revelation (D&C 94:91), was discontinued in 1979. See Irene Bates and E. Gary Smith, *Lost Legacy: The Mormon Office of Presiding Patriarch* (Urbana: University of Illinois Press, 1996).

7. What was (and is) implied in Mormonism's preservation of patriarchy is something more far-reaching than a particular pattern of male-female interpersonal relations that makes women subservient to men. That the preservation of patriarchy was critical to Mormonism's attempt to recover the Hebraic roots of Christianity is made obvious by the fact that it was an important part of recovering and revitalizing not just affinity with but a lineal connection through bloodline to the patriarchs of ancient Israel.

8. This effort is described by Gordon Wood in *The Radicalism of the American Revolution* (New York: Vintage Books, 1993); see particularly the section on "Patriarchal Dependence," 43–56.

9. The largest and longest-lived organized group of Mormons who rejected the esoteric doctrines and rituals that were added to Mormonism in the 1840s is the Reorganized Church of Jesus Christ of Latter Day Saints, which is headquartered in Independence, Missouri.

10. The characterizations of non-Mormon concerns in this paragraph are drawn from my study of articles about Mormons and Mormonism published in the periodical press between 1860 and 1960. The results of that study were presented in "From Satyr to Saint: American Attitudes toward the Mormons, 1860–1960," presented at the annual meeting of the Organization of American Historians, Chicago, April 1973. The paper reported the outcome of a detailed analysis of a substantial sample, stratified by date of publication, of one of every four articles in the periodical press indexed in *Poole's Index* and the *Reader's Guide* under "Mormons," "Mormonism," "Latter-day Saints," "Utah," and "polygamy" from 1860 to 1960. See also Richard O. Cowan, "Mormonism in National Periodicals, " Ph.D. diss., Stanford University, 1961; Dennis L. Lythgoe, "The Changing Image of Mormonism in Periodical Literature," Ph.D. diss., University of Utah, 1969; and Charles A. Cannon, "The Awesome Power of Sex: The Polemical Campaign against Mormon Polygamy," *Pacific Historical Quarterly* 43 (Feb. 1974): 61–82.

11. The critical importance of the Book of Mormon as a signal of the imminent opening of the millennium is clearly indicated in accounts of early Mormon preaching found in the writings of an LDS apostle, William E. McLellin. The dominant topics of sermons described in his missionary journals for 1831 and 1832 were the Book of Mormon and the judgments of God to be made at the impending return of Christ to the earth. See *The Journals of William E. McLellin: 1831–1836,* ed. Jan Shipps and John W. Welch (Urbana: University of Illinois Press, 1994).

12. In the second chapter of *Mormonism: The Story of a New Religious Tradition* (Urbana: University of Illinois Press, 1985), I argue that in the early years the Book of Mormon was the primary support undergirding Smith's standing as prophet, seer, and revelator. The key Book of Mormon passages that describe how a prophet (whose name, like that of his father, will be Joseph) will arise when the Book of Mormon comes forth are found in 2 Nephi 3.

13. Clyde Forsberg makes the anti-evangelical case in "The Quest of the Historical Nephi: The Book of Mormon in American Culture," Ph.D. diss., Queen's University, 1994.

14. Even before the Book of Mormon was printed, a derisive reference to the golden plates appeared on the title page of *Mother Goose's Melodies. The only Pure Edition. Containing all that have ever Come to Light of Her Memorable Writings, together with those which have been discovered among the MSS. of Herculaneum. Likewise Every One Recently Found in the Same Stone Box Which Held the Golden Plates of the Book of Mormon . . .* (New York: C. S. Francis, n.d.). Other examples include a parody of the book published in the Palmyra *Reflector* in June and July 1830. Called "The Book of Pukei," it was prepared by the newspaper's editor, Abner Cole. The first of many book-length exposés making use of interviews with neighbors and acquaintances of the Smith family in Manchester and Palmyra, New York, was Eber D. Howe, *Mormonism Unvailed; or, A Faithful Account of That Singular Imposition and Delusion . . .* (Painesville, Ohio: Printed and published by the author, 1834). Howe, the editor of the *Painesville Telegraph,* was assisted in his investigations by a Mormon apostate, Philastus Hurlbut. The often-repeated charge that the Book of Mormon was plagiarized from a manuscript written by Solomon Spaulding was one of the many charges against Joseph Smith put forward in this work.

15. By far the best known and most significant response to early Mormonism, and to the Book of Mormon in particular, is Alexander Campbell, *Delusions: An Analysis of the Book of Mormon* (Boston: Benjamin H. Greene, 1832).

16. The journals of William McLellin are filled with accounts of such opposition to the work of Mormon missionaries, as are the diaries of Wilford Woodruff in *Waiting for the World's End,* ed. Staker, and the *Autobiography of Parley Parker Pratt,* ed. Parley P. Pratt (1938, repr. Salt Lake City: Deseret Book Co., 1979). See also, D. Michael Quinn, trans. and ed., "The First Months of Mormonism: A Contemporary View by Rev. Diedrich Willers," *New York History* 54 (July 1973): 317–33.

17. This description of the national denominational pattern is based on a map prepared by Philip L. Barlow and his associates for the revision of Edwin Gaustad and Philip L. Barlow, *Atlas of Religion in America* (New York: Oxford University Press, in press). The map, based on exhaustive research, describes the breakdown as determined by denominational majorities in every county in the United States.

18. R. Laurence Moore, *Selling God: American Religion in the Marketplace of Culture* (New York: Oxford University Press, 1994) is an account of how religion maintained its significant position within the culture after disestablishment. Only in passing does this important work describe the internal workings of the religious marketplace. The best-known effort to do that is Roger Finke and Rodney Stark, *The Churching of America* (New Brunswick: Rutgers University Press, 1992). A particularly compelling account of the nature of the religious marketplace in a slightly earlier period has been provided by Alan Taylor in "The Paradox of Popular Religion on the Yankee Frontier: Otsego County, New York, 1785–1820," presented at the annual meeting of the American Historical Association, San Francisco, Jan. 8, 1994.

19. Ironically, opposition to Mormonism was one point on which the nation's Roman Catholics and Protestants agreed.

20. A systematic statement of Mormon belief would not come until 1835, when the "Lectures on Faith" were published in a volume of the D&C. A photographic reprint of this rare volume was issued in 1970 by Herald House, the publishing arm of the Reorganized Church of Jesus Christ of Latter Day Saints.

21. Accounts of the experience of the Mormons in Kirtland are part of every standard history of the Latter-day Saints. See James B. Allen and Glen M. Leonard, *The Story of the Latter-day Saints* (Salt Lake City: Deseret Book Co., 1976); and Leonard J. Arrington and Davis Bitton, *The Mormon Experience: A History of the Latter-day Saints* (New York: Alfred A. Knopf, 1979). A useful work is Milton V. Backman, Jr., *The Heaven's Resound: A History of the Latter-day Saints in Ohio, 1830–1838* (Salt Lake City: Deseret Book Co., 1983).

22. Rigdon's sermon was later reprinted as a pamphlet. It is described, and a long excerpt quoted from it, in Stephen C. LeSueur, *The 1838 Mormon War in Missouri* (Columbia: University of Missouri Press, 1987), 47–53.

23. What the prophet wrote in answer to the inquiry of John Wentworth, editor of the *Chicago Democrat,* is a good indication of the way he presented Mormon belief to the world. His letter concluded with a statement that amounted to a Mormon creed spelling out the primitivist Christian base of the faith, and he adds, "We believe in the literal gathering of Israel and in the restoration of the Ten Tribes [and] that Zion will be built on this continent." The full text of the letter is in *The Encyclopedia of Mormonism,* ed. Daniel H. Ludlow (New York: Macmillan, 1992), 4:1750–55.

24. For details on the pattern of Mormon voting, see chapter 3, "Illinois: A Land of Promise," and chapter 4, "A Land of Broken Promises," in Jo Ann B. [Jan] Shipps, "The Mormons in Politics: The First Hundred Years," Ph.D. diss., University of Colorado, 1965.

25. There are many books on Nauvoo, but the standard work is still Robert Flanders, *Nauvoo: Kingdom on the Mississippi* (Urbana: University of Illinois Press, 1975).

26. If their disagreement was great enough to cause a break between them and the rest of the community, such people were regarded as apostates. If they simply grumbled while remaining with the community, they were called "Jack Mormons."

27. This was a reference to the fact that, in a move that made it clear that the prophet anticipated a practically immediate opening of the millennium, Joseph Smith had entered the lists as a candidate for president of the United States, and he directed LDS missionaries to campaign for him throughout the nation. The connection between his candidacy and the imminent end of time was made by Robert Flanders in his presidential address to the John Whitmer Historical Association in 1972.

28. Smith's brother Hyrum, assistant president and patriarch of the church, was also murdered. Apostle John Taylor, visiting in the cell at the time of the attack, was wounded, but the bullet that might have killed him struck his watch instead.

29. Examples of rhetoric used against Mormonism generally and against Joseph Smith in particular abound in biographies of the prophet and histories of the church.

30. Although not always recognized, the movement atomized after the murder of the prophet. By no means did all of the Saints hold to all aspects of LDS theology and doctrine. For a catalog of the various LDS movements, see Steven L. Shields, *Divergent Paths to the Restoration: A History of the Latter Day Saint Movement,* 3d rev. ed. (Bountiful: Restoration Research, 1975).

31. On Mormon ethnicity, see Jan Shipps, "Making Saints in the Early Days and the Latter Days," in *Contemporary Mormonism: Social Science Perspectives,* ed. Marie Cornwall, Tim B. Heaton, and Lawrence A. Young (Urbana: University of Illinois Press, 1994), 64–83.

32. The part of the intermountain region where the Saints settled was in Upper California, which became U.S. territory as one of the conditions of the Treaty of Guadalupe Hidalgo that ended the Mexican War.

33. The term *deseret,* meaning "honey bee," came from the Book of Mormon.

34. In view of the importance of naming in religion discussed by Phyllis Trible in her rereading of Genesis 2–3, the refusal of Congress to accept the name the Latter-day Saints proposed indicates suspicion about the program the Mormons might be pursuing to create a separate religious culture. See Trible's article from *Andover Newton Quarterly* 13 (March 1973), reprinted in *Womanspirit Rising: A Feminist Reader in Religion,* 2d ed., ed. Carol P. Christ and Judith Plaskow (San Francisco: HarperCollins, 1992), 74–83.

35. Rumors about plural marriage among the Mormons had circulated ever since the 1830s, and it is quite possible that some covenants of plural marriage were entered into during that decade. The rumors about the practice spread rapidly after the prophet's murder. Although clandestine, marriage of Mormon men to more than one wife was openly practiced in Utah before the public announcement in 1852. Most marriages had been performed in the Nauvoo Temple before the Saints left Illinois. Before the completion of LDS temples in the intermountain West, the Saints established temporary "endowment houses" in which the ordinance of celestial marriage could be performed. For the religious and theological dimension of plural marriage, see Lawrence Foster, *Religion and Sexuality: Three American Communal Experiments of the Nineteenth Century* (New York: Oxford University Press, 1981), ch. 4. A convenient account of the history of the practice is in Richard S. Van Wagoner, *Mormon Polygamy: A History* (Salt Lake City: Signature Books, 1986).

36. This gave first wives an advantage, but this advantage was typically compromised because men entering the patriarchal order in order to comply with the principle had to have the permission of their original spouses. The requirement was often ignored.

37. Standard works on Mormon political and economic innovations are Klaus J. Hansen, *Quest for Empire: The Political Kingdom of God and the Council of Fifty in Mormon History* (1967; repr. Lincoln: University of Nebraska Press, 1974); and Leonard J. Arrington, *Great Basin Kingdom: An*

Economic History of the Latter-day Saints, 1830–1900 (Cambridge: Harvard University Press, 1958).

38. This generalization is based on an examination of a large variety of books that survey the history of the Mormons and the history of Utah, as well as specialized works such as Gustive O. Larson, *The Americanization of Utah for Statehood* (San Marino: Huntington Library, 1970); Edward Leo Lyman, *Political Deliverance: The Mormon Quest for Utah Statehood* (Urbana: University of Illinois Press, 1986); Frank Cannon and Harvey J. O'Higgins, *Under the Prophet in Utah: The National Menace of Political Priestcraft* (Boston: C. M. Clark, 1911); Gary L. Bunker and Davis Bitton, *The Mormon Graphic Image, 1834–1914* (Salt Lake City: University of Utah Press, 1983); and Cannon, *The Awesome Power of Sex.* The reason is obvious: The religious press is seriously under-represented in reference works that index periodicals and newspapers.

39. In the 1850s the non-Mormon population was primarily made up of merchants and their families and persons in or connected to the military unit assigned to Fort Douglas, an army post on a bench of the Wasatch Mountains above Salt Lake City after the conflict between the Saints and the federal government (the "Utah War"). In the 1860s large numbers of non-Mormons came to Utah in connection with building the transcontinental railroad and the development of mining in the territory.

40. The two best sources for information on non-Mormon religious activities in Utah are both by T. Edgar Lyon: "Religious Activities and Development in Utah, 1847–1910," *Utah Historical Quarterly* 35 (Fall 1967): 292–306, and "Evangelical Protestant Missionary Activities in Mormon Dominated Areas, 1865–1910," Ph.D. diss., University of Utah, 1962.

41. The *American Catholic Quarterly Review* published five long, negative articles about the Mormons during the territorial period; see especially, "Forty Years in the American Wilderness," *American Catholic Quarterly Review* (Jan.–Oct. 1890): 123–50.

42. Examples of popular pamphlets written by Protestant clergy, all found in the outstanding Mormon collection in the Beineke Library, Yale University, include: "Methods of Mormon Missionaries" by William R. Campbell, who, according to the title page, spent twelve years as a "Christian" missionary to Utah Territory; "Present Aspects of Mormonism" by R. G. McNeice, D.D., who was engaged in "Christian work in Utah" for twenty-one years; "Historical Sketch of Mormonism" by D. J. McMillan, D.D., who spent ten years in Utah; and "Articles of Faith of the 'Latter-day Saints' with Mormon Explanations" by the Rev. J. D. Nutting and D. J. McMillan, D.D., who together had fifteen years of experience in Utah. "Ten Reasons Why Christians Can Not Fellowship the Mormon Church" was issued by the Presbytery of Utah and endorsed by both the Congregational and Baptist Associations of Utah.

43. Historians of nineteenth-century Mormonism disagree about whether its exceptional political and economic systems or polygamy generated more opposition. Klaus Hansen, for example, has long argued that it was Mormon-

ism's seemingly un-American character, particularly of the political system, that incited the greater antagonism. This argument, initially made in Cannon and O'Higgins in *Under the Prophet in Utah*, is restated and expanded in Lyman, *Political Deliverance*, and in Edwin Brown Firmage and R. Collin Mangrum, *Zion in the Courts: A Legal History of the Church of Jesus Christ of Latter-day Saints, 1830–1900* (Urbana: University of Illinois Press, 1988). But my analysis of what was written about the Mormons in the periodical press and elsewhere suggests that plural marriage cannot be sufficiently disentangled from the political and economic elements of Mormon practice to make a strong argument one way or the other. Nevertheless, it seems likely that most members of the non-Mormon religious community saw plural marriage as un-American and un-Christian.

44. The literature on the Reynolds case is extensive. For an account devoted to its legal aspects, see Orma Linford, "The Mormons and the Law: The Polygamy Cases," Ph.D. diss., University of Wisconsin, 1964, and in *Utah Law Review* 9 (Winter 1964-Summer 1965): 308–70, 543–91. In *Religious Liberty in the United States: The Development of Church-State Thought since the Revolutionary Era* (Philadelphia: Fortress Press, 1972), Elwyn A. Smith makes an effort to place the case in the context of the history of interpretation of the First Amendment. See also Catharine Cookson, "Myths, Mormons, and Moral Panics: A Critique of Governmental Processes and Attitudes in the Free Exercise Case of *Reynolds v. United States*," master's thesis, University of Virginia, 1992, 54–57; and Firmage and Mangrum, *Zion in the Courts*, 151–53.

45. Accounts of the Saints' refusal to accede to federal legislative prohibitions against the practice of plural marriage are legion, the stuff of Mormon pioneer history. In addition to the history summarized in Van Wagoner, *Mormon Polygamy*, see Foster, *Religion and Sexuality*, ch. 5. For the story from the point of view of plural wives, consult the selections by plural wives included in *Women's Voices: An Untold History of the Latter-day Saints, 1930–1900*, ed. Kenneth W. Godfrey, Audrey M. Godfrey, and Jill Mulvay Derr (Salt Lake City: Deseret Book Co., 1982); Annie Clark Tanner, *A Mormon Mother: An Autobiography* (Salt Lake City: University of Utah Press, 1976); Maria S. Ellsworth, ed., *Mormon Odyssey: The Story of Ida Hunt Udall, Plural Wife* (Urbana: University of Illinois Press, 1992); and the essays in *Mormon Sisters: Women in Early Utah*, ed. Claudia L. Bushman (Cambridge: Emmeline Press, 1976). For a Mormon polygamist's view of the experience, see the Diary of Charles Ora Card, Special Collections Division, Utah State Library, Logan.

46. Holding that religious opinion alone may be held without constitutional inhibition, whereas actions hostile to good civil order are subject to such inhibition no matter how sincere the religious opinion undergirding such acts, the Court set forth "the true distinction between what properly belongs to the Church and what to the State" in this opinion. Because it clarified the meaning of the Jeffersonian concept of a "wall of separation" between church and state, the Reynolds decision is important to American religious history. But it seemed a travesty against religious freedom to Latter-day Saints at the time. See Firmage and Mangrum, *Zion in the Courts*, 151–59.

47. 95 U.S. 167, 164. The decision of the Court was written by Chief Justice Morrison R. Waite. In illustrating the necessity of controling religiously motivated behavior, he referred to human sacrifice and pointed out that religion in some cultures supported a wife's belief that it was her duty to burn herself on her husband's funeral pyre. The implication was that such a barbaric practice could not be outlawed if the government were prevented from making laws about religious behavior.

48. Cookson, "Myths, Morals, and Mormon Panics," 62.

49. Larson, *The Americanization of Utah*, esp. chapter 1, contains the standard account of the raid.

50. President Woodruff's remarks were made in the Cache Stake Conference, November 1, 1891. They were reported in the November 14, 1891, issue of the *Deseret Weekly* and are printed in the D&C as one of the "Excerpts from Three Addresses by President Wilford Woodruff regarding the Manifesto." The excerpts follow the text of Woodruff's statement.

51. Arrington, *Great Basin Kingdom*, ch. 13.

52. An even more liberal amnesty was signed by President Cleveland the following year.

53. The other major obstacle, denial of priesthood to blacks, was removed by a 1978 revelation to President Spencer Kimball that opened the priesthood to all worthy male Saints.

FOUR

Protestant Immigrants and the Protestant Mainstream

James D. Bratt

In October 1918 two Mennonite meeting houses in Inola, Oklahoma, were burned by an angry mob. The same month, the parochial schools of two Missouri Synod Lutheran churches were also destroyed: one in Lincoln, Missouri, by fire, and one in Schuum, Ohio, by dynamite. These joined the Lutheran school in Herrington, Kansas, that had been burned the month before and the main building of the Mennonites' Tabor College in Hillsboro, Kansas, torched in April. The same fate befell Christian Reformed churches in Peoria, Illinois, and Sully, Iowa.[1]

These incidents were the flash points in a storm of hostility that rolled across the American Midwest near the end of World War I. Of course, all things German had come under attack when the United States entered the war the year before, but of particular interest were the religious targets of that attack. Scores of mob demonstrations against German American Lutherans have been documented: ministers forced to kneel and kiss the American flag; prominent laity forced to buy Liberty bonds; church sanctuaries planted with unwelcome flags; the barns and homes of suspected "slackers" splashed with yellow paint; and clerics and laity alike subjected to tar and feathers, mock hangings, and malicious serenades. Mennonites and Amish suffered all these and more. Some of their farms and animals were seized and sold for war bonds, and 130 of their young men were court-martialed for defying military regulations. Two of these, of Hutterite affiliation, died in prison from maltreatment. The Christian Reformed suffering resembled the Lutheran more than the Mennonite, but then most of its members were of Dutch descent, and the Netherlands was not allied with the Central Powers but neutral in the war.[2]

How was it that these three groups—Mennonites and Amish, Missouri Synod Lutherans, and Christian Reformed—came under patriotic attack in 1918? After all, they were not Reds or Wobblies or radicals of any sort; on the contrary, they were renowned for their

conservativism. Although they were of immigrant background, whatever lingering affection they had for their old country did not extend
to its government, whose harassment had helped trigger their emigration in the first place. Besides, they showed all the markings of "good
Americans." Their forebears had been welcomed to the neighborhood
years before (perhaps by the mobs' own ancestors) just because of their
promising character, and they had not disappointed. Diligent, frugal,
industrious, and law-abiding, they epitomized the dominant American
ethic. They even shared Americans' ideal immigrant origin, being of
northwestern European, Teutonic, Protestant stock.

For all these qualities, however, they had quite deliberately kept themselves apart from the larger society and defied key American norms. Upon
that the mobs of 1918 were taking vengeance. My purpose is to explore
why such self-segregation occurred, how it was effected, with what consequences it was attended, and how the process taken as a whole alters
the understanding of American religious history.

Historians have usually categorized the three groups either by their
ethnicity or by their place in one of the three families of Protestantism:
Anabaptist, Lutheran, and Reformed or Calvinist. And so the groups
regarded themselves. They gave most of their attention to their sib-
lings—to other Germans, to fellow Anabaptists—and regarded each
other as distant cousins if not complete strangers. Yet some shared
dispositions make Mennonites, Missouri Synod Lutherans, and the
Christian Reformed resemble each other as often as their ethnic/theo-
logical kin. They followed a historical course different from the strict
sectarianism and broader ecumenicism that scholars usually notice, but
this third way has not yet been systematically clarified. In any case they
merit attention within the chronological bounds of this book because
they absorbed more of the immigrant stream between the Civil War and
World War I than did their sibling denominations.

The groups' common profile was compounded of four shared characteristics: they were continental in origin, confessionalist in theology,
restorationist in program, and tribal in culture and social structure. Of
course, what they confessed and what they would restore differed, with
important consequences for their American ventures. But they all bore
a common stamp of ambivalence: toward the old world and the new,
toward tradition and innovation, toward people of the same ethnicity
but (sometimes slightly) different religion, and toward people of the
same religion but different ethnicity. If the burden of ambivalence could
be heavy, it also spurred the creative adaptations that were the best part
of their achievement.

Their continental origins did not endow these communities with the elegance that adjective usually connotes; their origins did, however, give them a heritage significantly different from that of the British dissenting tradition that informed the American Protestant mainstream. As a result, they had their own slant on everything from the grand sweep of church history to behavioral niceties involving tobacco, alcohol, and secret societies. The most obvious difference probably lay in their confessionalism. If nineteenth-century Americans were notoriously noncreedal, these three groups took the formal testimonies of the sixteenth-century Reformation and its seventeenth-century aftermath as definitive summaries of divine truth and the seals of their own identities. In consequence, the subjects were all suspicious of inter-confessional ecumenism on the one hand; of subjective, emotional revivalism on the other; and of parachurch organizations in between.

The three were also enmeshed in a restorationist program and its paradoxes.[3] They were committed to following old paths and restoring a golden age that existed mythically in their memories if not in historical fact. Precisely this yearning for an old world guided them to the new: North America afforded the space to carry on a way of life that their former lands were closing off. As tribalists they were determined to carve out one part of that space for their own projects. They proselytized little among people who did not share their roots, but they built up separate worlds with complete sets of institutions and all-absorbing meaning systems. The separateness made them appear to be sects, and the completeness made them appear as churches; taken together, the two seemed to be the first fruits of the kingdom of God that the Bible promised and that history, in the golden time, had verged on opening.

Perhaps this desire to have things both ways at once helped trigger the rage against them during World War I. But 1918 was hardly the first time nor the United States the first place these groups had met persecution. In fact, they had become distinct before immigration, during confrontations with European governments over religious loyalties. The nineteenth-century state's rationalizing tendencies militated against the confessional particularities that these groups insisted on keeping, and the fines, threats, and imprisonment they suffered endowed them with the core memory that they brought to America, a memory of resisting an encroaching state and/or corrupted church that wore the cloak of progress. The old world they wished to restore, therefore, was not simply the world they had left. Yet their European suffering did not incline them toward making a wholesale identification with America. In fact, they resisted both of the assimilationist routes historians have defined:

that of liberal, secularist progressivism suggested by Oscar Handlin and that of millennial, biblicistic evangelicalism outlined by Timothy L. Smith.[4] Both options entailed the modernization they had rejected in Europe. Committed to preserving correct Christianity as they understood it, they could be profoundly suspicious of the sort of Christian America they saw in the late nineteenth century.

They were wary of their closest kin, especially on this score. The groups all received aid from some of "their own" who had immigrated long before, but those benefactors also displayed the changes that America might demand. Such acculturation could strike the new arrivals as a forfeiture of too much of the heritage, and so it often became a benchmark of purity—or impurity—and a rallying point for solidarity. The groups' contest with the American mainstream thus started out as an intra-ethnic quarrel over "purity" and "progress" and intensified over time. All three groups saw reformist innovators rise in their own circles during the 1890s and gain near ascendancy by 1910, only to become discredited in World War I and fall to a fundamentalist reaction in the early 1920s. That same reaction fixed certain elements of tradition as a permanent badge of group identity—ironically, a proposal the Progressives themselves had first suggested.

Resisting America, in sum, became one mode of adjustment while opening up to the new land usually proceeded in accordance with old values. Americanization was a two-way street that had some surprising U-turns, collisions in the passing lane, and a complex traffic pattern. Ethnic Protestants controlled the traffic sometimes better, sometimes worse than they intended. But the effort of doing so entailed a cultural diagnosis that the new land needed as much as the newcomers. A Christian Reformed minister said it best in launching a new journal in 1897—hard on the heels of an industrial depression, on the verge of new imperial ventures for the United States, and amid Anglo self-congratulation: "We are not and will not be a pretty piece of paper upon which America can write whatever it pleases."[5]

The preceding character profile described Mennonites from the very start of their history. Of all the Reformation streams, the Anabaptist was the one most committed to restoring the apostolic church in specific usages as well as general principles. As often happens, the restoration ideal promoted modernizing functions—in this case a commitment to separating church and state and to basing church membership upon the free choice of conscience. Just those features, of course, prompted an immediate and thoroughgoing persecution by the established order. Some Anabaptists died in the assault, and others quailed. The rest created a community that persisted by instituting some degree of physical separation from the world and taut discipline against it. The experience was crystallized in key documents: the Schleitheim Confession (1527) on the Swiss-German side; the Dordrecht Confession (1632) on the Dutch wing; and the *Martyrs Mirror* (1660), which served Mennonite memory much as Foxe's *Book of Martyrs* did the English Puritans'.[6]

Although concerted persecution ended with the Wars of Religion, Anabaptist migrations did not. Some Swiss Germans headed to North America and some of the Dutch to Prussia and then into Russia and the Ukraine. The two streams would reconnect in the United States in the nineteenth century, but by then they subscribed to different codes. As one Mennonite historian puts it, the Swiss Germans had learned to hold their heads down, the Dutch Russians to hold theirs up.[7] When Dutch Russian assertiveness arrived on the Great Plains after the Civil War, Swiss German deference that had been cultivated since colonial days in Pennsylvania could neither accept nor ignore it.

The Swiss Germans, says Mennonite historian Theron Schlabach, defined themselves by the indelible lesson of their history: "to be faithful meant to suffer." Early America presented them an unusual challenge, then, in "offering ever more comfort and toleration."[8] The old lesson came back for a time with the American Revolution, when the Mennonites' pacifism cost some of them punitive taxation and confiscated property. But for the most part they did not pursue the old Anabaptist option of confronting the powers; they simply tried to stay out of the powers' way. Nor were they yet set off from other Pennsylvania Germans in dress or language. Tolerated, somewhat patronized, they were accepted as minor exceptions so long as they remained "the quiet in the land."[9]

Yet being quiet proved exceptional enough in a young republic that was, in Schlabach's words, "boastful, expansionist, pragmatic, and all too oriented to power."[10] In lieu of the reality of suffering, the Mennonites cultivated a distinct style of humility that at once recovered an ancient virtue and effected group differentiation. Humility encouraged devotion to family farming and militated against the greed and disloyalty of individualistic frontiering; Mennonites did participate in the westward land rush but stayed better linked with each other than with their new and alien neighbors. Humility looked askance at evangelical revivalism, with its seeming presumptions upon the will of God and self-absorbed personal testimonies; Mennonites did base church membership upon free choice but absorbed individual decisions in a communal discipline that went well beyond mainstream norms in regulating behavior. They participated some in the Republic's democratic politics but with clear group purposes; if other Pennsylvania Germans voted Democratic in the antebellum period, the Mennonites backed Whigs and Republicans. Humility forswore officeholding and also cultivated important patrons who gave protection in time of stress; one of these was Thaddeus Stevens, who owed his perennial margins of victory to the Mennonites of Lancaster County.[11]

Mennonites thus participated in the larger American conversation but translated it by their own lexicon. The dynamic was clearly at work when the community was caught up in the fragmenting forces that struck American Protestantism in the 1840s. The Mennonites suffered simultaneous departures on both sides.[12] To the left, a fair number quit the Franconia Conference in 1847 under the lead of John H. Oberholtzer; to the right, the first Old Order schism occurred in 1845 under the lead of Jacob Stauffer. Oberholtzer wanted to institute reforms to strengthen the church; Stauffer resisted them for the same reason. Oberholtzer encouraged education to retain the youth, missions to affect the world, and written constitutions and greater congregational autonomy to reflect the American political climate. His group lowered barriers by allowing greater variation in dress yet promoted Mennonite unity by joining with German immigrants in Iowa to form the General Conference (1860) on a reformist platform. Stauffer, and three other Old Order groups who left between 1872 and 1893, argued exactly the contrary.[13] Group strength demanded higher, not lower, barriers and more, not fewer, differences. The Old Order restored such stringent enforcement measures as shunning and excommunication. It maximized distinctive dress and language, asserted oral tradition over written records, and redoubled communal authority over individual variants. It enumerated new behavioral restrictions in the name of tradition and then redoubled the irony by dropping these prohibitions once the worldly ways in question no longer threatened group solidarity.

Given Mennonite ideals of church unity and the group's small size in the first place, this fragmentation seemed lamentable. Yet it also had some positive functions. The controversies fixed everyone's attention upon the claims of tradition and thus strengthened Anabaptist consciousness. They generated a broader range of Mennonite options, enabling the like-minded to cluster together, to advance their own particular path, and finally to curtail their quarreling.[14]

The Dutch Russians' arrival on the Great Plains would push all the possibilities of this dynamic. Their distinctive style had its roots in the greater tolerance the Netherlands had shown the Anabaptist cause at the start and in the welcome its members had received as they resettled across Eastern Europe. Valued there as doughty farmers who would contribute to national development, the Dutch Russians negotiated deals with their hosts that gave them effective autonomy in their own districts—and thus separation from national development. They ran their own schools, governed their own villages, achieved economic prosperity, and verged on an Anabaptist form of the "Christendom" that Anabaptists were born to oppose.

Critics within the faith thought such folly deserved punishment, and it came in the 1860s. Widening social stratification raised some Mennonites to the status of Russian land barons but left others in the community landless. This fed a religious renewal that grew into the separation of the Mennonite Brethren movement, which insisted on experiential conversion and baptism by immersion as antidotes to formalism and complacency. Meanwhile, the imperial government mounted the "reform" program of Russification, mandating Russian-language instruction in the schools, threatening Mennonite military exemptions, and reducing the group's insulation from the world. The reaction was swift and bold. One-third (eighteen thousand) of the Dutch Russians left for North America, ten thousand of them to the Great Plains of the United States and Canada. By the 1936 federal religion census their descendants represented between 25 and 33 percent of the 114,000 Mennonite/Amish believers in the country.[15]

Although eastern Mennonites gave the new immigrants substantial monetary aid, the two sides hardly evinced sweet harmony. Most obvious were the quarrels over the question of whether the money was a gift or a loan. The easterners also suspected the Dutch Russians' real motivations; after all, the United States offered them even less than Russia had on the moral end (no military exemptions or village autonomy) but more on the material side (cheap, boundless land). The basic clash, however, involved maintenance strategies. The Dutch Russians set out to replicate their old commonwealth. They might have only congregations instead of whole villages to build around in America, but build they did: school systems, newspapers, and political networks. They celebrated the German language as a positive cultural vehicle not just as a defensive social wall. They showed clear sympathies with the Progressive tides of the 1890s, forming a teachers' association to run their schools more effectively and founding hospitals and deaconess homes that echoed the mainstream Social Gospel and woman's suffrage campaigns. Naturally, they joined the General Conference, which encouraged both cooperative institution-building and local church autonomy.[16]

Before labeling them progressive modernizers, however, we should remember that the Dutch Russians were trying to rebuild a traditional folk world. Their hopes and energies thrived in autonomous space; when Americans invaded that space, they would resist quite as much

as their forebears had in Russia. Furthermore, the midwesterners renewed a critical part of the Anabaptist heritage. During the Civil War
the eastern Mennonites, for all their peaceable rhetoric, had paid taxes, hired substitutes for their conscripts, and seen a good number of
their members bear arms. The new arrivals articulated a firmer pacifism.
As James Juhnke has said, if rebaptism catalyzed the tradition in the
sixteenth century, the "refusal of military participation . . . [proved] the
flashpoint in the twentieth."[17] The Dutch Russians had found a bolder issue than that of flashy dress by which to set themselves apart.

In addition, modernizing trends were appearing in the easterners'
Old Mennonite Church as well. As early as 1864, John Funk, sometime follower of Dwight L. Moody, began publishing the *Herald of
Truth,* which functioned as a denominational magazine. By the 1880s
revivalism was in full flower in Mennonite circles. It proceeded in properly humble style and aimed to reinforce group distinctiveness, but it
represented a critical opening to American evangelical notions. Soon,
Sunday schools (long resisted as a para-church wedge) and the English
language caught on, followed by Bible conferences, colleges, and mission enterprises. In the first decade of the twentieth century official
denominational boards were instituted to run the ventures. Although
Old Order devotees protested against all these, the loyalists' youth
eagerly enlisted in them, stanching the generational hemorrhage Mennonites had suffered for most of the nineteenth century.[18]

This Mennonite "quickening" had mixed results. Mennonite colleges
posed the incongruity of "farm-bred [youth] coming to small towns to
study under professionals trained in city universities in order to renew
rural congregations."[19] Students were being indoctrinated in Anabaptist distinctiveness and also inducted into the culture of professional-
ism. The faculties were too harried to systematize their philosophy of
education, however, and so practiced a lot of folk tradition. Mennonite missionaries burst their insular bounds to witness worldwide for
a suffering Christ, but they absorbed mainstream Protestantism's rhetoric of conquest in the process. Mennonite Bible conferences borrowed
teaching techniques from their American dispensationalist inventors
with the intent of teaching pacifism rather than prophecy. Even so, the
format—propositional and systematic—tended to separate personal
salvation from communal ethics in contradiction to the Mennonite way.
Everywhere, what had been organic custom was being codified and
rationalized, yet the ancient mode of personal leadership was probably more influential than ever.[20]

Whatever mixtures acculturation had bred were quickly reseparat-
ed by World War I. Eastern Old Mennonite circles again took to submissive suffering and reliance upon outside protectors. The Dutch

Russians had neither strategy in their repertoire and suffered the consequences. Worse yet, some of them were overtly pro-German. During the years of putative American neutrality the Kansas Mennonite *Herold* and *Vorwaerts* magazines regularly published German propaganda. A month before the *Lusitania* sinking, for instance, the *Vorwaerts* cover featured "a nine-inch picture of Bismarck with spiked helmet, bushy eyebrows, stern countenance, prominent paunch, and the quotation, 'We fear God and nothing else in the world.'"[21] These journals did not speak officially for the community but did speak regularly to it, a fact its neighbors did not ignore. In 1917, then, midwestern Mennonites came under especially vigilant scrutiny. Nor were only male conscripts at risk. Everyone was supposed to buy war bonds, but because doing so was voluntary not mandatory, the purchase did not fall under Jesus' command to "render unto Caesar" his due. Some Mennonites refused to buy bonds at all; more did so but under great duress. Accordingly, the entire midwestern Mennonite community came under attack, suffering more than any other church group in the nation.[22]

The war's aftermath produced two ironies that fittingly cap this narrative of ambivalence. The first was the more charming. Many Mennonite households donated the obligatory war bonds to denominational agencies, providing the capital for a remarkable institutional resurgence in the 1920s. Mennonite benevolence crested exactly as the Protestant mainline's venture in that direction, the Interchurch World Movement, evaporated. In relocating their starving kin from the Ukraine, Mennonites acted on the distinctive identity the war had retaught them. In coordinating disparate ventures into their first interdenominational agency, the Mennonite Central Committee, they proved themselves capable of the systematic philanthropy that progressive Americans had claimed for the war. Mennonites thus learned modern means to serve the world peaceably and to seal their separate identity in the bargain.[23]

The second irony Mennonites shared with others. If World War I had been a Progressive crusade, it spawned a reactionary backlash. In Protestant circles this registered as the fundamentalist offensive. Among Mennonites, denominational periodicals unleashed invective upon suspected liberals, and regional boards purged the Goshen (1918) and Bethel (1919) college faculties, finally shutting down Goshen entirely for the 1923–24 academic year. At issue was not theological modernism, of which these circles had but the slightest trace. Rather, the fundamentalist hunt weeded out individuals who had identified too enthusiastically with the American cause at war or with secular Progressivism in general. The purge was feasible, ironically, only because of the new communications and rationalized administrative structures that progressives themselves had introduced over the previous decades.[24]

Yet the Mennonite purge did not mark a total coalescence with Protestant fundamentalism. Some Bible Institute revivalists visited Mennonite colleges, and some Mennonites borrowed biblical inerrantist and dispensationalist rhetoric. But these were glosses on a different set of convictions. At bottom, Mennonites in the 1920s were more concerned with the doctrine of the church than the theory of scripture, and they imposed communal, not textual, authority in adjudicating disputes.[25] They were punishing conformity to American culture as fundamentalists were punishing deviance from it. And their intellectuals set out to escape the impasse of the 1920s by the same strategy the neo-orthodox would soon propose in the mainstream: returning to the Reformation heritage. As the Niebuhr brothers rediscovered Luther and Calvin, younger Mennonites sought to restore the original Anabaptist vision that would confess Christ by suffering in history.[26]

Some of the German Lutherans whose ancestors had persecuted Anabaptists in the 1520s had their turn three centuries later. Theirs were the trials of privilege, the canker of formalism and social complacency that came with being the established church. But the malaise would take a new and intolerable form in the early nineteenth century. Orthodox as they were, confessional Lutherans detested the Enlightenment; conservatives, the French Revolution; and patriots, Napoleon's invasion, especially as that brought the other two in its train. But the Restoration seemed even worse because it betrayed their rising hopes. Two grievances stood out. In church polity, King Frederick William III's proposal in 1817 to merge Lutheran and Reformed fellowships in an "evangelical union" seemed to them a state usurpation of church prerogatives. Theologically, the proposal looked to abet Enlightenment rationalism and the countervailing but symbiotic pietism that had risen against Lutheran orthodoxy in the eighteenth century.[27]

In response, a confessionalist protest arose in the king's Prussian domains and the German states that copied him. The movement drew largely from common people with the help of some key aristocratic and professional mentors. Soon it had a cadre of clergy to lead it as well, young men trained in the post-Napoleonic era, suffused in its Romantic Sturm und Drang, hostile to "desiccated rationalism," and also convinced that "subjective pietism" offered insufficient counterweight to it. Whatever their rank, the disaffected found in classic Reformation statements—the Book of Concord, especially the Augsburg Confession and its seventeenth-century commentaries—the clear definitions that could anchor religious experience and shape a true church.[28]

Restoring old standards required new organization. Out of old conventicles, house-churches, and their own congregations the restless cler-

ics formed a grass-roots network to which the devout from other parishes would travel for preaching and sacraments. Such irregularities,
added to their theological defiance, earned them scorn, fines, and some
prison terms. Little wonder that this circle felt the lure of emigration.
The leader of the dissenters in Saxony, Pastor Martin Stephan, demanded that all "true Christians" leave the "Babel of the State Church" for
his quasi-theocratic colony in Perry County, Missouri. Some seven
hundred did so in late 1838, establishing the nucleus of what would
become the largest German religious body in the United States. At the
same time, immigrants from Prussia, Silesia, Bavaria, and Pomerania
settled across the Great Lakes region. Some affiliated with the Missourians, others did not, but all shared the same confessional slant. From
these roots descended two bodies that a century later would constitute
half of American Lutheranism.[29]

From the start, the "Old Lutherans" showed as deep an ambivalence
toward their new country as toward the old. On the one hand, Stephan's
"Emigration Regulations" declared "the United States of North America" to be "a country where this [true] Lutheran faith is not endangered
. . . for there, as nowhere else in the world, perfect religious and civil
liberty prevails." On the other hand, the Prussian pastor Johannes A. A.
Grabau opened his church in Buffalo by crying, "Rejoice, America, the
Church comes to thee!"[30] The logical conclusion might have been that
America offered a free field for recruiting any and all into the true
church. But logic does not always apply. Exactly such aggressiveness
angered the confessionalists about the Methodists, champion prosely-
tizers of the new world. Accordingly, Methodist "sectarianism" was
one evil that the Missouri Synod singled out for condemnation in its
founding statement of 1847. Another was "unionism and syncretism,"
the joint ventures that colonial-descended Lutherans were carrying on
with Reformed people in the East and Midwest. Tertiary threats came
from Catholics, Masons, nativists, anti-clerical German '48ers, and
WASP moralizers. As one famous summary of Missouri Synod history
puts it, "No matter which way he turned, the German Lutheran immigrant leader saw potential hostility and harassment."[31]

Missouri's leaders made the source of their anxiety its solution. Fully
as much as revivalistic evangelicals, they sought the marks of authentic conversion. Unlike them but quite like the Mennonites, they found
these in the objective standards of the religious community—for the
Missouri Synod, the creeds and polity of the Book of Concord. Articulating these had made Lutheranism the only true church on earth;
restoring them made the Missouri Synod the only true church in America. Other fellowships contained true Christians, but only the synod

had the conjunction of confession and constitution that made it, as an institution, the visible body of Christ.[32] To settle for less like sectarians, or to dilute purity with syncretists, deformed that body. To ward off deformation and all hostile forces nothing more or less was needed than cultivating, maintaining, and reinforcing confessional consciousness.

The Missouri Synod well realized that consciousness availed little without communal structures to support it. Quickly and steadily its members built a set of interlocking institutions to make that support ready, unrivaled, and perpetual. From the start they erected parochial schools next to their churches so the young would receive the same message weekdays as Sundays. They built their own seminaries to supply church and school with leadership properly trained. Both preachers and teachers were supplied with reading materials that issued from the publishing house the synod founded in St. Louis in 1869. The seminaries, the publishing house, and the ten junior colleges that the synod would build by the end of World War I were all named Concordia in honor of the Lutheran book of confessions. Thus, the Missouri Synod's members could grow from childhood to old age in a complete communications network premised upon Lutheran orthodoxy.[33]

Well into the twentieth century the synod's parochial school system, publishing house, and St. Louis seminary would be the largest of their kind in American Protestantism and served a denomination that stretched from coast to coast. The synod's most remarkable achievement may not have been building a complete social world but bringing so many people into it. It accomplished this by a combination of old means and new. The synod itself originated out of a theological magazine, *Der Lutheraner,* founded in St. Louis in 1844, just five years after the Saxons arrived there. The journal was the means by which like-minded immigrants in Ohio, Michigan, and Indiana came into contact with the St. Louis band. The Missouri Synod also kept good contacts with German allies, particularly the Revs. J. K. Wilhelm Loehe of Neuendettelsau, Bavaria, and Frederick Brunn of Steeden, Nassau, in Germany. The two recruited orthodox young men from their areas and sent them on to Missouri institutions for finishing. By this means the fledgling synod received more than two hundred clergy who piloted fleets of German immigrants into the denomination's harbor.[34]

In this effort the synod showed new world savvy. Like its Methodist rivals, it developed a circuit-riding system spearheaded by lay book agents who would roam new areas of settlement, locate interested German families, and encourage them to send for a pastor. The *reiseprediger* (traveling preacher) would then organize these as a congregation while serving other groups in the area until they, too, could be formally constituted. The Missouri Synod followed the immigrant flow back to its spout and located ministers at welcome centers in the ports of New York and Baltimore. The New York agent alone contacted some twenty-seven thousand immigrants between 1870 and 1883, directing many to destinations along the Missouri network.[35]

Because Old Lutheran fellowships composed a small fraction of the German population, most new arrivals had to be of state-church background. Why did so many join a church far stricter than the one they had left behind? The Missouri Synod's loyalty to language was one reason; in fact, the synod kept German as much for evangelistic purposes as for its richer confessional resources. The synod's rigor also met immigrants' needs for discipline amid the potential chaos of transplantation. But the synod was also American-born, not German-born, and had no desire to replicate the church situation it had left.[36]

Its most controversial innovation was a quasi-congregational polity devised on the Missouri frontier. Within a year of landing, the Saxon colony expelled its leader, the Reverend-become-"Bishop" Stephan, for sexual and financial malfeasance. With the colony's religious integrity, not to mention its temporal affairs, in jeopardy, the young immigrant pastor Carl Ferdinand Wilhelm Walther seized the command he would exercise over the synod for the next fifty years. In a series of public debates he showed the colony from scripture and the confessions that it still harbored the true church because such consisted not in ordained clergy, much less in apostolic bishops, but in the devout laity of the local congregation. These delegated some of their powers to a minister via ordination, Walther argued, but kept sovereignty—under God—over their own affairs. Walther thus rescued the settlers by offering, no doubt unconsciously, an ecclesiastical analog to Locke's social contract. The confessions served as the synod's constitution while the laity was summoned by their churchly citizenship to meet the moral and financial obligations they faced under America's voluntary conditions. The denomination was thus set to flourish as a nation within the nation to which it had thus adapted.[37]

Its congregationalism cost the Missouri Synod the support of Wilhelm Loehe in Bavaria and provoked a long, intense argument with J. A. Grabau of the Buffalo Synod. Rather than backing down, however, the synod grew adamant in combat, a strategy it followed thereafter with great success. A dispute over predestination went on for a quarter century and stalled a promising move toward bringing all the Lutheran confessional groups into one synod. That fate was perhaps inevitable because dogmatic rigor was of the essence to all concerned. Besides, as Mennonites were discovering in these same decades, "exactly the violent polemics . . . kept people existentially involved in religious issues and served to strengthen self-identity."[38] Polemics against outsiders, in turn, served the purpose of self-preservation. The battle was well called for, too, because Methodism in 1850 had more followers among German immigrants than did the synod and was determined "to preach their religion out of their heads in order to preach Bible religion into their hearts." Finally, polemics with a third party, neither insiders nor outsiders but the middle band of Americanized Lutherans, won the synod some new adherents, steeled its self-definition, and helped promote confessionalist renewal within "lukewarm" synods.[39]

Assertive as they were in religion, in politics Missouri Synod members ranged from the apathetic to the defensive. Lutheran two-sphere theory taught them not to expect too much from law, and the "reforms" of German Restoration regimes had given that word a permanent taint. Thus they doubted crusades that would have governments bring in either progress or the Kingdom of God, were skeptical of mainline Protestants' equation of the two, and were concerned with guarding their liberties against the nearest threat. When the threat was Catholicism, they voted Republican. When, as was more often the case, it was WASP evangelicalism seeking to impose Prohibition, public schools, or sober Sabbaths by law, they voted Democratic. In the early 1890s they took the latter tack with a vengeance in Wisconsin and Illinois, driving out Republican administrations that had threatened the autonomy of parochial schools.[40]

The Progressive political movement that arose soon after could hardly look for support among the synod's leaders. Yet these leaders could hardly miss innovations occurring in their own house. For all their reputation as rural people, synod members were just as urban as other Americans and quite more so than other Lutherans. Their city churches introduced American innovations: using English in worship, replacing traditional *christenlehre* (catechesis) with Sunday school, and starting up special age and gender societies against traditionalists' warnings that such would fracture congregational solidarity. In 1911 a new day seemed at hand when an English-language affiliate long kept at arm's length was fully incorporated into the synod. Quickly, Concordia Publishing House redoubled its English productions.[41]

Shortly, the language change was proceeding at a gallop under the wartime whip. The synod dropped "German" from its official title in 1917, bought $94 million of Liberty bonds, sent thirty-seven thousand of its members into the armed forces, and, most remarkably, acceded to state encroachment upon the pulpit by preaching on the government's suggested weekly topics. Missouri Synod members also began speaking to their neighbors, arguing (before 1917) that anti-German propaganda violated American neutrality and (in 1917 and 1918) that their own ancestors had battled the German government long before American patriots knew of its existence.[42]

This counteroffensive turned out to be the real legacy of the war in the Missouri Synod. A thousand of its parochial schools disappeared from the rolls, but all save fifty had been Saturday or summer makeshifts. More than 1,300 of the real article remained, and commitment to them was redoubled by the synod's battle against mandatory public school legislation proposed in the early 1920s in Oregon and Michigan. The Walther League of young people's societies exploded from 310 chapters in 1918 to 1,182 in 1923. The urban model of a multiple-societies church spread to rural congregations as the denomination created a full flight of activities to ward off the lure of culture in the 1920s. Progressive innovations thus bolstered a traditional loyalty tested under wartime assault. Some neglected standards were resuscitated as well, particularly the old ban on secret-society membership.[43]

Given the economic boom of the 1920s, the synod reasserted itself most creatively in money matters. It had long frowned on members' purchasing life insurance but did accept lay initiatives—the Aid Association for Lutherans and the Lutheran Brotherhood—that filled the same need in the mode of fraternal benevolence societies. The membership and assets of these agencies soared during the 1920s as members sought social security by moral, communal means in an amoral, market-driven world. At the same time, the synod went through a financial and administrative revolution that drew off wartime fundraising schemes and the new managerial techniques of the 1920s. The result was an explosion of giving that in two years raised $2 million for endowment and benevolence—the greatest outpouring American Lutheranism had ever seen. This effort, like the simultaneous school-defense campaign, went forward under the auspices of two new laymen's associations that brought vibrant denominational consciousness to every rank and pocket. When their original goals were achieved, one of these bodies, the Lutheran Laymen's League, redirected its energies toward radio ministry.[44] And so the Missouri Synod in the 1920s bore an uncanny resemblance to the Old Lutherans in the 1820s, harnessing youthful vigor and new techniques to revitalize an old orthodoxy in the face of a hostile nation.

The Christian Reformed Church's origins resemble the Missouri Synod's as closely as Dutch does Deutsch. The same animus against

Enlightenment and Revolution, the same sense of betrayal by a Restoration king, and the same constitutional and theological protests against
his church reforms prompted some confessionalists in the Netherlands
to leave the National Reformed Church in 1834. These Seceders were
also led by freshly minted pastors, relied on a new organization that
wove together old conventicles and flagship congregations, and suffered
the same ridicule, fines, and imprisonment that Old Lutherans knew.[45]
The two groups had a like proclivity for emigration and moved at the
same time; seed groups came to the United States in the 1840s, and the
flow peaked in the 1880s. Once in America the two built analogous
communication grids and parochial school systems. Both forbad secret-
society membership and battled political liberalism. One might almost
have expected the two to merge except that, of course, the Old Lutherans were rejecting the very Calvinism that the Dutch prized.

Like the Old Lutherans, the Reformed Seceders always constituted
a minority of their nation's immigrants to the United States. But their
percentage among immigrants was remarkable in light of their minute
fraction of the population of the Netherlands. The Seceders were the
only sector of Dutch society to catch America fever, creating the psychological precedents and personal connections that skewed Dutch
immigration permanently toward the confessional Calvinist pole. Their
advantages in the information and transportation networks of the process meant that many National Church people emigrated through Seceder channels. With their early arrival and their ideological rigor, the
Seceders set the tone and structures of the enduring Dutch American
community.[46]

Like the Missouri Synod and the Mennonites, the Dutch confessionalists scrapped with each other as much as with the oppressive establishment. In the Seceders' case this had immediate ramifications for
emigration. The Seceder movement had three branches: one rooted in
the northern Netherlands and given to centralized polity and doctrinal precision; a second in the east, more decentralized and concerned
with pious experience; and the third in the southern river region, influenced by British evangelicalism and tending toward congregationalist, biblicistic, and millennarian ideas. By the mid-1840s the first had
gained sway in the Seceders' synod, and the leaders of the other two,
Albertus C. van Raalte and Hendrik P. Scholte, respectively, began the
Seceder trek to the United States.[47]

Van Raalte set down in western Michigan and quickly joined his
group to the East Coast Reformed Church in America (RCA), descended from New Netherland. By that move he blazed a path of ready assimilation, for the RCA was comfortable with much of the regnant

Protestantism of antebellum America. Scholte's settlement, in Pella, Iowa, would seem an even better fit, given his British bent. To the despair of these dominies, however, Dutch America chose a route of greater resistance. Scholte's design fell to his own difficult personality and congregational system; most of his group quickly followed van Raalte into the RCA, preferring consistently Reformed structures. But van Raalte met trouble, too, as doubts about the purity of the RCA arose in western Michigan and produced a schism in 1857. After passing through several permutations on True, Dutch, and Reformed, the group settled upon the name of the Christian Reformed Church (CRC).[48]

The new denomination had a fitful existence during its first twenty years. Its members were few, its clergy fewer, and defections by both were plentiful. But after the Civil War immigration resumed, now with a northern Netherlandic tilt toward the CRC. Then, in the early 1880s, the western Michigan colony was convulsed with a furor over secret societies. The RCA had long tolerated Freemasons in its eastern churches and left the matter for local congregations to decide. Many in the Midwest thought that intolerable. To their Continental eyes, Masonry registered not as a business club with ritual, as it did for British Americans, but as an underground religion surfeited with rationalism and revolution and hostile to Christianity. Their protests unavailing, the dissidents switched denominations. The CRC thereby gained several entire congregations, many individual families, key clerical leaders, and—after the dispute had aired back in the Netherlands—the endorsement of the Seceder church there, and that on the eve of the peak decade of Dutch immigration. The CRC's membership soared, surpassing that of the RCA's midwestern sector by 1895. The strict confessionalism, taut polity, and resistance to all rivals so evident in the Masonic controversy predominated in Dutch America thereafter.[49]

Still, maintaining distinctiveness would pose a harder challenge for the Dutch than for the Missouri Synod or the Mennonites. The Reformed tradition lay at the deepest roots of American Protestantism and mandated entry into public life. The Christian Reformed, therefore, had to give more concerted attention to criticizing the American scene and made that critique a prime mode of self-distinction. Evaluating every aspect of American life by distinctly Reformed principles became a summons in group discourse as frequent as, and closely linked to, the defense of theological orthodoxy.

All those declarations, however, required social solidarity. Well into the 1920s the Christian Reformed followed one order of worship and sang only Psalms, imbuing everyone with a common ritual language. They established parochial schools early on and put pressure on parents who enrolled their children elsewhere. They did not centralize their publishing operations, as did the Missouri Synod, until after World War II, but their church journals functioned as paper popes. The CRC's formal communications grid, in brief, was saturated and homogeneous. But its informal networks were more remarkable still. Most national-ities exhibited chain migration, but the Dutch cords were especially tight. Almost 75 percent of Dutch immigrants between 1820 and 1880 came from just 12 percent of Dutch municipalities, 50 percent from 5 percent, and 33 percent from 2 percent.[50] Because Catholics and Prot-estants chose different destinations and because Dutch American set-tlements were often distinguished by provincial origin, the new world neighborhoods were very much like the old. The latest arrivals knew and were known by someone immediately upon landing and soon picked up the gossip about everyone else. Leadership linkages were just as strong. Four-fifths of the CRC's nineteenth-century clergy were from the northern Netherlands, and all had their theological training in the Seceder school there or in the CRC's seminary in Grand Rapids.[51]

Perhaps because their tribalism was so strong, the Christian Re-formed could officially ignore it and put all their emphasis upon reli-gious purity. They spoke reflexively of "us," "our people," and "our school," but the Dutch in these was ritually subordinated to the Re-formed. The danger (and most assumed it was a danger) of American-ization is not that we will cease being Dutch, ran the standard line. "That must be. The danger is this, that our people will also lose their Reformed character. And that must not be."[52] "We and the world" thus became the favorite topic of Christian Reformed conversation, and guarding the first from the second became its primary object.

To the rank and file of Seceder background the world was, well, worldly. A "thousand and one" forms of pollution bedecked the Amer-ican cityscape, complained one pastor. "Theaters and vaudettes. Intox-ication in saloons and card-playing. Dance-halls and clubhouses. Au-torides and immorality. Excursions on the Sabbath." America's prime attractions bred its worst dangers: Its freedoms begat license, and its prosperity, materialism. How were "we" to respond? The Reformed pietist tradition sprang to hand. "Let us earnestly beseech God . . . that *we* do not fall into these sinful practices!" urged one pastor.[53]

But one could invade the world with political campaigns to elimi-nate sites of sin as well as flee it. The Christian Reformed forgot their suspicions of state power and their contempt for environmental theo-ries of evil when anti-saloon measures made the ballot in the 1910s. Both prayer and politics assumed a third measure, an itemization of signal sins as the code of group allegiance. For the CRC these were not the revivalists' smoking (virtually mandatory for Dutch males) and drinking (tolerated at home) but gambling, dancing, and theater attendance—violations of economic rationality or sexual restraint. While the Dutch in Grand Rapids split along class lines over Prohibition, they joined by a 75 percent majority to support stricter regulation of theaters.[54] But the ethical code required deeper wellsprings: the cultivation of Reformed consciousness. This entailed saturating everyone in the Heidelberg Catechism, requiring clergy to subscribe as well to the Belgic Confession and Canons of Dort, and honoring the seventeenth-century commentaries on all three as the apex of Reformed theology. Thus piety, politics, ethics, and doctrine formed a complete circle of crystal-clear definition.[55]

Because faith was the center of this circle, it was critical that Reformed consciousness be applied, especially to American religion. Again, the virtue-vice linkage seemed striking. How was it, the Christian Reformed asked, that the United States could be at once so pious and so immoral? It was because the nation's faith reflected its character: superficial, pragmatic, and self-centered. Calvinism had once reigned in the land but had long since devolved into liberalism. Arminian Methodism had taken over, a perfect fit for the American climate. Methodism's "sound organization" appealed to businessmen, its "social service" to their wives. When it took thought, Methodist theology necessarily went liberal; when it stayed with revivals, it left a fleeting thrill and broken promises.

America's fundamentalist option looked little better to the Christian Reformed than did its modernism because the two were rooted in the same Arminian pride and flowered in the same cult of personal experience.[56] Against it the Christian Reformed elevated the standards of classic orthodoxy nurtured in community. Their favorite theological topic was the covenant, understood as the descent of salvation along family lines. The new birth that the Christian Reformed insisted on no less than did their neighbors was to come to children by an intensive nurture that sent down deep roots and sent up broad branches. Let the rest of America go agog over Billy Sunday, said one CRC pastor after the revivalist's 1915 Michigan tour; such a spiritual "icebreaker" was good for the Arctic Ocean of American materialism but could never bring in the "full fleet" of Reformed thought and action.[57]

But could Reformed orthodoxy do any better? A growing band of CRC progressives were voicing their doubts by the turn of the century. Orthodoxy in itself had no purchase on public life they charged, and its defensive ethics bred an insularity that betrayed Calvinism's comprehensive vision. Just such a vision was the upstarts' passion, and just that they had learned from the eminent Dutch theologian-politician

Abraham Kuyper. Kuyper, too, venerated the Netherlands' seventeenth century as the golden age, but for its cultural as well as its theological achievement. Calvinism had bred both, he argued, and Calvinism could do so again if (echoes of restorationism) its "root principles" were transplanted into modern soil. Neo-Calvinism aimed to jar the devout out of their pious slumbers and take power back from the secularists. But Kuyper was also committed to fair play. No group might oppress another by monopolizing public space; rather, the adherents of every worldview should develop their own community, sending the tribal chieftains to the Dutch parliament for negotiations. Thus Kuyper anticipated the pillarized system that marked Dutch society after World War I—each faith community having its own schools, newspapers, and political party.[58]

Kuyper's vision was perfect for the young and restless in the CRC. It attacked Modernism without following the fundamentalist retreat from public life. It burst the bonds of cautious confessionalism. It accorded with immigrants' separate identity, yet would have "our people" engage fully and fearlessly in American life. It had grand philosophical sweep, leaving behind petty lists of sins to link root principles with social forces. Under its inspiration the rising generation could add to the critique of America a critique of the tribe and renew their appropriation of tradition.

But Kuyper was full of ambiguities, as befit a pilgrim in modernity and immigrants in a new world. Contrary to confessionalist worries, neo-Calvinism did not necessarily spawn progressivism. Some did take that path on the authority of Kuyper's principle of common grace; God had endowed the unconverted with virtue and talent that made Christian-secularist cooperation feasible in certain ventures. Others followed the master's antithetical doctrine that contrary commitments separated Christians from all others and necessitated distinct Christian organizations in every domain of activity.[59] The more cooperative neo-Calvinists rose with the national Progressive tide into the 1910s, as Michigan and the CRC endorsed Prohibition, woman's suffrage, and secular labor unions. Along with RCA leaders, they championed American entry into World War I. The confessionalists and antithetical neo-Calvinists opposed all of these, especially the civil-religious crusading by which the mainstream made demons out of rum and Huns.[60]

When the crusades failed, the aggrieved parties had their revenge. The CRC progressives' journals failed in the early 1920s, their point man on the Calvin Seminary faculty went down in a heresy trial in 1922, and the reconstructed America they had expected out of the war was a disappointment. Thus, they joined with their erstwhile opponents at the CRC's 1928 synod to pass a formal ban on the old-worldly tri-

ad of dancing, gambling, and theater.[61] It was a progressive who penned
the synodical statement that set the denomination's course for the next
thirty years: "Against all these and more pernicious influences, which
press upon us from all sides, there is a crying necessity that the church
mount a guard on principle; that she . . . fight tooth and nail for the
spiritual-moral antithesis. . . . with holy seriousness may she call . . . her
people and especially her youth not to be conformed to the world."[62]

But the conservative triumph was no more complete in the Dutch
case than in those of the Missouri Synod or the Mennonites. To keep
their children safe and Calvinism's cultural claims alive, the CRC by
1921 made Calvin College into a four-year institution and hired William Harry Jellema to create its philosophy department. Jellema would
not only revive the progressive cause for another generation but would
also mint half a dozen philosophers of international impact. Dozens
more would carry his Kuyperian vision into other disciplines, staking
claims for a distinctive Christian ground in broader academic discourse.[63] Perhaps all these were postmodern before they knew it. Perhaps they were refracting their own Reformation commitments through
a lingering ethnic ambivalence. Or, perhaps, in their case these two
sentences are redundant.

So why did their neighbors' wrath descend on these groups in 1918?
Why have religious historians typically put these denominations at the
margins of the national narrative? And what are they doing in a book
on religious outsiders? After all, they are Protestant, and does not Protestant historically equal mainstream? The last question holds the answer to the others. Protestant these denominations surely are, but
mainstream they consciously decided not to be, setting themselves off
from the neighbors who welcomed them for being so much like themselves. This deliberate separation bred the offense that the war fever
of 1918 avenged. The separation has puzzled historians who wrote
anticipating assimilation, expecting minorities to be set apart against,
never by, their own will.

But why the determination to be separate? Why choose to be an
outsider? It is because becoming insiders would have been so easy yet
so costly for these groups. Their old homelands had demanded conformity at the price of religious integrity, and they had no reason to
think that America's price would be any less. If the mainstream scold-
ed them for not taking the last, logical step—being Protestant they
should become wholeheartedly American—the groups thought the
mainstream had gone a step too far. To them, America and the Protestant mainstream valued Reformation religion as a prelude to the real
prize: political liberty, individualism, economic growth, and the right

of self-determination. These groups insisted, on the contrary, that Reformation faith was the prize, and the rest of it was baggage that could be taken or left as circumstances required.

Their intent to restore or fulfill the Reformation dream led these groups into a thicket that was by turns puzzling, comic, or downright contradictory. They mixed innovation with retention and blended elements of the old land, the new land, and the kingdom to come. Their rough jostling in World War I seemed to change things but did not, fundamentally. They put on American clothes—denominational colleges, the English language, radio programs, or benevolent agencies—but for the protection of their old body, the confessional community. Over time they would recognize that the clothes do make the person. But in the post-Protestant era the erstwhile mainstream might learn from their stories to attend as well to the body that fills out the clothes.

Notes

1. Frederick C. Luebke, *Bonds of Loyalty: German-Americans and World War I* (DeKalb: Northern Illinois University Press, 1974), 81; James D. Bratt, *Dutch Calvinism in Modern America: A History of a Conservative Subculture* (Grand Rapids: Eerdmans Publishing, 1984), 89, 257.

2. Luebke, *Bonds of Loyalty,* 15, 225, 253–59, 273–82; Bratt, *Dutch Calvinism,* 83–92.

3. I have taken my cues about restorationism from Richard T. Hughes and C. Leonard Allen, *Illusions of Innocence: Protestant Primitivism in America, 1630–1875* (Chicago: University of Chicago Press, 1988), 1–24, 205–25; and Richard T. Hughes, ed., *The American Quest for the Primitive Church* (Urbana: University of Illinois Press, 1988), 1–15. The application here is my own.

4. Oscar Handlin, *The Uprooted* (New York, 1951); Timothy L. Smith, "Religion and Ethnicity in America," *American Historical Review* 83 (Dec. 1979): 1155–85. Given the European origin of their sense of peoplehood, these groups deviate from the model of ethnic consciousness as a postmigration phenomenon articulated in recent scholarship.

5. Foppe M. Ten Hoor, in the inaugural article of *De Gereformeerde Amerikaan* 1 (Feb. 1897): 130.

6. James C. Juhnke, "Mennonite History and Self-Understanding: North American Mennonitism as a Bipolar Mosaic," in *Mennonite Identity: Historical and Contemporary Perspectives,* ed. Calvin W. Redekop and Samuel J. Steiner (Lanham: University Press of America, 1988), 89–91. Although Mennonites often downplay creeds and formal theology, their confessional heritage is well spelled out in Howard John Loewen, *One Lord, One Church, One Hope, and One God: Mennonite Confessions of Faith in North America, an Introduction* (Elkhart: Institute of Mennonite Studies, 1985).

7. Juhnke, "Mennonite History," 95.

8. Theron F. Schlabach, *Peace, Faith, and Nation: Mennonites and Amish in Nineteenth-Century America* (Scottdale: Herald Press, 1988), 20; Theron F. Schlabach, "Mennonites and Pietism in America, 1740–1880," *Mennonite Quarterly Review* 57 (July 1983): 228. The centrality of historical memory to Mennonite faith and identity is amplified in Dennis B. Kraybill, "Modernity and Identity: The Transformation of Mennonite Ethnicity," in *Kingdom, Cross, and Community*, ed. John R. Burkholder and Calvin W. Redekop (Scottdale: Herald Press, 1976); and in Rodney J. Sawatsky, "Defining Mennonite Identity," *Mennonite Quarterly Review* 57 (July 1983): 282–92.

9. Schlabach, *Peace, Faith, Nation*, 19–32. Calvin W. Redekop discusses the foresworn Anabaptist option in "The Sociology of Mennonite Identity: A Second Opinion," in *Mennonite Identity*, ed. Redekop and Steiner, 173–92.

10. Schlabach, "Mennonites and Pietism," 233.

11. Joseph C. Liechty, "Humility: The Foundation of Mennonite Religious Outlook in the 1860s," *Mennonite Quarterly Review* 54 (Jan. 1980): 5–31; Schlabach, *Peace, Faith, Nation*, 33–59, 96–105, 148–50.

12. The following summary of this fragmentation is based on Schlabach, *Peace, Faith, Nation*, 117–42, 173–229; and James C. Juhnke, *Vision, Doctrine, War: Mennonite Identity and Organization in America, 1890–1930* (Scottdale: Herald Press, 1989), 58–79.

13. The other three schisms were Jacob Wisler's (1872) in Elkhart, Indiana, Abraham Martin's (1889) in Ontario, and Jonas Martin's (1893) in Lancaster County, Pennsylvania.

14. Juhnke, *Vision, Doctrine, War*, 54, 110.

15. Juhnke, "Mennonite History," 91–92; Juhnke, *Vision, Doctrine, War*, 36–38, 83–84, 304–5.

16. Juhnke, *Vision, Doctrine, War*, 85–101, 177–79; Juhnke, "Mennonite History," 91–96.

17. James C. Juhnke, "Mennonites in Militarist America: Some Consequences of World War I," in *Kingdom, Cross, Community*, ed. Burkholder and Redekop, 171. On Mennonite behavior during the Civil War, see Schlabach, *Peace, Faith, and Nation*, 180–200.

18. Juhnke, *Vision, Doctrine, War*, 107–32, 139–77, 202.

19. Ibid., 171.

20. Ibid., 119–20, 141–45, 156–61; Kraybill, "Modernity and Identity," 171; Schlabach, *Peace, Faith, Nation*, 295–321.

21. James Juhnke, *A People of Two Kingdoms: The Political Acculturation of the Kansas Mennonites* (Newton, Kans.: Faith and Life Press, 1975), 89.

22. Juhnke, *Vision, Doctrine, War*, 208–42.

23. Ibid., 246–57; Juhnke, "Mennonites in Militarist America," 171–74.

24. Juhnke, "Mennonites in Militarist America," 174–78; Juhnke, *Vision, Doctrine, War*, 257–74.

25. Juhnke, *Vision, Doctrine, War*, 262–74; Paul Toews, "The Fundamentalist Conflict in Mennonite Colleges: A Response to Cultural Transitions?" *Mennonite Quarterly Review* 57 (July 1983): 241–56.

26. This was the project of the "Goshen school" led by Harold S. Bender, who began work in the 1920s and gained considerable notice outside and in-

side the community with "The Anabaptist Vision," his 1942 presidential address to the American Society of Church History. Juhnke, *Vision, Doctrine, War,* 277–82; Juhnke, "Mennonite History," 87.

27. This and the next two paragraphs draw from Ralph Dornfeld Owen, "The Old Lutherans Come," *Concordia Historical Institute Quarterly* 20 (April 1948): 4–26; Walter A. Baepler, *A Century of Grace: A History of the Missouri Synod, 1847–1947* (St. Louis: Concordia Publishing House, 1947), ch. 1; and Walter H. Conser, Jr., *Church and Confession: Conservative Theologians in Germany, England, and America, 1815–1866* (Mercer, Ga.: Mercer University Press, 1984), 15–68.

28. The biographical pattern was particularly clear in the case of C. F. W. Walther, who would lead the Missouri Synod for its first two generations in the United States. See Baepler, *Century of Grace,* 41–45; and Lewis W. Spitz, *The Life of C. F. W. Walther* (St. Louis: Concordia Publishing House, 1961), 15–44. The Book of Concord (1580) contains the Augsburg Confession (1530) together with its Apology (1531), the Smalcald Articles (1537), Luther's Small and Large Catechisms (1529), and the Formula of Concord (1577).

29. Stephan quotation in Baepler, *Century of Grace,* 24; statistic from Owen, "Old Lutherans," 3. On the immigration process, see ibid., 12–16, 19–21, 27–30; Abdel R. Wentz, *A Basic History of Lutheranism in America* (Philadelphia: Muhlenberg Press, 1955), 116–20; and E. Clifford Nelson, ed., *The Lutherans in North America* (Philadelphia: Fortress Press, 1975), 151–59, 176–85.

30. Quotations from Wentz, *Basic History,* 116, and Owen, "Old Lutherans," 16, respectively.

31. Quotation from Frederick C. Luebke, *Germans in the New World: Essays in the History of Migration* (Urbana: University of Illinois Press, 1990), 11. On the founding of the Missouri Synod, see the thorough discussion in Baepler, *Century of Grace,* and the summary in Wentz, *Basic History,* 210. On anti-Methodism, see F. Dean Lueking, *Mission in the Making: The Missionary Enterprise among the Missouri Synod Lutherans, 1846–1963* (St. Louis: Concordia Publishing House, 1964), 37–38, 55; August C. Stellhorn, *Schools of the Lutheran Church-Missouri Synod* (St. Louis: Concordia Publishing House, 1963), 34; and Baepler, *Century of Grace,* 54, 61.

32. Walther spelled out this position in "The Evangelical-Lutheran Church the True Visible Church of God on Earth" (1866), distilled and with commentary in *Walther and the Church,* ed. William Dallmann, W. H. T. Dau, and Theodore Engelder (St. Louis: Concordia Publishing House, 1938).

33. Wentz, *Basic History,* 217–19; Baepler, *Century of Grace,* 126–27, 196, 209–10, 224–26; Stellhorn, *Schools,* 58, 66, 79–80, 279–80. Carol K. Coburn, *Life at Four Corners: Religion, Gender, and Education in a German-Lutheran Community, 1868– 1945* (Lawrence: University Press of Kansas, 1992) is a fine study of a rural example of this saturation.

34. Baepler, *Century of Grace,* 57–69; Owen, "Old Lutherans," 33–39.

35. Nelson, ed., *Lutherans in North America,* 196–98; Lueking, *Mission,* 54–60; Judith W. Meyer, "Ethnicity, Theology, and Immigrant Church Expansion," *Geographical Review* 65 (April 1975): 180–97.

36. Robert M. Toepper, "Rationale for Preservation of the German Lan-

guage in the Missouri Synod of the Nineteenth Century," *Concordia Histori-cal Institute Quarterly* 41 (Nov. 1968): 156–67; Lueking, *Mission,* 19.

37. Baepler, *Century of Grace,* 47–48, 137–44; Wentz, *Basic History,* 118–19, 217; Leigh D. Jordahl, "American Lutheranism: Ethos, Style, and Polity," in *The Lutheran Church in North American Life,* ed. John E. Groh and Robert H. Smith (St. Louis: Clayton Publishing House, 1979), 45–47.

38. Wentz, *Basic History,* 212–16; quotation from Jordahl, "American Lutheranism," 47. Jon Gjerde remarks of this controversy among Norwegian Lutherans affiliated with the Missouri Synod: "They argued predestination in the saloon with their tongues . . . and settled in the alley with their fists." "Conflict and Community: A Case Study of the Immigrant Church in the United States," *Journal of Social History* 19 (Summer 1986): 689.

39. Lueking, *Mission,* 23, 37–38 (quotation from a Methodist missionary on 37); Wentz, *Basic History,* 118.

40. Frederick C. Luebke, "Politics and the Missouri Synod Lutherans: A Historiographical Review," *Concordia Historical Institute Quarterly* 45 (May 1972): 141–58; Stellhorn, *Schools,* 240–46.

41. Alan Graebner, *Uncertain Saints: The Laity in the Lutheran Church-Missouri Synod, 1900–1970* (Westport: Greenwood Press, 1975), 16–22, 79–88; Baepler, *Century of Grace,* 254–60. Demographic data are available in Neil M. Johnson, "Lutherans in American Economic Life," in *Lutheran Church,* ed. Groh and Smith, 137.

42. Baepler, *Century of Grace,* 219, 263–66; Neil M. Johnson, "The Patriotism and Anti-Prussianism of the Lutheran Church-Missouri Synod, 1914–1918," *Concordia Historical Institute Quarterly* 39 (Oct. 1966): 108–15.

43. Stellhorn, *Schools,* 275, 302–5, 318–19; Baepler, *Century of Grace,* 261; Graebner, *Uncertain Saints,* 79–84; Nelson, ed., *Lutherans in North America,* 444.

44. Graebner, *Uncertain Saints,* 30–53; Johnson, "Lutherans and Economic Life," 142–43 (quoted phrase on 143); Baepler, *Century of Grace,* 148–49, 221, 310–11.

45. Bratt, *Dutch Calvinism,* 3–10.

46. Robert P. Swierenga has rendered the most thorough demographic analysis of Dutch immigration in this era; a fine summary is "Dutch Immigration Patterns in the Nineteenth and Twentieth Centuries," in *The Dutch in America: Immigration, Settlement, and Cultural Change,* ed. Robert P. Swierenga (New Brunswick: Rutgers University Press, 1985), 15–42. A more traditional account is Henry S. Lucas, *Netherlanders in America* (Ann Arbor: University of Michigan Press, 1955). For a summary of the process, with attention to these authors' differing views, see Bratt, *Dutch Calvinism,* 8–10, 226–27.

47. Bratt, *Dutch Calvinism,* 7.

48. Ibid., 38–40.

49. Ibid., 39–40, 222–23; Elton Bruins, "The Masonic Controversy in Holland, Michigan, 1879–1882," in *Perspectives on the Christian Reformed Church,* ed. Peter De Klerk and Richard R. De Ridder (Grand Rapids: Baker Book House, 1983), 52–72.

50. The statistics are taken from Swierenga, "Dutch Immigration Patterns," 32–34.

51. On provincial enclaves, see David Vander Stel, "The Dutch of Grand Rapids, Michigan, 1848–1900: Immigrant Neighborhood and Community Development in a Nineteenth Century City," Ph.D. diss., Kent State University, 1983. On CRC clergy, see the comparative statistics of Robert Swierenga and Herbert J. Brinks discussed in Bratt, *Dutch Calvinism*, 40, 240.

52. Barend K. Kuiper, *Ons Opmaken en Bouwen* (Grand Rapids: Eerdmans-Sevensma, 1918), 5. For broader treatment of the Americanization question, see Bratt, *Dutch Calvinism*, 40–66.

53. John W. Brink, *Banner*, Sept. 28, 1911, 605; Peter Ekster, *Gereformeerde Amerikaan* 16 (July 1912): 297, and 17 (April 1913): 164; for a broader discussion, see Bratt, *Dutch Calvinism*, 62–66.

54. Anthony B. Travis, "Mayor George Ellis: Grand Rapids Political Boss and Progressive Reformer," *Michigan History* 58 (Summer 1974): 101–30, analyzes Dutch voting patterns in Grand Rapids in this era. Class standing had some but hardly absolute correlation with denominational membership. Both officially and in public pronouncements, the RCA was for Prohibition loud and early, the CRC later and with more dissent.

55. Bratt, *Dutch Calvinism*, 49–50.

56. Ibid., 57–62; Henry Zwaanstra, *Reformed Thought and Experience in a New World: A Study of the Christian Reformed Church and Its American Environment* (Kampen: J. H. Kok, 1973), 43–49.

57. John Van Lonkhuyzen, *Billy Sunday* (Grand Rapids: Eerdmans-Sevensma, 1916), 150–51, 133–34 for the covenant's meanings to this group.

58. Kuyper's thought and career are summarized in Bratt, *Dutch Calvinism*, 14–33.

59. Ibid., 17–20, 50–54; Zwaanstra, *Reformed Thought*, 95–131.

60. Bratt, *Dutch Calvinism*, 73–92; Zwaanstra, *Reformed Thought*, 193–294.

61. Bratt, *Dutch Calvinism*, 105–19.

62. [Clarence Bouma], "Witness to the Churches," *Acta Synodi van der Christelijke Gereformeerde Kerk*, 1924 (Grand Rapids: Christian Reformed Church, 1924), 149.

63. The philosophers are William Frankena, Cornelius Van Til, Carl Henry, Alvin Plantinga, Peter Kreeft, and Nicholas Wolterstorff. Calvin graduates have taken the lead since the early 1970s in the formation of Christian professional organizations in history, philosophy, psychology, natural science, and economics.

FIVE

Exodus Piety: African American Religion in an Age of Immigration

DAVID W. WILLS

The story of American religion has often been told as a struggle between an initially dominant Anglo-Protestantism and the late-arriving but ever more powerful religious diversity of European immigrant groups. As recounted by the descendants of the Puritans (whether literal or spiritual), this story can sometimes seem a melancholy tale indeed. Americans began their history, we are told, with a collective dedication to shared religious and moral values but gradually degenerated into a mean-spirited crowd of contentious subgroups and relativistic, self-seeking individuals. Descendants of later European immigrants, or "cultural pluralists" of whatever origin, tend to see the same story in a more hopeful light—as the struggle of an initially repressive and conformist people to welcome freedom and embrace diversity. Either way, the late nineteenth and early twentieth centuries are often seen as a critically important period of transition, when successive waves of European immigrants shifted the numerical balance of power away from the Anglo-Protestant majority toward a more pluralistic mix of Jews, Catholics, and continental Protestants. Thoroughly Protestant New England towns were during these years displaced as the definitive landscape of American religious life, it has sometimes been said, by the ever more pluralistic city of the industrial Northeast and Midwest. Although the floodgates of immigration were closed by the restrictive immigration laws of 1921 and 1924, a new, urban, pluralistic America had been born and, for good or ill, in the long run it would triumph over its small-town, Protestant predecessor.[1]

It is a revealing feature of this familiar story that the narrative seldom strays below the Mason-Dixon line. Home neither to the most potent symbols of America's Protestant past nor the best known icons of its ever more pluralistic future, the South typically lies, half-forgotten, at the edge of the best-known accounts of American religion during this period. The South is, however, no less American than the rest of the United States. The roots of its Protestantism lie largely in the same

soil as the Protestantism of the northern states, and it is more internally diverse, religiously and otherwise, than is sometimes imagined. Above
all, it has been throughout most of our history the primary arena for a
confrontation as indelibly impressed on our religious life as that between Anglo-Protestantism and other forms of Euro-American religion:
the encounter of Europeans and Africans, of whites and blacks.[2]

This encounter at its heart reveals the deepest fissure in American
culture—the gap between characteristically white ways of interpreting
the American experiment and sharply contrasting views of American
reality more predominant among blacks. The issues at stake are those
of power and meaning—especially the conjunction of these two things
in the history of the United States. Catholic and Jewish immigrants
found much to lament in the late nineteenth and early twentieth centuries about the American structure of power. Religiously, they had
frequent cause to complain about the way an informally established
Protestantism—the First Amendment to the Constitution notwithstanding—repeatedly turned the power of the state to its own advantage. At
the same time, however, the avenues for contesting this Protestant exercise of power, through the courts and the electoral process, were remarkably open even to relatively recently arrived immigrants. The franchise was readily accessible, and the formal (although not the informal)
barriers that had blocked Catholic and Jewish access to public office
in several states in the antebellum period were eliminated in the postwar era. The heavy burdens of poverty and life in a largely unprotect-
ed working class were also throughout the nineteenth century significantly alleviated by the widespread (if incomplete), formal (if not
informal) openness of the American economy to the upwardly mobile
striving of European American immigrants of whatever religious persuasion. Accordingly, it was possible for Catholics and Jews, in significant numbers, to see the organization of power in America as at bottom beneficent—and even to see in it a structure of liberty expressive
of their own deepest religious and moral convictions. As early as 1856
the Catholic Americanist Orestes Brownson could argue—even in the
face of the Know-Nothing movement—that "our Protestant ancestors
founded the American order, not on their Protestantism, but on the
natural law, natural justice and equity as explained by the Church, long
prior to the Protestant movement." He could even claim that America's "manifest destiny" was to realize "the Christian Idea of Society"
as it had been defined in the Catholic tradition.[3] Jews also, from the
beginning of the nation's history, "recognized and rejoiced in the [reli-
giously neutral] Constitution as a liberating document" and could argue throughout the nineteenth century that their determined resistance

to any political privileging of Christianity was precisely a defense of—
not an attack against—the essence of the American experiment. Isaac
Mayer Wise, the great institution-builder of nineteenth-century Reform
Judaism, could in 1869 describe the United States as "our promised
land, the home and fortress of freedom, the blessed spot which flows
with milk and honey."[4]

It was considerably harder for mid-nineteenth-century blacks to see
the United States as the promised land, to find in the constitution a
guarantee of their equal status, or to imagine that American institutions had unknowingly been founded on their ancestors' most cherished
ideals—ideals the country was manifestly destined to realize. Although
currents of cultural and religious alienation and resistance ran deeply
in American Catholicism and Judaism, they ran far deeper in African
American religion—above all because the exercise of white power in
America bore down more pervasively and relentlessly on blacks than
it ever did on Catholics or Jews. Although African cultural and religious patterns were by no means entirely extinguished in North America, the involuntary character and brutal realities of the slave trade and
slavery itself presented barriers to the transplantation of African traditional religion of a different order than those faced by Catholic or
Jewish immigrant traditionalists. In the Dred Scott decision the U.S.
Supreme Court ruled that from the standpoint of the Constitution, "The
Negro has no rights the white man is bound to respect"—something
the Court never said of Catholics or Jews, much less European Protestant immigrants. It is no wonder, then, that for African Americans the
meaning—the religious meaning—of America was more often conceived as a problem than a promise. What kind of world could this be,
as a young black religious leader experiencing a crisis of faith asked
himself in 1835, where "one race [is allowed by God] to oppress and
enslave another, to rob them by unrighteous enactments of their rights,
which they hold most dear and sacred"?[5] Nor is it any surprise that
for many black followers of biblical religion the typological clue to
answering that question was not that of Israel in the promised land but
Israel in Egypt—the land of captivity.[6]

For most African Americans between the end of the Civil War and
the mid-1920s, the Egypt of their captivity was primarily the southern
states and the power relations there that tightly circumscribed their lives
and constrained their hopes. In 1870, according to the U.S. Bureau of
the Census, 91 percent of all black Americans lived in the South. Forty years later, the figure had dropped only slightly to 89 percent. Even
the Great Migration of the World War I era, when hundreds of thousands of southern blacks moved to the North, did not alter the funda-

mentally southern character of black life. As late as 1940, 77 percent of all black Americans still resided in the South. The southernness of blacks, moreover, had profound implications for the blackness of the South. In 1870, when African Americans constituted a mere 2 percent of population in the North and 1 percent of the population of the West, they represented 36 percent of the population of the South. (In 1940 these numbers still stood at 4 percent, 1 percent, and 24 percent, respectively.) In several states, moreover, blacks were in 1870 a majority or near majority of the population. They were 59 percent of the population of South Carolina, 54 percent of Mississippi's, and 50 percent of Louisiana's. In Florida, Alabama, Georgia, and Virginia, the population of blacks ranged from 49 to 42 percent.[7]

In these places and across the South as a whole, the presence of a black population of such size was inevitably of decisive importance in shaping the region's political economy and culture. The great question in the aftermath of the Civil War concerned how much the racial power relations previously imbedded in the institution of slavery would be truly transformed and how much they would simply be transferred to new institutional forms. Particularly in the late 1860s, important steps were taken toward a significant increase in black power—especially in the political realm, where newly enfranchised blacks voted and held office across the South. In a long, bitterly contested, and often violent struggle, however, these gains were largely rolled back. Political reconstruction was effectively ended in some states as early as 1870. In 1877, when the remaining federal troops were withdrawn from the South (as part of the political compromise that resolved the disputed election of 1876 and allowed Rutherford B. Hayes to assume the presidency), the North clearly signaled its unwillingness any longer to contest with force the political terrorism through which white rule had been restored in so many places. In a further wave of repression in the 1890s the restoration of a thoroughgoing system of racial domination was completed. Largely stripped of the vote by literacy tests, poll taxes, and other devices of turn-of-the-century southern political "reform," locked by poverty and political pressure into dead-end forms of agricultural labor, separated—with the Supreme Court's sanction (*Plessy v. Ferguson,* 1896)—into an underfunded and inferior system of public schools, segregated from or subordinated to whites in all aspects of social life by a pervasive and demeaning structure of racial caste, and recurrently subjected to brutal mob violence, black Americans were by the end of the century a subjugated people.[8]

This political reality—and "political" is here to be taken in its broadest sense—is critical to the understanding of African American religious life during this era. The story of black religion during these decades is not, however, one of unrelieved defeat and despair. Far from it. The seeming evidence of the newspapers and their daily lives notwithstanding, many blacks found in their religious faith cause for hope. A righteous God, they believed, still ruled and would in time overturn segregation as He had slavery. Some were also—at least when things were not at their very worst—simply optimistic. Like so many other Americans, they believed in progress and took encouragement from such signs of the time as advancing black literacy and the gradual enlargement of a more prosperous black middle-class—especially if they were themselves members of that class.[9] Yet such optimism remained more fragile and such hope harder won than the optimism and hope of the immigrants and Yankees. Bound more by poverty and coercion than by love to the land in which they had been slaves, African Americans experienced America as a religious—as well as a practical—problem in a way (whatever their own very real troubles) both older and new European Americans did not. And when, toward the end of the era, blacks increasingly made their way out of the South to the northeastern and midwestern cities that the descendants of the Puritans and the generations of immigrants had together built, this pilgrim people discovered they had still not arrived in the promised land.

On March 21, 1878, five thousand South Carolinians, mostly black, thronged a Charleston wharf to witness the consecration of the bark *Azor.* The ship had been purchased a month before by the Liberian Exodus Joint-Stock Steamship Company, a recently formed enterprise whose president was a black clergyman and whose purpose was to carry African American emigrants to Africa. According to the Charleston *News and Courier,* the "crowds of colored people" that gathered for the day's festivities represented "all ages and classes." "The gray-haired 'mauma' or 'daddy' tottered slowly along in company with young and middle-aged, many of whom bore their children in their arms," the paper reported, "the high-toned octoroon and the quadroon were there, together with the coal-black chimney sweep and laborer, and all moved together." The ceremonies in which they shared included the singing of the missionary hymn "From Greenland's Icy Mountains," a fiery address by the nationally prominent black church leader Henry McNeal Turner, prayers for the success of the company and its ship by a black bishop, and the unfurling of the Liberian flag. Some among the crowd were also able to board the *Azor,* where—according to Turner—"the more impulsive" broke into "odd manifestations of joy." "Some would go aboard and thank God," he reported; "others raise their hands to heaven and bless God for the sight, others jump up a few times, and others would kiss the vessel." It was, Turner thought at the time, "the grandest day I ever witnessed, or ever expect to."[10]

In the logic of biblical imagery, a people who sees itself as Israel in Egypt must make an exodus, and it is no surprise that exodus—as both practical program and religious symbol—held an important place in African American life during this period. Especially in the late 1870s, when the terminal political defeats of the Reconstruction era were a fresh memory, economic hard times a present reality, and the fear of imminent re-enslavement genuine, black interest in an escape from the southern states surged. For some, including the founders of the Liberian Exodus Joint-Stock Steamship Company, black Israel's promised land was to be found—as in the Bible—by a return to the pre-captivity homeland, to Africa. For others, including the "Exodusters" gripped by "Kansas fever" in the spring of 1879, a habitable space was to be found in the American West. In either case, religious ideas, clergymen, and church organizations played an important role in the search for geographical deliverance.

The idea that Americans of African descent were destined eventually to return to their ancestral homelands was not in 1877 a new one. It can be traced at least as far back as the 1770s, when John Quamino and Bristol Yamma, two African-born former slaves who were church members in Newport, Rhode Island, developed with the city's prominent Congregational pastors, Samuel Hopkins and Ezra Stiles, a plan by which they would be educated and returned to West Africa as Christian missionaries. The upheaval of the Revolutionary era prevented the implementation of the plan, but the idea lived on, especially among blacks in New England, and developed into the more ambitious program of establishing in Africa whole missionary colonies of American ex-slaves—a vision encouraged by Great Britain's launching of a similarly conceived venture in Sierra Leone in 1792. These dreams finally produced tangible results in 1816, when Paul Cuffee, a black Yankee sea captain and merchant, transported thirty-eight African Americans to Sierra Leone. Just at this moment, however, the meaning of such emigration was changed—or at least confused—by the founding (in 1817) of the American Colonization Society. A white organization that enlisted the support not only Protestant clergy and church members committed to foreign missions but also major figures in the American political establishment, the Colonization Society's program of resettling freed blacks in Liberia (a country it established for just this purpose) was intended as much to de-Africanize the United States as to Christianize Africa. Its work rested on the premise—espoused by Jefferson and (through most of his public career) Lincoln and central to American political culture throughout the antebellum period—that blacks and whites could never live side by side as equals in a biracial society. If social order were to be maintained, eliminating slavery would therefore require the elimination of blacks as well—by relocating them to Liberia or some other suitable location, perhaps in Central America or the Caribbean.

Although colonizationism was to its proponents a kind of antislavery, most blacks—or at least most of their outspoken leaders—saw it as an aggressive form of racism. For much of the nineteenth century, black resistance to this program of forced repatriation obscured, although never obliterated, the earlier interest in voluntary emigration. Especially in the 1850s, when the grip of slavery on American life seemed unbreakably tight, some black leaders returned to the idea with fresh enthusiasm. Their efforts, however, produced little in the way of tangible results. Meanwhile, by 1860, unable either to enlist massive numbers of blacks or to command the vast resources that a large-scale program of emigration would have required, the American Colonization Society and its Maryland state auxiliary had after four decades of work sent only about eleven thousand African Americans to West Africa.[11]

During the early years of the Civil War, the Lincoln administration nonetheless adhered to the colonizationist program. An Office of Emigration was established in the Interior Department, the State Department sought out appropriate sites for a black colony in Central America, and Congress voted $600,000 to support the venture. Emancipation—and the postwar constitutional establishment of black citizenship rights through the Thirteenth (1865), Fourteenth (1868), and Fifteenth (1870) amendments—created, however, a new optimism about the possibility of a racially inclusive society in America, and interest in emigration correspondingly declined. Black leaders such as Martin R. Delany, who had actively pursued the emigrationist vision in the 1850s, threw themselves into Reconstruction politics in the late 1860s and early 1870s. When the American Colonization Society, faced with a sharp decline in voluntary contributions, persuaded Congress early in 1867 to consider appropriating $50,000 in support of its work, the measure was debated rather lightheartedly and then voted down by a three-to-one margin.[12] A little more than ten years later, in April 1878, the ACS reported that it had, since the end of the war, colonized only 3,190 additional black Americans in Liberia.[13]

Still, even in these years, African American interest in emigration persisted—often under explicitly religious auspices. Indeed, according to one historian, the "most successful groups [of emigrants to Liberia during these years] were those organized by colored churches . . . ; led by men of initiative and determination they usually were able to hold together despite every kind of obstacle imaginable."[14] The tenacity of Cornelius Reeves, a Baptist preacher from Mullens Depot, South Carolina, was, for example, essential to the success of one such group of 116 emigrants who sailed for Liberia under the auspices of the American Colonization Society in April 1867.[15] Four years later another group of emigrating South Carolina blacks, this time from York County, was led by the remarkable Elias Hill. Crippled since childhood by disease so that he could neither use his badly twisted limbs nor move his jaw, this self-taught but highly knowledgeable preacher and local political activist was regarded by his followers, said one observer, "with a superstitious reverence."[16]

Religious images and ideas were also an essential part of the rhetoric by which such groups defined and explained themselves. The organizers in 1871 of the Freedmen's Emigrant Aid Society of Elizabeth City, North Carolina, knew that their cause had many critics who routinely emphasized the many obstacles to successful colonization in Liberia. "We do not desire that any should go to Africa who feel contented with the present state of things," they observed, "but would caution them to remember the fate of those who saw giants in the promised land in the time of Joshua."[17] Of course, religious leadership and religious rhetoric were applied with equal force—and more often during these years—by the opponents of emigration. Lecturing on Liberian emigration in Petersburg, Virginia, in April 1866, John Orcutt, a white colonizationist, was dismayed when a black minister countered his remarks with what Orcutt angrily described as "an incoherent, boisterous, untruthful, mischievous harangue on *human rights* and things in general."[18]

The terms of the debate did not change much in the late 1870s. Emigrationists convinced that the promised land for blacks lay somewhere else than America—or at least elsewhere than the American South—contended with proponents of a continuing effort to win full human rights in the United States, even in the former Confederate states. The bitter struggles and brutal defeats of the late Reconstruction period seem, however, to have won for the emigrationists a much larger share of black sentiment than they had previously commanded. Between 1876 and 1880 the number of blacks writing to the secretary of the American Colonization Society, applying for aid in emigrating, was more than three times what it had been between 1871 and 1875.[19] The creation in Charleston, in the summer of 1877, of the Liberian Exodus Joint-Stock Steamship Company, and it subsequent purchase of the *Azor,* was evidence, moreover, that the currents of emigrationism among African Americans were running too strong and deep to be any longer confined to the narrow channels of the ACS.[20]

The American Colonization Society regarded this surge of independent black emigrationism with ambivalence. S. D. Alexander, the president of the New York Colonization Society, saw in all this activity "the plain indications of Providence" and spoke with approval of "the great exodus the symptoms of which are becoming more distinct every day."[21] Yet by April 1878 the *African Repository* (the ACS periodical) expressed a strong note of caution. "It is a serious question," the paper worried, "whether emigration to Africa shall be carefully organized and controlled by those who know the country and the climate, and who can provide for the best welfare of the emigrants, or whether they shall plunge indiscreetly into all the perils of a miscellaneous and mismanaged exodus." It is easy to see why the ACS, now barely able to transport a thousand emigrants a decade, thought the situation had gotten out of control. The Liberian Exodus Company of Charleston claimed that a hundred thousand persons had "signified their desire to go to Liberia," while the Colonization Council of Shreveport, Louisiana reported "71,000 names enrolled for settlement in Liberia." Citing such reports, the *African Repository* declared in early 1878 that a "quarter of a million of people are estimated to be looking to Africa as their home and distinct nationality."[22] Not satisfied even by such numbers as these, Richard Harvey Cain, a South Carolina black emigrationist, member of the clergy, and two-term member of Congress, maintained in his paper the *Missionary Record* a standing editorial headlined "Ho for Africa! One million men wanted for Africa."[23]

As events unfolded, it soon became clear that black groups such as the Liberian Exodus Company were no more able to move masses of blacks across the Atlantic than the ACS had been. The *Azor* made only one voyage to Liberia under its auspices. Carrying 206 emigrants— twenty-three of whom died at sea—it ran up so many unanticipated expenses that it had to be sold to liquidate the debt before it could make another trip. It would be a mistake, however, to judge the significance of the Liberian exodus of 1878 by the paucity of its tangible results. When the *Azor* sailed from Charleston harbor in April, 175 would-be emigrants were left ashore because the ship simply could not hold them—a fitting symbol of the frustrating gap between the movement's desperately eager constituency and its severely limited carrying capacity.[24] Although it may be doubtful, moreover, that the number of those seriously prepared to go to Liberia ever rose to 250,000 as claimed, it is certain that fascination with the idea was widespread among blacks and that thousands more would have gone to Africa if they could. It is also certain that the despair that fed such emigrationist dreams was far less ephemeral than some of the organizations that sought to implement them. No sooner had the "Liberian fever" of 1878 run its course than there appeared a seemingly massive outbreak of Kansas fever.

Like the idea of a return to Africa, the notion that blacks might find deliverance in the West was not an entirely new one. The Northwest Ordinance of 1787 had blocked the legal expansion of slavery westward into the territories north of the Ohio River, and thereafter there was a recurrent hope among some blacks that states with no history of legal slavery might eventually offer a haven from racial discrimination as well. In the antebellum period these hopes were repeatedly disappointed. Western whites were often as concerned to keep their new states free of blacks as free of slavery, and the "Black Laws" they adopted were not only discriminatory in their provisions but also exclusionary in their spirit. Some antebellum blacks accordingly looked further north, promoting colonization of Lower Canada with the hope of finding in British-controlled territory a freedom unavailable in the United States. The numbers attracted were, however, few, and in the war and Reconstruction era black optimism about the West once more focussed on the United States.[25]

By the 1870s the rapidly growing state of Kansas, richly associated with memories of John Brown and the antebellum struggle against the westward spread of slavery, had become particularly attractive.[26] Early in the decade, for example, Benjamin "Pap" Singleton, a Tennessee ex-slave frustrated in his postwar attempts to help freedmen purchase small farms in their home state, began promoting settlement in Kansas as the best path to black landowning and economic self-determination. Some of the black migrants Singleton assisted settled in established towns and cities, such as Wyandotte, (later part of Kansas City, Kansas) and Topeka, where they formed the Tennesseetown settlement. Singleton led others, however, to black colonies he established at Baxter Springs in Cherokee County in the southeastern corner of the state and at Dunlap in Morris County southwest of Topeka. In 1877, moreover, a group of Kentucky blacks established in Graham County, in northwestern Kansas, another all-black colony, the town of Nicodemus.[27]

In all these efforts, religious influences were notable. The secretary— and only literate person—among the incorporators of the Nicodemus Town Company was S. P. Roundtree, a black minister, and at least three of the subgroups that early populated the colony were Kentucky or Mississippi congregations led westward by their pastors. Providing handbills to traveling preachers was one of the main ways Pap Singleton sought to publicize his colonies across the South, and his and other colonization efforts often achieved further publicity when letters home from Kansas migrants were read aloud in churches. Churches were also frequently the sites for the promotional meetings of Singleton's Tennessee Real Estate and Homestead Association—meetings that included the singing of specially composed migration songs such as "The Land That Gives Birth to Freedom":

> We have Mr. Singleton for our President, he will go
> before us, and lead us through. (Repeat).
> Chorus: —Marching along, yes we are marching along, to
> Kansas City we are bound. (Repeat).
> Surely this must be the Lord that has gone before him,
> and opened the way. (Repeat).[28]

Singleton himself was a religious visionary. "The great God of glory has worked in me," he declared: "I have had open air interviews with the living spirit of God for my people; and we are going to leave the South."[29] He eventually took to signing his handbills and publicly designating himself as the "Father of the Exodus" or the "Moses of the Colored Exodus."[30]

What gave exodus imagery a special currency in the spring of 1879 was not, however, the direct result of Singleton's efforts—which were primarily devoted to helping small, well-organized groups of blacks from the Upper South make carefully planned migrations westward. Rather, widespread talk of a general black exodus was occasioned by a sudden and seemingly pell-mell rush of thousands of poor blacks from the river counties and parishes of Mississippi and Louisiana up the Mississippi to St. Louis and then westward to Kansas. By late 1878 there had been signs that Kansas fever was rapidly spreading in the lower Mississippi Valley, but authorities in St. Louis were nonetheless unprepared in early March when river steamers began depositing hundreds of migrants on the city's wharves. Convinced by rumors that the federal government would provide free transportation to Kansas, land, tools, and a year's provisions, these mostly impoverished and largely unorganized migrants arrived in St. Louis with only the vaguest ideas about where they were going and exactly how they would get there. Although city officials offered the migrants little help, casting the burden of relief work instead on the local black community, the migrants continued to come. By mid-April, as "the fever" spread and newspaper coverage mounted, reports appeared that thousands of Louisiana and Mississippi blacks were gathering along the river, seeking passage north. Some observers thought a massive exodus of African Americans from the South was underway—a phenomenon evaluated largely along politically partisan lines. Stalwart Republicans tended to see the exodus as a telling commentary on the brutality with which Democratic rule had been restored in the post-Reconstruction South, whereas Democrats tended to see the migrants as hapless innocents manipulated by unscrupulous land agents and Republican politicians eager to relocate their votes out of the hopelessly lost South to closely contested northern states.

Eventually, in the spring of 1880, a U.S. Senate committee was appointed to investigate the matter, but after hearing the testimony of dozens of witnesses it filed majority (Democratic) and minority (Republican) reports divided along strictly partisan lines. By that time, however, Kansas fever had subsided. As early as late April 1879 St. Louis merchants and Louisiana and Mississippi planters hostile to the exodus persuaded steamboat companies simply to refuse passage to the migrants—even if they could pay full fare. A violation of the Civil Rights Act of 1875, which forbade such discrimination on common carriers, this denial of service to black passengers was sustained for only a month. That was enough, however, to break the movement's momentum, for poor blacks with minimal resources could not tarry indefinitely at the riverside as boats sailed unresponsively past them—especially since they were meanwhile subject to other forms of harassment from local whites. The upriver flow of Exodusters did resume in late May, and there was a comparable surge overland from Texas later in the year. More carefully planned black migrations to Kansas also continued throughout 1879 and into the early 1880s. But the peak of excitement had been passed.[31]

Once again, the numbers involved were small relative to the ferment and publicity that had been generated. It has been estimated that "the much publicized migration of 1879 [to Kansas] netted no more than about 4,000 people from Mississippi and Louisiana."[32] Yet it is also clear that the exodus impulse touched the lives of thousands who were unable to act on it—most obviously those waiting at the riverside as the boats passed them by and thousands of others who entertained the idea of escape and made emotional investments in it, even if they could not or would not in the end pursue it. It is equally clear that exodus as a concrete program of action drew part of its compelling power from exodus as a religious symbol. One aged Exoduster, interviewed in St. Louis by the *Globe-Democrat* in March 1879, found both insight and a determination to persist by comparing the impoverished migrants' precarious situation to that of the fleeing Israelites:

> we's like de chilun ob Israel when dey was led from out o' bondage by Moses. De chilun ob Israel was a promised to be sot free by Pharoah, but wen Pharoah got over his skear he sot 'em back agin to makin' bricks

out o' straw. Den Moses he said dat shouldn't be de case, an' he took
'em out o' bondage, and wen dey was all awaverin' an' mighty feared
he took 'em 'cross de Red Sea an' den day was safe. Now chile, jes' listen to me. Dis is our Red Sea, right hyah in St. Louis, atween home an'
Kansas, an' if we sticks togeder an' keeps up our faith we'll git to Kansas and be out o' bondage for shuah. We's been sot free by Massa Lin-
kum, but it war jes' sich another sot free as Pharoah gib de chilen of
Israel. You heah me, chile, dem as is awaverin' an' is a'feared is goin' to
sink in dis hyah Red Sea.[33]

Nor were such views eccentric among the Exodusters. One newspaper reporter described the spring 1879 migrants as gripped by "a sort
of religious exaltation, during which they regarded Kansas as a modern Canaan and the God-appointed home of the negro race."[34] One
historian of the 1879 exodus, Nell Painter, has in fact contended that
it was precisely this intensity of religious conviction that gave the spring
1879 exodus its special character. These migrants—so distinctively
careless of the details of their future and so certain of government support—were, she has argued, "millenarians," believers in a "collective,
. . . terrestrial, . . . imminent, [and] . . . total" salvation of their people
through escape to the promised land.[35]

Yet it is unwise to draw too sharp a distinction between these seemingly impulsive migrants and those, before and after them, who moved
north more cautiously—or not at all. One white Texan, writing to the
governor of Kansas in August 1879, complained that ever since their
emancipation the former slaves had believed "some general movement
would eventually be made to take them out of the South." He attributed this expectation to "religious fanaticism." "All freedmen seemed
to be imbued," he lamented, "with the idea that god has foreordained
that they shall be made a great people whereby he will manifest to all
nations His great power, etc."[36]

If the numbers involved in the Liberia exodus of 1878 or the Kansas exodus of 1879 were small, the significance of these episodes was
not. Like a match struck to the tinderbox of black alienation, the idea
that a geographical deliverance was at hand in these moments vividly
illuminated a larger landscape of both despair and hope. Although the
cold waters of practical reality in both cases soon extinguished the
flame, they dampened but did not wash away the combustible realities of African American life in the American South. The smoke of
smoldering black despair—and hope—hung over the religious landscape of the southern states as a more or less permanent cloud.

At the time of the sailing of the *Azor* in 1878 and the great Kansas
exodus of 1879, by far the most common religious affiliation among

black Americans was Baptist or Methodist—with the Baptists just slightly in the lead. Black Baptists in the United States were much slower, however, to create enduring, independent, nationwide organizations than were black Methodists. The African Methodist Episcopal Church and the African Methodist Episcopal Zion Church, the two largest independent black Methodist denominations, had been founded in 1816 and 1821, respectively. Kept out of the Deep South by the repressive laws of the slave regime, they had remained in the antebellum period relatively small, northern-based organizations. Seizing the opportunity afforded by the Civil War and Reconstruction, however, they had both rapidly expanded southward in the 1860s and 1870s and were by 1880 sizable and genuinely nationwide churches, with the larger AMEs counting four hundred thousand members and the Zion Methodists perhaps a hundred thousand less.[37] Meanwhile, a third major black Methodist denomination, the Colored Methodist Episcopal Church, had been organized in 1870 out of the remaining black membership in the Methodist Episcopal Church, South and by 1880 likely had about a hundred thousand members.[38] (More than two hundred thousand blacks also belonged to the northern-based, predominantly white, Methodist Episcopal Church.)[39] Although they had formed numerous state conventions, regional associations, and special, task-oriented national organizations, black Baptists did not achieve full denominational status until the creation of the National Baptist Convention in 1895. Perhaps that was why they were so surprised in the mid-1880s when their first systematic census attempt produced a figure of 1,066,131. Apparently, they had thought the Methodists outnumbered them.[40]

The mistake could easily have been made by anyone present at the consecration of the *Azor* in the spring of 1878. Harrison N. Bouey, the secretary of the Liberian Exodus Joint-Stock Steamship Company and by some accounts one of the *Azor* emigrants, was a Baptist minister, but he seemed everywhere surrounded by black Methodists.[41] Especially noticeable were prominent members of the African Methodist Episcopal Church, not only the largest but also the most influential—and by many accounts the most militant—of the independent black Methodist denominations. Benjamin F. Porter, the president of the Liberian Exodus Company, was pastor of Morris Brown AME Church in Charleston. Richard Harvey Cain, the member of Congress whose *Missionary Record* had so enthusiastically summoned "one million men" for Africa, was the same denomination's missionary secretary, and Henry McNeal Turner, who gave the main address at the *Azor's* consecration, was manager of the AME Book Concern. John Mifflin Brown, the bishop who prayed over the ship, was also an AME.[42] Indeed, the AME prominence in the movement was so pronounced that anti-emigrationist African Methodists seemed on the defensive in recording their opposition. In Philadelphia, the denomination's historic center, the local AME Preachers Meeting adopted in March 1878 a resolution declaring their "unfaltering opposition" to "the absurdity of the colored people of America attempting to build up a nationality in Africa." They had been moved to speak, they said, because "this enterprise of African emigration is looked upon by many as having the support of the leading minds of our people by the intense interest manifested in it by persons holding high official positions in the AME Church, so much so as to misguide the masses of the people."[43]

It is yet another measure of the power of the exodus idea, even in the lives of thousands who never sailed east to Africa or rode westward to Kansas, that it was so widely and intensely debated across black America in the late 1870s. Nowhere is this more evident than in the AME Church, where the debate was especially fierce in the spring of 1878. As the pages of the denomination's newspaper, the *Christian Recorder*, make clear, the Philadelphia preachers were not the only group who felt obliged to take a stand on emigration. Reports appear of special public meetings to address the issue, resolutions passed at annual conferences, and even school-room debates.[44] It would be a mistake, however, to see this especially intense moment in isolation from a more extended process of political and ecclesiastical self-definition. Emigration, whether to Africa or the West, was the subject of recurrent controversy from the end of Reconstruction through the first quarter of the twentieth century. Deciding exactly how the biblical exodus story applied to the emigration issue, moreover, was for black church folk intimately connected with the question of how the analogy applied to their religious institutions. Consider the case of the AME Church in 1887, as it celebrated what many AMEs regarded as the centennial of their originating moment—when a group of black Methodists, in protest against racial oppression, made their exodus from the white-controlled St. George's Methodist Episcopal Church in Philadelphia.

"Reading carefully the history of the Jews," the Rev. W. H. Yeocum wrote in a September 1887 issue of the *Christian Recorder*, "it is observed that, through all their peculiar conditions, which commenced after their departure from Egypt, they thought it worthwhile to hold celebrations and jubilees on past events. These were continued . . . as a recognition of God's favor and divine blessings [and] to keep the events fresh in the minds of the children, that they might be handed down by history or tradition to unnumbered generations." A Trenton, New Jersey, pastor, Yeocum wrote to exhort his fellow AMEs to take seriously their imminent centennial anniversary. "We call upon every member of the African M.E. Church," he declared, "to observe the . . . anniversary . . . in November . . . because one hundred years from that time God, in his wise providence, raised up the sainted Richard Allen and a few others to launch this old ship." The ship's perilous passage through the stormy waters of oppression and warfare "should be written so indellible upon the hearts of the ministry, the laymen and the children of the African M.E. Church that time itself cannot erase it; that tradition and history will cause it to be explained to the children of every succeeding generation. If there ever was a time for grand evidence of Church patriotism," he announced, "it is now."[45]

Yeocum was scarcely alone in calling for a major expression of AME "Church patriotism" in November of 1887. In January of that year, the denomination's Council of Bishops had adopted a resolution to that effect prepared by John Mifflin Brown—an Oberlin graduate and the same bishop who had invoked God's blessing on the *Azor* nine years earlier. Quoting the historical preface to the denomination's first *Discipline* (1817), Brown's resolution identified the originating occasion to be celebrated as that moment a hundred years before in Philadelphia when "the colored peoples belonging to the M.E. Society convened to take into consideration the evils under which they labored, arising from unkind treatment of their white brethren, who considered them a nuisance in the house of God, and even pulled them from their knees, while in the act of prayer, and ordered them to the back seat."[46] The resolution recalled what is probably the single best known event in all African American church history. Sometimes referred to as the "gallery incident," the event, traditionally dated to November 1787, occurred in St. George's Methodist Episcopal Church, the historic, initial congregation of Philadelphia Methodism, which by that time had a sizable black membership. The *locus classicus* for the story is the late-in-life autobiographical recollections of Richard Allen, the Delaware Methodist convert and former slave who was a leader among St. George's black members and eventually became the AME Church's founding bishop. As Allen remembered it:

> A number of us usually attended St. George's Church in Fourth Street; and when the colored people began to get numerous in attending the church, they moved us from the seats we usually sat on, and placed us around the wall, and on Sabbath morning we went to church and the sexton stood at the door, and told us to go in the gallery. He told us to go, and we would see where to sit. We expected to take the seats over the ones we formerly occupied below, not knowing any better. We took those seats. Meeting had begun, and they were nearly done singing, and

just as we got to the seats, the elder said, "Let us pray." We had not been
long upon our knees before I heard considerable scuffling and low talking. I raised my head up and saw one of the trustees, H_____
M_____, having hold of . . . Absalom Jones, pulling him up off his
knees, and saying, "You must get up—you must not kneel here." Mr.
Jones replied, "Wait until prayer is over." Mr. H_____ M_____
said "no, you must get up now, or I will call for aid and force you away."
Mr. Jones said, "Wait until prayer is over, and I will get up and trouble
you no more." With that he beckoned to one of the other trustees, Mr.
L_____ S_____ to come to his assistance. He came, and went to
Mr. William White to pull him up. By this time prayer was over, and we
all went out of the church in one body, and they were no more plagued
with us in the church. . . . We then hired a store-room and held worship
by ourselves.[47]

Brown's resolution identified this withdrawal from St. George's and
beginning of independent worship as the "most decisive act of our religious colored people in the United States." It also declared—in a statement that speaks volumes about the late-nineteenth-century AME
Church's understanding of itself—that there was "nothing like [this act]
in the world except the resolutions of the Haitians, under Toussaint,
Christophe, Petion and Boyer." "These men"—the leaders of Haiti's
revolution of the 1790s and early national history—"were to Hayti and
San Domingo what Allen [and his co-workers] were to the colored
Christians of the United States." This linking of the creation of a black
church with the creation of a revolutionary black nation-state makes
clear that Yeocum's call for "Church patriotism" was an apt phrase.
Religion and a sense of nationality, so often associated in the experience of white Protestants and other American religious and ethnic
groups, were combined with specific reference to African American
experience. What was to be celebrated in November 1887 was not simply an incident in ecclesiastical history but the emergence of a self-de-
termining black people in the Americas.[48]

    Considered in this light, it is clear that the gallery incident, as remem-
bered by AMEs and other African Americans, was a type of exodus.
"We all went out of the church in one body, and they were no more
plagued with us," Allen had declared.[49] Sometimes, moreover, within
a wide-ranging commemorative rhetoric that found several notable
precedents and parallels for the dramatic egress of the black Methodists from St. George's, this implicit analogy to the biblical exodus was
made explicit. In an early 1888 address honoring Allen as "the Second
Reformer," the Rev. J. A. Jones was primarily concerned to place Allen
alongside Martin Luther as the leader of a new Reformation. But in
developing his general thesis that Allen, as "the God-send of the sons

of Ham on the Western Continent," stood in a long line of divinely appointed deliverers he not surprisingly began his story with Moses— a connection other AME speakers and writers sometimes explicitly made as well.[50] In a January 1888 editorial in the denomination's recently established quarterly magazine, the *AME Church Review,* for example, Benjamin T. Tanner observed with regard to the origin of separate black churches that Richard Allen "was as a Moses to them."[51] Sometimes, more detailed comparisons were drawn. In retelling the gallery incident in a February 1888 article in the *Christian Recorder,* Edward A. Clark suggested that the efforts of St. George's white Methodist authorities to restrict their burgeoning black membership by confining them to a limited number of seats along the wall failed because "like the Israelites of old, oppression only increased their numbers." When the determined white authorities then assigned the black members seats in the gallery, their action became, in Clark's tale, the "second edict of Pharoah."[52]

At other times the denomination's early history was more broadly sketched as a passage from Egyptian bondage to religious nationhood. An example is the story told by H. C. C. Astwood, an AME clergyman and superintendent of the denomination's mission in San Domingo, in an article published in the January 1888 issue of the *AME Church Review:*

> Whilst the then so-called Church of Christ proclaimed the doctrine of the Redeemer, yet it held with the tenacity of Pharaoh to the heresy of human bondage, and refused to let the people go. They had no nationality save that brought from their fatherland, no Government to which they could look for protection, no fraternity with which they could identify themselves . . . until the African Methodist Episcopal Church was founded. Bishop Allen battled on and prayed on. He and his coadjutors became encouraged and strengthened; they saw the cloud disappearing day by day; they were led, as it were, by Divine inspiration until a religious government of their people was formed, as firm and lasting as that of the Nation.[53]

The exodus analogy was also put to work to promote self-conscious efforts at preserving the denomination's historical memory. "There is rising a generation who knew not Pharoah nor the fathers," observed John T. Jenifer, a prominent AME pastor, two months before the church's November 1887 centennial. "Let us commemorate this event by refreshing the memory of the fathers, and"—he added—"do not forget the fore-mothers . . . ; thanks to God for his many mercies in aiding us in our efforts at self-help, self-government, and independent ecclesiastical government."[54]

If the egress from white Methodism was an exodus, moreover, the logic of the analogy could suggest as well that "independent ecclesiastical government" was a kind of promised land. When Richard Allen had left the Egypt of St. George's Methodist Episcopal Church after the gallery incident, he had found his ecclesiastical Canaan in Bethel African Methodist Episcopal Church. Founded by Allen in 1794, initially as a separate black congregation within the white-controlled Methodist Episcopal Church, it led the way in 1816 in the creation of an entirely independent black Methodist denomination—the AME Church. "Mother Bethel," as it came to be known, was to many AMEs the primal site where their autonomy had first been realized and where it remained most tangibly present.[55]

Henry McNeal Turner was by 1889 one of the denomination's bishops. Called upon to speak in November of that year, when the cornerstone was laid for a new building erected on the original site, he declared that "the spot on which Bethel stands is the most sacred spot in America."[56] Invited back in May 1901, when the bones of Richard Allen—and his wife—were reinterred in "the depths of the mammoth edifice" in a new tomb, the now seventy-year-old Turner made the point even more forcefully. According to the *Christian Recorder,* "The old hero's eyes flamed with leaping fire, his stalwart form became erect and his voice vibrated with deep feeling as he said,'young people, never give up this spot of ground; hold it, hold it forever. In the trying days of the future, here brave Negroes can come and rekindle the torch of Negro manhood at Allen's tomb.'" A younger colleague, Bishop Abram Grant, then placed the occasion and the site in a biblical context. "Seventy years after his death the bones of Joseph were borne from Egypt to their final resting place," Grant observed, "seventy years after his death we bear to the tomb below the bones of Richard Allen." Here Allen became a patriarch whose body had been brought home to rest in the promised land.[57]

Whatever their respect for Richard Allen or reverence for Mother Bethel, however, not all the denomination's leaders were prepared to equate "independent ecclesiastical existence" with arrival at a final resting place in Canaan. The AME missionary H. C. C. Astwood was ready to see the denomination's early history in exodus terms, but he thought the analogy no longer ought to define the church's sense of itself in 1888. Accordingly, he proposed that the denomination change its name from the African to the Allen Methodist Episcopal Church. Blacks during the age of slavery, he contended, had been denied American citizenship and had of necessity embraced the term *African* as the mark of a separate nationality—"the only nationality to which people of color were entitled in the United States." The abolition of slavery and the enactment of the great constitutional amendments of Reconstruction had, however, changed all that, and "when the race became citizens of the United States, and accepted that citizenship, the mission of the word 'African' had ended." Allen's name was an appropriate substitute because he was, in the end, better thought of as a religious reformer, like Luther or Wesley, than as the Moses-like leader of a people, and to name the church for him would be to march under a potentially more inclusive banner. Different scriptural reference points now should define the church's sense of itself. Astwood wrote:

> Christianity can tend to but one end: to fit men for that spiritual kingdom founded by our dying Lord. There can be no nationality or race discriminating influences attached to it. The Church Militant must be a type of the Church Triumphant, pictured by the Revelator on the great day of final assizes. "And after this I beheld and lo a great multitude, which no man could number, of all nations and people and tongues, stood before the throne, and before the Lamb, clothed in white robes and palms in their hands, and cried with a loud voice, saying Salvation to our God which sitteth upon the throne and unto the Lamb forever." African and Anglo-Saxon and all other races of people, all united in the City of our God, around one common Throne, singing one song, praising one God, serving one Christ, without respect to race, people, or condition; this is Heaven, and this is the destiny of all good men; this is the teaching of all true Christian Churches.

Astwood was clear about the practical ways this vision of the end time impinged on the present. "Christians must fraternize. Race prejudices must become extinct. . . . Congregations much be presided over indiscriminately by white and black ministers. Conferences must be held by white and black Bishops alike." The predominantly white Methodist churches and the independent black Methodist denominations were all "discriminating Churches" that must repent of their ways and prepare for "one general amalgamation of all Protestant denominations."[58]

Astwood was not a figure of sufficient power in the AME Church for his views to weigh heavily in its deliberations. The same could not be said of Daniel Alexander Payne (1811–93), the church's senior bishop from 1873 until his death twenty years later.[59] The denomination's single most important leader in the decades since Richard Allen's death, Payne too believed that "the future development of the AME Church [must] be unlike its past." Writing in July 1884 in the inaugural issue of the *AME Church Review,* Payne began by observing that "about sixty-seven years ago the blasphemous spirit of American slavery and American caste compelled the organization of the African M.E.

Church." If its existence had been a religious necessity, he continued, its accomplishments had also been great. "When the terrible civil war was begun, especially when slavery was overthrown," he recalled, "all eyes of thoughtful men were turned toward this Church, and she was found to be in possession of more talent, more pluck, and more general intelligence than in other combinations of colored men existing within the Republic." He warned his readers, however, that such a glorious past did not necessarily imply an equally glorious future, for the future lay in the hands of a God who could work powerfully through a particular form and then discard it in favor of a better one. In Payne's reading of the Bible, this was evident in God's successive gathering and disbanding of the "Patriarchal Church" and the "Mosaic Church." Once these—or any other religious or social form—had fulfilled their missions, Payne thought, no human effort to preserve them could succeed in the face of God's onrushing providence. Indeed, drastic measures to preserve such forms often had the ironic effect of hastening their demise. "The rejection of Jesus was doubtless done to preserve the Jewish Church, as viewed by the eyes of the High Priests," Payne suggested, "but that very act destroyed it utterly. . . . So also," he continued, "the Southern leaders chose the sword to preserve slavery, but that very act destroyed it utterly." The Christian Church as such, Payne believed, was never to be disbanded, but only because "it was not made like the others for a particular time, nor a particular privileged race. . . . No!" he continued, "it was made for all time and for all the races—not for colored men, nor for white men; but *for humanity.*" The same could not be said for the specific branches of Christianity, however, especially in the United States—and this was true even of the AME Church. *"Like all the American Churches, the AME Church is a race Church,"* Payne declared, and he did not hesitate to draw the consequences of that statement. "The 'ultimate development and perfection' of the Church of the Living God will not be on the plane of race; but on the plane of humanity. All the present ecclesiastical organizations in America must either leap upon that plane or be swept out of the way of Christian progress. The non-progressive Churches . . . will be annihilated. . . . *The Eternal sets little value upon races,* but *much upon humanity. . . . Races perish. Humanity lives on forever."*[60]

Unlike Astwood, Payne did not issue a call for the merging of all Methodists—much less all Protestants—into a single, racially inclusive, and nondiscriminatory church.[61] Rather, he urged the denomination to prove it was not a "barren fig tree" ready to be cut down by soberly and humbly rededicating itself to the two basic forms of Christian work: those addressed to the body (feeding the hungry, clothing the naked, and housing the homeless), and, more important, those addressed to the mind (educating the ignorant and taking the gospel to the heathen). This could only be done, he warned, if the denomination resisted the rancorous and contentious spirit he thought had dominated its most recent national assembly. "The General Conference of 1880," he lamented, "seemed often like the Atlantic when a hurricane is sweeping over its surface." "No assembly of ambitious politicians," he continued, "could have been more excited and boisterous." Indeed, he thought the ambition manifested by candidates for church office was so "impious . . . they lost all respect and reverence for . . . the discipline . . . and the infallible Word of God." Equally dangerous, he warned, was a kind of collective vanity evident in some of his fellow AMEs' more grandiose visions of global outreach. This he labeled the "Don Quixotic idea of 'Ecclesiastical Imperialism'—the intention of making African Methodism embrace the world—of bringing every negro on the earth under our Discipline—controlled by our Government." Payne was a strong supporter of his church's missionary work in Haiti and believed it should begin a new mission in the Congo, but to imagine that the AME Church, with its limited resources, could reach out to black Christians all across Africa and the Caribbean was to him *"an idea* [that] *savors of religious insanity."*[62] More pointedly, he vigorously opposed the idea of any special commitment to work in Liberia—and to the whole idea of a transatlantic exodus to which Liberian missions was so often linked. When the *Azor* had been consecrated in 1878 Payne had not been among the church leaders who had prayed and preached over the ship. Indeed, the "Liberian Exodus" was in many ways an exceptionally vivid expression of precisely what worried him most in the AME Church.

Payne did not hesitate, moreover, to make his views known. Writing in the *Christian Recorder* not long after the *Azor* sailed, he characterized the "Liberian Exodus" as misnamed, impractical, and of dubious motivation. He thought the analogy to the biblical exodus was utterly misdrawn. He wrote:

> The new departure of our brethren in South Carolina has been unfortunately called an "Exodus." I say unfortunately, because, if they mean what that historic name implies, then, they have given utterance to a great fallacy. The "Exodus" implies two things, the perfect emancipation of an enslaved people, and the immediate destruction of their enslavers, and both accomplished by a miracle, in which the former, as a race, is forever separated from the latter as a race. These ideas became facts in the case of Egyptian bondage—they can never be realized in the case of American slavery. The enlightenment and *salvation* of *humanity* is in-

volved and needed in the former; no salvation of humanity is involved or needed in the latter.

He also thought the emigrationists had misread African realities as badly as they had misapplied the exodus analogy. "The hope of escaping from the oppression of the white man in America, and of finding an *asylum* from his power in Africa has doubtless influenced tens of thousands of the dupes of the 'Exodus' movement," Payne declared, "This hope is . . . vain . . . because, on their arrival . . . they will ascertain that . . . the white man has gone ahead and taken possession of the best portions of Africa." The whole quest for a racial promised land was in Payne's judgment hopeless, for "the races were never made for isolation, but for fraternity." In the past, "God has tested Ham by himself, Shem by himself, Japhet by himself," but "He the Omnipotent God is now about to test these three brothers abreast of each, for the benefit of each other and for the reconstruction of society, in order that He might develop in them a history, brighter, purer, more glorious than the past." The utterly misdirected plea for an "exodus" was the "offspring of disappointed political ambition. . . . Just so long as the leaders or this 'Exodus' held their seats in the Legislatures of Georgia and South Carolina, or played a successful part in the politics of these States," Payne contended, "not a word was heard from their lips concerning African Emigration."[63]

Richard Harvey Cain definitely "played a successful part" in Reconstruction era politics in South Carolina, while Henry McNeal Turner had been comparably active, if less successful, in Republican politics in Georgia, so there could be little doubt whose "disappointed political ambition" Payne thought was fueling the exodus. Payne also held this same pair largely accountable for turning the 1880 General Conference into something akin to an "assembly of boisterous politicians."[64] It is therefore a telling measure of the balance of opinion in the denomination that both Cain and Turner were elected bishops in 1880. The AME Church had been in the antebellum era an essentially northern institution, but by 1880 its constituency was overwhelmingly southern and seems not to have shared Payne's reading of the politics, practicality, or religious meaning of the exodus. Although itself scarcely monolithic, the AME southern constituency provided a ready and responsive audience for the militantly nationalistic rhetoric of Henry NcNeal Turner, who became—as Payne's power waned—the single most influential leader of the AME Church.[65]

Turner was, moreover, widely influential outside the denomination. For nearly the entire period from the end of Reconstruction to the beginning of World War I he was the most notable promoter of black

American emigration to Africa. When Daniel Payne claimed that Turner's embrace of emigrationism was the opportunistic act of a disappointed office-seeker, Turner replied that he had embraced the cause as early as 1849, when a white preacher's missionary sermon had persuaded him that "God would ultimately use the Negro of this country to aid in the civilization of Africa."[66] Turner's support for an exodus to Africa, moreover, outlived even that of the American Colonization Society, which effectively ceased emigration work in the early 1890s and entirely went out of business in 1910.[67] In 1883, when the U.S. Supreme Court ruled the Civil Rights Act of 1875 unconstitutional, Turner advised his fellow blacks to "prepare to return to Africa or get ready for extermination."[68]

In the 1890s Turner was able to tie his emigrationism to his denomination's growing African missions program, making the first of four visits to the continent in 1891 and promoting the cause after 1893 in the *Voice of Missions,* an AME missionary publication he edited. At the same time, he worked directly with the International Migration Society and the Colored National Emigration Association, two short-lived and largely ineffective attempts at turning emigrationist hopes into practical realities.[69] Slowed considerably by a stroke in 1899 and less directly involved in emigrationist organizations after the early 1900s, Turner nonetheless remained the movement's most implacable advocate. "I wish to say that hell is an improvement upon the United States where the Negro is concerned," he observed in 1906.[70] He died in Windsor, Canada, in May 1915, and it was said by some that he crossed to Canada with his last bit of energy to avoid dying in the United States.[71]

During the same turn-of-the-century decades in which Turner's influence among the AMEs and in black America generally was at its zenith, black Baptists were also enacting their own historically fateful version of exodus piety. The landmark event was the formation in 1895 of the National Baptist Convention, the first enduring black Baptist attempt at nationwide denominational organization. In an apt rephrasing of G. K. Chesterton's often-quoted aphorism that America is a "nation with the soul of a church," black Baptist historian James M. Washington has termed the new denomination "a church with the soul of a nation."[72]

Like the racial nationalists within the AME Church, the founders of the National Baptist Convention saw their new church as an expression of black self-determination and peoplehood—as a new ecclesiastical exodus. Because black Baptists had long been organized into separate congregations and independent local associations and state conventions, the originating events in the founding of the National Baptist Convention did not center on a walkout from a white church—in the manner of Allen and his colleagues from St. George's—but the disruption of longstanding patterns of "cooperation" with the white-controlled and northern-based American Baptist Publication Society and American Baptist Home Mission Society. In 1889, when the ABPS, which supplied Sunday school and other literature to the black Baptist churches, withdrew its recently made invitation to Walter Henderson Brooks, Emanuel K. Love, and William J. Simmons—three prominent black Baptist leaders—to write for its magazine the *Baptist Teacher,* the event was seen as a racial insult akin to the black Methodists at St. George's being dragged from their knees while at prayer. The ensuing exodus was in the direction of an independent black Baptist publishing house. Meanwhile, intense conflicts, centered on the ABHMS's continuing control over the black southern colleges it funded led in 1893 to schisms in the black state conventions in Texas and Georgia between those favoring continuing cooperation with the white-controlled agency and those more insistent on black control of at least some black Baptist colleges. The various streams of separatist sentiment converged in 1895 when three black Baptist organizations—the Baptist Foreign Mission Convention, the American National Baptist Convention, and the Baptist Education Convention—were merged into the National Baptist Convention, which quickly established a publishing board. Immediately the largest of the independent black denominations, the National Baptist Convention soon displaced the AME Church as the preeminent body among the black churches.[73]

In the same years that conflicts over publishing and higher education were pushing black Baptists toward a new degree of denominational independence, their missionary efforts—like those of the AMEs—were also increasingly entwined with African emigrationism. Harrison Bouey, one-time secretary of the Liberian Exodus Joint-Stock Steamship Company, was in 1879 designated by the black South Carolina Baptist Convention as its representative in Liberia. Returning to the United States in 1881, Bouey became an influential promoter of missionary interest among American black Baptists—eventually working for the Mission Board of the National Baptist Convention before himself returning to Liberia in 1902.[74] Benjamin Gaston, a Georgia black Baptist minister who had emigrated to Liberia in 1866, returned twenty years later and spent the late 1880s and early 1890s promoting a series of mostly unsuccessful emigration efforts among southern blacks.[75] A sense that blacks in the United States had a special racial destiny to lead in the redemption of Africa also strengthened black Baptist resolve to create and maintain missionary programs independent of white control. A year before he was involved as one of the rejected authors in the celebrated controversy with the American Baptist Publication Society, Emanuel K. Love, pastor of the historic First African Baptist Church in Savannah and president of the black Baptist Foreign Mission Convention, declared, "There is no doubt in my mind that Africa is our field of operation, and that [as] Moses was sent to deliver his brethren . . . God's purpose is to redeem Africa through us." Like Turner, he saw in this the "evils of slavery [being] turned to gracious account."[76] Meanwhile, black Baptists were also to be found among the ranks of those promoting emigration within the United States. When Love and several other black Baptists traveling with him to the Mission Convention's 1889 meeting were beaten by a white mob for taking seats in a "white" first-class railroad coach, two committees were dispatched by a group of Baptist organizations to convey a protest to President Harrison. The first committee declared that the beatings were part of a more general "reign of terror . . . in several of our southern states that is unparalled since the days of kukluxism," while the second—led by William J. Simmons, another of the principals in the dispute with the American Baptist Publication Society—suggested that it was "useless to hope for a change of sentiment in these sections of the South" and urged the president to ask Congress for $50,000,000 to "be appropriated to aid those who are thus situated to leave the South and settle on western lands." "The exodus of the Israelites from Egypt," they warned the president, "will be a small sized excursion compared to the move there will be [from] the South."[77] Clearly, such Baptist leaders as Emanuel Love and W. J. Simmons were the kindred spirits of Henry McNeal Turner rather than Daniel Alexander Payne. Indeed, when Simmons in 1887 published *Men of Mark: Eminent, Progressive and Rising*, a major collection of black biographical sketches, it included an entry on Simmons himself prepared by Bishop Turner, who praised him as a man whose motto was "God, my race and denomination."[78]

Yet for all its apparent triumph in the rise of the National Baptist Convention, a Turner-style version of exodus piety did not entirely carry the day among black Baptists—any more than it did among AMEs. The schisms in Texas and Georgia in 1893—as in Virginia in 1899—occurred because there were "cooperationists" and well as "separatists." In 1897 black Baptists (centered in North Carolina and Virginia), concerned to maintain a kind of black-white foreign missions collaboration that the National Baptist Convention Foreign Missionary Board opposed, formed the Lott Cary Foreign Mission Society, known after 1903 as the Lott Cary Foreign Missions Convention. Even Baptist congregations and associations affiliated with the National Baptist

Convention were, moreover, not always so willing as their national leaders to leave behind the old ways. Some continued to get their literature from the American Baptist Publishing Society rather than the Publishing Board of the new convention and to work more closely with the American Baptist Home Mission Society than some of their leaders thought wise. As Evelyn Brooks Higginbotham has shown, black Baptist women—even as they formed separate organizations of their own in the late nineteenth century—also maintained an "unlikely sisterhood" with white Baptist women organized in the Chicago-based Women's Baptist Home Mission Society and the Women's American Baptist Mission Society (of New England). Information, money, and personnel moved widely over a biracial Baptist women's network organized around a shared concern with soul-winning, moral development, and educational advancement.[79]

A common commitment to the perspectives and practices of evangelical Protestantism—as well as a continuing need among blacks for material, political, and cultural resources controlled by white religious organizations—similarly worked against complete racial separation in other denominational families as well. Black and white Methodists, who otherwise kept their distance from one another, seem to have been drawn together more commonly in late-nineteenth-century camp meetings than has sometimes been realized.[80] Blacks went to hear Dwight L. Moody and Sam Jones, the leading white revivalists of the time, and when Frank Bartleman set out across the South in 1897 with a "Bible wagon" sponsored by the proto-fundamentalist Moody Bible Institute of Chicago he initially found a more ready audience among blacks than among whites.[81] Maria Woodworth-Etter, a white holiness evangelist who later became an important Pentecostal leader, was sometimes called "the voodoo priestess" because her style of "trance evangelism" seemed so similar to patterns of religious ecstasy common among blacks. She also sometimes worked with a black song leader and spoke under black sponsorship.[82] The ability of radical revivalism to erode racial barriers was even more vividly demonstrated by the striking—if short-lived—biracialism of early Pentecostalism, so evident when the movement erupted into public view at the Azusa Street meetings in Los Angeles in 1906.[83] Meanwhile, a significant minority of black Christians eschewed the idea of an exodus church and remained, however uncomfortably, within the organizational structures of predominantly white denominations.[84]

Even within and among the black-controlled denominations themselves, moreover, the quest for a religiously grounded sense of black peoplehood often foundered on the hard rocks of ecclesiastical rivalry and self-interest. Just two decades after the National Baptist Convention was organized, the very enterprise that had most symbolized its dedication to racial solidarity and self-development—the Publishing Board—became the occasion for a major schism. Richard H. Boyd, the Texas Baptist who "ran the board as if it were his personal enterprise," resisted attempts to bring it more firmly under denominational control and in 1915 led in the creation of a second black Baptist denomination, the (similarly named) National Baptist Convention of America.[85] Meanwhile, repeated efforts to effect a merger of the three major independent black Methodist bodies—the AME Church, the AME Zion Church, and the Colored Methodist Episcopal Church—proved equally fruitless. The Zion Methodists were consistently willing to join such a new church, but in each case—the major efforts were in the Reconstruction period, the 1890s, and the World War I era—either the CMEs or the AMEs or both were unwilling. It may seem unsurprising that, when H. C. C. Astwood called in 1888 for the merger of all Methodist bodies—both black and white—as a fitting preparation for the racial inclusiveness of the end time, his appeal was unpersuasive. It is important to note, however, that appeals for a black Methodist merger to promote racial solidarity were equally ineffective. Indeed, when a serious plan was developed in 1892 to merge the AME and AME Zion denominations into a new African Zion Methodist Episcopal Church, even Henry McNeal Turner was unmoved by the prospect of a larger church with "African Zion" in its name. It would "blot out our individuality," Turner declared. Similarly, a CME leader who argued against another serious merger possibility in 1920 warned that it would "ask us to forget the past and traditions of our fathers." The cornerstones at Mother Bethel in Philadelphia, as at the comparable AMEZ and CME sites—Varick Temple in New York and Miles Chapel in Washington, D.C.—would have to be chiseled off and "United Methodist Episcopal Church" (the proposed name of the new denomination) carved in its place. "Forbid it Almighty God," he exclaimed.[86] Like the Israelites of old, who could not long live together in one kingdom even in the Promised Land, black Methodists and Baptists divided the Canaan of "independent ecclesiastical government" into several principalities.

Evelyn Brooks Higginbotham has argued that the separate organizations of black Baptist women—especially the Woman's Convention of the National Baptist Convention, founded in 1900—were not spaces for cultivation of either a racial or gender isolation but zones of empowerment from which black Baptist women could move out to collaborate with both black Baptist men and white Baptist women and participate effectively in the public life of America generally.[87] Something similar can be said of independent black religious organizations generally in the late-nineteenth- and early-twentieth-century United States. When the independent black churches saw their own life in exodus terms, they tapped deeply into the exodus piety that so profoundly informed African American religion. Yet the image masked some realities of their collective life even as it revealed others; it also set a standard of collective aspiration that was sometimes difficult to live up to. In the end, no single church was able to embody the black nation's soul, and the warning that Daniel Payne had given to those who sought an African exodus held true for those who pursued an ecclesiastical exodus as well. Wherever blacks went in the organizational world of American religion they found no place where they could entirely escape the presence of white people or the effects of their power. Like the Woman's Convention, the exodus churches were in the end less a way to escape religious interaction with whites than a means of restructuring that interaction, both practically and symbolically, and as such they were also powerfully effective. These zones of racial empowerment could also easily become, however, spaces for the cultivation of personal power and privilege; black denominational leaders, like their white counterparts, were not immune to the temptation to become, ironically, "at ease in Zion."

While black church leaders pursued or resisted the development of their denominations as exodus churches, ordinary southern black folk continued to suffer under the oppressive racial regime of the late-nineteenth- and early-twentieth-century South—and to seek some deliverance from it. One measure of this was the persistence throughout these decades of the migratory impulse itself—always smoldering and recurrently in flame. Quite apart from the episodic, highly visible, and politically controversial efforts of some blacks to relocate themselves en masse to Africa or the West, there was in the post-Reconstruction decades a steady, unobtrusive, but restless movement among individual black southerners—and their families—to find a less confining space for themselves. One recent student of black migration, William Cohen, has noted "how central mobility was to the concept of freedom" held by late-nineteenth- and early-twentieth-century black southerners. "Deprived of many of the most basic rights of citizenship," he observes, "they clung tenaciously to that most important of rights, the right to move." Hard economic realities, above all their extreme poverty, usually made long-distance moves more the stuff of dreams than a practical option. But local movement was a different matter. Every winter at the end of the crop year, thousands of black sharecroppers left the farms where they had been working and moved to new ones in the usually vain hope that they would find better treatment and a better income working for a different landowner. They also "moved back and forth between the agricultural and semi-industrial sectors of the economy," temporarily seeking better wages and more freedom in such activities as railroad building, the turpentine industry, lumbering, and sawmilling.[88] Throughout most of the period, moreover, there was a steady shift of the southern black population westward. In 1870, 45.4 percent of American blacks were to be found in the South Atlantic states (those lying along the East Coast from Maryland and Delaware to Florida), whereas only 15.2 percent lived in the West South Central area (Louisiana, Arkansas, and Texas). In the next forty years this 3:1 ratio declined to 2:1. By 1910 the percentage of the black population living in the South Atlantic states had fallen to 41.8 percent while that in the West South Central states (now also including the new state of Oklahoma) had risen to 20.2 percent.[89]

Meanwhile, throughout the era emigrationist dreams of a more organized and collective exodus persisted. In *Black Towns and Profit* Kenneth Marvin Hamilton has identified forty-five black communities founded in the Trans-Appalachian West between 1877 and 1915.[90] Thirty-two of those towns were in Oklahoma. When the federal government divided the Indian Territory in 1889 and opened the Oklahoma District to non-Indian settlement, some blacks—perhaps encouraged by the example of Mormon Utah—apparently cherished the hope that a rush of black homesteaders might take political control of the area and turn it into an all-black state.[91] Alarmist stories in the *New York Times* early in 1890 claimed that members of a black brotherhood organized the year before in Nicodemus, Kansas, had taken "an oath which declared eternal enmity to the white race, and bound its members to aid politically only the man who has negro blood." When interviewed, the reputed head of the organization insisted that its members did not "propose to impose upon the whites nor abuse our power. . . . We will simply stand by our people, and there can be but one result . . . a solid Negro State, the grandest in the Union."[92] Emigration activists hoped that Republican politician Edward McCabe, a founder of Nicodemus, promoter of the new black town of Langston City in Oklahoma, and the only black ever to hold statewide office in Kansas (he was auditor from 1882 to 1886) would be named governor of the new territory, but he was not. The *Times*'s sources claimed he would have been "assassinated, within a week after he enter[ed] the Territory . . . [because] of the rapidly growing . . . anti-negro sentiment caused by the aggressiveness of the blacks . . . which bids fair to unite the whites irrespective of party." Blacks saw McCabe's non-appointment and this newfound white political unity in a different light. "Oh, we were so sorry," a black Georgia preacher wrote to his denomination's weekly newspaper. He continued:

> This is a white man's country and government and he is proving it North, South, East and West, democrats and republicans. For my part, I am tired of both parties: The Negro's back is sleek where they have rode him so much.
> . . . In fighting for the rule of government the North and South are divided; when they reach the suppression of the Negro they are one. I am already a Christian and the first thing you know I will be voting the prohibitionist ticket. I love no one who does not love me.[93]

Disappointment with early developments in Oklahoma and disillusionment with the Republican Party did not, however, end the hope for a black state in the West. In the worsening racial climate of the 1890s the idea even found new supporters in unlikely places. The Colored Methodist Episcopal Church was the most politically cautious of the independent black Methodist denominations, with a reputation—undeserved its apologists claimed—for subservience to southern white Methodists. Of no one was this more true than Lucius H. Holsey, one of the denomination's leading bishops. Yet by the turn of the century the patient Holsey had given up hope for justice in a biracial society. Lamenting "the constant and universal tendency in the south to gradually reduce the great bulk of the negro race to a state of serfdom and peonage," to create in effect "a second form of old slavery," Holsey could "see no chance for the black man to arrive at his best and highest possibilities . . . in the same territory with the white people of the south." Blacks' only hope was to have entirely for themselves territory "from the western part of the public domain, such as a part of the Indian territory, or New Mexico, or other parts of the great West."[94]

As some blacks looked West, however, others once again turned East—to Africa. Not infrequently, in fact, African emigrationism recruited followers—and sometime leaders—from disillusioned participants in the westward movement. In 1885, after briefly promoting black emigration to Cyprus, "Pap" Singleton, the self-declared Moses of the 1879 exodus to Kansas, led in organizing the United Trans-Atlantic Society. This African emigrationist group declared that "we will . . . bridge the ocean, that the sons and daughters of Ham may return to their God-given inheritance, and Ethiopia regain her ancient renown, and be enhanced with modern splendor . . . the God of heaven marches with us and will manifest his power. The waters of adversity will tumble as did the walls of Jerico at the approach of Israel."[95]

Early in 1892, when Oklahoma still represented the promised land to many southern blacks, some black Oklahomans were already abandoning the area and turning their hopes to Africa. One such group, led by Prentiss H. Hill, an AME pastor and follower of Bishop Turner, arrived in New York in February 1892 expecting to board a ship for Liberia. The necessary arrangements with the American Colonization Society had not been made, however, and the group found itself literally on the Manhattan streets before being given temporary shelter in a Methodist mission. The New York press, which gave extensive coverage to the migrants' plight, reported on the efforts of Solomon Buckaloo, one of the older members of the group, to keep the exodus hope alive among his fellow Oklahomans. A reporter filed this account:

> After breakfast, Brother Buckaloo addressed the meeting and urged all to keep heart.
>
> "Yesterday mornin', chillen, Brother Brower was a-tellin' you to keep a trustin'. I can't give you no bettah 'vice dan dat, brudders and sisters. so to what Brother Brower said to you den I now jus' says. Heah! Heah! We is de Lord's chillen of Israel of de nineteenth centery: dere ain't no doubt at all about dat," cried Brother Buckaloo, bringing his fist down upon the table with a thump of affirmation.
>
> "If we can't get to Liberia any oder way, de Lord he'll just open up a parf through the ocean jes' as he did for dem oder chillen through the Red Sea. The 'Lantic Ocean is a mighty big pond, they tells me, and Liberia it lies a heap ob a way oft, but de Lord's equal to the occasion, brudders: don't you go and be forgettin dat. Liberia is so far that there ain't a man in the party—not even Brother 'Dolphus Kindle, and he's de best swimmer we'se got, as could swim more'n half way dah.
>
> "It's so long that none of us couldn't walk it even if the parf frough the sea was all ready made. We ain't got no mules like the oder chillen had, but that makes no difference, breddern.
>
> "De day ob de miracles ain't done yet, and if we get the road made for us dere will be street car tracks goin' along wif it, shuah as you live. An' then, breddern, we won't have to wait very long on de cornah before one ob them jingle-bell cabs ull be comin' along 'jes as dey do up on de avenue. The cornductor 'll say, 'All aboard from Liberia,' and we'll get on."[96]

The waters never parted, the trolley never arrived, and most of these would-be Liberians never reached their promised land, but the exodus hope persisted among blacks who failed to find their Zion in the American West. Two decades later, when disillusionment with their state's increasing segregationism (after its admission to the union in 1907)

again stirred African dreams among black Oklahomans, Solomon
Buckaloo's spiritual descendants made their presence known. When
Chief Albert C. Sam, a Gold Coast black, appeared in the state in the
summer of 1913, recruiting emigrants for his homeland, hundreds of
blacks responded to his appeal. As with the *Azor* in 1878, when Sam's
ship made its one voyage from Galveston it left hundreds of disappointed would-be emigrants standing on the shore.[97]

Oklahoma also produced during this period a new variation on the
black exodus tradition—or at least on the longstanding black Protestant habit of reading their own experience in relation to that of the
biblical Hebrews. Williams Saunders Crowdy (1847–1908), a Maryland former slave, Union Army veteran, and longtime resident of Kansas City, arrived in Oklahoma in September 1891. Taking up a farm
near Guthrie, he became a captain in the local black militia (at a time
when a violent racial confrontation over political control of the state
seemed a serious possibility), a Baptist deacon, and an active member
of the black, Prince Hall Masons. A year later he began to feel called
by God to some special mission. By the following spring, his visionary
experiences persuaded him that all existing churches—especially the
Baptist churches—were polluted and that God was calling him to found
the one true church. Itinerating in Texas and then traveling to Chicago and on to the Northeast, this "Black Elijah" formally established
the Church of God and Saints of Christ in Emporia, Kansas, in November 1896. The teachings and practices of the new church were highly eclectic. They included, for example, large elements of Masonic symbolism. Central to Crowdy's teaching, however, was the proposition
that blacks were the literal—not figurative—descendants of the lost
tribes of Israel. The true church was an inclusive one that rejected neither blacks nor the Hebrew tradition. In the new church, therefore,
Saturday was celebrated as the Sabbath, an annual Passover was observed, months were referred to by Jewish names, and officers were
given such titles as "Father Abraham." The group was never a large
one, and it quickly fell into the pattern of previous exodus groups by
purchasing some land in Virginia to serve as a literal promised land. It
did, however, set a pattern that would recur in later years of small
African American groups coming to see themselves as the literal and
distinctively authentic descendants of the ancient Israelites.[98]

At the end of the period, however, it is not the West, nor Africa, nor
a racial identification with the people of the Bible that moved multi-
tudes of African Americans. Rather, it was the prospect of an exodus
northward, to the states of the Northeast and old Midwest. With the
coming of World War I, and the unprecedented economic opportunity

it created for blacks in the North, the steady stream of black migration that had been flowing mostly to the Southwest turned northward and became a flood. In the forty years between 1870 and 1910 the percentage of blacks living in the tier of northern states stretching from New England and the Middle Atlantic area westward to the Mississippi had barely risen, from 9.3 percent to 10.5 percent. The Great Migration of 1916 to 1918 dramatically changed that. By 1920, 14.1 percent of American blacks lived in these northern states, and by 1930 that number would rise to 20.3 percent.[99]

Emmett Scott, whose *Negro Migration during the War* was the most important contemporary study of this upheaval, thought the exodus of 1916–18 bore "such a significant resemblance to the migration to Kansas in 1879 and the one to Arkansas and Texas in 1888 and 1889 that . . . [it could] be regarded as the same movement with intervals of a number of years." He also noted that the wartime migration, like its predecessors, "was hailed as the 'Exodus to the Promised Land' and characterized by the same frenzy and excitement." "The devout and religious," he observed, "saw God in the movement"—for example in the droughts, floods, and boll weevil infestation that plagued the South just as new economic possibilities had been opened by the labor shortage in the North. Scott cited one observer's report that train stations in some places struck by the exodus fever were so crowded that people were "like bees in a hive." "One old lady and man had gotten on the train," the observer noted; "They were patting their feet and singing and a man standing nearby asked, 'Uncle, where are you going?' The old man replied, 'Well, son, I'm gwine to the promised land.'" Scott also relayed reports of a group of 147 blacks from Hattiesburg, Mississippi, who "held solemn ceremonies" when they had crossed the Ohio River: "These migrants knelt down and prayed; the men stopped their watches and, amid tears of joy, sang the familiar songs of deliverance, 'I done come out of the Land of Egypt with good news.' The songs following in order were 'Beulah Land' and 'Dwelling in Beulah Land.' One woman of the party declared that she could detect an actual difference in the atmosphere beyond the Ohio River, explaining that it was much lighter and that she could get her breath more easily."[100] Reverdy C. Ransom, a Northern-based black social gospeller and editor of the *AME Review,* declared in 1917 that "we have already passed from the wilderness and have begun our victorious march around the Jericho walls of American prejudice and opportunity. Let the exodus from the South rise to the flood tide of multiplied thousands."[101]

It was this migration that finally brought blacks in very large numbers to what has so often been seen as the definitive terrain of post-

Protestant American religion—the industrial city of the Northeast and
Midwest. The ethnic and religious diversity of these cities' Euro-American
populations did not, however, make them an unproblematic
Canaan for newly arrived blacks. With the single exception of Chicago,
the polyethnic urban machines that increasingly governed the urban
North had little inclination to add blacks to their ranks. Trade
unions were often no more hospitable, and where they were black suspicions
of their intentions were not easily overcome. Blacks were aware,
moreover, that it was the shortage of immigrant labor that had provided
them with their economic opening during the war—an opening
that might well close if prewar immigration patterns reasserted themselves.
Nor were blacks bound to the newer immigrants—or many of
the older ones—by ties of a closely shared religious faith. Although the
number of black Catholics in the urban North would grow significantly
in the decades following 1930, it was initially very small. Judaism exerted
a fascination evident in a handful of converts and the continuing
elaboration of the "black Jewish" tradition that Crowdy had apparently
begun. But blacks initially experienced the pluralism of their new
environment as more alien than reassuring.[102]

Not surprisingly, the language of religious alienation that had flourished
in the South did not disappear in the northern city. Eventually,
new religious movements, identifying themselves in some way with
Islam, would become the most notable bearers of a rhetoric of deliverance
from white American space. The Nation of Islam, emerging out
of Detroit's black ghetto in the early 1930s, combined older desires for
a separate black state with newly minted doctrines and distinctive images
of a coming racial apocalypse. An earlier Islamicizing movement,
emerging in the period of the Great Migration itself, was the Moorish
Science Temple. Organized in Newark, New Jersey, in 1913 by a North
Carolina black who took the name Noble Drew Ali, the Moorish Science
Temple was in its beliefs and practices a highly eclectic combination
of elements from several Eastern religions, harmonial piety, Masonic
symbolism, and Islam. It called on blacks to recover their ancient
identity as Asiatics and to live in the United States as "Moorish Americans"
who defined themselves in relation to the world of Islam, not
European or Euro-American Christianity.[103]

Far more important than this movement in the aftermath of World
War I, however, was the Garvey movement, which represented the
culmination—but also the transformation—of the transatlantic exodus
tradition. A Jamaican journalist and racial activist, Marcus Mosiah
Garvey first came to the United States in 1916, a year after Henry
McNeal Turner's death. Two years later, he officially relocated to Har-

lem the headquarters of his recently formed (1914) Universal Negro Improvement Association and African Communities League. Launching local chapters in hundreds of small towns as well as all the major metropolitan centers, the UNIA quickly became the "largest mass-based protest movement in black American history."[104] With a motto of "One God! One Aim! One Destiny!" and a program that included the creation of the Black Star Steamship Line, the UNIA sought to promote black pride and self-determination by binding "Africa abroad" more closely to "Africa at home." Garvey particularly sought to mobilize the black Diaspora's support for Africa's postwar struggles for political independence and socioeconomic development. "Our Fatherland, Africa, is bleeding," he declared in 1919, "and she is now stretching forth her hands to her children in America, the West Indies and Central America and Canada to help her."[105] Alarming both political authorities in the United States and the colonial rulers of Africa, Garvey and his movement quickly became the target of governmental surveillance and undermining. Convicted on mail fraud charges in connection with the Black Star Steamship Line, Garvey was imprisoned in Atlanta in 1925, and the movement suffered a fragmentation and loss of momentum from which it never recovered.[106]

In some ways, Garveyism represented a direct extension of the older emigrationist tradition. Garvey sometimes promoted his steamship company by noting that "if you want to leave America, the West Indies, South and Central America for more prosperous fields, the Black Star Line will be at your service."[107] As Randall Burkett has observed, the Garvey movement also drew deeply on longstanding nationalist elements within African American religious traditions. Although sharply attacked by some segments of the black churches and their leaders, Garveyism was vigorously supported by others—and the movement itself had an important religious dimension. UNIA meetings followed a set ritual spelled out in the *Universal Negro Ritual,* whereas Garveyite doctrine was succinctly set forth in the *Universal Negro Catechism* written by George Alexander McGuire, one of the organization's chaplain-generals. Garvey himself can also seen, according to Burkett, "as a theologian concerned with constructing a coherent view of God, man, and the world." Some of the movement's religious elements were directly reminiscent of earlier emigrationist religion. One of the prescribed hymns for UNIA meetings was "From Greenland's Icy Mountains," the same missionary hymn that had been sung at the consecration of the *Azor* in 1878. Garveyite preachers on occasion compared Garvey to Moses, and it was even said that his pious Methodist mother had given him Mosiah as a middle name because she believed he had a special, God-given destiny.[108] Yet exodus imagery seems to have been marginal to most Garveyite rhetoric, and although the press often labeled the UNIA a "back-to-Africa" movement, its emphasis was far more on racial solidarity among a scattered people than their relocation to their ancestral homeland.[109] The Black Star Steamship Line was promoted primarily as a means of transatlantic black economic development, not a means of transporting emigrants. Buying stock was more important than buying a ticket, and to be in political solidarity with Africa one had to travel no further than one's local "Liberty Hall," where the UNIA held its meetings. Identifying with "Africa at home" did not mean that "Africa abroad" could no longer continue to make its home in America. But could it be truly at home there?

From the time of the Civil War and before, the emigrationist tradition had combined an exodus rhetoric with the acknowledged reality that most African Americans would continue to live in the United States—indeed, in the American South. In this respect, Garveyism shifted the emphasis within the tradition but did not fundamentally alter its basic structure. Henry McNeal Turner had insisted throughout his career that emigration to Africa was a realistic option for only a minority of black Americans. "I am no advocate for wholesale emigration," he declared, "such a course would be madness in the extreme and folly unpardonable." Those who stayed behind, however, had a critically important psychic stake in the emigrants' work, for those who went would "build a country and raise a national symbol that could give character to our people everywhere." African Americans' basic problem, Turner thought, was one of consciousness: they did not "respect black." Nothing would go farther toward curing that than the emigrants' creation of a fully autonomous modern black nation-state in Africa. It is a telling irony, however, that Turner, who declared that "to the negro in this country the American flag is a dirty and contemptible rag," nonetheless entertained an "African dream" that was in substance the American dream purged of racism—and assumed that Africans could not realize it without African American leadership.[110]

As many a disappointed late-twentieth-century reader of culturally relativistic proclivities has discovered to his or her chagrin, Turner—and others like him—had little interest in building anew on culturally African foundations. What they envisioned rather was an emigrant-built world of free market economy, liberal political institutions, and Protestant Christianity. Such themes carried over, moreover, into Garvey's UNIA, whose constitution announced that one of its aims was to "promote a conscientious Spiritual worship among the native tribes of Africa."[111] The Americanism of the West-oriented migration tradition was even more obvious. The hope for land that led many a southern black westward was often articulated in a language of economic autonomy and personal freedom commonly invoked by other migrants as well. Even more collectively defined visions of the black West also sometimes embraced America even as they rejected it. Bishop Holsey, sensitive to the turn-of-the-century mood of reconciliation between the North and the South, pled for a black state in the West on the grounds that this alone could bring the true national unity that all parties desired. "The Union of the States will never be fully and perfectly recemented with tenacious integrity," he argued, "until black Ham and white Japheth dwell together in separate tents."[112]

In one of his most celebrated essays, "Errand into the Wilderness," the literary and cultural historian Perry Miller contended that gloomy seventeenth-century American Puritan rhetoric about declension and apostasy had to be read as masking a deeper acceptance of the new land in which they had come to live. "Under the guise of this mounting wail of sinfulness, this incessant and never successful cry for repentance," Miller argued, "the Puritans launched themselves upon the process of Americanization."[113] The cases are in this respect similar, that late-nineteenth- and early-twentieth-century black exodus rhetoric was also a mode of implicitly coming to terms, albeit by way of explicit negation, with a life lived in American space. It remains a decisive difference, however, that African Americans' relation to the land was in its origins an involuntary one and that for the most part, even in this era, the land neither belonged to them nor they to the land. It is also a matter of no mean significance that in this great age of immigration, when millions of European immigrants found in the Atlantic Ocean a highway to their promised land, many African Americans saw it as a wall of water, shutting them up in the American Egypt. Africa abroad was not yet at home in the United States, and exodus piety was a way of embracing the land, but only as a stranger.[114]

Notes

1. The Puritan and pluralist tellings of the story of American religious history have appeared in myriad forms and innumerable places—from survey textbooks to highly influential cultural tracts. As examples of the latter, see Robert Bellah et al., *Habits of the Heart: Individualism and Commitment in American Life* (Berkeley: University of California Press, 1985); and Horace M. Kallen, *Culture and Democracy in the United States: Studies in the Group Psychology of the American People* (New York: Boni and Liveright, 1924).

2. I have previously addressed this characteristic exclusion of the South from the defining narratives of American religious history in "The Central Themes of American Religious History: Pluralism, Puritanism, and the Encounter of Black and White," *Religion and Intellectual Life* 5 (Fall 1987): 30–41; and "Forum: The Decade Ahead in Scholarship," *Religion and American Culture* 3 (Winter 1993): 15–22.

3. Orestes Brownson, "Mission of American," *Brownson's Quarterly Review*, New York series, 1 (Oct. 1856): 409–44, as excerpted in Aaron I. Abell, *American Catholic Thought on Social Questions* (Indianapolis: Bobbs-Merrill 1968), 19–37, quotations on 28 and 25.

4. Morton Borden, *Jews, Turks, and Infidels* (Chapel Hill: University of North Carolina Press, 1984), 21; Isaac Mayer Wise, "Our Country's Place in History," in *God's New Israel: Religious Interpretations of American Destiny*, ed. Conrad Cherry (Englewood Cliffs: Prentice-Hall, 1971), 218–28, quotation on 218.

5. Daniel Alexander Payne, *Recollections of Seventy Years* (Nashville: AME Sunday School Union, 1888, repr. New York: Arno Press, 1969), 28.

6. The exodus theme has long attracted the attention of students of African American religious history. I am especially indebted to the work of Albert J. Raboteau. See, for example, his "African-Americans, Exodus, and the American Israel," in *African-American Christianity: Essays in History*, ed. Paul E. Johnson (Berkeley: University of California Press, 1994), 1–17, where he contends that "no single symbol captures more clearly the distinctiveness of Afro-American Christianity than the symbol of Exodus" (9). This and other of Raboteau's essays touching on the exodus theme are also included in *Fire in the Bones: Reflections on African American Religious History* (Boston: Beacon Press, 1995). See also Theophus H. Smith, *Conjuring Culture: Biblical Formations of Black America* (New York: Oxford University Press, 1994), 55–80.

7. U.S. Department of Commerce, Bureau of the Census, *The Social and Economic Status of the Black Population in the United States: An Historical View, 1790–1978*, Current Population Reports, special studies series P-23, no. 80 (Washington: Government Printing Office, 1979), 13, 17. It is important to note that the South, as the Census Bureau defines it, includes Delaware, the District of Columbia, Maryland, West Virginia, Kentucky, and Oklahoma as well as the states of the Confederacy.

8. The most important recent account of the Reconstruction era is Eric Foner, *Reconstruction: America's Unfinished Revolution, 1863–1877* (New York: Harper and Row, 1988). A succinct account of the collapse of the Reconstruction and the consequent "triumph of white supremacy" may be found in John Hope Franklin and Alfred A. Moss, Jr., *From Slavery to Freedom: A History of Negro Americans*, 6th ed. (New York: Knopf, 1988), 229–38.

9. One evidence of this is the publication during these years of many works reporting on "the progress of the race." See, for example, G. F. Richings, *Evidences of Progress among Colored People* (Philadelphia: Geo. S. Ferguson, 1896), which was eventually published in twelve editions. The most impor-

tant recent study of the upper strata of black America during this period is Willard B. Gatewood, *Aristocrats of Color: The Black Elite, 1880–1920* (Bloomington: Indiana University Press, 1990).

10. The *News and Courier* story of March 22, 1878, was reprinted with a brief introduction in the April 4, 1878, edition of the *Christian Recorder* (hereafter cited as *CR*) under the headline "Consecration of the Exodus Bark, 'Azor.'" Turner's comments were made in his column "Wayside Dots and Jots," *CR*, April 18, 1878. See also George B. Tindall, "The Liberian Exodus of 1878," *South Carolina Historical Magazine* 53 (1952): 133–45.

11. The literature on emigrationism and colonizationism is extensive. Floyd J. Miller, *The Search for a Black Nationality: Black Emigration and Colonization, 1787–1863* (Urbana: University of Illinois Press, 1975), remains a sound survey and analysis of these movements in the antebellum period. On Quamino, Yamma, Hopkins, and Stiles, see also Joseph A. Conforti, *Samuel Hopkins and the New Divinity Movement* (Grand Rapids: Christian University Press, 1981), 142–58. Another study of Cuffee is Lamont D. Thomas, *Rise to Be a People: A Biography of Paul Cuffee* (Urbana: University of Illinois Press, 1986), which was published in a paperback edition under the title *Paul Cuffee: Black Entrepreneur and Pan-Africanist* (Urbana: University of Illinois Press, 1988). Willis Dolmon Boyd, "Negro Colonization in the Reconstruction Era, 1865–1870," *Georgia Historical Quarterly* 40 (1965): 360, has observed that by "the late 1850's some eleven thousand" African Americans had been colonized by the ACS. William Cohen, *At Freedom's Edge: Black Mobility and the Southern White Quest for Racial Control, 1861–1915* (Baton Rouge: Louisiana State University Press, 1991), 139, gives a total of 10,802 for the period through 1865 and reports that another 1,227 were colonized during these same years by the Maryland Colonization Society.

12. Boyd, "Negro Colonization," 360–61, 374–74; Miller, *Search for a Black Nationality*, 262–63.

13. "Sixty-first Annual Report of the American Colonization Society," *African Repository* 54 (April 1878): 35 (hereafter cited as *AR*).

14. Boyd, "Negro Colonization," 377.

15. Cohen, *At Freedom's Edge*, 142–46.

16. Ibid., 153; "A Remarkable Man for Liberia," *AR* 47 (Sept. 1871): 280–82, quotation on 281; and "Departure of Our Fall Expedition," *AR* 47 (Dec. 1871): 353–54, 356–60. See also, on Hill's activity as a Union League leader and beating by the Ku Klux Klan, Herbert Shapiro, *White Violence and Black Response: From Reconstruction to Montgomery* (Amherst: University of Massachusetts Press, 1988), 22–23.

17. "Address of the Elizabeth City [N.C.] Freedmen's Emigrant Aid Society," *AR* 47 (May 1871): 156.

18. John Orcutt to William Coppinger, April 16, 1866, "Letters Received," American Colonization Society Papers, vol. 153, no. 43, Library of Congress, Washington, D.C., cited in Boyd, "Negro Colonization," 364.

19. Cohen, *At Freedom's Edge*, 155.

20. For a general discussion of Liberian emigration movements of the late

1870s, see Nell Irwin Painter, *Exodusters: Black Migration to Kansas after Reconstruction* (New York: Norton, 1976), 137–45, and Cohen, *At Freedom's Edge*, 154–67. See also Adell Patton, Jr., "The 'Back-to-Africa' Movement in Arkansas," *Arkansas Historical Quarterly* 51 (Summer 1992): 164–77.

21. S. D. Alexander, "Letter to the Editor of the World," *AR* 54 (Jan. 1878): 26.

22. "Contemplated Exodus," *AR* 54 (April 1878): 35–37.

23. Tindall, "Liberian Exodus," 135.

24. Ibid., 139–43.

25. William Loren Katz, *The Black West*, 3d ed. (Seattle: Open Hand Publishing, 1987), 12–15, 23–138, provides a highly impressionistic overview of black life in the antebellum West, with strong emphasis on "western colorphobia." For a general account see also W. Sherman Savage, *Blacks in the West* (Westport: Greenwood Press, 1976), especially 1–47. David A. Gerber, *Black Ohio and the Color Line, 1860–1915* (Urbana: University of Illinois Press, 1976), 3–24, presents a succinct but nuanced account that stresses the local variation of black life in the first state of the Old Northwest. Miller discusses Canadian emigration in *Search for a Black Nationality*, see especially 105–15, 157–59. For an increased sense of the importance of the West in the study of African American religious history I am greatly indebted to Laurie F. Maffly-Kipp.

26. The main studies of black migration to Kansas in the late 1870s are Painter, *Exodusters*, and Robert G. Athearn, *In Search of Canaan: Black Migration to Kansas, 1879–80* (Lawrence: University of Kansas Press, 1978). See also Cohen, *At Freedom's Edge*, 168–97, and John G. Van Deusen, "The Exodus of 1879," *Journal of Negro History* 21 (April 1936): 111–29.

27. On Singleton's early migration activity and later career, see Painter, *Exodusters*, 108–34, and Walter L. Fleming, "'Pap' Singleton, The Moses of the Colored Exodus," *American Journal of Sociology* 15 (July 1909): 61–82. On the founding and development of Nicodemus, see Glen Schwendemann, "Nicodemus: Negro Haven on the Solomon," *Kansas Historical Quarterly* 34 (Spring 1968): 10–31, and Kenneth Marvin Hamilton, *Black Towns and Profit: Promotion and Development in the Trans-Appalachian West, 1877–1915* (Urbana: University of Illinois Press, 1991), 5–42.

28. Simon P. Roundtree is consistently identified in all accounts as a member of the clergy but little information is provided regarding his prior or subsequent ministerial career. The Rev. M. M. Bell led three hundred blacks from Lexington, Kentucky, to Nicodemus in September 1877; the Rev. Daniel Hickman, a Baptist, brought another colony from the same state in March 1878; in the spring of 1879, a "Rev. Goodwin" brought fifty blacks from Mississippi to the town (Schwendemann, "Nicodemus," 14–15). Columbus M. Johnson, whom Painter, *Exodusters*, 111, describes as "associated with Singleton perhaps longer than any other man," is identified as "an itinerant preacher" by Roy Garvin, "Benjamin, or 'Pap,' Singleton and His Followers," *Journal of Negro History* 33 (Jan. 1948): 9. Katz, *Black West*, 169, reprints circular number 1 of the Edgefield Real Estate Association (with which Singleton was

also associated), which states, "We pray that every minister of the gospel of Jesus Christ will take an active part in this work, as we feel it their duty, irrespective of their denominations." The group's weekly meetings in Nashville were held in the Second Baptist Church. See also Fleming, "'Pap' Singleton,'" 63 (meetings in churches), 65 (giving literature to traveling preachers), and 67–68 (exodus songs); Painter, *Exodusters,* 129 (text of song), and 156 (letters read in churches); and Hamilton, *Black Towns,* 8–9 (circulars mailed to churches).

29. Testimony of Benjamin Singleton in U.S. Congress, Senate, *Report and Testimony of the Select Committee of the United States Senate to Investigate the Causes of the Removal of the Negroes from the Southern States to the Northern States, Part III,* Senate Report 693, 46th Cong., 2d sess. (Washington: Government Printing Office, 1880), 381.

30. Fleming, "'Pap' Singleton,'" 70.

31. Painter, *Exodusters,* 184–201, 250–55; Cohen, *At Freedom's Edge,* 176–81.

32. Painter, *Exodusters,* 147. For a careful analysis of the numbers of blacks migrating to Kansas throughout the 1870s, see Cohen, *At Freedom's Edge,* 301–11.

33. *St. Louis Globe-Democrat,* March 19, 1879, as cited in Painter, *Exodusters,* 195.

34. Nell Irwin Painter, "Millennarian Aspects of the Exodus to Kansas of 1879," *Journal of Social History* 9 (Spring 1976): 33, quotes this statement and cites the *St. Louis Globe-Democrat,* March 12, 1879. She quotes the same passage, however, in *Exodusters,* 187, and cites as the source F. R. Guernsey, "The Negro Exodus," *International Review* 7 (Oct. 1879): 375.

35. Painter, "Millennarian Aspects," 331. For a critique of Painter's view that the 1879 exodus to Kansas was a millenarian movement, see Cohen, *At Freedom's Edge,* 181–83.

36. S. A. Hackworth to Governor St. John, Brenham, Texas, Aug. 11, 1879, "Correspondence Received," St. John subject file, box 10, Kansas State Historical Society, Topeka, as cited in Painter, *Exodusters,* 196.

37. Reliable membership statistics for the late-nineteenth-century black denominations are not easily obtained. W. E. B. Du Bois, *The Negro Church: Report of a Social Study Made under the Direction of Atlanta University; Together with the Proceedings of the Eighth Conference for the Study of Negro Problems Held at Atlanta University, May 26th, 1903* (Atlanta: Atlanta University, 1903), reprinted in *The Atlanta University Publications: Nos. 1, 2, 4, 8, 9, 11, 13, 14, 15, 16, 17, 18* (New York: Arno Press, 1968), a pioneering sociological study of the black churches, probably contains the single best set of statistics and includes figures from the 1890 census. Du Bois gives AME Church membership as 402,638 for 1880 (126). He does not, however, provide comparable 1880 membership figures for the AME Zion Church. He does cite the 1890 census figures for the two denominations—452,725 and 349,788, respectively—and gives 1903 membership figures of 785,000 and 551,591 for the two churches (38, 153). These figures put AMEZ membership at around

178 DAVID W. WILLS

78 percent of AME membership in 1890 and about 70 percent in 1903. If the relationship between the two denominations was somewhere within this range in 1880, AMEZ membership would have been between about 280,000 and 315,000.

38. Du Bois, *Negro Church,* reports CME membership at 67,889 in 1872 (133), at 129,383 in 1890 (38), at 200,000 in 1896 (133), and at 207,723 in 1903 (153).

39. Ibid., 38. The 1890 census gives a membership of 246,249 for the black congregations within the ME churches; a small number of blacks also presumably belonged to predominantly white ME congregations.

40. James M. Washington, *Frustrated Fellowship: The Black Baptist Quest for Social Power* (Macon: Mercer University Press, 1986), 140, describes "the jubilation and surprise that greeted" this report. Du Bois, *Negro Church,* 38, reports 1890 census figures of 1,348,000 "Regular Baptists" and more than 50,000 members of smaller Baptist constituencies, which put a Baptist total of around 1,400,000 beside a Methodist total of about 1,200,000. Although blacks were also to be found among Episcopalians, Presbyterians, Congregationalists, Lutherans, and other Protestant groups, as well as among Roman Catholics, none of those constituencies—not even all of them together—remotely approached in numbers the black Baptists or Methodists.

A general survey of late-nineteenth-century black churches appears in William E. Montgomery, *Under Their Own Vine and Fig Tree: The African-American Church in the South, 1865–1900* (Baton Rouge: Louisiana State University Press, 1993), which omits the North, however, and is also much stronger for the Reconstruction era than for the period from 1877 to 1900. See also Carter G. Woodson, *The History of the Negro Church,* 3d. ed. (Washington: Associated Publishers, 1972), 180–289, for a general survey of black church history from Reconstruction to World War I.

41. Tindall, "Liberian Exodus," 135, identifies Bouey as secretary. The brief biographical sketch provided in William J. Simmons, *Men of Mark: Eminent, Progressive and Rising* (Cleveland: George Rewell, 1887, repr. Chicago: Johnson Publishing, 1970), 675–76, does not give a date for Bouey's ordination, saying only that it took place after he was "counted out" as sheriff of Edgefield County, South Carolina, in the election of 1876, but it seems probable that it occurred before March 1878. Walter L. Williams, *Black Americans and the Evangelization of Africa, 1877–1900* (Madison: University of Wisconsin Press, 1982), 40, identifies Bouey as an *Azor* migrant, but Simmons mentions no trip to Africa before 1879.

42. Tindall, "Liberian Exodus," 134–35 (Porter); Richard R. Wright, Jr., *The Bishops of the African Methodist Episcopal Church* (Nashville: AME Sunday School Union, 1963), provides brief biographical sketches of Cain (119–22), Turner (329–41), and Brown (111–14). Turner is also the subject of a modern biographical study: Stephen Ward Angell, *Bishop Henry McNeal Turner and African-American Religion in the South* (Knoxville: University of Tennessee Press, 1992). Both Cain and Turner were elected to four-year terms as denominational officers in 1876, but Cain was removed from office in 1879,

ostensibly because his service in Congress too much interfered with his job as missionary secretary; see Angell, *Bishop Henry McNeal Turner,* 141. Cain was elected to Congress in 1872 and again in 1876 and served in the Forty-fifth (1873–75) and Forty-seventh (1877–79) Congresses. For his career in South Carolina, see also Joel Williamson, *After Slavery: The Negro in South Carolina during Reconstruction, 1861–1877* (Chapel Hill: University of North Carolina Press, 1965), and Thomas Holt, *Black over White: Negro Political Leadership in South Carolina during Reconstruction* (Urbana: University of Illinois Press, 1977).

43. "Emigration: What Thought of It," *CR,* April 11, 1878.

44. Besides reporting on the resolutions of the Philadelphia Preachers Meeting, for example, *CR,* April 11, 1878, carried the following related articles: H. M. Turner, "African Movement" (reports on a Washington meeting where a resolution condemning Cain, Turner, and Porter "as traitors and enemies of their race" was introduced); Joseph E. Cook, "Emigration Discussion" (reporting on an emigration debate at Hampton Institute); and "Report of the Meeting of the Literacy Society of Bethel Church, Philadelphia, April 2, 1878" (also an emigration debate). For the debates and resolutions of three annual conferences—all unfavorable but none from the Deep South—see "Annual Session of the Baltimore Conference," *CR,* May 23, 1878; "Report on African Emigration–N.J. Conference," *CR,* July 4, 1878; and "The Exodus Movement in the N.E. Conference," *CR,* May 30, 1878. Painter, *Exodusters,* 268, reports that "the 1879 volume [of the *Christian Recorder*] has been absent, since the 1930s, from the files of both Mother Bethel A.M.E. Church in Philadelphia and Drew University," which makes it impossible to examine in an equally detailed way the debate within the denomination over the Kansas exodus of 1879. For a general discussion of the AME debate over emigrationism in the late 1870s, with an emphasis on Henry McNeal Turner's role, see Angell, *Bishop Henry McNeal Turner,* 133–41.

45. W. H. Yeocum, "The One Hundredth Anniversary," *CR,* Sept. 29, 1887.

46. An open letter containing this resolution, a list of the committees appointed to implement it, and recommendations for observing the centennial was published in every issue of the *Christian Record* between September 15 and November 24, 1887—and presumably through the earlier months of the year as well—under the title "Centennial of the African M. E. Church." See also *The Doctrines and Disciplines of the African Methodist Episcopal Church* (Philadelphia: African Methodist Connection in the United States, 1817, repr. Atlanta: n.p., 1917), 11–14.

47. Richard Allen, *The Life, Experience, and Gospel Labours of the Rt. Rev. Richard Allen. . . . Written by Himself* (Philadelphia: Martin and Budon, 1833, repr. Nashville: Abingdon, 1960), 25–26. Modern reprintings seem universally to omit the first comma in the title.

48. Quotation from "Centennial of the African M.E. Church," *CR,* Sept. 15, 1887, and subsequently. As is usually the case where "national" memory is being shaped or celebrated, very mundane interests and rivalries were also

at stake. Raising money to retire the debt of the AME publication department was one of the celebration's goals, and this seems to have occasioned some resistance. Apparently there were also complaints from a now largely southern church about the inevitably Philadelphia-centered character of the centennial. See, for example, the somewhat defensive editorial, "It's the Centennial of Our Church," *CR*, Sept. 29, 1887.

49. This arresting image of a united people marching out of ecclesiastical Egypt and never looking back seems to have influenced some of the older historical narratives of the AME Church's origins—at the price of some confusion about the actual chain of events. Woodson, *Negro Church*, 64, sees the gallery incident as antecedent to the creation of the Free African Society, a black voluntary association from which St. Thomas African Episcopal Church, the first black Episcopal congregation in America, and Bethel African Methodist Church eventually emerged. This version of events can be traced as far back as William Douglass, *Annals of the First African Church, in the United States of America* (Philadelphia: King and Baird, 1862), 9–13. Because the Free African Society was organized in April 1787, this would place the gallery incident in the spring of that year. The traditional date among AMEs has been November 1787—the date given in the historical preface to the denomination's first *Discipline*.

Either date, however, seems problematic. Arguing in part from records showing that the gallery at St. George's Methodist Episcopal Church was not completed until the early 1790s, Milton Sernett, *Black Religion and American Evangelicalism: White Protestants, Plantation Missions, and the Flowering of Negro Christianity, 1787–1865* (Metuchen: Scarecrow Press, 1975), 117, has contended that the gallery incident must have occurred "around the middle of 1792." If so, it occurred some five years after the creation of the Free African Society, and the latter cannot therefore have been a "post-exodus" first step in institution-building.

Allen, *Life Experience, and Gospel Labours*, 24, observes that as early as 1786 he wanted to build "a place of worship for the colored people" but was blocked in doing so by "the most respectable people of color" in Philadelphia. These "respectable people of color" were presumably not Methodists and in any case were not prepared to fall in line behind the young (twenty-six), newly arrived Allen. The Free African Society, which Allen never dominated, was apparently organized in 1787 as a more acceptable alternative to a black Methodist church—and even after the gallery incident the latter never became the common project of all black Philadelphians, or even of all black Philadelphia Methodists, some of whom stayed in the ME Church. The lesson here is that the traditional origin narratives of the earliest black churches must be read on at least two levels: as sources for a critical reconstruction of events and also as community-creating stories with their own inner logic.

50. J. A. Jones, "Richard Allen, the Second Reformer," *CR*, March 29, 1888. The image of Allen as a second Luther could lead to a less nationalistic picture of Allen than that usually associated with the exodus motif—but not necessarily so. See, for example, the comparison of Luther and Allen offered

in A. J. Moore, "The A.M.E. Church and Its Relation to Race Elevation," *CR*, Dec. 1, 1887, which concludes with the statement "Allen occupied the same relation to the negroes of America that Luther did to the Anglo-Saxons." In any case, as important as the exodus analogy was, it was by no means the sole nor always even the dominant image used by AMEs in defining themselves. A full study of the range of biblical and historical precedents employed in this process has yet to be made.

51. Benjamin T. Tanner, "Crimes of Caste against Christ," *AME Church Review* 4 (Jan. 1888): 336 (hereafter cited as *AMECR*).

52. Edward A. Clark, "The A.M.E. Church and the Colored Race," *CR*, Feb. 2, 1888.

53. H. C. C. Astwood, "Shall the Name of the African Methodist Episcopal Church Be Changed to That of the Allen Methodist Episcopal Church?" *AMECR* 4 (Jan. 1888): 319; Daniel A. Payne, *History of the African Methodist Episcopal Church*, ed. Charles S. Smith (Nashville: Publishing House of the A.M.E. Sunday School Union, 1891, repr. New York: Johnson Reprint, 1968), 481, briefly discusses Astwood and the state of the San Domingo mission in late 1887. Astwood was also U.S. consul there at the time.

54. John T. Jenifer, "The Centennial of African Methodism," *CR*, Sept. 8, 1887.

55. Much information on the life of this historic congregation in the late nineteenth and early twentieth centuries is to be found in Robert Gregg, *Sparks from the Anvil of Oppression: Philadelphia's African Methodists and Southern Migrants* (Philadelphia: Temple University Press, 1993). On the role of the site itself, see especially 185–86 and 256n47.

56. "The Bethel (Phila) Cornerstone Laid," *CR*, Nov. 14, 1889.

57. "Reinterment Services," *CR*, May 11, 1901.

58. Astwood, "Shall the Name . . . Be Changed?" 318, 319, 321, 320.

59. The standard accounts of Payne's life are his own *Recollections of Seventy Years* (Nashville: AME Sunday School Union, 1888, repr. New York: Arno Press, 1969), and Josephus R. Coan, *Daniel Alexander Payne: Christian Educator* (Philadelphia: AME Book Concern, 1935). These are supplemented by two unpublished dissertations: Charles Denmore Killian, "Bishop Daniel Alexander Payne: Black Spokesman for Reform," Ph.D. diss., Indiana University, 1971, and Arthur Paul Stokes, "Daniel Alexander Payne: Churchman and Educator," Ph.D. diss., Ohio State University, 1975. See also David W. Wills, "Womanhood and Domesticity in the A.M.E. Tradition: The Influence of Daniel Alexander Payne," in *Black Apostles at Home and Abroad: Afro-Americans and the Christian Mission from the Revolution to Reconstruction*, ed. David W. Wills and Richard Newman (Boston: G. K. Hall, 1982), 133–46.

60. Daniel A. Payne, "Thoughts about the Past, the Present and the Future of the African M.E. Church, *AMECR* 1 (July 1884): 1–8, and 1 (April 1885): 314–20, emphasis in the original. Payne appears to have taken a conventional Christian attitude toward Judaism as the relic of an earlier divine dispensation now displaced by Christianity. It is also clear that his thinking about the history and destiny of the AME Church was importantly shaped by

his views on what, for Christians, is the relation between the Old and New Testaments. Questions about the proper interpretation of this relation are inevitably raised, of course, implicitly if not explicitly, any time Christians draw analogies between themselves and ancient Israelites.

61. He did, however, argue with regard to the selection of faculty at AME colleges that "ignoring the miserable, puerile and heathenish question of color, the Professors must not be chosen because they be black, or white, but because they be *competent.*" Payne, "Thoughts about the Past," 6, emphasis in the original.

62. Ibid., 4–5, 319.

63. Daniel A. Payne, "African Emigration, or Colored Americans and Africa—Colored Americans and America," *CR*, July 25, 1878.

64. On the controversy surrounding Cain and Turner at the General Conference of 1880, see Angell, *Bishop Henry McNeal Turner*, 145–56.

65. Ibid., 157–252, examines Turner's career as an AME bishop, with special attention to the regional politics of the denomination.

66. Henry McNeal Turner, "Reply to Bishop Payne," *CR*, Aug. 22, 1878; see also Edwin S. Redkey, *Black Exodus: Black Nationalist and Back-to-Africa Movements, 1890–1910* (New Haven: Yale University Press, 1969), 27–28. *Black Exodus* remains the fullest account of Turner's career as an emigrationist.

67. Redkey, *Black Exodus*, 73–149. Turner was offered the secretaryship of the ACS in 1892 (128).

68. *CR*, Dec. 13, 1883, as cited in Redkey, *Black Exodus*, 42.

69. Ibid., 194–286. Turner was after 1900 no longer in control of the *Voice of Missions*, the official paper of the AME missionary department. He therefore launched a new paper, the *Voice of the People*. Redkey, *Black Exodus*, 261; Angell, *Bishop Henry McNeal Turner*, 239.

70. *Atlanta Constitution*, Feb. 16, 1906, as reprinted in *Respect Black: The Writings and Speeches of Henry McNeal Turner*, comp. and ed. Edwin S. Redkey (New York: Arno Press, 1971), 196–97.

71. Mungo M. Ponton, *Life and Times of Henry M. Turner* (Atlanta: A. B. Caldwell, 1917, repr. New York: Negro Universities Press, 1970), 137, reports simply that Turner was found unconscious on a wharf at Windsor on the morning of May 8 and died just after noon. Lerone Bennett, *Before the Mayflower: A History of the Negro in America, 1619–1964*, rev. ed. (Baltimore: Penguin, 1966), 226, quotes, without direct citation, Lawrence D. Reddick's view that "when [Turner] felt that his last days on earth were near, he deliberately dragged himself off to Canada, in order not to die on American soil." Angell, *Bishop Henry McNeal Turner*, reports that a fellow AME bishop, Joseph S. Flipper, claimed that Turner had a premonition that he would die during the Canadian trip but proceeded with it against advice to the contrary—which is perhaps the source of Reddick's judgment.

72. This phrase appears as one of the chapter titles in Washington, *Frustrated Fellowship*, the most reliable account of the nineteenth-century black

Baptist institution-building that culminated in the creation of the National Baptist Convention.

73. Ibid., 159–85; see also Montgomery, *Under Their Own Vine*, 239–51.

74. Williams, *Black Americans and the Evangelization of Africa*, 66. Bouey's career also receives passing mention in Sandy D. Martin, *Black Baptists and African Missions: The Origins of a Movement, 1880–1915* (Macon: Mercer University Press, 1989).

75. Redkey, *Black Exodus*, 152, 161–69.

76. Baptist Foreign Mission Convention, *Minutes*, 1889, 7–8, as cited in Washington, *Frustrated Fellowship*, 137. The idea of a special black American destiny to Christianize or "redeem" Africa was often linked to Psalm 68:31: "Princes shall come out of Egypt and Ethiopia shall soon stretch forth her hands unto God." For a general discussion of this motif, often referred to as "Ethiopianism," in nineteenth-century African American religious history, see Albert J. Raboteau, "'Ethiopia Shall Soon Stretch Forth Her Hands': Black Destiny in Nineteenth-Century America," in *Fire in the Bones*, ed. Raboteau, 37–56. Although black Baptists and Methodists played an important role in developing and promoting this idea, major contributions were made as well by Edward Wilmot Blyden, a black Presbyterian from St. Thomas, and black American Episcopal priests Alexander Crummell and James Theodore Holly. See Hollis R. Lynch, *Edward Wilmot Blyden: Pan-Negro Patriot 1832–1912* (New York: Oxford University Press, 1967); Wilson Jeremiah Moses, *Alexander Crummell: A Study of Civilization and Discontent* (New York: Oxford University Press, 1989); and David Dean, *Defender of the Race: James Theodore Holly, Black Nationalist Bishop* (Boston: Lambeth Press, 1979).

77. "The Baptist Demand," *Washington Bee*, Nov. 9, 1889, partially cited in Washington, *Frustrated Fellowship*, 155.

78. Simmons, *Men of Mark*, 5–19, quotation on 15.

79. Montgomery, *Under Their Own Vine*, 239–51; Washington, *Frustrated Fellowship*, 193–96; Williams, *Black Americans and the Evangelization of Africa*, 70; Evelyn Brooks Higginbotham, *Righteous Discontent: The Women's Movement in the Black Baptist Church, 1880–1920* (Cambridge: Harvard University Press, 1993), 88–119.

80. See, for example, John W. Bishop, "The Good of Camp Meetings," *CR*, Oct. 10, 1878; and Willard B. Gatewood, Jr., ed., *Slave and Freeman: The Autobiography of George L. Knox* (Lexington: University Press of Kentucky, 1979), 122–30.

81. See, for example, Dorothy Sterling, ed., *We Are Your Sisters: Black Women in the Nineteenth Century* (New York: Norton, 1987), 483 (excerpt from Ida B. Wells's diary, Feb. 8, 1886, on Moody); "Jones and Small in Baltimore, Md.," *Star of Zion*, May 21, 1886; and Frank Bartleman, *From Plow to Pulpit, from Maine to California* (Los Angeles: n.p., 1949), 39–63, reprinted in *Witness to Pentecost: The Life of Frank Bartleman*, ed. Cecil M. Robeck, Jr. (New York: Garland, 1985).

82. Wayne E. Warner, *The Woman Evangelist: The Life and Times of Char-*

184 DAVID W. WILLS

ismatic Evangelist Maria B. Woodworth-Etter (Metuchen: Scarecrow Press, 1986), 47, 79, 82, 150, 214–15, 245.

83. The most complete account of the black role in early Pentecostalism is Douglas J. Nelson, "For Such a Time as This: The Story of Bishop William J. Seymour and the Azusa Street Revival," Ph.D. diss., University of Birmingham, England, 1981. For a different view, see James R. Goff, Jr., *Fields White unto Harvest: Charles F. Parham and the Missionary Origins of Pentecostalism* (Fayetteville: University of Arkansas Press, 1988), 106–46. Much useful information on the role of blacks in early Pentecostalism is also to be found in *Dictionary of Pentecostal and Charismatic Movements,* ed. Stanley M. Burgess and Gary B. McGee (Grand Rapids: Regency, 1988). A better understanding of the early history of blacks in the Pentecostal movement is dependent on a fuller examination of their earlier involvement—in both biracial and black settings—in the holiness movement. An important contribution is David Douglas Daniels III, "The Cultural Renewal of Slave Religion: Charles Price Jones and the Emergence of the Holiness Movement in Mississippi," Ph.D. diss., Union Theological Seminary, 1992. See also Michael Mullins, "Re-Envisioning the Borders of the Sanctified Church: The Holiness Idea in the African Methodist Episcopal Tradition," B.A. thesis, Amherst College, 1996. More study is also needed of the role in late-nineteenth- and early-twentieth-century black piety of images of a future deliverance other than those associated with exodus imagery or Ethiopianism, for example, the curious case of the "Christ Craze" in Liberty County, Georgia: see "Calls Himself Christ" and untitled story on the same subject, *Savannah Tribune,* June 29, July 20, 1889.

84. For a sketch of the history of blacks within—and in relation to—the "Protestant establishment" from the end of the nineteenth century to the civil rights era, see David W. Wills, "An Enduring Distance: Black Americans and the Establishment" in *Between the Times: The Travail of the Protestant Establishment in America, 1900–1960,* ed. William R. Hutchison (New York: Cambridge University Press, 1989), 168–92.

85. Montgomery, *Under Their Own Vine,* 335–36.

86. Dennis C. Dickerson, "Black Ecumenism: Efforts to Establish a United Methodist Episcopal Church, 1918–1932," *Church History* 52 (Dec. 1983): 479–91, quotations on 482, 484.

87. Higginbotham, *Righteous Discontent,* 1–18 and following.

88. Cohen, *At Freedom's Edge,* xiii, xvi (quotations), 131–35 (end of the year and seasonal movement). See also Nicholas Lemann, *The Promised Land: The Great Black Migration and How It Changed America* (New York: Knopf, 1991), 1–21, which, however, focusses primarily on the 1930s and the massive northward migration that began around 1940.

89. U.S. Department of Commerce, Bureau of the Census, *Negroes in the United States, 1920–1932* (Washington, D.C.: Government Printing Office, 1935), 5.

90. The list is given in Hamilton, *Black Towns,* 153. Hamilton's concern is to see these towns "as an integral part of the frontier urban settlement process" and to argue that "the promotional processes used by new predominantly

black towns paralleled those used by promoters of new white towns in the Trans-Appalachian West" (1, 4).

91. Cohen, *At Freedom's Edge*, 254. Hamilton, *Black Towns*, 99–137, discusses Langston City and Boley, Oklahoma.

92. "To Make a Negro State: Western Black Men Organizing in Oklahoma," *New York Times*, Feb. 18, 1890; "The Proposed Negro State: Excitement Created in Kansas and Oklahoma," *New York Times*, March 5, 1890. The *Times* identified the black organization involved as the "First Grand Independent Brotherhood." Hamilton, *Black Towns*, 115–16n10, suggests "the reporter must have been in error [because an] organization called the First Grand Independent Benevolent Society of Kansas and Missouri did exist and had eleven lodges in Kansas, including one in Nicodemus, but it was not politically active." He also indicates, however, in discussing its activities in Nicodemus, that it was "best known for its sponsorship of an annual August 1 celebration commemorating England's 1834 emancipation of slaves in the West Indies" (18).

It seems curious—and possibly a matter that had political implications—that the group would perpetuate the celebration of this event, which seems to have generally gone out of fashion after the Civil War, into the late nineteenth century. See Will B. Gravely, "The Dialectic of Double-Consciousness in Black American Freedom Celebrations, 1808–1863," *Journal of Negro History* 67 (Winter 1921): 304–5. The complex interrelationships of black voluntary associations, secret societies, churches, and politics in the late nineteenth and early twentieth centuries deserve far more attention than they have so far received. Such study might illuminate, for example, additional aspects of the black use of the exodus analogy. A. E. Bush and P. L. Dorman, *History of the Mosaic Templars of America* (n.p., n.p., 1924), for example, reports that "the oppressed conditions of the Negro at the time of organization [1883] were in such deep resemblance to the conditions of the Children of Israel that, in designing the Mosaic Templars of America, the founders were moved to make the selection of the life of Moses as the basic for the principles around which to build the Order" (152–53). John E. Bush, the moving figure in organizing the Mosaic Templars, was an active Baptist and a Republican officerholder. See also the discussion in the text and in note 98 concerning William Saunders Crowdy.

93. "To Make a Negro State," *New York Times*, Feb. 28, 1890; A. B. B. Gibson, "Is the Negro Capable of Self-Government?" *CR*, June 26, 1890.

94. L. H. Holsey, "Race Segregation," in *The Possibilities of the Negro in Symposium: A Solution of the Negro Problem Psychologically Considered. The Negro Not "a Beast"* (Atlanta: Franklin, 1904, repr. New York: Negro Universities Press, 1969), 111, 112, 114, 116. See also Glenn T. Eskew, "Black Elitism and the Failure of Paternalism in Postbellum Georgia: The Case of Bishop Lucius Henry Holsey," *Journal of Southern History* 58 (Nov. 1992): 637–66.

95. Benjamin Singleton Scrapbook, 56, Kansas State Historical Society, Topeka, as quoted in Painter, *Exodusters*, 128–29.

96. "Stranded Colored Emigrants"; this clipping is included on reel 322 of the microfilmed American Colonization Society Papers, Library of Congress, Washington, D.C., where a handwritten entry identifies it as coming from the *New York Sun,* Feb. 23, 1892. I have not been able to locate the story in the microfilm files of the *New York Sun,* however, and believe it is misidentified. I am indebted to Edwin S. Redkey for help in attempts to track this elusive citation. For a narrative of the episode and its consequences for the American Colonization Society, see Redkey, *Black Exodus,* 99–126.

97. Ibid., 292.

98. The Historical Committee of the Church of God and Saints of Christ, *History of the Church of God and Saints of Christ,* (Suffolk: Church of God and Saints of Christ, 1992), vol. 1: *The Re-Establishing Years (1847–1908),* 4–6, 11–13, 19–33, provides basic information on Crowdy's life. See also Elly Wynia, *The Church of God and Saints of Christ: The Rise of Black Jews* (New York: Garland, 1994), 19–32 (which must, however, be used with caution on Crowdy's life), and 45–77 (on the church's beliefs and practices). On the threat of armed racial confrontation in Oklahoma in late September 1891, see "To-day's Rush for Homes: Trouble Likely to Follow the Oklahoma Invasion," *New York Times,* Sept. 22, 1891, and "The New Land Occupied: No Serious Disturbances in Oklahoma Yesterday," *New York Times,* Sept. 23, 1891.

99. U.S. Department of Commerce, Bureau of the Census, *Negroes . . . 1920–1932.* In *At Freedom's Edge,* 78–108, Cohen discusses northward migration throughout the era from the end of Reconstruction to World War I, emphasizing the importance of increased economic opportunity during the war. See also Lemann, *Promised Land,* 6 and throughout, on the importance of the numerically larger northward migration that occurred during and after World War II.

100. Scott, *Negro Migration,* 3, 6, 40, 41, 45–46.

101. Ransom, "The Exodus," *AMECR* 33 (Jan. 1917): 151, as cited in Albert J. Raboteau, "Black Americans" in *With Eyes toward Zion,* vol. 2, ed. Moshe Davis (New York: Praeger, 1986). Milton C. Sernett discusses the use of exodus imagery as part of a far-ranging analysis of the religious dimensions of the migration in "'Bound for the Promised Land': African American Religion and the Great Migration," unpublished typescript.

102. Martin Kilson, "Political Change in the Negro Ghetto, 1900–1940's," in *Key Issues in the Afro-American Experience,* ed. Nathan Huggins, Martin Kilson, and Daniel M. Fox (New York: Harcourt Brace Jovanovich, 1971), 2:170 (on exclusion of blacks from urban machines); James R. Grossman, "The White Man's Union: The Great Migration and the Resonance of Race and Class in Chicago, 1916–1922," in *The Great Migration in Historical Perspective,* ed. Joe William Trotter, Jr. (Bloomington: Indiana University Press, 1991), 83–105; and David J. Hellwig, "Strangers in Their Own Land: Patterns of Black Nativism, 1830–1920," *American Studies* 23 (Spring 1982): 94–95 (on black support for immigration restriction in the 1920s). Arthur Huff Fauset, *Black Gods of the Metropolis: Negro Religious Cults in the Urban North* (Philadelphia: University of Pennsylvania Press, 1944, 1971), 31–40, contains an early

study of Prophet F. S. Cherry's "Church of God"; see also Howard M. Brotz, *The Black Jews of Harlem: Negro Nationalism and the Dilemmas of Negro Leadership* (New York: Schocken, 1964). Some of the subsequent literature on these and related movements is cited by Wynia, *Church of God*, 13–17.

103. An account of the Moorish Science Temple may be found in Yvonne Yazbeck Haddad and Jane Idleman Smith, *Mission to America: Five Islamic Sectarian Communities in North America* (Gainesville: University Presses of Florida, 1993), 79–104. Martha F. Lee, *The Nation of Islam: An American Millenarian Movement* (Lewiston: Mellen, 1988), stresses the apocalyptic dimension of the movement's teaching.

104. Randall K. Burkett, *Black Redemption: Churchmen Speak for the Garvey Movement* (Philadelphia: Temple University Press, 1978), 3.

105. Robert A. Hill, ed., *The Marcus Garvey and Universal Negro Improvement Association Papers* (Berkeley: University of California Press, 1983), 1:256 (motto and preamble of constitution), 1:374 (Africa abroad and Africa at home), and 1:461 (Africa bleeding).

106. Burkett, *Black Redemption*, 19–26, provides a succinct summary of Garvey's career and the history of the UNIA.

107. Hill, ed., *Garvey Papers*, 1:461.

108. Burkett, *Black Redemption*, 24 (quotation), 19 (middle name). For an extended use of the comparison between Garvey and Moses by a Garveyite member of the clergy, see George Alexander McGuire, "What Is That in Thine Hand," in Burkett, *Black Redemption*, 165–80. Burkett summarizes his interpretation of the religious dimensions of Garveyism (ibid., 3–18), but for its full development see Randall K. Burkett, *Garveyism as a Religious Movement* (Metuchen: Scarecrow Press, 1978).

109. Judith Stein, *The World of Marcus Garvey: Race and Class in Modern Society* (Baton Rouge: Louisiana State University Press, 1986), 108–9, argues that "black leaders . . . who wished to denigrate the movement, chose to call it an exodus," while in fact "Garvey's Pan-Africanism stemmed from the elite tradition of ambition and uplift, not the mass desire for land." This, however, overstates the distance between Garvey and the earlier exodus tradition. A related issue concerns black response to early Zionism. See Robert G. Weisbord and Richard Kazarian, Jr., *Israel in the Black American Perspective* (Westport: Greenwood Press, 1985), 7–19, which includes a brief discussion of Garvey and Zionism.

110. Henry McNeal Turner, "Emigration to Africa," *CR*, Feb. 22, 1883, as cited in Redkey, *Respect Black*, 55–56 (quotation); Redkey, *Black Exodus*, 24–46 (Turner's "African Dream").

111. Hill, ed., *Garvey Papers*, 1:257.

112. Holsey, "Race Segregation," 119.

113. Perry Miller, *Errand into the Wilderness*, (Cambridge: Harvard University Press, 1956), 9.

114. For suggestions concerning pertinent source material and many conversations regarding the interpretation of African American religion during this period I am greatly indebted to Albert J. Raboteau, Laurie Maffly-Kipp, and

Judith Weisenfeld, my fellow editors in "Afro-American Religion: A Documentary History Project," an undertaking funded by the Lilly Endowment and the Pew Charitable Trusts. Albert Raboteau and Laurie Maffly-Kipp also gave helpful critical readings to an earlier draft of this chapter. I owe a comparable debt to my Amherst College colleagues David W. Blight and Robert Gooding-Williams, not only for their insightful reading of the penultimate version of this chapter but also for many illuminating discussions of black life and thought in late-nineteenth- and early-twentieth-century America. I am also deeply grateful to the National Humanities Center, whose hospitality I enjoyed in the spring of 1994 when part of the writing of this chapter was completed.

PART 2

Arenas of Conflict

The Bible, Minority Faiths, and the American Protestant Mainstream, 1860–1925[1]

MARK A. NOLL

Between the age of Abraham Lincoln and the age of Woodrow Wilson, the Bible hovered over the civilization of the United States as in primordial time "the spirit of God hovered over the face of the waters."[2] Use of the Bible by no means escaped the more general changes occurring in the nation during this period, but Scripture remained a central feature of American culture. Mainstream Protestants assumed that their Bible was *the* American Bible. They were at least half right, but no more than half. Other religious groups—populating eddies at the margins of the mainstream, flowing along in currents largely unconnected to the mainstream, or self-consciously working to divert the mainstream into new channels—felt differently about the Scriptures. These other perspectives—especially as they resulted in political controversy, stimulated new translations of the Bible, or put Scripture to use to define minority communities against the mainstream Protestant flood—are the first concerns of this chapter. I will then dwell at greater length on the situations of African American Christians and white Protestant women reformers. Those situations were more complicated because, in different ways, the two groups employed the mainstream Protestant Bible for purposes to which the Protestant mainstream objected. Although study of the Bible and religious minorities in the United States between the Civil War and the mid-1920s reveals a great deal about American religious history, it reveals even more about the Bible.

To the extent that a self-conscious interpretive framework informs this discussion, it is provided by the missiologists Lamin Sanneh and Andrew Walls who, in a series of scintillating works, have described the implications for culture formation in the history of Christianity when Scripture is translated into local languages. The acquisition of the Bible in the vernacular often turns out to be powerfully associated with, as Sanneh puts it, "cultural understanding, vernacular pride,

social awakening, religious renewal, [and] cross-cultural dialogue."[3] To
Walls, this feature of cross-cultural religious communication is a specific instance of a more general phenomenon whereby "Africans have
responded to the gospel from where *they* were, not from where the
missionaries were; they have responded to the Christian message as they
heard it, not to the missionaries' experience of that message."[4] The
work of Sanneh and Walls would suggest that study of the Bible and
American minority faiths will be most productive when it concentrates
on the circumstances that prompted indigenous translations of the Bible
or those effects, such as new vernacular translations produce, that arise
when a minority group appropriates the mainstream Bible for its own
purposes.

In order to gauge the stake for minority faiths in Scripture during
this period, it is necessary first to sketch the dimensions of the Bible
within mainstream culture.[5] New people, new cities, new industry, and
new learning—the litany is no less true for having become a cliché of
the historians—were changing the face of American life in the years
between the outbreak of the Civil War and the Scopes trial. Such changes could not take place without affecting the appropriation of Scripture. The subjects of Lewis Saum's intriguing studies of the nation's
"popular mood"—"humble but literate white Protestant Christians"
who had been profoundly shaken by the experiences of the Civil War,
who were rapidly filling up the Continent, and who were being transformed into the first mass-consumer society—seem not to have quoted Scripture as readily in the generation after the Civil War as in the
generation before.[6] In this period the names that Americans gave their
cities, organizations, and children were also not as likely to be taken
from the Bible as had once been the case.[7]

The most significant religious development affecting the place of the
Bible in the mainstream culture, however, was the gradual decline of
mainstream Protestantism—the white, English-speaking, British-derived, broadly Reformed evangelicals who had acted as the nation's
cultural arbiters since early in the century. The decline came about for
two reasons. First, the proportion of such Protestants in the general
population was decreasing; one estimate suggests that while in 1860
Roman Catholics, Lutherans, African-American Baptists and Methodists, Jews, and the Eastern Orthodox had made up barely 30 percent
of the religious adherents of the United States, by the mid-1920s they
constituted close to 60 percent.[8] Second, and more important, the Protestant mainstream was itself dividing, with polarized contenders for the
nineteenth-century evangelical legacy (representing a learned academic culture of moderates and liberals against a traditional popular cul-

ture of reactionaries and moderate conservatives) becoming so prominent as to render nearly invisible the broad mass of undifferentiated Protestants who remained in the middle. The result of these two developments was what Robert Handy has called the "second disestablishment" in the United States, when evangelical Protestants who had constituted the unofficial national religion since the early nineteenth century lost their cultural hegemony.[9]

Diverging attitudes toward Scripture within mainstream Protestantism both contributed to this second disestablishment and were stimulated by it. Biblical higher criticism from Europe and the application of evolutionary models to biblical study were especially prominent wedges dividing the old Protestant mainstream.[10]

Having made all necessary qualifications, however, white, English-speaking, British-derived, broadly Reformed, evangelical Protestants remained unusually influential throughout this period. This was the Protestantism to which all presidents of the period deferred in some way; it was the Protestantism that created American public education and dominated it into the twentieth century.[11] It was the Protestantism that, until much later in the twentieth century than once was thought, established the ethos for American higher education, research universities and colleges alike.[12] It was the Protestantism that, of all American faiths, enjoyed closest connections with mainstream publishing, and it was the form of religion that foreign visitors such as Lord Bryce and André Siegfried, along with such articulate immigrants as Philip Schaff, always singled out as a (if not the) driving force of the culture.[13]

The Mainstream Protestant Bible

For this kind of Protestantism, the Scriptures, as Robert Handy has written, were central: "These Protestants shared a common devotion to the bible, very evident in their patterns of preaching, worship, and Sunday school education. Familiar biblical phrases and cadences informed the way they spoke and wrote. They could, and often did, disagree over ways of interpreting 'the word of God,' yet it continued to operate as the central written point of reference for Christian life in church and world."[14]

A brief catalog of incidents and testimonies suggests the dimensions of the biblical presence among these mainstream Protestants.

• On both sides, the Civil War was fought in order to vindicate attitudes toward Scripture as well as to the Constitution. So it was that late in that conflict a southern editor offered this exhortation to troops weary with the struggle: "Above all, the providence of God has made it their [Confederate soldiers'] special privilege to defend with their lives the right of freedom of conscience, the essential issue of the war; the right to interpret the Bible for ourselves, without the prescription of creeds for us by synods, councils, or congresses."[15]

· Throughout the period, American presidents routinely testified to the centrality of Scripture in the national consciousness, from Lincoln's ironic observation in his Second Inaugural Address—"Both read the same Bible, and pray to the same God"—to Woodrow Wilson's straightforward affirmation before a Denver audience in 1911 that "part of the destiny of America lies in their daily perusal of this great book of revelations—that if they would see America free and pure they will make their own spirits free and pure by this baptism of the Holy Scripture."[16]

· It was an era when the nation's leading newspapers devoted considerable space to their readers' lively debates on the merits and demerits of biblical higher criticism.[17]

· It was an age when the American Bible Society (ABS), despite a shift in mentality from Christian crusading to rational business, still accomplished prodigies in producing and distributing Scripture—more than three million Bibles and Testaments to combatants on both sides during the Civil War, nearly five million to armed forces personnel during World War I, and (by the time the ABS finally closed its own printing operation, the Bible House, in 1922) a total of 76,051,112 volumes of Scripture in sixty-eight languages and six kinds of embossed printing for the blind over the previous seventy years.[18]

· During this period, novels based on biblical characters or situations— from William Ware's *Julian: Or, Scenes in Judea* (1856) to Lew Wallace's phenomenally popular *Ben Hur, A Tale of the Christ* (1880) and many more to follow—were sure-shot best-sellers.[19]

· Popular painting was suffused with biblical subjects.[20]

· Enthusiasm of the sort that in the late twentieth century is reserved for rock stars and sports celebrities greeted some biblical milestones, especially the publication of the English Revised Version of the New Testament in May 1881. So intense was interest in this first major effort to touch up the King James Version that a million American orders were awaiting its publication, two Chicago papers ran the entire Testament in their May 22 issues, two hundred thousand copies were sold in New York alone in the first week after publication, and at least three million copies in twenty-six different editions were marketed by the end of the year.[21]

• Besides its literary virtues, the Bible was also prized as an icon. Tales of pocket Bibles that stopped bullets were common during the Civil War and World War I. In order to show that a southern publisher could compete with the major houses of the North, the Southern Methodist Publishing House in Nashville prepared a Bible printed in gold on sheepskin to be exhibited at Chicago's World Columbian Exhibition in 1893.[22]

• This period also witnessed the founding of dynamic new organizations to distribute the Scriptures. When in 1898 a raucous crowd of lumberjacks at the Central Hotel in Boscobel, Wisconsin, drove together traveling salesmen John H. Nicholson and Samuel Hill, the two discovered a common love of the Scriptures, organized a voluntary association, and, ten years later, began the work of the Gideons that has distributed more than a half billion Bibles or testaments in seventy-five countries since.[23]

• So widespread was the mainstream Bible that even those who were not in the mainstream sometimes celebrated its influence in America, as Solomon Schechter did when dedicating New York's Jewish Theological Seminary in 1903: "This country is, as everybody knows, a creation of the Bible, particularly the Old Testament, and the Bible is still holding its own, exercising enormous influence as a real spiritual power in spite of all the destructive tendencies, mostly of foreign make. . . . The bulk of the real American people have, in matters of religion, retained their sobriety and loyal adherence to the Scripture, as their Puritan forefathers did."[24]

The Bible, in other words, was a central, defining element of the mainstream national culture through at least the two generations after the Civil War. The power of the Bible, and of the Protestant mainstream, by no means came to a complete end in the 1920s. But—as much as the American Bible Society, the Gideons, the talismanic use of Scripture, and other manifestations of biblical consciousness have remained alive in recent decades—the salience of such phenomena in the wider culture has been much reduced.

The mainstream conception of the Bible—although rarely, if ever, stated in so many words—included several distinct convictions. They may not have been as widely shared in 1925 as in 1860, but they none-

theless dominated the era. Mainstream Protestants, if they had stated
these convictions explicitly, might have summarized them as follows:

1. The Bible was a unique revelation from God that told its readers both
how to find eternal life and how to live in this world.

2. The Bible of mainstream Protestantism was the Authorized or King
James Version (KJV), or one of the KJV's successors, the English Revised Version of 1881–85 and the American Standard Version of 1901.
The KJV provided the cadences and phrases for public speech and a
vocabulary for political mobilization.[25] It also provided an incredibly
rich field for commercial exploitation. Between 1860 and 1925 American publishers brought out at least 448 editions of the KJ, English
Revised, and American Standard versions (with the overwhelming
majority the King James).[26] Mainstream Protestants were not entirely
blind to other Bibles or the biblical scholarship of non-Americans.
Moses Stuart (1780–1852) of Andover Seminary, who almost by himself brought into existence the advanced academic study of Scripture
in the United States, was thoroughly committed to using the best European (usually German) scholarship of his day. His many students
followed in their master's train. More generally, throughout early
American history Protestants eagerly turned to Jewish scholarship, and
sometimes Jewish scholars, for training in Hebrew. Most of the colleges
in the United States founded before 1800 provided some sort of support for studying that language as an aid to understanding the Bible.[27]
Due allowance having been made for some breadth of interest, *the* Bible
for mainstream Protestants was never anything but the KJV.

3. Mainstream Protestants held that truths of the Bible were compatible with, or perhaps even the basis for, the highest American ideals of
republican freedom. Earlier in the century, some Old School Presbyterians had mounted a campaign to establish a parochial school system,
motivated at least in part by their belief that the nonsectarian reading
of the KJV, which was then the norm in American schools, did not
provide enough confessional guidance to the students. For their pains,
they were attacked as "sectarian, divisive, narrow, clannish, and *anti-
republican.*"[28]

4. Biblical and American loyalties combined in another conviction that
emerged from a Christian republican calculus: public acknowledgment
of the Bible's teachings was critical for the well-being of the Republic.
One of the first significant court cases involving the Bible in the public
schools took place during 1869 and 1870 in Cincinnati, where daily
readings from the KJV had been the practice since the schools were

founded in 1829. One of the lawyers arguing for the continued use of Scripture succinctly summarized a widely held opinion: "This recognition of Christianity—and I wish to say that I use that term in a very broad sense, as meaning the religion of the Bible, not in any limited or narrow sense—this recognition of Christianity or the religion of the Bible, results from propositions which are at the foundation of and necessary to the constitution and stability of society."[29]

5. White evangelical Protestants also felt they were the divinely appointed stewards of the Bible and the Bible-based civilization in the United States. The era's active anti-Catholicism was sparked in large measure by the belief that the Catholic hierarchy discouraged, or even prohibited, the use of Scripture among the laity. This belief, in turn, led to the conclusion that Catholicism was inimicable to the American way of life, a conclusion set out with disarming frankness by an attorney arguing in 1887 to preserve the right of a Wisconsin school board to continue daily readings from the KJV: "The decrees of the councils, the encyclicals of the Popes, the pastoral and other letters of the Archbishops and Bishops, and the writings of learned Catholics furnish abundant evidence that the Catholic church is opposed to popular government, that it is opposed to liberty of conscience, and of worship, and that it is opposed to our public school system."[30]

6. Finally, mainstream Protestants held that interpretation of the Bible was a fairly straightforward exercise dependent only upon common sense, proper scientific method, and the judicious exercise of reason. Where a person or group failed to display these characteristics, mainstream Protestants concluded that they were guilty of moral failure, because all humans by nature simply had to be equipped with these capacities. In 1865, Phoebe Palmer, the holiness evangelist, expressed this sentiment with special clarity: "The Bible is a wonderfully simple book; and, if you had taken the naked Word of God as . . . your counsel, instead of taking the opinions of men in regard to that *Word,* you might have been a more enlightened, simple, happy and useful Christian."[31] Mainstream Protestants may not have followed their own principles concerning the simplicity of interpretation, but it remained a central feature of American biblicism that both strengthened Protestant self-confidence and aggravated tensions with groups that felt otherwise about what the Bible taught clearly.[32]

The combination of convictions about the mainstream Protestant Bible turned out to be unstable historically.[33] It also was incoherent when measured by some historical expressions of Protestantism itself.[34] But, instability and incoherence notwithstanding, these convictions about the mainstream Protestant Bible exerted a telling impact on American culture.

They also set up an adversarial situation between the Protestants who held these convictions and Americans who did not. Thus in 1885, Josiah Strong, the Congregationalist executive of the Evangelical Alliance, identified "immigration, Romanism, Mormonism, intemperance, Socialism, wealth, and the city" as "perils" threatening the civilization defined by mainstream Protestantism.[35] In return, these immigrants, Roman Catholics, Mormons, socialists, and city-dwellers—only a few were wealthy or unusually intemperate—had to come to terms with a culture in which Protestants like Strong, along with the mainstream Protestant Bible, were prominent. Jews, Mormons, Catholics, Mennonites, many Lutherans, some Baptists, Christian Scientists, Jehovah's Witnesses, and members of other minority faiths faced a situation where the American-Bible synthesis threatened their civil, religious, political, or social rights, and also one in which the effort to employ Scripture for their own purposes was imperiled.

When examining minority responses to mainstream Protestantism, however, it is well to remember that throughout this entire period both "the Bible" and "minority faiths" were extraordinarily elastic.

Never in American history—and certainly not in the period under consideration here—did *the* Bible exist in America. Even in the heyday of the KJV, when the appearance of biblical hegemony was strongest, there always existed numerous Bibles in numerous languages and translated from numerous Hebrew, Greek, and Latin originals. Publishing figures, like all such enumerations, do not interpret themselves. But it nonetheless says something about the pluriformity of Scripture in American life that, during the sixty-five years treated here, American publishers brought out at least 136 non-KJV English-language editions of 42 separate translations of the Scriptures. The Douay-Rheims-Challoner Bible for Roman Catholics was most prominent among these versions, but it was hardly by itself, even among Catholic Bibles. During the same period, American publishers also produced at least 316 editions of complete Bibles (or complete Hebrew Scriptures) in forty languages other than English. To show by comparison what this foreign language publishing meant, there were more editions of complete German-language Bibles (one hundred) in this period than editions of the Revised Version and American Standard Version combined (sixty-seven).[36] "The" Bible was always polyglot and never conformed strictly to the KJV.

The notion of "minority faiths" is just as plastic. Jews, Catholics, and some European sectarian movements were etched fairly clearly in opposition to the mainstream Protestant Bible. America's indigenous "scripture religions"—like Mormonism, Christian Science, or the Restorationist movement of Disciples and "Christians"—shared much of the mainstream's respect for Scripture. Nevertheless, by adding new accounts of divine revelation or by emphasizing a single aspect of the mainstream hermeneutic, these movements diverged from both the mainstream and the European-based religions. African American Christians and women Protestant reformers represented still other ways of expressing minority challenges to the mainstream Bible.

Numerous as the minority alternative were, however, some problems were common. The Bible served as a lightening rod that attracted defenses against, and assaults on, the Protestant mainstream. The prominence of the mainstream Protestant Bible lay behind some efforts by minority groups to provide their own biblical translations. Translation was itself an instance of a more general effort by minorities to define a biblicism for themselves as distinct from the biblicism of the mainstream culture. Among African American Christians and women Protestant reformers the Bible played a critical role in a process that combined conformity to the mainstream with opposition to it.

The Bible as Political Lightening Rod

Strife over Bible reading in public schools has always been much more a political issue than a religious question; it is thus canvassed thoroughly in other chapters in this book.[37] But the issue cannot be entirely passed by here, because such strife helped bring into the open attitudes toward the Bible held by minorities and because it shows that the public use of the Bible was directly related to the minorities' own use of Scripture.

For Jews, mandated readings from the KJV in public schools were almost always felt as a civil and religious imposition.[38] Before the Civil War, Isaac Leeser (himself a notable translator of the Scriptures) had complained that making Jews obey Sunday legislation was the same thing as forcing them to attend church or receive baptism.[39] Much the same reasoning was applied to Bible reading in public schools, especially after the great increase in Jewish immigration during the last third of the nineteenth century.

To be sure, at least a few leaders in the antebellum period were able to make somewhat light of the issue. Isaac Wise, an influential leader of American Reform Judaism, did oppose Bible reading in public school and also suggested that, if the practice was deemed necessary for the health of the Republic, the best solution was the most thoroughly neutral solution, which to Wise meant readings, without comment, in Hebrew and Greek.[40] Wise's solution was ingenious, but it also illustrated the weight of the mainstream Protestant Bible, even on those who opposed its public hegemony, because Wise apparently overlooked the fact that for many contemporary Roman Catholics the Latin of the Vulgate also functioned as an authoritative original language of Scripture.

In the famous Cincinnati case of 1869–70, the two Jews on the Cincinnati school board divided over the board's decision to exclude Bible readings. But Isaac Wise was joined by another of Cincinnati's prominent Reform rabbis, Max Lilienthal, to support the board's effort to eliminate Bible readings altogether from the public schools. As Wise put his position about that time, "We are opposed to Bible reading in the schools. We want secular schools and nothing else. . . . Having no religion [the state] cannot impose any religious instruction on the citizen."[41]

Jewish sensitivity to the way Bible reading in public schools imposed civil and religious burdens remained keen through the period. In 1906 the Central Conference of American Rabbis published a pamphlet setting out its reasons why, as the title had it, *The Bible Should Not Be Read in Public Schools*. The next year the Union of Orthodox Jewish Congregations succeeded in having the New York City Board of Education end the teaching of religion in the city's public schools.[42] For several years near U.S. entry into World War I, *The American Jewish Yearbook* cataloged instances where courts or legislators mandated, eliminated, or discussed Bible reading in the schools. In its listings— alongside notices concerning legal action on general religious education in public schools, the observance of Sunday as a holy day, and provision for Jewish religious observances—the *Yearbook* noted twenty-six Bible rulings in thirteen states over just three years.[43]

Readings from the KJV in public schools joined other Bible-related offenses (like rampant anti-Semitism in popular biblical fiction) and more general efforts of mainstream Protestants to define the United States as a Christian nation (like the National Reform Association's effort to amend the Constitution and recognize the rule of Christ over the nation) to sharpen Jewish understanding of what they desired from the Scriptures themselves.[44] Separate, privately financed Jewish schools, in which study of the Scriptures in Hebrew figured prominently, were one of the responses to the imposition of mainstream Protestantism and American patriotism.[45]

Catholic opposition to Bible readings from the KJV in public schools appeared before Jewish protests.[46] Although the details of objection were different—Catholics wanted Bible readings but not from a translation condemned by the hierarchy—protests resembled arguments being made by the Jews. The Wisconsin court case previously mentioned provides a clear illustration of how that Catholic opposition could be expressed.

In 1886 Catholic parents in Edgerton, Wisconsin, petitioned their local school board to stop daily readings from the KJV. The board replied that reading the KJV without comment gave all children the right to interpret the Bible for themselves. To read the Bible without comment was nonsectarian; to stop reading it because it offended Roman Catholics was sectarian. This reasoning incensed Humphrey Desmond, for fifty years the editor of the *Catholic Citizen* of Wisconsin, who galvanized support to save the parents and their children "from the sectarian inquisition presently established in the tax-payers' public school." To suggest the absurdity of the mainstream position, he wrote in February 1887, "Where in the whole land is the Catholic Bible read in the public school each morning; where is the Ave Maria compulsorily recited by Protestant pupils . . . ? On the other hand, we have public Normal Schools in this state run as part of the Methodist Book Concern; public school establishments turned into Protestant ecclesiastical machines; . . . and proselytism at the expense of Catholics whose children are being proselytized." A local judge ruled against the parents, stating that the KJV's "very presence, as a believed book, has rendered the nations having it, a chosen race; and then too, in exact proportion as it is more or less generally known and studied." It is "beyond compare the most perfect instrument of humanity." But then the Wisconsin Supreme Court reversed that ruling in favor of the parents and forbade local boards to mandate readings from the KJV.[47]

To Jews and Catholics, such court rulings represented only good logic. They could not see how the United States could both promote civil liberty and bestow special privileges on the mainstream Bible. But having made this point well enough for at least some recognition in court and legislature by the early twentieth century, it remained for scriptural religions such as Judaism and Catholicism to define what positive steps could be taken in the American context to promote a proper use of the Bible. That effort often led to the production of biblical translations that were supposed to alleviate the taint of the KJV.

Indigenous Translations

The production of indigenous Bible translations represented one way in which scriptural religions could create space for themselves in an environment dominated by the mainstream Bible. The urgency behind the drive to make such translations varied from minority to minority, but it was widespread.

For American Jews, the dominance of the KJV posed a special problem because of the way that Protestant marginal notes and Protestant traditions of interpretation Christianized the Hebrew Scriptures. One of the impulses stimulating Isaac Leeser to his pioneering English trans-

lation of 1853 was the Christianizing propensity he found in the KJV:
"wherever it was possible for the translators to introduce Christianity
in the Scriptures, they have uniformly done so" in order "to assail Israel's hope and faith."[48] Leeser objected particularly to headings and
marginal comments such as "The Prediction of Christ" for Psalm 110,
"A Description of Christ" for the Song of Solomon, and "Christ's Birth
and Kingdom" for Isaiah 9. He felt that uneducated Jews had "no
means of knowing what is Scriptural and what is not" when reading
such headings.[49] As Jonathan Sarna has summarized the Jewish com-
plaint, "These theologically charged translations do not . . . capture the
literal meaning of the biblical idiom. Instead, they distort the text, reduce the sanctity and significance of the Hebrew Bible, and engender
interreligious hostility."[50]

The dissatisfaction with the way that the KJV and other English language versions of the Old Testament compromised Jewish understanding of the Hebrew Scriptures was a major factor in efforts to produce a
new English-language, but also self-consciously Jewish, Bible. To that
end, the Jewish Publication Society of America appointed a committee
in 1892 to prepare a new translation. But progress was slow, with only
the Psalms appearing (1903) before the group was reorganized to function as an editing committee to supervise Max Margolis, who took on
the task of preparing a draft for the entire Hebrew Bible.[51]

As the work under the committee and Margolis went on, Jewish
leaders articulated clearly what was at stake. In 1913 Solomon
Schechter, a member of the editorial committee who died only shortly
before the full project was completed, looked forward to the forthcoming translation, "which the Jew of the future will use habitually, sometimes crying over a Psalm in it, or deriving comfort from a chapter of
Isaiah, or reading a story to his children—his own Bible, not one mort-
gaged by the King James Version." The new translation would be "a
Jewish translation, instinct with Jewish tradition and Jewish sentiment."
But a translation was not enough for Schechter. He also wanted to
promote "the publication of a commentary to the Bible," because "our
people should know the Bible from the Jewish point of view." It was
necessary to "be a Jew and have a Jewish soul to understand the passage fully." Schechter did not see how Judaism could "be made intensive if there are no Jewish Bible commentaries[.] If sentiment is borrowed from others? . . . All efforts through synagogue extension,
Chautauqua classes, or Talmud Torahs will be futile so long as the very
life of Judaism is not written for Jews and by Jews."[52]

When *The Holy Scriptures According to the Masoretic Text* finally
appeared in 1917, the surviving members of the editorial committee
carried Schechter's argument further. To them it was clear that the times

demanded a translation of the Bible like Schechter described. The editors could have mentioned, but did not, that since the end of the nineteenth century a Christian Zionism based on dispensationalist readings of the Old Testament had been growing rapidly in strength among the Populist and conservative wings of the Protestant mainstream.[53] The dispensationalist interpretation seemed pro-Jewish, but its main themes were part and parcel of mainstream hermeneutical practice and so could bring no comfort to Jews wary of being coopted by the mainstream Protestant Bible.

If the particular implications of this specific hermeneutic were not uppermost in the mind of the committee, the more general situation facing American Jews certainly was. The committee thought "the English language, . . . unless all signs fail," would soon "become the current speech of the majority of the children of Israel." The new work, regarded strictly by itself, "gives to the Jewish world a translation of the Scriptures done by men imbued with the Jewish consciousness." But regarded in competitive biblical context, the work meant even more. The committee went out of its way to praise the KJV and the English Revised Version but added the telling reservation—"they are not ours." And it spelled out clearly what was at stake for minorities such as the Jews in a culture dominated by an alien Scripture:

> The repeated efforts by Jews in the field of biblical translation show their sentiment toward translations prepared by other denominations. The dominant feature of this sentiment, apart from the thought that the christological interpretations in non-Jewish translations are out of place in a Jewish Bible, is and was that the Jew cannot afford to have his Bible translation prepared for him by others. He cannot have it as a gift, even as he cannot borrow his soul from others. If a new country and a new language metamorphose him into a new man, the duty of this new man is to prepare a new garb and a new method of expression for what is most sacred and most dear to him.[54]

Not the least of the new translation's virtues in Jewish eyes was its rescue of Scripture from the phraseology of the KJV. In the 1917 translation of Isaiah 7:14, for example, "the young woman shall conceive" replaced the KJV's "and a virgin shall conceive." The translators also left no doubt about their intention to avoid the string of messianic titles in Isaiah 9:5–6 that Christians routinely applied to Jesus:

> For a child is born unto us,
> A son is given unto us;
> And the government is upon his shoulder;
> And his name is called
> Pele-joez-el-gibbor-
> Abi-ad-sar-shalom.[55]

For American Jews, in short, a translation of their own was one way of asserting independence over against the dominant presence of the mainstream Protestant Bible.

For Roman Catholics, neither the same need nor desire was present for a fresh translation. The Douay-Rheims-Challoner version, which in its preparation by several hands over nearly two hundred years had been sanctioned at each step by the church, seemed to have served English-speaking American Catholics quite well. Nonetheless, three fresh English translations were attempted, of which the most learned was by Francis Kenrick, Bishop of Philadelphia and later Archbishop of Baltimore. With the Douay-Rheims-Challoner version already functioning as the Catholics' KJV, the purpose of Kenrick's work was more theological in its effort to defend the integrity of the Vulgate by correcting infelicities of the standard Catholic translation. He even paid the KJV the compliment of having "deferred to its usage, although of Protestant origin, feeling that, in things indifferent, conformity is desirable, and that every approach to uniformity in the rendering of the inspired word, without sacrifice of principle, or violation of disciplinary rules, is a gain to the common cause of Christianity."[56]

If Kenrick's work was not overwhelmingly innovative as a translation, it was a decidedly Catholic venture that allowed him to defend his tradition's readings of Scripture against the Protestant commentary regularly provided with editions of the KJV—as, for example, in his comment on "the woman" of Genesis 3:15: "The woman is not Eve only, or principally, although she no doubt detested the tempter, the occasion of her fall; but Mary, the mother of Him who came to repair the ruin."

It was not, however, just Jews and Catholics who, by providing themselves with their own translations, sought the twin goals of self-definition and protection from the Protestant mainstream. Of several other efforts, the most interesting were a number of "immersion" translations. Baptists and Restorationists, eager to carry on their antipaedobaptistic polemic against Catholics, Lutherans, Methodists, Episcopalians, and Methodists, published a series of translations in which the New Testament's *baptizo* was regularly translated "immerse" instead of "baptize." Alexander Campbell, a founder of the Restorationist movement, published one of the first of these in 1826 as an edited version of an earlier composite British translation. These translations often followed the KJV closely except for words regarding baptism. But they carved out a secure niche for themselves, with eight different "immersion" translations appearing between 1849 and 1928 and with some of those versions attaining considerable popularity. Campbell's translation was republished ten more times in its first century, and the Baptist-sponsored American Bible Union translation appeared in fifteen different editions between 1862 and 1912.[57]

Scripture and Community Self-Definition

Translations were a special case of the more general effort to establish or preserve a community's own scriptural identity over against the biblicism of mainstream Protestantism.

Roman Catholics mounted persistent efforts to rebut Protestant charges that their tradition disregarded Scripture, a charge repeated endlessly in pedestrian accounts and sometimes spectacularly, as in the *Awful Disclosures of the Hotel Dieu Nunnery of Montreal* by "Maria Monk" in 1836.[58] Catholic apologists responded regularly to that charge in order to prove themselves freedom-loving Americans as well as faithful Catholics. In the process, they also defined what a proper Catholic use of Scripture amounted to, which was a reading of the Bible, not as autonomous individuals but under authority. In 1871 a writer in *The Catholic World* made these points brusquely: "Does the Catholic Church condemn the Bible and forbid her people to circulate and read it? We answer: NO! On the contrary, the Catholic Church believes the Bible to be the inspired word of God himself, and constantly incites her people to its diligent perusal."[59]

The most effective apology of the era, which sold more than two million copies in its first forty years and was translated into all of the major European languages, was Cardinal James Gibbons's *The Faith of Our Fathers*. In this work, the Archbishop of Baltimore showed how the Vulgate had shaped every stage of his own education, and he explained to the uninitiated that Catholic priests were required to study the Bible for an hour each day. Gibbons also provided prooftexts liberally throughout his work to illustrate the sincerity of his profession. Negatively, Gibbons took direct aim at mainstream Protestant biblicism by arguing that the evangelical Protestant notion of a self-interpreting Bible open to all was both foolish and anti-Christian. He pointed out that discord over the meaning of the Bible had emerged with the Reformation as proof positive of the problems in private interpretation. In sum, Gibbons concluded "that God never intended the Bible to be the Christian's rule of faith, independently of the living authority of the Church."[60]

A few years later, after higher critical conclusions had become more prevalent in the United States, Hugh Pope, O.P., combined a defense of traditional Catholic views on the Bible with criticism of Protestant capitulation to the intellectual fashions of the day: "It is not the Bible that is condemned [by the hierarchy], nor the use of it, but the abuse of it. . . . Ironically enough, it is the Catholic Church which (outside a comparatively small body of men who still base themselves on an exact literal interpretation of the English translation made three hundred years ago) is, in the modern world, the defender of Scriptural authority."[61]

Catholic apologists who countered the threat of the mainstream Protestant Bible did not so much define an indigenous Catholic biblicism as create the space for one to develop. At the same time that Cardinal Gibbons was setting a largely Protestant world straight on how Catholics regarded the Bible, other leaders were encouraging the faithful to use the Bible in an appropriately Catholic way. John Joseph Keane, then bishop of Richmond, in 1880 produced "A Sodality Manual for the Use of the Servants of the Holy Ghost," which hundreds of Catholics in his region used for several years thereafter. When the complete office was recited at monthly gatherings, or when parts of it were used in private devotionals, Catholics read many portions of Scripture from the Douay version (forty-one different passages in the complete office), and read them, moreover, in the context of a historic Catholic spirituality. Similar efforts with the Bible, such as Thomas F. Hopkins's "Novena of Sermons on the Holy Ghost" (published in 1901), which featured the Virgin Mary in its exegesis of various biblical texts, again showed Catholics how they could use the Bible for their own, rather than mainstream Protestant, purposes.[62]

Other minority faiths also had to negotiate with the mainstream Protestant Bible if they wished to retain their distinct identities. The strategies employed were probably as diverse as the groups employing them, but several broad categories did exist: historic European Protestants who were neither British nor descendants of Reformed traditions, English-speaking Protestants who had been marginalized in the culture, and faiths that added other sacred writings to the Bible.

HISTORIC EUROPEAN PROTESTANTS

Lutherans made up the largest Protestant family that did not share the mainstream Bible or its conventions of interpretation. Until the first decades of the twentieth century, many Lutherans were able to avoid direct confrontation with the mainstream Bible because of the continued use of European mother tongues. The Lutherans maintained a religious tradition strong enough to sponsor most of the one hundred German-language Bibles of the period (including editions from Muscatine, Iowa, Erie, Pennsylvania, Ravenna, Ohio, Joliet, Illinois, and Nashville, as well as from the major publishing centers); twenty-two

Swedish Bibles (including editions published in Rockford and Rock Island, Illinois, and Worcester, Massachusetts); ten Danish editions; seven Norwegian editions; and four Finnish editions.

When English finally became unavoidable, Lutherans did not produce their own translations, as the Catholics and Jews had attempted. Rather, the path of Americanization lay in choosing one of the American Protestant alternatives as an ally in maintaining the Lutheran heritage. The results of such choices were the production of Lutheran variations on Protestant liberalism, as with Charles Michael Jacobs (1875–1938), or on Protestant fundamentalism, as with Michael Reu (1869–1943).[63]

It is speculation, but one of the reasons for the ambiguous character of Lutheran identity in the United States may have something to do with Lutherans being suspended between Luther's German translation (or its Scandinavian equivalents) and the competing biblicisms of the fragmenting nineteenth-century Protestant mainstream. The absence of a distinct translation of the Bible may help explain why American Lutherans, despite large numbers and exemplary individuals, have not yet succeeded in communicating a sense of Lutheran distinctiveness in the culture at large.

The situation with the Mennonites was not quite as complex. Anabaptist biblicism had always stressed a literal application of New Testament commands and a strict fidelity to "following Christ." The problem of biblical self-definition for Mennonites at the start of the twentieth century was a problem of how to respond to the broader culture's changing views of Scripture. Norman Kraus, the best student of the subject, has described the alliance between Mennonites and fundamentalists as both natural (given the Mennonites' historic fidelity to the New Testament literally applied) and incongruous (given their historic rejection of the nationalism, patriotism, and militarism that made up such a large part of the mainstream biblical hermenuetic). In Kraus's phrase, "As [Mennonite leaders] began to be aware of the issues in modern theology, they knew that they were not liberals or Modernists, and in the heat of the moment they simply assumed that they were Fundamentalists."[64] Community identity was, therefore, set on a new course because of Mennonite decisions on the character of Scripture.

MARGINALIZED AMERICAN PROTESTANTS

Among several minority faiths arising out of the Protestant mainstream during the second half of the nineteenth century, the Holiness tradition had one of the most distinctive biblical emphases.[65] Holiness leaders who left the main Methodist denominations regarded themselves as outcasts providentially commissioned to preach the doctrine of entire sanctification. As they did so they developed what Stephen Lennox has called "the holiness hermeneutic" that stressed subjective appropriation of entire sanctification as the central theme of the Bible. The struggle for a Holiness identity soon became a two-front biblical battle, where Holiness preachers defended their exegesis against the traditional mainstream (which rejected their notion of sanctification) and the even newer Pentecostal movement (which carried Holiness exegesis to unacceptable conclusions about the baptism of the Holy Spirit). Given the emphasis on a right understanding of the Bible as the key to Holiness identity, it is not surprising that one of the leading Holiness evangelists, W. B. Godbey (1833–1920), after years of preaching entire sanctification from his Greek Testament, eventually in 1902 published his own translation of the New Testament "Dedicated to the Holiness People in All Lands."[66] Godbey's Testament did not differ substantially from the KJV, but its presence was an indication that religious self-definition often meant ownership of a distinctive translation of the Bible.

RELIGIONS WITH OTHER SCRIPTURES

The United States was also home to several minority faiths that followed additional divine revelations besides the Bible. It is striking that during this period virtually all of these faiths found it necessary to defer, in some fashion or the other, to the mainstream Protestant Bible even as each continued to promote its own special revelation as a key to defining the meaning of its community. Given this pattern, religions with alternative or supplemental Scriptures were also testifying to the influence of the mainstream Bible even as they made space for their own use of Scripture.

In southeastern Iowa, the Amana Society was left largely alone by its more conventionally religious neighbors for most of the period from its arrival from New York in 1855 to its dissolution as a religious community during the depression. The Community of True Inspiration, which had been formed in Germany and then guided in America by *Werkzeuge* (leaders who received prophetic revelations from God) and which practiced a religious communism far outside mainstream American conventions, nonetheless tried in its first communications with English-language interpreters to stress the conformity of its faith with the traditional Christian Scriptures. At the turn of the century, one of the first full histories of the Amana Society noted that in the society's literature, "the phraseology of the [German] Bible is frequently used or imitated" and that the record of divine communications through the

Werkzeuge was always "in common with the written word of the prophets and apostles." Moreover, the society wanted interested outsiders to know that it had never "acknowledged any basis of faith other than the literal word of God as contained in the Scriptures and in *Bezeugungen* [the revelations from *Werkzeuge*]," and that, in a restorationist idiom common in America, rejected "all sects and point to Jesus Christ alone as the living foundation."[67]

Christian Science was considerably more visible than the Amana Society, but its scripturalism resembled that of the Inspirationists in several ways. Like the Amana communists, who used a German translation of the Bible from the early eighteenth century as their Scripture, Christian Scientists also came up with their own version of the Bible. The edition was published in the mid-1920s by Arthur E. Overbury, who set it forth as interpreting "the New Covenant . . . from a Spiritual or Meta-Physical Standpoint, and Recognizes Healing as well as Teaching as a Component Part of True Christianity." Overbury wanted this version to be "unhampered by So-Called Ecclesiastical Authority" and also to be "based on the premise of 'Scientific Statement of Being' as given in 'Science and Health,' by Mary Baker Eddy."[68]

Overbury's translation does not seem to have been nearly as important, however, as Christian Science efforts to show the compatibility of Mrs. Eddy's revelations with the mainstream Bible. Thus, in the 1906 edition of Eddy's *Science and Health with Key to the Scriptures,* Christian Scientists were committed, "as adherents of Truth," to the "inspired Word of the Bible as our sufficient guide to eternal Life." The argument prefacing the book's "glossary," moreover, was a historically American one that people, if only they understood the Bible correctly, would have all the religion they needed: "In Christian Science we learn that the substitution of the spiritual for the material definition of a Scriptural word often elucidates the meaning of the inspired writer. . . . [This chapter] contains the metaphysical interpretation of Bible terms, giving their spiritual sense, which is also their original sense."[69] New revelations had led to the formation of Christian Science as a distinct faith, but, given the cultural influence of the mainstream Protestant Bible, these additional revelations were as likely to be accommodated within the conventions of mainstream biblical interpretation as they were to lead, in cases like Overbury, to a new translation.

Study of the Bible among Latter-day Saints enjoys the great advantage of a fine book devoted to the theme. Philip Barlow's *Mormons and the Bible* sets out clearly the way in which Mormonism can almost be defined by its adaptations and additions to the mainstream Protestant Bible. The most obvious conclusion from Barlow's study is that Mormonism has always been typically American in its reliance on Scripture but distinct in its own faith for how that reliance has taken shape. In Barlow's succinct summary:

> Since the time of Joseph Smith, the Mormon use of scripture has combined a traditional faith in the Bible with more "conservative" elements (like a more than occasional extra dose of literalism), some liberal components (such as Joseph Smith's . . . insistence on the limitations of human language), and, at least in an American context, some radical ingredients (an open canon, an oral scripture, the subjugation of biblical assertions to experimental truth or the pronouncements of living authorities). This peculiar recipe links the Saints sometimes with Catholics, sometimes with Jews, sometimes with more exotic groups like the Jehovah's Witnesses, and sometimes with others of the world's religions. It links them often with evangelical protestants. Yet taken as a whole, the combination constitutes the "difference" in the Mormon use of the Bible.[70]

Mormon scripturalism was made more interesting by the fact that Joseph Smith himself revised the KJV through selective abridgment and emendation. The resulting text, however, was not published until 1867, when it appeared under the auspices of the Reorganized Church of Jesus Christ of Latter-Day Saints. Perhaps it is this provenance that explains the main Mormon Church's hesitancy about elevating that version to the status of Scripture or the Book of Mormon.[71] The central matter for our purposes is that Mormonism flourished as a religion of written revelation and that, although never replicating the mainstream Bible entirely, Mormon scripturalism, as it developed, was brought into closer and closer connection with the KJV and the interpretive conventions of the Protestant mainstream. The Book of Mormon and other revelations to Joseph Smith gave Latter-day Saints their distinct identity, but that identity was also materially shaped by the form and texts of mainstream Protestant biblicism.

African American Christians and White Women Reformers

The most complicated instances of minority biblicism during this period were the uses of Scripture by African American Christians and the women (mostly white and Protestant) who sought to reform the patriarchialism that then dominated public life and the church.

In important ways the task was the same for both groups. Both faced a situation in which arguments from the mainstream Protestant Bible were a major weapon of those who wanted to reinforce the traditional status quo. The KJV, that is, was a major resource for demonstrating the inferiority, even the animality, of blacks as well as for keeping women from speaking in church and voting in the nation.[72]

Yet even in these circumstances, African Americans and women reformers were as fully steeped in the stories, wording, and style of the KJV as the Protestant mainstream. With a few exceptions, both also were deeply committed to the religious and social messages they found in the KJV, even as they used the mainstream Bible for purposes opposed by dominant elements in the Protestant mainstream.

The way in which the mainstream Bible was a means for both constriction and self-definition makes even more remarkable the fact that neither African Americans nor reforming women prepared their own translations of the Bible. These groups were like the Scots in Great Britain who, also without their own version of Scripture, nonetheless created a biblical civilization from a text prepared by the English who were, at best, indifferent to the culture of Scotland.[73]

Among African Americans, an occasional voice was raised for a new translation, but without fruition. In 1899, A.M.E. Bishop Henry Mc-Neal Turner extended his criticism of white oppression by appealing for a fresh version of the Scriptures:

> The white man's digest of Christianity or Bible doctrines are not suited to the wants, manhood, growth, and progress of the Negro. Indeed he has colored the Bible in his translation to suit the white man, and made it, in many respects, objectionable to the Negro. And until a company of learned black men shall rise up and retranslate the Bible, it will not be wholly acceptable and in keeping with the higher conceptions of the black man. . . . We need a new translation of the Bible for colored churches.[74]

With most African Americans, however, the more general sentiment was to use the narratives and phrases of the KJV with little thought for a new version.

Reform-minded women raised more complaints against the KJV. Sarah Grimké had sounded this note first, with characteristic force, in 1837:

> In examining this important subject [concerning the equality of the sexes], I shall depend solely on the Bible to designate the sphere of woman, because I believe almost every thing that has been written on this subject, has been the result of a misconception of the simple truths revealed in the Scriptures, in consequence of the false translation of many passages of Holy Writ. My mind is entirely delivered from the superstitious reverence which is attached to the English version of the Bible. King James's translators certainly were not inspired. I therefore claim the original as my standard, *believing that to have been inspired.*[75]

Something of the same note appeared in one of the resolutions from the Seneca Falls conference in July 1848. This time the animus was not against the KJV per se, but against how it had been put to use: "*Resolved,* That woman has too long rested satisfied in the circumscribed limits which corrupt customs and a perverted application of the Scriptures have marked out for her, and that it is time she should move in the enlarged sphere which her great Creator has assigned her."[76]

Such protests did not, however, lead to distinctly women's translations of the Bible. To be sure, there were at least three "Bibles by women" during the period, but none was what would be called today a feminist translation. In 1876 Julia Evelina Smith published her own "literal" translation of the whole Bible, which she had first begun to prepare to adjudicate the claims of William Miller and the Adventists several decades before. The circumstances of publication were definitely feminist. Smith and her sisters had refused to pay local taxes in Glastonbury, Connecticut, on the American principle that, since they were prohibited from voting, they should be exempt from taxation. When local officials sold off part of their property and appropriated some of their cattle to pay the tax, Smith and her sister sued. She also published her translation, because, she wrote, "it might help our cause to have it known that a woman could do more than any man has ever done" (i.e., in translating the Bible by herself). The translation itself, however, was remarkable only for its effort to use the same English word for each Greek and Hebrew word in original, not for the nature of its contents.[77]

The Woman's Bible of 1895 and 1898 represented a decidedly feminist approach to Scripture, but it was not a fresh translation. Elizabeth Cady Stanton, who organized the project, was joined by a team of coworkers in producing a commentary on passages relevant to women's issues. While the book made many suggestions concerning weaknesses in the KJV, it was not designed as a substitute for that version.

In 1924, the American Baptist Publication Society issued a translation of the New Testament by Helen Barrett Montgomery (1861–1934), a Baptist minister from Rochester, New York. This version did contain renderings more in keeping with feminist understandings of Scripture. For example, although the prohibition in I Timothy 2:12 against women exercising authority over men appeared substantially as in earlier versions, the Pauline injunction from I Corinthians 14:34 that women should keep silent was rendered as a quotation from the Corinthians rather than a command from Paul: "'In your congregation' [you write], 'as in all the churches of the saints, let the women keep silence in the churches, for they are not permitted to speak.'" But Montgomery's

Centenary Translation of the New Testament was published, as its title suggests, primarily to memorialize one hundred years of labor by the Baptist Publication Society. It was a New Testament translated by a woman, but not a "woman's New Testament."[78]

African Americans and women resembled each other in not producing their own versions of the Bible and in their consistent appropriation of the mainstream Protestant Bible. But in other ways they were quite different.

Reforming women were of the religious world of mainstream Protestantism but not comfortable in it. Through techniques, precedents, methods, and habits of mind cultivated by the mainstream Protestant tradition, reforming women tried to show that "the American Bible" promised a reality to women that the Protestant mainstream had not yet recognized.

By contrast, African American Christians were perforce in the world of mainstream Protestantism, but their religion was not of it. Through capacities of cultural creation arising from an African past and their experiences as slaves—that is, from circumstances almost completely alien to the Protestant mainstream—African American Christians used "the American Bible" to construct a religion substantially different from the Protestant mainstream.

WOMEN: OF BUT NOT IN

The situation for women reformers in the two generations after the Civil War was not the same as that faced by religious women in the late twentieth century.[79] An essay by Carolyn Osiek on "hermeneutical alternatives" now employed by women who oppose traditional female subordination provides a helpful point of comparison. Beginning with modern positions closest to those of the nineteenth-century Protestant mainstream, Osiek differentiates six possibilities of feminist biblical interpretation: (1) loyalists who accept but redefine traditional hierarchical notions; (2) loyalists who, to avoid hierarchy, reinterpret what they consider still to be an infallible text; (3) revisionists who feel that Judeo-Christian patriarchialism is historically but not theologically necessary; (4) sublimationists who find "the eternal feminine in biblical symbolism"; (5) liberationists who propose a radical reinterpretation of biblical eschatology to promote universal standards of justice; and (6) rejectionists who feel that the Bible has oppressed women throughout history.[80] In the late nineteenth and early twentieth centuries, loyalist and revisionist stances dominated, with only an occasional person such as Elizabeth Cady Stanton rejecting the authority of the

Bible entirely. Overwhelmingly, Protestant women reformers favored an approach that was both loyal to a traditional Protestant Scripture and eager to reinterpret it for the sake of equity for women. In fact, the main reforming impulse was to show that the "American Bible" could as easily support new activities like voting and the participation of women in public life as it had earlier been used to deny them.

The mainstream character of these debates is suggested by the character of opposition to a reforming use of the KJV. On the left, Elizabeth Cady Stanton wanted to do away with the Bible, which was certainly not a mainstream disposition. But the way she wanted to do it—with a commitment to the "scientific" conclusions of the new higher criticism along with her unflagging optimism about a new day of liberty and equality for all—marked her arguments as quintessentially of the mainstream.[81]

On the right, opponents of reform regularly cited the Scriptures, interpreted in traditional American fashion, as the source of their opposition. In 1871, for example, "Mrs. General Sherman" was joined by "One Thousand Ladies" in a petition to the U.S. Senate to oppose the vote for women. Their reason was that "Holy Scripture inculcates a different, and for us higher, sphere apart from public life."[82] The biblical traditionalists and fundamentalists who came to oppose the reform of women's roles exercised mainstream conventions of common-sense interpretation and straightforward empirical exegesis most vigorously of all.[83]

Reformers used the same weapons but to a different end. For many of them, the Bible was a key support. Or, as Aileen Kraditor has put it, "Most suffragists found all they sought in the pages of the Old and New Testaments."[84] In their work, moreover, white Protestant women discovered ample precedents in how the mainstream (or at least northern Whig representatives of mainstream Protestantism) had earlier used American intellectual methods to reinterpret the Scriptures for reforming purposes. Theodore Dwight Weld's *The Bible against Slavery* (1837) was the most important of many similar works that showed how the bare propositions of Scripture, which seemed to support slavery, could yield abolitionism. Similar exegetical gymnastics had transformed the Bible into a temperance tract.[85]

Protestant women reformers could also draw on deeply ingrained mainstream habits of mind in using the Bible to defend suffrage or a woman's right to preach. Once again, Sarah Grimké led the way. When in 1837 she attacked the mistakes of the KJV, she also affirmed the competencies of the American individual: "I . . . claim to judge for myself what is the meaning of the inspired writers, because I believe it to be the solemn duty of every individual to search the Scriptures for themselves, with the aid of the Holy Spirit, and not be governed by the views of any man, or set of men." Later that year she said much the same thing: "I examine any opinions of centuries standing, with as much freedom, and investigate them with as much care, as if they were of yesterday. I was educated to think for myself, and it is a privilege I shall always claim to exercise."[86]

The reformers' foundational commitment to the mainstream Bible, their knowledge of precedents allowing for reinterpretations within that mainstream, and their expertise in mainstream habits of mind help explain why Elizabeth Cady Stanton's *Woman's Bible,* which rejected biblical authority, received such lukewarm support from other women reformers.

Soon after the appearance of the first volume of *The Woman's Bible,* the twenty-eighth annual convention of the National American Woman Suffrage Association adopted the following resolution by a vote of 53 to 41: "That this Association is non-sectarian, being composed of persons of all shades of religious opinion, and that it has no official connection with the so-called 'Woman's Bible,' or any theological publication."[87]

With the second volume of *The Woman's Bible,* Stanton herself published a series of intriguing responses to two questions she had posed to a wide circle of woman's rights leaders: "(1) Have the teachings of the Bible advanced or retarded the emancipation of women? (2) Have they dignified or degraded the Mothers of the Race?"[88] Most of those who responded, if they supported the notion of a "woman's Bible" at all, did so from revisionist rather than rejectionist standpoints. One or two respondents, such as M. A. Livermore, even defended the Apostle Paul, "the advice, or the commands, to women given by Paul in the Epistles, against which there has been so much railing, when studied in the light of the higher criticism, with the aid of contemporary history and Greek scholarship, show Paul to have been in advance of the religious teachers of his time."[89]

The most telling defense of Scripture as an agent of reform came from Frances Willard, long-time head of the Women's Christian Temperance Union. Her response to Stanton's questions was an eloquent apology for Scripture as well as a summary of mainstream reforming approaches to the use of the Bible:

> No such woman as Mrs. Elizabeth Cady Stanton, with her heart aflame against all forms of injustice and of cruelty . . . has ever been

produced in a country where the Bible was not incorporated into the thoughts and the affections of the people and had not been so during many generations.

I think that men have read their own selfish theories into the Book, that theologians have not in the past sufficiently recognized the progressive quality of its revelation, nor adequately discriminated between its records as history and its principles of ethics and of religion, nor have they until recently perceived that it is not in any sense a scientific treatise; but I believe that the Bible comes to us from God, and that it is a sufficient rule of faith and of practice. . . .

To me the Bible is the dear and sacred home book which makes a hallowed motherhood possible because it raises woman up, and with her lifts toward heaven the world. This is the faith taught to me by those whom I have most revered and cherished; it has produced the finest characters which I have ever known; by it I propose to live; and holding to the truth which it brings to us, I expect to pass from this world to one even more full of beauty and of hope.[90]

Even Susan B. Anthony upbraided Stanton for letting her rejection of the Bible stand in the way of addressing the terrible inhumanities of the present, such as mistreatment of blacks: "Now this barbarism does not grow out of ancient Jewish Bibles—but out of our own sordid meanness!! And the like of you ought to stop hitting poor old St. Paul—and give your heaviest raps on the head of every Nabob—man or woman—who does injustice to a human being—for the crime! of color or or sex!!"[91] In 1930 Alice Stone Blackwell summed up a predominant attitude to efforts such as *The Woman's Bible* to remove Scripture as a key to the reforming impulse: "Mrs. Stanton was really more interested in attacking orthodox religion than in promoting equal rights for women."[92]

Most women reformers, in other words, wanted to use the mainstream American Bible for new purposes, but they also wanted to preserve that Bible, traditions for interpreting it, and its centrality in the culture. For them, a better use of the American Bible would lead to a fulfillment of the highest American ideals for all humans, female as well as male. The situation for African American Christians was considerably different.

AFRICAN AMERICAN CHRISTIANS: IN BUT NOT OF

It is difficult to overestimate the importance of the KJV for African American religion.[93] Personal accounts of the period are often saturated with a biblical presence. In her autobiography, published in 1886, Julia A. J. Foote, repeatedly testified to the centrality of the KJV in her experience. It was, for instance, a key element in her conversion:

Such joy and peace as filled my heart, when I felt that I was redeemed and could sing the new song. Thus was I wonderfully saved from eternal burning.

I hastened to take down the Bible, that I might read of the new song, and the first words that caught my eye were: "But now, thus saith the Lord that created thee, O Jacob, and he that formed thee, O Israel, fear not, for I have redeemed thee; I have called thee by thy name; thou art mine. When thou passest through the waters, I will be with thee, and through the rivers they shall not overflow thee; when thou walkest through the fire, thou shalt not be burned, neither shall the flame kindle upon thee." (Isaiah xliii.1,2)

The form of her experience was almost the same on the sad day that Foote's husband left for the sea: "While under this apparent cloud, I took the Bible to my closet, asking Divine aid. As I opened the book, my eyes fell on these words: 'For thy Maker is thine husband.' I then read the fifty-fourth chapter of Isaiah over and over again. It seemed to me that I had never seen it before. I went forth glorifying God."[94]

The same pattern appeared elsewhere. The sermon notes of Virginia W. Broughton, a holiness evangelist in Tennessee and Arkansas, leave a record of undeviating commitment to a biblical message.[95] Amanda Smith's spiritual autobiography did not cite Scripture as explicitly as did the writings of Foote and Broughton, but the message she proclaimed on several continents was thoroughly informed by "the holiness hermeneutic" as well as the phraseology of the KJV.[96]

Black poetic expressions of the period were likewise suffused with scriptural phrases, and they sometimes presented versified renditions of Old Testament narratives.[97] Even more clearly did African American spirituals testify to a steady contemplation of biblical experiences.

Sermons in black churches invariably began with biblical readings and continued on to apply the meaning of these passages in ways adapted to particular audiences.[98] Even black leaders, such as W. E. B. Du Bois, who had stopped attending church and who sometimes criticized the escapism of African American spirituality, showed a remarkable familiarity with the Bible. Du Bois was quoting the KJV accurately in his extreme old age, and as a younger man he once wrote a series of prayers to use privately that were keyed to appropriate scriptural texts.[99]

African American immersion in the KJV, the American Bible, was thorough, but the religion expressed in the cadences of the KVJ was not the religion of mainstream Protestantism. African Americans found something different than mainstream Protestantism when they read the Bible mediated to them by the Protestant mainstream. Occasionally, blacks found a millennialism in the Bible that was Afro-centric rather than American, especially as they contemplated what Albert Raboteau has called "without doubt the most quoted verse in black religious history": Psalm 68:31—"Princes shall come out of Egypt; Ethiopia shall soon stretch out her hands unto God."[100] Sparked by mediations on that text, J. Augustus Cole in 1888 called upon the black church to "make it her duty to instruct the race as to the right principles of religion by expunging from African Christianity all idolatrous imitations, which we have acquired from the white man." If this could be done, Cole anticipated a truly eschatological result: "God will be honored, the Church will be powerful, and we will no more 'do evil that good may come.' Then the millennium of the Negro will be near, when the sheep of other folds in Africa shall be united with those in America and the West Indies by the cord of Christianity, and then there shall be one flock under one Shepherd, Jesus Christ."[101]

More generally, however, African American use of the Bible led not so much to a self-conscious counter-religion as to a set of emphases largely unknown in mainstream Protestantism. Thus, A.M.E. Bishop W. J. Gaines observed in 1897 that "history presents no sublimer spectacle than the patience and non-resistance of this race who, though smarting under the wrongs of more than two hundred years, refused to take revenge into their own hands and rebel with violence and bloodshed against their oppressors. No race ever acted more like Jesus Christ, whose life was one long patient non-resistance to wrong."[102] This kind of emphasis went along with a Christian faith in which sacred and secular distinctions, as construed by the Protestant mainstream, broke down, where Old Testament narratives prevailed over New Testament doctrines, and where Jesus was defined as much through the experience of Moses as through the letters of Paul.[103]

Thus, from the resources of the Protestant mainstream, especially "the Protestant Bible," arose a minority faith—still biblical, still evangelical, still Protestant, but only barely the same religion that white Protestant preachers and teachers thought they were communicating when they read the words of the KJV to their slaves. Lawrence Levine has put the matter very well:

> Because Protestant churches failed to protect the slave's inner being from the incursions of the slave system, it does not follow that the spiritual message of Protestantism failed as well. Certainly the slaves themselves perceived the distinction. Referring to the white patrols which frequently and brutally interfered with the religious services of the slaves on his plantation, West Turner exclaimed: "Dey law us out of church, but dey couldn't law 'way Christ." Slave songs are a testament to the way in

which Christianity provided slaves with the precedents, heroes, and future promise that allowed them to transcend the purely temporal bonds
of the Peculiar Institution.[104]

The circumstances contributing to African American religion have
been well chronicled by Albert Raboteau, Lawrence Levine, Eugene
Genovese, and other perceptive historians. Almost certainly an African legacy provided a rich nutritive medium for black faith. Beyond
doubt the experiences of slavery shaped religion, along with every other
facet of African American life. But African American religion was also
a product of the mainstream Protestant Bible which, in the process of
passing from white to black, remained no longer simply mainstream
or simply Protestant.

From the 1860s to the 1920s, religion in the United States was overwhelmingly scriptural. The power of the mainstream Protestant Bible
was great, but neither the KJV nor the mainstream interpretive conventions ever monopolized scripturalism during this period. Through
a variety of means—use of the Bible in languages other than English,
fresh translations of the Bible into English, or employment of the mainstream Bible in ways unsanctioned by the mainstream—religious minorities defined themselves biblically just as effectively as did that
mainstream. The Bible, in other words, was always more, or other, than
the mainstream Protestant Bible.

But it was also never less. To a remarkable degree, the KJV and conventions of mainstream Protestant biblical interpretation exerted an
immense sway in America's diverse religious communities. This sway
was exercised unreflectively for many white Protestants; with a critical edge for some women reformers; as a threatening presence demanding alternative translations from Jews, Roman Catholics, and some
Baptists; as a religious given incorporated into new revelations for
Mormons, Christian Scientists, and some European sects; and as a
dynamic source of liberation for many African Americans.

Given the hereditary position of the KJV, it is worth asking if another sign of the decline of Protestant America may not have been the
modern English translations by Edgar J. Goodspeed and James Mof-
fatt that appeared in 1923 and 1924–25. By no means were these the
first, or necessarily even the best, new translations of the period, but
they did become popular, and in their popularity anticipated the flood
of extraordinarily successful new translations (several with sales in the
tens of millions) that have appeared in their train. If the mainstream
Protestant Bible was a substantial part of mainstream Protestant hegemony, then the decline of the mainstream Bible—for whatever wor-

thy religious purposes—quite naturally indicated, or even hastened, the decline of the Protestant mainstream.

Especially people who believe that the Bible is from God—even if they cannot agree among themselves on how much is in that Bible, who should interpret it, or what it means in whole or parts—will also conclude about this period that the Bible was always bigger than any of the uses to which any American community put it. To be sure, the Bible often functioned as a tame book—dignifying cultural proprieties, shoring up the exercise of power, serving the ambitions of leaders, and even sanctioning inhuman treatment of human beings. At the same time, messages from the Scriptures—however they were received in local cultures and also because they were received in local cultures— retained the capacity to renew individuals, transform groups, and confound the intentions of those who felt they owned the Scriptures.

Nowhere was this capacity more evident than among African Americans who in the handsbreadth of liberty gained after the Civil War reaped a harvest of experiences, like that described by Albert Raboteau, which had been sown in slavery: "One visitor to a night school for freemen in Beaufort, North Carolina, learned from the teacher the story of a fugitive slave 'who carried a big Bible about with her through the woods and swamps.' Though she was unable to read, she 'had got her old mistress to turn down the leaves at the verses she knew by heart, and often she would sit down in the woods and open the big Bible at these verses, and repeat them aloud, and find strength and consolation.'"[105]

If African Americans did not fit the pattern described by the missiologists Sanneh and Walls—in that the biblical translation that allowed them to define their own religious identity was the very translation employed by their oppressors to keep them in oppression—African Americans fit the missiological picture remarkably well in other respects, as they, along with other American minorities, were nerved by their own Bibles (or their own appropriation of some one else's Bible) to fashion community in the face of a religiously dominant mainstream culture.

What these specific Bibles offered was something cultural but also something transcendent. That reality was rarely expressed with greater piety, but also rarely with greater exception to the conventional vocabulary promoted by the Protestant mainstream, than in the preface to the Jewish Publication Society's 1917 translation when the committee "in all humility" submitted "this version to the Jewish people in the confident hope that it will aid them in the knowledge of the Word of God."[106]

Appendix

Table 6.1. English Editions of the Bible and the New Testament in the United States, 1860–1925 (Keyed to the Publication of the RV and ASV)

	1860–81	1881–1900	1901–25	Total
KJV	185	84	102	371
RV or RV plus KJV		57	2	59
ASV or combined with KJV, RV			18	18
Douay-Rheims-Challoner	25	13	13	51
Other Catholic editions	3	1	1	5
Jewish editions			4	4
Editions of other translations	26	23	27	76[a]
Total	239	178	167	584

Key: RV: English Revised Version; ASV: American Standard Version

a. 33 separate translations

Source: Enumerations are from Margaret T. Hills, ed., *The English Bible in America: A Bibliography of the Bible and the New Testament Published in America, 1777–1956* (New York: American Bible Society and New York Public Library, 1962).

Table 6.2. Complete, Foreign-Language Editions of the Bible Published in the United States, 1860–1925[a]

100	German
37	Hebrew
35	Spanish
22	Swedish
12	French
10 each	Dakota, Danish
9	Portuguese
8 each	Hawaiian, Italian
7	Norwegian
6	Welsh
4 each	Finnish, Gilbertese, Polish, Zulu
3 each	Arikara, Czech
2 each	Anglo-Saxon, Armenian, Dutch, Estonian, Gothic, Kalispel, Kussaie, Russian
1 each	Arabic, Bulgarian, Burmese, Cheyenne, Choctaw, Hidatsa, Hungarian, Lithuanian, Marshall, Nauru, Navaho, Romanian, Sheetswa, Winnebego
316	Total

a. The totals do not include editions published jointly with foreign firms, editions where the card in the National Union Catalog was totally in a non-roman script, or American Bible Society editions published outside the United States.

Source: Enumerations are from *The National Union Catalogue, Pre-1956 Imprints* (Chicago: American Library Association, 1980), vols. 53 and 54.

Notes

1. The role of the Bible is one of the most seriously under-researched topics in American religious history. In particular, the question of minority faiths and the Bible deserves to be studied from the sources; such study should also be integrated into the scholarship now burgeoning for the religious histories of African Americans, women, Mormons, Jews, Roman Catholics, and other minorities. This chapter offers, instead, a preliminary probe that skims sources and integrates material on the Bible only partially into the substantial literature that exists for the various minorities. A full treatment of the subject would also be alert to comparisons with the history of the Bible in other North Atlantic societies that have a strong Protestant influence, for example, English Canada and the regions of Britain and Australia. For a sense of how fruitful such comparisons can be, see Christiane d'Haussy, "Bible et société en Grande Bretagne," in *Bible de tous les temps*, vol. 8: *Le monde contemporain et la Bible* (Paris: Beauchesne, 1985), 161–86. I would like to thank Jason Mitchell for industrious research assistance on this project.

2. Genesis 1:2, from *The Holy Scriptures According to the Masoretic Text: A New Translation* (Philadelphia: Jewish Publication Society of America, 5677 [1917]), with lower-case "spirit" self-consciously revising the King James Version.

3. Lamin Sanneh, *Translating the Message: The Missionary Impact on Culture* (Maryknoll, N.Y.: Orbis, 1989), 2; see also Lamin Sanneh, "Gospel and Culture: Ramifying Effects of Scriptural Translation," in *Bible Translation and the Spread of the Church*, ed. Philip C. Stine (Leiden: E. J. Brill, 1990), 1–23.

4. Andrew Walls, "The Evangelical Revival, the Missionary Movement, and Africa," in *Evangelicalism: Comparative Studies on the Popular Protestantism of North America, the British Isles, and Beyond*, ed. Mark A. Noll, David W. Bebbington, and George A. Rawlyk (New York: Oxford University Press, 1994), 326; see also Andrew Walls, "The Translation Principle in Christian History," in *Bible Translation and the Spread of the Church*, ed. Stine, 24–39.

5. Of general surveys, F. F. Bruce, *The English Bible: A History of the Translations from the Earliest English Versions to the New English Bible* (New York: Oxford University Press, 1970), has much helpful information on the United States; by contrast, the essays in S. L. Greenslade, ed., *The Cambridge History of the Bible*, vol. 3: *The West from the Reformation to the Present Day* (New York: Cambridge University Press, 1963), although useful for other subjects, are almost valueless for understanding the cultural place of Scripture in the United States. I have attempted a survey in "The Bible in American Culture," in *Encyclopedia of the American Religious Experience*, ed. Charles H. Lippy and Peter W. Williams (New York: Charles Scribner's Sons, 1988), 2:1075–87.

6. Lewis O. Saum, *The Popular Mood of America, 1860–1890* (Lincoln: University of Nebraska Press, 1990), 3, and, on the decline of biblical quotation, 79–83.

7. Mark A. Noll, "The Image of the United States as a Biblical Nation, 1776–1865," in *The Bible in America,* ed. Nathan O. Hatch and Mark A. Noll (New York: Oxford University Press, 1982), 40 and notes. Eleven of the first sixteen American presidents (from Washington through Lincoln) had biblical first names; only three of the next thirteen did (from Andrew Johnson through Coolidge and counting Wilson as "Woodrow" instead of "Thomas"); and only two of the last twelve did (from Hoover through Clinton).

8. Mark A. Noll, *A History of Christianity in the United States and Canada* (Grand Rapids: Eerdmans, 1992), 361, which makes use of E. S. Gaustad, *Historical Atlas of Religion in America,* 2d ed. (San Francisco: Harper and Row, 1976); Roger Finke and Rodney Stark, "Turning Pews into People: Estimating Nineteenth-Century Church Membership," *Journal of the Scientific Study of Religion* 25 (1986): 180–92; Arthur A. Goren, "Jews," in the *Harvard Encyclopedia of American Ethnic Groups,* ed. Stephan Thernstrom (Cambridge: Harvard University Press, 1980); various reports of the U.S. Census.

9. Robert T. Handy, *A Christian America: Protestant Hopes and Historical Realities,* 2d ed. (New York: Oxford University Press, 1984), ch. 7. Some of the insights in this book are developed further in Robert T. Handy, *Undermined Establishment: Church-State Relations in America, 1880–1920* (Princeton: Princeton University Press, 1991). Also helpful on this "second Protestant disestablishment" is Martin E. Marty, *Modern American Religion,* vol. 2: *The Noise of Conflict, 1919–1941* (Chicago: University of Chicago Press, 1991).

10. Orientation for the polemical effects of the new biblical scholarship is provided by Grant Wacker, "The Demise of Biblical Civilization," in *The Bible in America,* ed. Hatch and Noll, 121–38; Paul A. Carter, *The Spiritual Crisis of the Gilded Age* (DeKalb: Northern Illinois University Press, 1971); Stephen John Lennox, "Biblical Interpretation in the American Holiness Movement, 1875–1920," Ph.D. diss., Drew Univesity, 1992; and Mark A. Noll, *Between Faith and Criticism: Evangelicals, Scholarship, and the Bible in America,* 2d ed. (Grand Rapids: Baker, 1991), 11–31. For a telling personal account of the struggle over the nature of Scripture, see William Newton Clarke, *Sixty Years with the Bible: A Record of Experience* (New York: Charles Scribner's Sons, 1909).

11. Lawrence A. Cremin, *American Education: The National Experience, 1783–1876* (New York: Harper and Row, 1980); Lawrence A. Cremin, *American Education: The Metropolitan Experience, 1876–1980* (New York: Harper and Row, 1988), 17–126.

12. See D. G. Hart, "Faith and Learning in the Age of the University: The Academic Ministry of Daniel Coit Gilman," and Bradley J. Longfield, "'For God, for Country, and for Yale': Yale, Religion, and Higher Education between the World Wars," both in *The Secularization of the Academy,* ed. George M. Marsden and Bradley J. Longfield (New York: Oxford University Press, 1992), 107–45, 146–69.

13. James Bryce, *The American Commonwealth,* 3d ed. (New York: Macmillan, 1893), 2:706–7, 714–27; André Siegfried, *America Comes of Age: A*

French Analysis (New York: Harcourt, Brace, 1927), 33–37; Philip Schaff, *America: A Sketch of Its Political, Social, and Religious Character*, ed. Perry G. Miller (New York: Charles Scribner, 1855, repr. Cambridge: Harvard University Press, 1961), 104–44.

14. Robert T. Handy, "Protestant Theological Tensions and Political Styles in the Progressive Period," in *Religion and American Politics from the Colonial Period to the 1980s*, ed. Mark A. Noll (New York: Oxford University Press, 1990), 283.

15. *The Army and Navy Messenger* [Shreveport, La.], March 16, 1865, 2, as quoted in Kurt Berends, "Proclaiming God's Cause: *The Army and Navy Messenger* in the Civil War," Wheaton College seminar paper, 1992.

16. Roy P. Basler, ed., *The Collected Works of Abraham Lincoln*, 9 vols. (New Brunswick: Rutgers University Press, 1953), 8:333; Arthur S. Link, ed., *The Papers of Woodrow Wilson*, vol. 23: *1911–1912* (Princeton: Princeton University Press, 1977), 20.

17. See, for example, a full column in the *New York Times*, July 9, 1905, 6.

18. Margaret T. Hills, ed., *The English Bible in America: A Bibliography of the Bible and the New Testament Published in America, 1777–1957* (New York: American Bible Society and New York Public Library, 1962), 255, 256, 363. (Hills is the indispensable authority for a chapter such as this.) For an account of the ABS's changing procedures, see Peter J. Wosh, *Spreading the Word: The Bible Business in Nineteenth-Century America* (Ithaca: Cornell University Press, 1994).

19. Allene Stuart Phy, "Retelling the Greatest Story Ever Told: Jesus in Popular Fiction," in *The Bible and Popular Culture in America*, ed. Allene Stuart Phy (Philadelphia: Fortress Press, 1985), 41–84.

20. Examples may be seen in Anita Schorsch and Martin Greif, *The Morning Stars Sang: The Bible in Popular and Folk Art* (New York: Universe Books, 1978).

21. Hills, ed., *English Bible in America*, 295–96.

22. Ibid., 317.

23. Carla Davidson, "The Traveler's Bible," *American Heritage* 42 (April 1991): 104–5; Hills, ed., *English Bible in America*, 329.

24. Solomon Schechter, *Seminary Addresses and Other Papers* (Cincinnati: Ark, 1915), 48–49, as quoted in Martin E. Marty, "America's Iconic Book," in *Humanizing America's Iconic Book*, ed. Gene M. Tucker and Douglas A. Knight (Chico: Scholars Press, 1982), 14.

25. The best example of such rhetoric was William Jennings Bryan's Cross of Gold speech before the Democratic Convention in Chicago in 1896.

26. Hills, ed., *English Bible in America*, 252–367. Everyone has realized, especially those such as Margaret Hills who work closely with biblical bibliographies, that totals for numbers of Bible editions are only approximations. For a tabulation of editions from *English Bible in America*, ed. Hills, as well as from Library of Congress catalogs, see table 6.1.

27. On Stuart's influence, see Thomas Olbricht, "Biblical Primitivism in

American Biblical Scholarship, 1630–1870," in *The Restoration Tradition in America,* ed. Richard Hughes (Urbana: University of Illinois Press, 1988). Jewish influence on mainstream Protestants is the theme of several chapters in *Hebrew and the Bible in America: The First Two Centuries,* ed. Shalom Goldman (Hanover: University Press of New England, 1993).

28. Quoted in Lewis Joseph Sherrill, *Presbyterian Parochial Schools, 1846–1870* (New Haven: Yale University Press, 1932), 38, emphasis added.

29. "Argument of George R. Sage," in *The Bible in the Public Schools: Arguments before the Superior Court of Cincinnati . . . (1870),* introduction by Robert G. McCloskey (Cincinnati: Robert Clarke, 1870, repr. New York: Da Capo Press, 1967), 152.

30. Quoted in John O. Geiger, "The Edgerton Bible Case: Humphrey Desmond's Political Education of Wisconsin Catholics," *Journal of Church and State* 20 (Winter 1978): 25.

31. Phoebe Palmer, "Witness of the Spirit," *Guide to Holiness* 47 (June 1865): 137, as quoted in Nancy A. Hardesty, *Your Daughters Shall Prophesy: Revivalism and Feminism in the Age of Finney* (Brooklyn: Carlson, 1991), 65–66. On how those conventions bridged theological divisions, see James H. Moorhead, "Prophecy, Millennialism, and Biblical Interpretation in Nineteenth-Century America," in *Biblical Hermeneutics in Historical Perspective,* ed. Mark S. Burrows and Paul Rorem (Grand Rapids: Eerdmans, 1991), 291–302, esp. 296–97.

32. The ironies of the situation were illustrated on both left and right. At the University of Chicgao, Shirley Jackson Case led the cheers for the new higher criticism as simply the recognition "that religion can be best understood by giving first attention, not to its theoretical aspects, but it its actual historical manifestations." Quoted in William J. Hynes, *Shirley Jackson Case and the Chicago School* (Chico: Scholars Press, 1981), 80, with many similar affirmations concerning the objectivity of scientific research.

On the other side of the ideological divide, Protestant fundamentalists, who prided themselves on the hermeneutical principle of "every man his own interpreter," produced during the period some enduringly powerful hermeneutical guides to the Scriptures, such as the first red-letter edition of the New Testament (1899), the first Thompson Chain Reference Bible (1908), and the first Scofield Bible (1909). On the Populist conservatives, see Timothy P. Weber, "The Two-Edged Sword: The Fundamentalist Use of the Bible," in *The Bible in America,* ed. Hatch and Noll, 101–20. "Modernists" and "fundamentalists" were united in their allegiance to nineteenth-century ideas of proper scientific method and Populist interpretive procedures, even as they rushed apart from each other in the content of their convictions.

33. For a superb analysis of the instability over time of the mainstream amalgam of nonsectarian Protestantism, unfettered science, and democratic freedom, see George M. Marsden, *The Soul of the University: From Protestant Establishment to Established Nonbelief* (New York: Oxford University Press, 1994).

34. For a Protestant argument against the Protestant-scientific-patriotic

synthesis of the nineteenth century, see Mark A. Noll, George M. Marsden, and Nathan O. Hatch, *The Search for Christian America*, 2d ed. (Colorado Springs: Helmers and Howard, 1989).

35. Surprisingly, Strong referred only infrequently to the Bible in *Our Country: Its Possible Future and Its Present Crisis* (New York: American Home Missionary Society, 1885), although when he did cite Scripture it was in a characteristically mainstream way to emphasize the value of honestly gained wealth for defending Anglo-Saxon institutions (183–207).

36. Foreign-language Bibles are organized in *The National Union Catalog, Pre-1956 Imprints* (Chicago: American Library Association, 1980), vols. 53 and 54. For more detail on these foreign-language editions, see table 6.2.

37. An overview, keyed to legal decisions of the 1950s and 1960s, is found in Donald E. Boles, *The Bible, Religion, and the Public Schools*, 3d ed. (Ames: Iowa State University Press, 1965). Several contemporary arguments concerning Bible reading in the public schools are found in *Religious Teaching in the Public Schools*, ed. Lamar T. Beman (New York: H. W. Wilson, 1927).

38. For succinct orientation to the general subject, see Jonathan D. Sarna, "Christian America or Secular America? The Church-State Dilemma of American Jews," in *Jews in Unsecular America*, ed. Richard John Neuhaus (Grand Rapids: Eerdmans, 1987), 8–19.

39. Naomi W. Cohen, *Jews in Christian America: The Pursuit of Religious Equality* (New York: Oxford University Press, 1992), 5.

40. Cohen, *Jews in Christian America*, 80.

41. Ibid., 83.

42. Jacob Rader Marcus, *United States Jewry, 1776–1985* (Detroit: Wayne State University Press, 1993), 3:186.

43. *The American Jewish Yearbook* 16 (5675 [1914]): 138; 17 (5676 [1915]): 203–4; 18 (5677 [1916]): 84–85.

44. On anti-Semitism in fiction, see *Essential Papers on Jewish-Christian Relations in the United States*, ed. Naomi A. Cohen (New York: New York University Press, 1990), 112–13; on the Reform Association, see Howard M. Sachar, *A History of the Jews in America* (New York: Knopf, 1992), 81–82.

45. Virginia L. Brereton, "The Public Schools Are Not Enough: The Bible and Private Schools," in *The Bible in American Education*, ed. David L. Barr and Nicholas Piediscalzi (Philadelphia: Fortress Press, 1982), 43–45.

46. On that opposition, see Brereton, "The Public Schools," 45; Jay P. Dolan, *The American Catholic Experience* (Garden City: Doubleday, 1985), 267; and James Hennesey, *American Catholics* (New York: Oxford University Press, 1981), 122, 125, 166.

47. Geiger, "The Edgerton Bible Case," 13–28, quotations on 16, 19.

48. Isaac Leeser, *Occident* (1851): 480, (1853): iii, as quoted in Jonathan D. Sarna and Nahum M. Sarna, "Jewish Bible Scholarship and Translations in the United States," in *The Bible and Bibles in America*, ed. Ernest S. Frerichs (Atlanta: Scholars Press, 1988), 86.

49. Quoted in Sarna and Sarna, "Jewish Bible Scholarship and Translations," 86.

50. Jonathan D. Sarna, "Jewish-Christian Hostility in the United States: Perceptions from a Jewish Point of View," in *Uncivil Religion: Interreligious Hostility in America,* ed. Robert N. Bellah and Frederick E. Greenspahn (New York: Crossroad, 1987), 13.

51. Sarna and Sarna, "Jewish Bible Scholarship and Translations," 95–103; Hills, ed., *English Bible in America,* 338; Jonathan D. Sarna, "A Modern Jewish Bible Translation," "The Margolis Translation," "The Compromise Translation," and "The Bible Commentary Project," in *JPS: The Americanization of Jewish Culture, 1888–1988* (Philadelphia: Jewish Publication Society of America, 1989), 97–103, 103–8, 108–16, 116–20.

52. Solomon Schechter, "The Bible," *The American Jewish Yearbook* 15 (5674 [1913]): 173, 174, 176–77.

53. See Yaakov Ariel, *On Behalf of Israel: American Fundamentalist Attitudes toward Jews, Judaism, and Zionism, 1865–1945* (Brooklyn: Carlson, 1991); and David A. Rausch, *Zionism within Early American Fundamentalism, 1878–1918* (New York: Edwin Mellen, 1979).

54. "Preface," *Holy Scriptures According to the Masoretic Text,* iv, vii–viii.

55. See Sarna, *JPS,* 109–10, for a discussion of how this translation emerged from the Jewish Publication Society's Translation Committee.

56. Francis Patrick Kenrick, "Introduction," in *The Pentateuch. Translated from the Vulgate, and Diligently Compared with the Original Text, Being a Revised Edition of the Douay Version. With Notes, Critical and Explanatory* (Baltimore: Kelly, Heian and Piet, 1860), x. A full account of Kenrick's work is found in Gerald P. Fogarty, *American Catholic Biblical Scholarship* (San Francisco: Harper and Row, 1989), 14–34.

57. Hills, ed., *English Bible in America,* 260; Harold P. Scanlin, "Bible Translation by American Individuals," in *The Bible and Bibles in America,* ed. Frerichs, 49.

58. For thorough background, see Barbara Welter, "From Maria Monk to Paul Blanshard: A Century of Protestant Anti-Catholicism," in *Uncivil Religion,* ed. Bellah and Greenspahn, 49 and notes.

59. G. Dershon, "The Catholic Church and the Bible," *Catholic World* 7 (1871): 657.

60. James Gibbons, *The Faith of Our Fathers: Being a Plain Exposition and Vindication of the Church Founded by Our Lord Jesus Christ,* 110th ed. (1876, repr. New York: P. J. Kennedy, 1917), ch. 8, quotation on 63.

61. Hugh Pope, *The Catholic Church and the Bible* (New York: Macmillan, 1928), 93, 8.

62. Keane's and Hopkins's works are reprinted, along with a helpful introduction, in *Devotion to the Holy Spirit in American Catholicism,* ed. Joseph P. Chinnici (New York: Paulist, 1985).

63. James Kenneth Echols, "Charles Michael Jacobs, the Scriptures, and the Word of God: One Man's Struggle against Biblical Fundamentalism among American Lutherans," Ph.D. diss., Yale University, 1989. For an example from Johann Michael Reu of the American-Lutheran amalgam that resulted from this process, see *Two Treatises on the Means of Grace* (Minneapolis: Augsburg,

1952), where Reu repeats in "What Is Scripture and How Can We Become Certain of Its Divine Origin?" some of the best arguments made by American Protestant conservatives, for example, B. B. Warfield, for the inneracy of Scripture; but in "Can We Still Hold to the Lutheran Doctrine of the Lord's Supper?" he uses largely Continental sources to argue for a traditional Lutheran view of the eucharistic real presence.

64. C. Norman Kraus, "American Mennonites and the Bible," in *Essays on Biblical Interpretation: Anabaptist-Mennonite Perspectives,* ed. Willard M. Swartley (Elkhart: Institute of Mennonite Studies, 1984), 131–50, quotation on 146.

65. This paragraph depends almost entirely on Lennox, "Biblical Interpretation in the American Holiness Movement."

66. Hills, ed., *English Bible in America,* 336.

67. Bertha M. H. Shambaugh, *Amana: The Community of True Inspiration* (Iowa City: State Historical Society of Iowa, 1908), 8, 23, 264.

68. Hills, ed., *English Bible in America,* 366–67.

69. Mary Baker Eddy, *Science and Health with Key to the Scriptures* (1906, repr. Boston: First Church of Christ Scientists, 1934), 479, 579.

70. Philip L. Barlow, *Mormons and the Bible: The Place of the Latter-day Saints in American Religion* (New York: Oxford University Press, 1991), 227–28. A helpful typology of modern Mormon approaches to Scripture that reflects much of the larger Protestant spectrum is Anthony A. Hutchinson, "LDS Approaches to the Holy Bible," *Dialogue: A Journal of Mormon Thought* 15 (Spring 1982): 99–125.

71. Barlow, *Mormons and the Bible,* 46–61; Hills, ed., *English Bible in America,* 270. For later ambiguity toward this version, see Thomas G. Alexander, *Mormonism in Transition: A History of the Latter-day Saints, 1890–1930* (Urbana: University of Illinois Press, 1986), 222.

72. See the examples from 1867 through 1902 republished as volumes 5 (*The "Ariel" Controversy: Religion and "The Negro Problem,"* Part 1) and 6 (*The Biblical and "Scientific" Defense of Slavery: Religion and "The Negro Problem,"* Part 2), in *Anti-Black Thought, 1863–1925: "The Negro Problem,"* ed. John David Smith (Hamden: Garland, 1992). For conservative use of the Bible against women's reforms, a good summary is in Donna A. Behnke, *Religious Issues in Nineteenth-Century Feminism* (Troy, N.Y.: Whitston, 1982), 221–44.

73. David Ogston, "William Lorimer's *New Testament in Scots:* An Appreciation," and David F. Wright, "'The Commoun Buke of the Kirke': The Bible in the Scottish Reformation," in *The Bible in Scottish Life and Literature,* ed. David F. Wright (Edinburgh: Saint Andrew Press, 1988), 60, 176.

74. Quoted in Stephen Ward Angell, *Bishop Henry McNeal Turner and African-American Religion in the South* (Knoxville: University of Tennessee Press, 1992), 256.

75. Sarah Grimké, *Letters on the Equality of the Sexes and Other Essays,* ed. Elizabeth Ann Bartlett (New Haven: Yale University Press, 1988), 31–32, emphasis in the original.

76. Elizabeth Cady Stanton, Susan B. Anthony, and Matilda Joslyn Gage, eds., *History of Woman Suffrage,* 6 vols. (Rochester: Susan B. Anthony, 1881–1922), 1:72.

77. Madeleine B. Stern, "The First Feminist Bible: The 'Alderney' Edition, 1876," *Quarterly Journal of the Library of Congress* 34 (Jan. 1977): 24–31, quotation on 27; see also Hills, ed., *English Bible in America,* 288–89.

78. Hills, ed., *English Bible in America,* 365–66.

79. The literature on American women, the Bible, and related subjects is now very rich. I have found especially helpful Barbara Welter, "Something Remains to Dare: Introduction to *The Woman's Bible,*" in *The Original Feminist Attack on the Bible (The Woman's Bible)* (New York: European Publishers, 1895/1898, repr. New York: Arno Press, 1974) (hereafter cited as *The Woman's Bible*); Nancy Hardesty, Lucille Sider Dayton, and Donald W. Dayton, "Women in the Holiness Movement: Feminism in the Evangelical Tradition," in *Women of Spirit: Female Leadership in the Jewish and Christian Traditions,* ed. Rosemary Ruether and Eleanor McLaughlin (New York: Simon and Schuster, 1979); many sections of *Women and Religion in America: A Documentary History,* vol. 1: *The Nineteenth Century,* and vol. 3: *1900–1968,* ed. Rosemary Radford Ruether and Rosemary Skinner Keller (San Francisco: Harper and Row, 1981, 1986); Barbara Brown Zikmund, "Biblical Arguments and Women's Place in the Church," in *The Bible and Social Reform,* ed. Ernest R. Sandeen (Philadelphia: Fortress Press, 1982), 85–104; Behnke, *Religious Issues in Nineteenth-Century Feminism,* chs. 8, 13; Hardesty, *Your Daughters Shall Prophesy;* and Margaret Lamberts Bendroth, *Fundamentalism and Gender, 1875 to the Present* (New Haven: Yale University Press, 1994). Also helpful on its specific subject is James Smylie, "*The Woman's Bible* and the Spiritual Crisis," *Soundings* 59 (Fall 1976): 305–28.

80. Carolyn Osiek, "The Feminist and the Bible: Hermeneutical Alternatives," in *Feminist Perspectives on Biblical Scholarship,* ed. Adela Yarbro Collins (Chico: Scholars Press, 1985), 93–106, quotation on 102.

81. Elizabeth Cady Stanton, "Introduction," *The Woman's Bible,* 1:7–13.

82. Welter, "Introduction," *The Woman's Bible,* xv–xvi.

83. See Bendroth, *Fundamentalism and Gender;* and Betty A. DeBerg, *Ungodly Women: Gender and the First Wave of American Fundamentalism* (Minneapolis: Fortress Press, 1990).

84. Aileen S. Kraditor, *The Ideas of the Woman Suffrage Movement, 1890–1920* (New York: Columbia University Press, 1965), 77.

85. For solid treatment of these precedents, see Hardesty, *Your Daughters Shall Prophesy,* 69–73.

86. Grimké, *Letters,* 31–32, 81.

87. *The Woman's Bible,* 2:215–17.

88. Ibid., 2:185

89. Ibid., 2:199.

90. Ibid., 2:200–201.

91. Anthony to Stanton, Dec. 2, 1898, as quoted in Kraditor, *Ideas of the Woman Suffrage Movement,* 78.

92. Quoted in Behnke, *Religious Issues in Nineteenth-Century Feminism*, 128.

93. On the importance of Scripture for African American Christians, I have found the following to be of great use: James Weldon Johnson, ed., *The Book of American Negro Spirituals* (New York: Viking, 1925), 20–21; William H. Pipes, *Say Amen, Brother! Old-Time Negro Preaching: A Study in American Frustration* (Westport: Negro Universities Press, 1951); Lawrence W. Levine, *Black Culture and Black Consciousness: Afro-American Folk Thought From Slavery to Freedom* (New York: Oxford University Press, 1977); Albert J. Raboteau, *Slave Religion: The "Invisible Institution" in the Antebellum South* (New York: Oxford University Press, 1978), 239–43; Vincent L. Wimbush, "The Bible and African Americans: An Outline of an Interpretive History," in *Stony the Road We Trod: African American Biblical Interpretation*, ed. Cain Hope Felder (Minneapolis: Fortress Press, 1991); Timothy E. Fulop, "'The Future Golden Day of the Race': Millennialism and Black Americans in the Nadir, 1877–1901," *Harvard Theological Review* 84 (1991): 75–99; and Janet Duitsman Cornelius, *When I Can Read My Title Clear: Literacy, Slavery and Religion in the Antebellum South* (Columbia: University of South Carolina Press, 1992). Other relevant accounts for the antebellum period are mentioned in Noll, "The Image of the United States as a Biblical Nation," 48–51.

94. Julia A. J. Foote, *A Brand Plucked from the Fire: An Autobiographical Sketch by Mrs. Julia A. J. Foote* (1886), in *Spiritual Narratives*, ed. Sue E. Houchins (New York: Oxford University Press, 1988), 33, 61.

95. Virginia W. Broughton, *Twenty Years' Experience of a Missionary* (1902), in *Spiritual Narratives*, ed. Houchins, 130–40.

96. Amanda Smith, *An Autobiography: The Story of the Lord's Dealings with Mrs. Amanda Smith the Colored Evangelist*, ed. Jualynne E. Dodson (Chicago: Meyer and Brother, 1893, repr. New York: Oxford University Press, 1988).

97. See, for example, Priscilla Jane Thompson, "David and Goliath" (1900), in *Collected Black Women's Poetry*, ed. Joan R. Sherman (New York: Oxford University Press, 1988), 2:58–64.

98. Pipes, *Say Amen, Brother!* 72.

99. W. E. B. Du Bois, "Hail Humankind!" in *W. E. B. Du Bois Speaks: Speeches and Addresses, 1920–1963*, ed. Philip S. Foner (New York: Pathfinder Press, 1970), 321. Du Bois ends this address by quoting the KJV from Isaiah 55:1: "Listen to the Hebrew prophet of communism: Ho! every one that thirsteth, come ye to the waters; come, buy and eat, without money and without price!" W. E. B. Du Bois, *Prayers for Dark People* [ca. 1909–10], ed. Herbert Aptheker (Amherst: University of Massachusetts Press, 1980).

100. Raboteau, quoted in Fulop, "'Future Golden Day of the Race,'" 85. Fulop provides the best sustained coverage I have found on African American development of explicitly biblical themes.

101. Ibid., 87–88.

102. Ibid., 88.

103. Levine, *Black Culture and Black Consciousness,* passim, is excellent on the nature of this faith, as are, for an earlier period, Eugene D. Genovese, *Roll, Jordan, Roll: The World the Slaves Made* (New York: Random House, 1972), 159–284; and Donald G. Mathews, *Religion in the Old South* (Chicago: University of Chicago Press, 1977), 185–236.

104. Levine, *Black Culture and Black Consciousness,* 54.

105. Raboteau, *Slave Religion,* 240.

106. "Preface," *Holy Scriptures According to the Masoretic Text,* xii.

SEVEN

Missions and the Making of Americans: Religious Competition for Souls and Citizens

R. Scott Appleby

In 1922, C. A. Brooks, an apologist for the Protestant missionary enterprise, looked back upon a century of concerted efforts to evangelize America. He described an "irrepressible conflict" between Roman Catholicism, "a religion of autocracy and aristocracy with sensuous forms which appeal to the imagination and to superstitions which hold men in their power," and evangelical Christianity, whose proclamation of "the Open Word of God" has "everywhere been the Magna Charta of civil and social progress." Where Catholicism succeeds in winning souls, Brooks argued, "liberty is denied and ignorance and illiteracy reach their highest rate." Where Protestant Christianity has reigned, by contrast, "in the place of autocracy has reigned religious liberty; instead of aristocracy, religious democracy." As a citizen of the United States, Brooks acknowledged the right of Catholics to compete for converts and the right of potential converts to decide for themselves their religious destiny, but he also made it clear that liberty could lead to its own undoing were it to advance the cause of "Romanism."[1]

Roman Catholicism was not the only repugnant religious force threatening the moral and civic order of Protestant America. "The Mormon menace," as one of its former "dupes" termed it, was also among the miscreant faiths rearing their un-American heads. Nor were Protestants the only mudslingers in the field. The eminent leader of Reform Judaism, Isaac Mayer Wise, was incensed at the "rascality" of Protestant missionaries who seemed to deny Jews their right as Americans to practice their religion in peace. Indignant Jews accused the missionaries of bribery, fraud, hypocrisy, deception, impertinence, imposition, laziness, immorality, and false piety.[2] Catholic evangelists likewise abandoned the rhetoric of civility in castigating the "devilish" Native Americans who resisted their civilizing missions.[3]

The rhetoric of militant evangelism, reflected in the aggressive tactics of Christian missionaries, seemed justified by the high stakes involved in the competition for souls. The surge of immigration and the influx of millions of foreigners after the Civil War, until restrictions were imposed in 1920, made America in these decades seem a ripe, open field for harvest by energetic, idealistic, and dedicated home missionaries. Efforts to ensure the Christian identity of the United States also extended to missionary activity among Native Americans and African Americans.

A synoptic history of American religion between the Civil War and World War I depicts the period as a time of paradox and irony, of overwhelming promise and also dire conflict. Religion appeared to be headed in ecumenical, modernist, and cosmopolitan directions, but it also tended to be reactive and inward-turning as denominational boundaries proliferated and ethnoreligious enclaves served as protective cocoons.[4]

In comparing religious traditions in their missionary efforts, we can see clearly the tension between these two tendencies of American religion; indeed, the tendencies often coexisted within the same denomination. Further, we see a somewhat different picture than is presented by the conventional juxtaposition of a monolithic Protestant mainstream against several "outsider" or minority faiths. The study of comparative missionary efforts nuances this conventional portrait in two ways. First, it causes us to question the assumption that evangelical Christians—members of the Baptist Home Mission Society, for example—were somehow marginal to the Protestant mainstream. Although Protestantism did lay persuasive claim to the center of American religion and society, the missionary enterprise—so essential to mainstream Protestant identity—was embraced in the same ways and for the same reasons by a variety of Protestant Christians. Second, in observing missionary activity, the map of American religion is not divided into two distinct regions, with mainstream Protestants on one side and minority faiths on the other. Instead, it is configured in overlapping circles. On their terms, Catholics as well as evangelicals, Mormons as well as Jews, were intensely active in the competition for souls. Even if this was not a term or concept inherent in the religious imagination of a denomination, it was nonetheless drawn into the competition, if only in a defensive mode. This inevitability of conflict is best exemplified in the case of the Jews, who did not harbor historic or theological missionary impulses but were nonetheless impelled to counterattack in order to defend their religious identity.

Such unlikely players were drawn into the competition for souls because it was cast not only in religious but also in civic terms. Mainstream Protestants as well as American Catholics and Jews framed the competition in these terms. Missions were, in short, an important arena of religious and ethnic conflict over the true meaning of Americanism. Protestant and Catholic home mission literature after the Civil War reflects a concern with saving souls and winning converts and also making Americans. Each of these two major Christian traditions cast its net far and wide, potentially to encompass Jews, Mormons, Blacks, and Native Americans—and one another. Jews and Mormons in particular resisted the religious imperialism of the missionaries but accepted the Americanist assumptions underlying it.

The complex relationship between the two missionary goals—religious conversion and Americanization—as pursued in a pluralist religious culture is the central theme of this chapter.

Missionaries saw themselves as being responsible for the civic no less than the spiritual character of their "clients." This was a natural assumption for Protestantism, which had cast itself as the religious embodiment and public guardian of American values. Yet Protestantism faced internal diversity and a host of issues that demanded coherent response. Within the Protestant home mission field itself, for example, were significant disagreements over matters such as the acceptable degree to which new or potential converts should retain the language, culture, and ethnic affiliation of their past. Although many missionaries argued strenuously that ethnic customs and native language should be respected and preserved, others saw these traits as inseparably bound to a primitive form of religion and civic culture. In addition, developments such as the elaboration of premillennial thought and the rise of Pentecostalism midway through the period provided competing theological justifications for proselytism and further complicated the question of American identity.[5] Nonetheless, Protestants in their diversity were united by the otherness, the strangeness, of the "unwashed" immigrants, the so-called outsiders. By sheer numbers Catholic immigrants threatened to transform the United States and jeopardize the Protestant hegemony over its mainstream cultural values and institutions. However it was to be theologically construed and culturally constructed, the Protestant missionary enterprise must provide a powerful response to this challenge from "Romanism."

Each of the two major Christian traditions had its own vision of a Christian America, of course; each occupied its own unique place in American political and religious culture; and each responded to different challenges and opportunities. Roman Catholics struggled with their brand of internal diversity and pondered the meaning of "true Americanism." Like other outsiders, Catholics debated questions such as the appropriate response to Protestant missionary encroachments, the pace of accommodation to American culture, and the need for internal evangelization or self-proselytism, that is, missionary efforts designed to the renew and retain "the faith of our fathers."

Within and across these camps people argued over the definition of success. Is a successful missionary career measured in numbers of converts won? they asked. And how many? Or is it measured in terms of effective educational and reform work for general civic purposes? And they experienced the routine disappointments of any overly ambitious, inadequately staffed enterprise with limited resources: a crop of mediocre workers and leaders who sometimes undermined the work of the best and brightest; inconsistent application of principle; and, occasionally, incoherent principles of evangelization.

Indeed, countermissionary activism propelled the construction or reconstruction of religious identity and thereby served as a strategy for survival. American religious outsiders built enclaves, as that term is used in cultural anthropology: self-contained communities that assume certain organizational and behavioral patterns out of fear of losing members of a traditional religious community because "the number of defectors is on the rise, while the distinction maintained in the past between apostates and those faithful to the Covenant has gotten blurred."[6] Both Catholics and Jews bolstered their respective enclaves when Protestant missionaries came calling.

The consequences of pluralism and the competition for souls it fostered eventually compelled Protestant Christians in particular to regard missionizing in a new light. During the latter half of the nineteenth century the two conversions, the religious and the civic, were presumed to go hand in hand. By the turn of the century, however, denominational and interdenominational mission leaders were shifting their emphasis to civic culture rather than religious conversion. Americanism overtook creedalism. The assumption seemed to be that American civic culture could contain a prominent religious element. Social welfare and relief programs aimed at character-building claimed a larger percentage of missions' budgets and energies by the 1920s than they had in the 1880s, with foreign churches and explicitly religious programs and appeals playing a relatively diminished role. If we cannot make immigrant masses into the best kinds of Christians, one missionary concluded, at least we can make them into civilized Americans.[7]

Why did this shift in emphasis occur? In the following descriptions of competition for or among Catholics, Protestants, Jews, Native Americans, and African Americans two answers emerge. First, the vignettes depict the striking resilience of ethnoreligious groups and their resistance to proselytization. They took seriously the guarantee of religious liberty provided by the U.S. Constitution. Jewish and Catholic programs to counter Protestant missionary influence, for example, were based in part upon this awareness of constitutional rights. The barri-

ers to successful evangelization of immigrants and Native Americans
were formidable, and it became increasingly apparent that the wholesale creedal conversion of peoples was not to be.

Second, the reconciliation of the missionary ethos and American
values was increasingly seen as a problem. In this chapter, I examine
Catholic, mainstream Protestant, and Jewish responses to that problem, but Mormonism, which posed a particularly strong challenge to
Protestant and Catholic missionary apologists, also deserves mention.

The aggressive missionary campaigns of the Mormons both imitated and scandalized leaders of the Protestant mainstream and caused
them to rethink the "American-ness" of the missionary enterprise. The
Home Protection Association polemicist Alfred Henry Lewis attacked
Brigham Young in print, portraying the Mormon leader as an autocrat
and anti-democrat who sought to coerce not only his own followers
but unsuspecting Americans as well. In 1905 Lewis published the "confession" of the former Mormon "assassin" John Doyle Lee. The sala-
cious exposé sought "to warn American men and particularly American women of the Mormon viper still coiled upon the national hearth"
and "to give a sufficient picture of the Mormon Church in its hateful
attitude towards all that is moral or republican among our people."[8]

Polygamy came in for vigorous condemnation as a Mormon missionary ploy that was particularly un-American and intended "to mark the
Church members and set them apart from Gentile influences." Were it
not for the stigma incurred by polygamy, "Mormonism is the sort of
religion that children would renounce and converts, when their heat
had cooled, abandon."[9] Other polemicists, Catholics as well as Protestants, wondered about the probity of extending to Mormon missionaries the same freedoms and privileges enjoyed by "true Americans."[10]

In the sections that follow, I examine the often paradoxical Protestant and Catholic attempts to make Americans while winning converts,
the differing strategies of competition that resulted from the tension
between missionary zeal and American conventions of civility, and the
counterstrategies of the groups targeted by the missionaries.

Roman Catholics: Holding Their Own

"The losses which the Church has suffered in the United States of North
America number more than ten million souls." So proclaimed the Lucerne Memorial, a petition submitted to Pope Leo XII in 1891 by the
St. Raphaelsverein, an international organization dedicated to the care
of German Catholic emigrants. The petition charged the American
hierarchy and clergy, dominated numerically by the Irish, with gener-

al neglect of immigrant Catholics in the United States and recommended several measures to improve the deteriorating situation.[11] Notwithstanding its somewhat hysterical tone and inflated numbers, the memorial was a response to the pressure created by the influx of an estimated 2,475,000 Catholic immigrants from twenty or more countries between 1880 and 1900. Father Peter Abbelen of the Archdiocese of Milwaukee had sounded the alarm in 1886, claiming that grave losses to the faith were occurring in the absence of German Catholic parishes, priests, schools, and bishops. The Lucerne Memorial, designed to increase the pressure for national parishes and inspire other neglected immigrant groups to make similar demands, was published with great fanfare in the New York *Herald*.[12]

The signers of the memorial depicted the new immigrants as potential recruits to American Catholicism, recruits "who could contribute to the moral stature of their new homeland, as well as to the stimulation of religious consciousness in the old European fatherlands." Only "the true Church, of which Your Holiness is the highest shepherd" was capable of guiding the United States during this time of population growth and urban expansion "because it [the Church] is the true source of all progress and civilization." In order to harness the energies of the immigrant flock, the memorial continued, "It seems necessary to unite the emigrant groups of each nationality in separate parishes, congregations, or missions wherever their numbers and means make such a practice possible" and "to entrust the administration of these parishes to priests of the same nationality to which the faithful belong." Religion should be tightly bound to ethnicity. Priests in mixed areas, the memorial instructed, should provide catechetical instruction to each group in its own language; bishops should establish separate parochial schools for each nationality, with the curriculum of these schools taught in the mother tongue "as well as the language and history of the adopted country"; and all clergy should promote immigrant confraternities, charitable organizations, and mutual aid and protective associations. By these means "Catholics would be systematically organized and saved from the dangerous sects of Freemasons and organizations affiliated with it."[13]

The challenge of keeping immigrants faithful to the church produced a variety of American Catholic pastoral strategies; mission work and competition for souls unfolded within this larger context of concern for the retention of people transplanted from Europe. The bishops of the Third Plenary Council of Baltimore (1884) had this concern in mind when they mandated a separate, parochial school system and implemented measures to coordinate disparate Catholic organizations and

institutions in their various efforts to meet immigrant needs. By the time
the Lucerne Memorial was published, foreign missionaries had already
arrived; the Congregation of Missionaries of St. Charles Borromeo
(known as the Scalabrinis, after their founder), to take one example,
began work among New York's Italian immigrants in 1888 and expanded to Chicago in 1891.[14] And, as foreign missionaries and foreign-born
pastors addressed the concern for retention, immigrant parishes became
viable and vital institutions for preserving Catholic identity. They did
so by establishing the Catholic sacramental and devotional system, by
acting as a channel for immigrant assimilation into the workplace, and
thus by renewing the traditional European bonds between ethnicity and
religious affiliation.[15]

The emphasis in recent historical accounts of Americanism on the
conflict between conservatives and Americanists in U.S. Catholic hierarchy produces a distorted picture if one forgets that the "antagonists"
shared the same general set of assumptions and were working on the
same basic problem: How do we, as Roman Catholics, maintain a distinctive and exclusive religious identity without provoking religious
divisiveness or insulting non-Catholic Americans? Both camps, the
conservatives and the progressives alike, saw the need to convince other
Americans of the loyalty of American Catholics to the political institutions and values of the United States; both camps wished to assure
Rome of their loyalty to the temporal power of the pope at the same
time; and both camps believed that adopting an attitude of civility toward non-Catholics did not mean that religious divisions were acceptable or that Catholicism was not the only true church. The two camps
differed, however, on points of emphasis and on strategy. Conservative bishops such as Michael A. Corrigan of New York City and Bernard McQuaid of Rochester were reluctant to embrace American institutions such as schools and workers' associations as adequate means
to Catholic ends, and they believed that any religious association with
non-Catholics tended to compromise Catholicisms' doctrinal supremacy and exclusiveness. Americanist bishops such as John Ireland of St.
Paul and Cardinal James Gibbons of Baltimore were more confident
that the gap between American civic culture and Roman Catholic religious sensibilities was bridgeable, and they were more ready than the
conservatives to enter into pragmatic alliances with public school officials, labor unions, and other non-Catholic American institutions. It
is worth noting, however, that neither the conservatives nor the Americanists wished for Catholics to be perceived as violating the conventions of civil discourse.[16]

In part, the differing strategies of the two camps were based on different estimates of the relative strength of anti-Catholicism in the United States and the extent of Protestant missionary penetration into Catholic immigrant enclaves in New York, Philadelphia, Boston, Chicago, and elsewhere. In 1887 Catholic prelates, still smarting from the memory of the antebellum Know-Nothing movement, were alarmed when Henry F. Bowers and six associates (including a Methodist, a Lutheran, a Baptist, a Presbyterian, and a Congregationalist) founded the American Protective Association of Clinton, Iowa. Members swore a secret oath to "wage a continuous warfare against ignorance and fanaticism; . . . to strike the shackles and chains of blind obedience to the Roman Catholic church from the hampered and bound consciences of a priest-ridden and church-oppressed people; . . . [to] use my influence to promote the interest of all Protestants everywhere in the world; . . . [and] not [to] employ a Roman Catholic in any capacity if I can procure the services of a Protestant."[17] In 1896 the APA boasted a million members and had strongholds in the Midwest, where, they had warned in a particularly fantastic piece of propaganda, American Jesuits would lead a papal-inspired insurrection against the United States government.[18] Meanwhile, the Protestant Home Mission Society launched a concentrated campaign for the souls of immigrants in major urban areas, with New York City's Italian population high on the list of vulnerable enclaves.

To the conservative Catholic bishops this seemed a conspiracy of forces, the Protestant home missionary masquerading under the cloak of civil discourse and religious liberty, the APA nativist revealing the true face behind the mask. In such an environment, enclave-building seemed a prudent strategy. Americanists, by contrast, welcomed the competition, arguing that Catholicism, being the one true faith, would only prosper in an environment that allowed open and unrestricted competition of ideas.

The Protestant mainstream, in other words, evoked two types of reaction from the Catholic leadership. Not to be outdone by Protestant millennial enthusiasm or nativist identification of true Americanism with Protestantism, the Catholic Americanists produced a patriotic discourse in which the American republic, the age of science, and the promise of true liberty found fullest expression in the Catholic Church and vice-versa.[19] Conservatives, on the other hand, backed the Lucerne Memorial, nationalist churches, parochial schools, and parish missions that strengthened Catholic identity and prevented slippage rather than competing with Protestantism, either for souls or on ideological or rhetorical grounds. That the conservative strategy carried the day is apparent not only from the papal condemnations of Americanism (1899) and modernism (1907), and the subsequent shift of the progressives' energies from "the conversion of America" to social welfare programs, but also from the resistance of immigrant Catholics to Protestant missionary efforts. Immigrants did keep the faith, in large part because the church devoted its energies to enclave-building, a preoccupation within which missionizing usually meant competition for *Catholic* souls. This was a battleground where the Catholic Church exploited its natural advantage.[20]

"In the Catholic Church of the United States, the work of evangelization has been primarily directed within the boundaries of the church rather than extended out to non-Catholics and non-believers."[21] That statement is particularly compelling in that it was made by Paul Robichaud, archivist of the Missionary Society of St. Paul the Apostle (the Paulists), the first American male religious order and one oriented in its beginnings to the conversion of non-Catholic Americans. "We have tried Protestantism and found it wanting," the founder of the Paulists, Isaac Hecker, proclaimed in 1855, when he was still a Redemptorist priest. "It is inadequate to satisfy the needs of the heart or to meet the demands of the intellect."[22]

Hecker, the son of German immigrants in New York and a member of the transcendentalist community at New England's Brook Farm before his conversion to Catholicism in 1844, was convinced that Protestants in America would follow him into the Catholic Church. In 1858, however, his associates were divided over Hecker's insistence that their missionary efforts be directed to non-Catholics; as Redemptorists, they had helped immigrants keep the faith by specializing in missions to Catholics. Hecker, however, was less concerned with solidifying the faith of immigrant Catholics and protecting well-defined doctrinal borders than with reaching out to the elite, unchurched Yankees, to other "earnest seekers," and to middle-class Catholics. For Hecker, a "Catholic America" connoted a providential era in which the Holy Spirit would lead all Americans, Catholics and non-Catholics alike, to an orderly consensus and a universal brotherhood based on an interior experience of the Holy Spirit "speaking the same message of natural rights and natural laws in conscience, in the church, and in historical events."[23] Yet Hecker's associates felt that non-Catholic missions would be difficult to arrange, costly, and unattractive to busy Catholic priests and bishops.

Hecker won that early round, but his grand vision eventually succumbed to the realities of Protestant resistance to Catholicism, as well as to the unrelenting pastoral demands made upon his small missionary band by a burgeoning immigrant population. In his lectures and missions during the 1850s and 1860s, conducted in the Northeast and later in the Midwest, Hecker attracted hundreds (and, at times, thousands) of curious non-Catholics; very few of them converted to Catholicism. By 1869 he had turned his attention to other methods of reaching non-Catholics, including the journal *Catholic World* and the Perpetual Mission to Protestants located at the Paulist church in New York City; but his audience remained predominantly Catholic. Hecker miscalculated the strength of his opponent and underestimated the influence of the anti-Catholicism among nineteenth-century Protestants.[24]

From the 1860s to the 1890s the emphasis shifted to self-evangelization, to what Jay Dolan has termed "Catholic revivalism," which took the form of parish missions conducted by religious order priests for Catholics scattered in small towns and rural areas, as well as for immigrant laborers packed into the tenements of growing cities. The mission preacher evoked in individual listeners an intense personal experience of sin and grace, interpreted in the Roman Catholic religious idiom and framed by the sacraments of confession, communion, and confirmation. This "sacramental evangelicalism," as practiced by Jesuit, Redemptorist, and Paulist missionaries, "shaped the piety of the people and strengthened the institutional church" in the second half of the nineteenth century.[25]

Despite its similarities to the Protestant revival, however, the Catholic parish mission was modeled on European Catholic exemplars reaching back to the Counter-reformation. Catholic convert Orestes Brownson, scornful of Methodist-style camp meetings, claimed that any similarity between Protestant and Catholic missions indicated that the former had imitated the latter.[26] Although the religious order priests who conducted the parish missions no doubt had the European model in mind, their selective borrowing from the American model of revivalism was also apparent in the rhetorical style of the mission preaching, the stress placed on emotions and individual experience, and the demand that each person make a personal choice for Christ. The Catholic missionaries added the institutional element to the mix, of course: personal choice could be properly secured only by the Catholic sacraments, and the individual must interpret his or her personal experience in light of the European past of his or her family and friends.

The parish mission was well-suited to an immigrant people whose practice of the faith and devotion to the sacraments had not been particularly strong in Ireland, Italy, or Germany and who were in danger of drifting into religious apathy or, worse, into the clutches of the ubiq-

uitous Protestant soul-winner. In the 1890s, however, the Americanist
wing of the clergy, buoyed by apocalyptic expectations of a Catholi-
cized America and confident that immigrants were keeping the faith,
set out to convert non-Catholics. As in the case of the parish missions,
the primary model for Catholic "apocalypticism" was not Protestant
revivalism or premillennialism but developments in European Catholicism. Thomas Wangler has argued that Americanist bishops such as
John J. Keane and John Ireland were influenced more by the thinking
of the English Cardinal Henry Manning and Pope Leo XIII on the decay
of Catholicism in Europe and the providential destiny of the United
States than by any specific doctrines of mainstream American Protestantism.[27]

Nonetheless, the American religious climate was one of expansive
optimism about the providential role of the United States in renewing
the face of Christianity in the modern age, and the Protestant mainstream was decisive in shaping that climate. Given the Catholic Americanists' interaction with and awareness of developments in American
Protestantism, it seems accurate to conclude that the renewed interest
in Hecker's legacy and in non-Catholic missions emerged as a result of
a confluence of ideas, with the general American confidence in manifest destiny and the specific evangelical enthusiasm for milliennial ideas
serving as the backdrop for Ireland's and Keane's retrieval of the Roman Catholic tradition's distinctive version of salvation history.

The parallel experiences of the Americanists and liberal Protestants
are easier to discern. Both groups embraced the new learning, especially
the higher Biblical criticism, as a splendid, providential means of winning the world for Christ. Baptist editor and educator William Rainey
Harper, for example, saw biblical criticism as a powerful aid to missionizing; his journal *The Biblical World* and the adult education ventures he sponsored demonstrated the constructive side of critical studies. Similarly, William L. Sullivan, a Paulist missionary based at the
Apostolic Mission House in Washington, D.C., embarked on the path
to Catholic modernism after two years (1899–1900) of mission preaching in Tennessee, which was considered to be part of "the grandest work
before the church in this country." Sullivan became convinced that the
parish missions must be overhauled if Catholics were to reach Protestants and other non-Catholics. Needed was a new apologetic that spoke
to the everyday experience and values of Americans. Because his audiences were not receptive to the abstract metaphysics of the Catholic neo-
scholastic theological tradition, even when expressed popularly, Sullivan wanted to develop a new theological context for evangelization.
Americans seemed uncomfortable with any system or argument re-

moved from the concerns that they deemed meaningful, practical, and directly applicable to their lives as Americans. The evidence from this period suggests that Sullivan enjoyed his greatest success when he spoke to these basic questions in the context of the parish mission: the nature of right and wrong, the hope for redemption, the immortality of the soul, and the dignity of individual conscience. Yet he found Americans, especially non-Catholics, to be wary of authority that was not self-authenticating or respectful of cherished democratic values such as freedom of speech and liberty of conscience.[28] Returning to Washington in 1901, Sullivan devoted himself to study of the new critical sciences and strengthened his friendship with the Americanists. In 1907, after the papal condemnation of modernism, Sullivan began to drift away from institutional Catholicism.[29]

While Sullivan labored over the mission question, Hecker's biographer and closest disciple Walter Elliott led a new generation of Paulist missionaries in an effort to revive the mission to non-Catholics. Elliott encouraged diocesan bishops and priests to reach out to Protestants and the unchurched, and he attempted to institutionalize the non-Catholic mission by training seminarians at the Apostolic Mission House of the newly founded Catholic University in special procedures and techniques. In this training Elliott emphasized the conventions of civility, including a healthy respect for the religious sensibilities of his listeners. He cautioned prospective missionaries to wear street clothes rather than clerical garb during their presentations; to hold the initial lectures and missions in a public place (with the podium preferably draped by an American flag) rather than in a Catholic Church, where the majority of curious Protestants would feel uncomfortable (or would avoid altogether); to stress, wherever possible, the continuities between American values and Catholic religious principles; and to make use of a question box (with a few questions planted beforehand) designed to draw Protestant or unchurched Americans' fears and superstitions about Catholicism out into the open, where the missionary could presumably vanquish them.

Although the number of conversions to Catholicism increased as a result of the emphasis on missions to non-Catholics, this irenic effort met with essentially the same results as Hecker's earlier experience, and, beginning in about 1907, the Paulist mission to non-Catholics waned, even as it was transformed from an attempt to extend the faith to a defense of the faith conducted now in the church building itself and directed to a largely Catholic audience. This change in direction in Paulist missions was in part a response to the papal condemnation of Americanism and modernism. After 1909 all methodologies that sought

to engage or evangelize American culture on its own terms were potentially suspect in the eyes of church authorities. Frustrated in their
expansive optimism, Catholics turned back to their internal evangelism
and to shoring up the immigrant enclave.[30] Strategies for participation
in the mainstream now shifted to the Catholic social gospel as it came
to be expressed in the National Catholic War Council and in subsequent
vehicles of "public Catholicism." Catholics, therefore, chose to remain
religious, if not civic, outsiders: They would confine the missionary
impulse to internal catechesis and enclave-building in the neo-scholastic mold, and they would separate their particular religious identity
from their public role.

Jews: Fighting Back, American-Style

Nowhere was the tension between the American norms of civility and
the rhetoric of the enclave more evident than in the American Jewish
community, which found itself the object of Protestant Christian missions throughout most of the nineteenth century and with increasing
frequency after the Civil War. Like other European immigrants, Reform
Jews prided themselves on their fidelity to the constitutional principles
and cultural values of the United States: They were more American than
Americans, as one historian put it.[31] Although the Jewish community
was not without resources and skilled leadership, it felt even more
vulnerable than did Catholics to the threat of losing members to Protestant Christianity. Even a modest measure of missionary success could
make a statistical impact on the small community. Jews also worried
that the strong bond between peoplehood and religion might be weakened by the pressure to equate genuine Americanness with membership
in a mainstream religious denomination. Jewish conversions to Christianity could be interpreted in mission literature to imply that Jews had
seen the error of their ways in rejecting Christ; in short, that Judaism
had for centuries been based on a fundamental religious mistake. "In
Jewish eyes," Jonathan Sarna writes, "the war against missionaries
became a war of affirmation—a war to prove that eighteen-hundred
years of Jewish civilization had not been in vain."[32]

The civil response to missionary encroachment, represented in the
antebellum period by Jewish editor and publicist Isaac Leeser, proved
itself unsuccessful and gave way, after the Civil War, to a bolder strategy of confrontation that risked offending and alienating the Christian
majority. By the end of the nineteenth century, Jews had reserved their
most powerful polemics for a very specific segment of the Christian pop-

ulation: missionaries. Jews put missionaries on the defensive by pointing to Christian discord, doctrinal inconsistencies, infighting, and to the rapid progress of Unitarianism. They also made a great deal of Christian conversions to Judaism, thereby insisting "on their right to battle Christianity on equal terms. If Christians could convert Jews, Jews could convert Christians. The same voluntary system that permitted Protestant denominations to compete and permitted Catholics to make converts, must allow Jews to proselytize as well." Anti-missionary crusades, led by polemicists such as Adolph Benjamin, were quietly supported by socially active Jews like Jacob Schiff, who could thereby observe the conventions of civility publicly while violating them secretly. "The result was ambivalence: manners went one way, money the other."[33]

Part of the war to defend the Jewish heritage was fought over intermarriage. Although the number of Jewish men or women marrying Gentiles was very low, there were occasional losses, especially to Italian or Irish Catholics in New York. This was in no way a missionizing strategy on the part of the Christians involved, but Reform Jews worried nonetheless that the phenomenon might make them more vulnerable to Orthodox Jews, who were arriving in greater numbers from Eastern Europe after 1880 and who had long maintained that Judaism would die out if left in the hands of Reform rabbis and their permissive policies. Thus Isaac M. Wise's chest did not swell with fatherly pride when his daughter eloped with a Presbyterian of Irish descent.[34] Indeed, in the case of intermarriage, the real competition was between Reform and Orthodox rabbis to see who could compose the direst formulation of the problem. Reform leader David Einhorn railed that "each intermarriage drives a nail in the coffin of Judaism," while an Orthodox polemicist warned that marriage to a Christian violated the Jew's "instinctive protest against Jewish extinction."[35] Penalties were stiff, and it was common that family members who had intermarried were shunned, even in the second and third generations, although Reform were somewhat more lenient than Orthodox regarding punishment. Still, both camps agreed, as did the Conservatives, that intermarriage eroded the solidarity of the Jewish people and threatened the survival of the Jewish religion.

The response to Christian insinuations about, and infiltrations of, the Jewish community went beyond prohibitions of intermarriage and intellectual refutations of anti-Semitism. To reduce the appeal of the Christian institutions proliferating in their neighborhoods, Jews established their own presses, newspapers, Hebrew classes, and Sunday schools. Later in the nineteenth century, partially in response to Chris-

tian missionaries' strategy of proselytizing through social relief programs, Jewish leaders strengthened their own immigrant social welfare
and relief programs.[36]

The dynamic Sarna described, which persisted into the twentieth
century, was complicated, however, by a new development in the 1880s.
Before then, the evangelization of the Jews was not a top priority for
American evangelicals. A new motivation came after the Civil War,
when John Nelson Darby's exposition of premillennial theology began
to gain currency among evangelicals and displaced postmillennial scenarios, at least among conservatives. Dispensational premillennialism
emphasized the role of the Jews in God's plans for the final redemption: Some would be converted to Christ, others would perish alongside all unbelievers, but, before any of that could happen, Jews must
return to their homeland. Accordingly, many evangelical missionaries
supported Zionist initiatives. William Blackstone, founder of the Chicago Hebrew Mission and author of the best-seller *Jesus Is Coming*,
believed that history was entering *The Jewish Era*, as he named the
mission's journal.[37] Missions to the Jews were a prominent topic at the
Bible and Prophecy conferences (1878–1918), where premillennialists
tried to dispel prejudice against Jews and lamented the lack of support
and enthusiasm for the evangelization of the Jews as signs of indifference, ingratitude, and even malice toward Jesus' nation.[38]

Premillennialist missions presented the Christian belief to Jews in the
terms of this new understanding. Jews were not expected to turn their
backs on their Jewish heritage and identity as they had for centuries.
Their Jewishness was no longer looked upon by Christians as a deficien-
cy, an obstacle to be overcome. The new evangelical missions to the
Jews presented the acceptance of Christianity as the fulfillment of one's
destiny, not as a denial of one's Jewish roots. By accepting Jesus as lord
and savior, Jews were becoming truer to their Jewish selves. The missionary tactic was to persuade Jews that they were not betraying their
people or their faith by converting. Previous oppression of Jews or
discrimination against them was perpetrated by Roman Catholics or
Orthodox Christians, not true born-again Christians, who treated Jews
with kindness and appreciated the integrity of their religious tradition.
Indeed, Blackstone wrote, Jewish laws, customs, and rites had kept the
Jewish people intact by protecting the religion from disintegrating and
becoming part of distorted forms of Christianity. Now the Jews were
ready to fulfill their heroic destiny in the days to come.[39]

The premillennialists used Jewish symbols in decorating mission
houses and in their publications. Many of the missions' books and
journals were illustrated with scenes from traditional Jewish life, such

as women lighting candles, a rabbi teaching young children the Torah, or a Bar Mitzvah celebration.[40] Missionaries would also relate to the Jewish religious year in their services and sermons.[41] They often conducted services on Saturday so as to give Jews the feeling that they were not neglecting to fulfill their religious obligations by coming to hear a Christian service. Missionaries would often build their arguments on passages from the Hebrew Bible; Arno Gaebelein and the Hope of Israel Mission in New York even distributed unleavened bread to needy Jews on Passover.[42]

By 1913 forty-five Protestant missionary societies and two hundred individual missionaries worked in seventeen cities to evangelize Jews in America.[43] Many of these missions were sponsored by Protestant churches, while others relied on interdenominational support. One of the most successful missionaries, Leopold Cohn, operated officially under the auspices of the Baptist Home Missions Society, which also assisted him financially. The mission, however, was actually an independent enterprise rather than an agency of the Baptist church, and it conducted its affairs on its own, a situation which, at times, created tensions between Cohn and the Home Missions Society.[44] A similar although calmer relationship existed between Arno Gaebelein's Hope of Israel Mission and the Methodist Episcopal Church.[45] The Chicago Hebrew Mission listed a number of churches as its sponsors; nonetheless, the mission was nondenominational in its operation and character and had adopted a distinct premillennialist ideology.

Success was measured in a unique way in the premillennialist missions. According to the dispensationalist scheme, 144,000 Jews, 12,000 from each tribe, would accept Jesus as their lord and savior at the beginning of the Great Tribulation. It was essential, therefore, that there be 144,000 Jewish persons who would possess the knowledge of the Gospel, even if they had not accepted it, so that they could fulfill their role at the moment the rapture came. Thus the preaching of the Gospel to Jews need not result in immediate conversions; success was measured, rather, in how many Jews had given the preacher an honest hearing. "The premillennialist missionary attempt was based on the realistic assumption that only a small part of the Jewish people would accept Christ as their Savior in this age," Yaakov Ariel comments. " The converted Jews would remain a large enough mass of people to fulfill their part in God's plan for humanity and get the eschatological scheme going." In this view, witnessing to Jews was a manifestation of love and concern. "Jews, as might have been expected, viewed the matter differently."[46]

Indeed, Jews were in no way fooled by the new mission approach and reacted as vigorously as they had before the advent of the premil-

lennialists. They fought back in a variety of ways. They tried, for example, to make the evangelization of children declared illegal, but that
strategy failed even in the state of New York, where the Jewish population was relatively influential. And Jewish leaders discredited those
few who did convert to Christianity, arguing that they had converted
not on religious grounds but to enjoy the security, status, and privileges that the non-Jewish community could offer.[47] Jews tended to portray attempts to evangelize them as complete failures, yet they attacked
the missions vehemently, a pattern suggesting that missionaries posed
a real threat to Jewish solidarity. Reform Jews were concerned less
about actual conversions, however, than about the challenge that the
existence of Christian missions posed to their legitimacy and rights as
American citizens to be free from religious coercion. Although much
of Wise's countermissionary activity preceded the premillennialist
movement to evangelize Jews, other Reform rabbis depicted evangelical Christianity as a primitive form of religion and trumpeted an aggressive Jewish theology that matched Christian triumphalism step for
step. Jewish polemicists scoured missionary publications and found
disputable or clearly inaccurate accounts of conversion numbers, which
the Jewish countermissionaries then publicized to demonstrate that
missionaries were falsifying information. Similarly, they deried the
Christian biographical sketches of missionaries and converts, many of
which bordered on the hagiographic.[48] Jewish countermissionaries
could also point to prominent and well-to-do Reform Jews who were
living proof that Jews could prosper and gain acceptance in American
society, up to a certain point, without embracing Christianity.

In the campaign to discredit Christian missionaries, Jews received
unexpected help from the missionaries themselves, who fought with one
another over turf and tactics. For example, Arno Gaebelein attacked
Herman Warszawiak, a missionary who worked in New York, for what
he considered to be unethical methods of bringing Jews to hear the
Gospel.[49] Protestant missionaries and mission agencies also competed
with one another for the support of the larger evangelical community.
In New York the stakes were high, with numerous branches, dozens
of workers, and a number of publications in place by the mid-1890s.
Few questioned the integrity of non-Jewish missionaries; complaints
were mostly directed at Jewish converts who had become engaged in
evangelization work.[50]

Jewish countermissionary activity did not stem the tide of premillennial missions at the turn of the century, however. By the beginning
of the twentieth century there were missions to the Jews in virtually
every city in America that had a community of a few thousand or more

Jews. The missions became, in a sense, part of the surrounding scenery of Jewish neighborhoods in American cities.[51] In large Jewish areas such as Brooklyn or the Lower East Side of New York, as many as a few hundred might come to hear a sermon. For all this activity, however, the overall number of conversions was low. Between 1880 and 1920 no more than two hundred Jews a year converted to evangelical Christianity in America at a time when total Jewish immigration numbered more than two million. Examining evangelical Christianity was one thing, it seems; accepting it was another. Regarded as an act of betrayal of one's people and ancestors, conversion generally evoked guilt, inner turmoil, and pain. The "average" convert to evangelical Christianity was a young man in his early twenties from a traditional, Orthodox, Yiddish-speaking background who arrived as an immigrant from Eastern Europe without family or friends. It was among such individuals that the missions invested much of their efforts.[52]

Despite the low number of converts, especially when compared to the success of revivals in converting other groups (e.g., unchurched Americans of Protestant descent), the missionaries did not regard their work as a failure.[53] Their conversions filled the missionaries with pride and satisfaction. Although an average missionary might manage to convert no more than a few dozen Jews in a lifetime of work, he or she would typically be perfectly content with their achievements.[54] Conferences of Christian Jews began in the early twentieth century and led eventually to the creation of the Hebrew Christian Alliance in 1915.[55]

Protestant missions to the Jews thus provided unforseen benefits for both sides. If Christian premillennialists convinced themselves that success was not to be measured in numbers of converts but in numbers of hearers, Jewish leaders, alarmed by the attempt of evangelicals to gain a widespread hearing, took deliberate and sustained measures to ensure that Christians would not be able to exploit Jewish failures to meet the social, spiritual, and material needs of their people. Despite the incendiary rhetoric of a leader such as Wise, who attacked missionaries individually and in the strongest of terms, Jewish leaders did not cross the line of civility by advocating violence against missionaries, although some episodes of widespread rioting and violence did occur in the 1890s.[56]

Instead, Jewish leaders followed a pattern similar to that of Catholic countermissionaries: They cast the language of Americanism in their own religious idiom, aggressively refuted ideological challenges to their civic virtue and religious autonomy, and strengthened or created an institutional network of newspapers, schools, textbooks, hospitals,

synagogues, and relief agencies. To Christian missionary journals such
as *Israel's Advocate* and *The Jewish Chronicle*, Jews responded with
journals like *The Jew* and *The Occident* to rebut missionary claims.
Jewish catechisms were developed as direct counterparts to the Christian ones, and foreign rabbis were recruited to strengthen the bonds
between ethnicity and religion—bonds the Protestant missionaries
sought to sunder. Furthermore, like the Catholics, Jews turned inward
to their own needs rather than outward to compete with Protestants
for unchurched Americans. The few converts won by Jews or by Catholics from nominally Protestant populations were significant primarily as pawns in the strategy of demonstrating the fallibility of the Protestant religion and the appeal of the Jewish (or Roman Catholic) faith.
And, as with Catholics, Protestant missionizing did not inspire enclave-
building as much as it hastened a process already underway. For Jews
more than Catholics, however, the conversionist threat "proved a decisive argument—the one that convinced thrifty Jews to contribute their
hard-earned money."[57]

Protestant-Catholic Competition

Although Catholics and Jews focused the lion's share of their institutional
and ideological resources on retaining their immigrant faithful as well
as the second and third generations, Catholics did compete with Protestants directly for the souls of people whom both churches deemed vulnerable to mission appeals. These included Italian immigrants (most of
whom were nominal Catholics), black Americans, and Native Americans.

If they did not make significant inroads into nominal Protestant
populations, Catholic missionaries did manage to thwart the most
ambitious designs of Protestants dedicated to the evangelization of
immigrants. Among the new arrivals the Italians occupied a prominent
place in the mission strategies of both Catholic and Protestant missionaries, in large part because Italians were perceived as not being exceed-
ingly loyal to the institutional Roman Catholic Church. Providing
adequate pastoral ministry and social services for them was clearly
placing a strain on Catholic resources. The plight of the Italians was
well known abroad, and Pope Leo XIII addressed a special plea to the
American hierarchy in December 1888, in which he asked for assistance
in alleviating Italian unemployment and religious drift in the United
States.[58]

Given the apparent opening in the Catholic ranks, work among the
Italians initially seemed a promising field for Protestant evangelicals.
In 1916 the Home Missions Council, which represented thirteen Amer-

ican evangelical denominations, commissioned Antonio Mangano of Colgate Theological Seminary, Brooklyn, to research and survey the progress of the missions to the 3.5 million Italian immigrants concentrated in the Northeast, with large colonies also in West Virginia, Ohio, Illinois, and California. Italians were represented in almost every line of work: They were farm laborers, manufacturers, merchants, servants, barbers, carpenters, gardeners, jewelers, mechanics, painters, stoneworkers, engineers, tailors, and shoemakers, with a smaller number of professional actors, architects, clergymen, editors, lawyers, scientists, and musicians.[59] Mangano found these people to be commendably industrious workers well on their way to becoming financially successful Americans. Religiously, however, their identity was unsettled. "Ninety-nine percent of the Italians landing on our shores would give 'Roman Catholic' as their religious belief," he reported, "but if questioned, a large number would add that they were not faithful to its celebrations nor its services except perhaps in times of births, deaths, and marriages."[60]

Mangano's report emphasized the Protestant concern to make Americans, and to proceed civilly in doing so. Eager to refute "the common charge of proselyting which all evangelical mission work among the Italians meets," he described in detail the anticlerical attitudes of the Italians and declared them ripe for conversion from the autocratic, un-American, Roman church. "These newcomers ought not to be allowed to blunder in their conceptions of liberty," he warned the Mission Board. "If they continue to come a million or more a year they will soon rule America through the ballot box. How will they rule? By what standards? According to what ideals? It is for us to determine while yet there is time." The Catholic Church is guilty of "Italianizing rather than Americanizing these newcomers," and its strategy "is to make them more at home as if this is a little Italy."[61] The tone of urgency reflected Mangano's concern that the first wave of Protestant missions, begun in the 1880s and 1890s, had succeeded only in alerting the Catholic leadership:

> For a number of years the Roman Church paid little attention to the Italians in America. Consequently the work of Italian evangelization was much easier than at the present time. The common report among Protestants throughout the length and breadth of our land was, "When we opened our mission the Catholics were doing nothing for the Italians. Now they have built a church are building a parochial school and are copying our various social activities." Realizing that the majority of Italians and priests weren't able to hold the people, ten years ago young American seminarians, mainly Irish, were sent to Rome to learn the Ital-

252

R. Scott Appleby

ian language and to become familiar with Italian thought and feeling. They are now taking part in this new aggressive campaign.[62]

Mangano cited case after case in which Catholics rolled back Protestant initiatives. In Lawrence, Massachusetts, a Protestant mission preacher had begun to attract crowds, so "a new Catholic Church has just been reared and seven nuns have been brought into town to overcome the 'devilish influence of the Protestants.'" In Providence's Italian colony of forty thousand, the Catholics built "a beautiful copy of the church of Saint John and Saint Paul in Venice . . . where the religion of the fatherland will be taught in *Italianita,* which means Italian feeling, and which can hardly be conducive to Americanization." In many other localities, "the Catholic church conducts sewing schools, music classes, gymnasiums, athletic activities, English classes, kindergartens, day schools, and Boy Scout troops, homes and protectorates for foundling, orphans, and wayward boys and girls. . . . All of these helpful ministries [which] are the direct result of the example of Protestant work."[63]

Lack of Protestant success in planting ecclesial roots in these Italian communities, Mangano asserted, was due not only to the vigorous countermeasures of Roman Catholics but also to prejudices against Italians by Protestants who would otherwise support the missions financially and to Italian misconceptions that all American Christians were like the Irish bosses who lorded it over them in the workplace. To overcome these prejudices Protestant missions must also graduate from the "experimental stage" to permanent work with systematic strategic features, including missionaries who speak Italian and honor Italian culture but who also teach and insist upon English and American values. Mangano suggested that "the great work to be done during the next ten or fifteen years"—what he elsewhere termed "the intensive stage" of competition with Catholics—would put the existing works upon more solid foundations by projecting an image of Protestants that was contrary to the negative images most Italians had of Catholic priests. Thus Protestant missionaries must be totally free of personal corruption and must avoid any appearance of seeking money from the Italians, who were tired of all the devices, from masses for the dead to indirect collections, by which Catholic priests "extort" immigrants. Most important, Protestant missionaries must concentrate on winning Catholic women by personal contact, for the women controlled the home and the education of the children—and thus they controlled the future.[64]

Yet all this must be achieved, Mangano concluded, without violating the norms of civility. "Our Italian missionaries should be taught as far as possible to refrain from railing at the Catholic church. Preaching should be constructive and practical," he advised. Missionaries must be familiar with Roman Catholic views, doctrines, and practices—and even respectful of some of these. In America, Mangano assumed, reasoned discourse would ultimately win the day. "When the message of Christ is presented in all its simplicity and power and the moral side of religion is given imminent emphasis and prominence, the Italian, whether a zealous Catholic or no, says, yes, you were right, that is true and in many cases he is willing to confess." The Mission Board should fund this new phase of missions, confident that Italian immigrants would see that "the Protestant teaching is better than the Roman Catholic teaching and that the Protestant ethics are better than Roman Catholic." Having seen this, immigrants would convert to the true American religious faith.[65]

Sixteen years later, at the end of the "intensive stage," however, Theodore Abel issued a similar type of progress report to the Protestant Home Missions Boards, which concluded that:

> The unimpressive results of fifty years of formal church work among immigrants clearly show that it has failed to fulfill the expectation of serving as an adequate means of evangelizing a mass of Catholic immigrants. The approach through the organization of missions and foreign-language churches with their methods of mass appeal and individual work has failed to create a movement toward Protestantism among immigrants. Mission Centers established at great cost in money and energy, have not grown into large churches as expected. Many mission churches today are struggling for their very existence and are attempting to combat financial difficulties . . . [and] the growing apathy of the community. An unpublished report of the leader of the work of his denomination among foreign born says, "We must be sensible of the many mistakes which have been made, of sins of commission and omission, and must realize that with all the efforts that have been expended we have scarcely made an impression upon the field that lies before us.[66]

By this indictment, Abel included the sweep of activity of ministers, missionaries, and social workers appointed by local or national boards of Protestant denominations to conduct religious, educational, recreational, and general service programs for Catholic immigrants and their children. These programs were carried on in special centers organized, staffed, and financed by the denominations; by the end of the period, one thousand such centers were in operation in the East, Midwest, and the Pacific Region, nearly 80 percent of them under the auspices of the Presbyterian, Baptist, and Methodist denominations. These missions, and Abel's indictment, included work not only among Italians but also among Mexicans, Czechs, and Hungarians. Abel's study for the Missions Board, like Mangano's, was based on extensive fieldwork, in this case with 150 Mission Centers over a year and a half. These included institutions fashioned after the pattern of the Social Settlement and the YMCA; churches; neighborhood houses; and Christian centers in New York, Chicago, Cleveland, Los Angeles, Buffalo, Philadelphia, Baltimore, Denver, San Francisco, and the coal fields and iron ranges of Pennsylvania and the iron range of Michigan.[67] Yet within that large sample, "It is very probable that there has been no loss of Catholics at all beyond the defections of Catholics which ordinarily takes place among any population due to the weakness of human nature and the usual manifestations of the same."[68]

What had gone wrong in the undertaking? Abel lists several pitfalls, summarized in the phrase: "the difficulties that inhere in the religious nature of work and in the obstacles that are due to the resistance of social forces operating in the immigrant community." Most important was the fact that the conversion of immigrants with a Catholic background proved far slower than expected, with the evangelist's emotional appeals attracting the curious listener who was "lacking the background that would enable him to comprehend the meaning and significance of the Protestant message unless he has been subjected to a prolonged period of reconditioning." Such "reconditioning" Abel deemed necessary because the immigrant would inevitably fall back on Catholic sacramentalism in times of crisis or in life's important moments, such as the birth of a child or the death of a family member. Only indifferent Catholics were susceptible to such reconditioning, but these were people who were likely to be indifferent to any religion.

Two types of obstacles to effective Protestant mission work recurred. First was immigrant hostility to missionaries on the grounds that the very idea of mission work was condescending; this mode of response was similar to that adopted by American Jews insulted at the preacher's implication that the Jewish religious tradition and culture were somehow inferior. Closely related was the immigrant anger directed at the puritanical emphasis in Protestant mission preaching, and the linkage established between "false religion" and immigrant behavior such as drinking, dancing, or theater attendance. A second, related pattern of immigrant response may be termed the resistance to differentiation, that is, the resistance to breaking down the integral relationship between ethnic identity, politics, and religious affiliation. In most immigrant communities, Abel reminded his board, the Catholic Church occupied an important position as the arbiter of public opinion, "for the church fulfills not only a religious function, but it serves as the nucleus around which the immigrant community organizes itself and it promotes many of the social activities and institutions that play a vital role in immigrant life." Among groups such as the Poles, the church also had significance for nationality. Abel concluded that to change one's religion, therefore, "implies the capital offense of disloyalty and the violation of national solidarity."[69]

In such an environment competition for souls would give way to social service. The difficulty in reaching indifferent Catholics, Abel reported, led some missionary leaders to abandon the formal church work approach in favor of an approach through social and cultural activities.[70]

Racism on the part of Christians inhibited Protestant support for missions to Italians, and it impeded the efforts of Catholic and Protestant missionaries to integrate black Americans into one, unified church body. Protestants expended far greater resources and energies in this mission field than did Catholics, but the language of separation carried the day in both cases, with acrimony arising within each mission camp. Baptist missionaries working at the turn of the century among unchurched Alabama blacks, for example, could not have welcomed the statement by the *Alabama Baptist* that the Negro should "stay absolutely in his own sphere and let us [whites] manfully, religiously, and patriotically maintain our dignity, supremacy, and social status in our own sphere." Martin Marty notes that mention of blacks largely disappeared in white Baptist church convention proceedings after 1900.[71] The "separate but equal notion" also made its way into Methodism, even though some 280,000 blacks remained in the Methodist Episcopal Church, and some Presbyterians in 1900 considered black education to be a question completely beyond their reach.[72] Across the denominations, a policy of separation and neglect bordering on indifference became characteristic. In this atmosphere effective mission work was an unlikely possibility.

For their part, black churches were engaged in internal debates about what it meant to be African American. Black religious leaders contemplated an appropriate response to the racism of white co-religionists and the racism simmering in their own ranks. Some argued that the history of slavery and white oppression precluded the possibility of blacks joining with the mainstream Protestant churches. Others resisted the formula inspiring Protestant missionaries, Americanization through evangelization.

Catholics and Protestants were concerned with their rivalry, however, at least as much as they were with the attitudes of blacks themselves. Advocates of mission work among blacks resented but also at-

tempted to exploit the competitive posture on the part of their religious
superiors. The case of the Roman Catholic priest John R. Slattery provides a brief illustration of this point. Slattery felt that the most effective Catholic challenge to Protestant proselytizing among blacks was
the development of a black clergy. Confronting deep-seated prejudices, from which he was not entirely free himself, Slattery embarked on
a campaign to make American Catholicism more responsive to the
black community.[73] To succeed, however, he had to fight an uphill battle
for the acceptance of blacks and the resources to evangelize them.

His religious superiors in England found Slattery arrogant and "un-
disciplined" in his approach to the problem, and by a vote his brother
missionaries in the United States dismissed him from the office of provincial of the Mill Hill Fathers (Josephites) in 1882. Retreating to Richmond, Virginia, at the invitation of Bishop John Keane, Slattery opened
a Josephite mission there and wrote numerous articles for *Catholic
World* advocating greater institutional support for the Negro missions
and battling white stereotypes about blacks. On the eve of the Third
Plenary Council in Baltimore, Slattery sent a memorandum to Herbert
Vaughan, his superior in England, with copies to Keane and Cardinal
James Gibbons, Archbishop of Baltimore. The memorandum made
several specific recommendations for the evangelization of black Americans, including the establishment of a Josephite seminary in Baltimore.
Although the bishops did not follow this recommendation, they decreed
an annual collection for the Negro and Indian missions and formed a
Commission for Catholic Missions among the Colored Peoples and Indians. Despite these victories Slattery continued to criticize the mea-
ger Catholic missionary efforts and published articles documenting the
much greater investments of Protestant churches in the evangelization
of blacks.[74]

At the same time, Slattery pressed his Mill Hill superiors for an American college to train missionaries. He argued that the seminary in England
produced missionaries who understood neither the United States nor the
Negro missions.[75] Black missionaries would be much more effective than
whites. In this cause Slattery enlisted the aid of Bishop Francis A. Jans-
sens of Natchez, who was the first bishop to publicly advocate "colored
priests for colored people."[76] Cardinal Gibbons dedicated St. Joseph's
Seminary in 1888. Three years later one of the seminary's first students,
Charles Uncles, became the first African American ordained in the United
States. In 1893 Slattery became the first superior of the Josephites (St.
Joseph's Society for Colored Missions).[77]

Encouraged by the recognition and respect that his new post brought
him within the American church and by his friendships with members
of the progressive wing of the American hierarchy, Slattery continued

his campaign to strengthen Catholic commitment to the black missions. In "The Negroes and the Baptists," published in the *Catholic World*, he took issue with an article from "an irresponsible quarterly review published in New York City, and edited by one who claims to be a Catholic." In this article, Eugene Didier misrepresented Catholic teaching on slavery. "Everything in Mr. Didier's paper against the Negro is directly contrary to Catholic truth or ethics," Slattery protested, contrasting Didier's statement that "slavery was a blessing to the slave" with Leo XIII's condemnation of it as a "dreadful curse."[78] Writing as a Catholic, Didier had slandered the Negro as "a natural born and habitual liar" and as "shiftless, shameless, brutal . . . ungrateful, immoral." Slattery was infuriated not only by the language used but also by its identification with Catholicism.[79]

Because he was in direct competition with Protestant evangelists for the souls of black Americans, Slattery was doubly dismayed at any display of Catholic racism. He reported that Thomas Jefferson Morgan, corresponding secretary of the American Baptist Home Mission Society and a Baptist minister, had taken extracts from Didier's article and "with conscious duplicity has made them appear as the teaching of representative Catholics." Unfortunately, Slattery lamented, "some of the more simple of the colored people . . . were inclined to take Morgan's misstatement for the truth, and consequently these least of the kingdom were deeply scandalized at what they in their simplicity believed to be the opinions of the Catholic Church." Slattery responded with a castigation of Southern Baptists, who "show no such friendship for the black man."[80]

As superior of the Josephites, Slattery presided over the expansion of the Negro Mission to seven southern states served by twenty-one priests. By 1899 the Josephites had founded churches, a seminary, an orphanage, and an industrial school and were in need of catechists for the South. Slattery issued a plea for institutional support for a proposed Catholic college for Negro catechists:

> Unless fortified by negro catechists and negro priests, we shall always be at a disadvantage in dealing with the negro millions beyond the pale of Holy Church. The negro looks with suspicion upon white men. The impression left from slavery; the many dishonest tricks upon them; unpaid wages . . . these and countless other wrongs make the negroes suspicious of the whites. . . . How can one say the negroes do not want their own priests since the experiment has never been tried, for we have but two, one of whom is dead?[81]

At this juncture, despite his misgivings about some of the black students at St. Joseph's Seminary and concerns about the supposed "moral weakness" of blacks, Slattery remained hopeful that the church would provide adequate support for the cause.[82] "The nineteenth century brought them emancipation, right of ownership, education, citizenship," he wrote. "Let the twentieth century crown all by imparting to them the truths of our Holy Religion, in which glorious task, with God's blessed help, no small part shall be played by St. Joseph's College for Negro Catechists."[83] In April 1899 Slattery journeyed to Rome and submitted a memorial to the Congregation of the Propaganda, requesting a grant of funds and farm land for the college. The request was approved, and Slattery proceeded with the foundation of St. Joseph's College for Negro Catechists in Mobile, Alabama.[84]

From his ordination in 1877 to 1899 Slattery was engrossed in efforts to evangelize black Americans. He traveled extensively, especially in the South, visiting the schools and missions established by the Josephites. His diverse experiences as an administrator and church leader, and as a missionary to missionaries, shaped his intellectual growth. In the 1890s he became increasingly frustrated by the Catholic hierarchy's seeming indifference to the Negro missions. Resources for Catholic mission work in the South were being directed toward the immigrant population from Europe, with little left for the Josephite missions and Catholic Church Extension Society missions to rural areas mostly populated by blacks.

Roman Catholicism's failure to evangelize a sizable number of black Americans can be attributed to a variety of causes. Most American Catholics hailed from European immigrant stock, and Catholic missionaries did not always conquer racist attitudes within themselves, much less in their co-religionists. Furthermore, many Catholic missionaries, including Slattery, were inexperienced in dealing with African Americans, and they learned the same lesson as did white, Anglo-Saxon Protestants who attempted to convert southern Italian immigrants: Cultural barriers could be insurmountable, especially when missionaries failed to adjust their approach by taking into account the specific needs, expectations, and cultural heritage of the people they sought to reach. Slattery later complained, for example, that the standard missionary presentation of Catholic doctrine relied too heavily on the terminology and concepts of neo-scholastic theological tradition endorsed by the Vatican. Scholastic theology, however essential to the training of priests in the Roman system, proved to be a narrow, arid, and culturally unappealing framework within which to promote Catholic teaching and practice to rural black Americans.[85]

In the case of the efforts to evangelize blacks, unlike their missionary enterprise among Italians, Catholics apparently were not stimulated by a sense of competition with mainstream Protestants. Based on his observations of Protestant missionaries in the South, Slattery concluded that they succeeded in their work among blacks when the latter formed churches and participated in ministries. Thus he argued strenuously for a black Catholic clergy and bishops.[86] Catholic bishops by and large did not feel the same urgency toward unbaptized blacks as they did toward wayward Italians, most of whom were nominal Catholics. Some liberal bishops supported Slattery's plan to recruit and train a native black clergy, but seminaries generally refused to admit blacks. Eventually Slattery decided that the U.S. Catholic Church had gone as far as it would go in committing resources to the Negro missions. Disappointed and angry, he became increasingly involved with the nascent modernist movement in Catholicism and eventually renounced his priesthood and the Roman Catholic Church itself.[87]

Native Americans and American Nativism

The dynamics of civility in tension with religious nationalism shaped the competition between Protestants and Catholics for the souls of Native Americans. In their attitudes toward each other, and toward the tribes they sought to convert to the gospel, Catholic and Protestant missionaries, despite their different approaches and traditions, were inspired by a familiar blend of patriotic nationalism and religious triumphalism. Each tradition claimed to offer the best hope for "civilizing" the Native Americans.

Civilizing, of course, meant transforming Native Americans into law-abiding, democracy-loving citizens of the United States.[88] That was also an important goal of missionary work with immigrants. In the case of Native Americans, however, Protestants and Catholics competed not only for the soul of the individual but also for the blessings of the state. By turning over the tribes to the ministrations of the churches in 1872, the Grant administration cast the U.S. government in the unprecedented role of religious judge. Which religious communities would best succeed in "pacifying" the tribes? the government asked. The answer turned on the assumption that Christianizing and Americanizing efforts were mutually reinforcing—and so the competition between the denominations was framed as a contest over "true Americanism." For some contestants, "true Americanism" was an indivisible quality that could not be apportioned among diverse religious traditions; it was identified with a particular religious worldview and organizational structure. Thus the government's reliance on and manipulation of the churches in its Native American "peace policy" not only fostered competition among denominations but also deepened animosities and mutual an-

tagonisms. In this regard the Christian mission to Native Americans
revealed the limits of civil religious discourse as it developed at the turn
of the century.

In this competition Catholics labored under a burden imposed by
their Protestant rivals. It was the age of nativism, and episodes of anti-
Catholicism occurred before and after the Civil War. Although Catholics had the more impressive record of success in serving and pacifying
the tribes, they were forced to defend themselves against a Protestant-
inspired nativism that called their very American-ness into question.
The anti-Catholic American Protective Association became involved in
the Indian question after its founding in 1887. Its polemicists pointed
to the reputedly unsavory and undemocratic masses of Eastern Europeans pouring into the United States and huddling together in urban
immigrant enclaves. If Roman Catholicism could not successfully
Americanize its own people, the argument went, how could it pretend
to civilize Native Americans?

The Protestant mainstream had already entered the mission field
when the Presbyterian Church, U.S.A., established a Board of Foreign
Missions (BFM) in 1838 and inaugurated a long-term campaign to
evangelize Native Americans. In 1893, after sending over 450 men and
women to work with nineteen tribes, the agency was transferred to the
Presbyterian Board of Home Missions.[89] The assignment to "foreign"
missions reflected the nineteenth-century assumption that Indians were
not Native Americans in the proper sense of the term but uncivilized
"aliens" who spoke a foreign tongue and worshipped strange gods. It
would take almost sixty years of "progress" before Presbyterian missionaries were sufficiently satisfied that Native Americans were rejecting their tribal past and "heathen" ways. Cultural intolerance combined
with simple racism as the missionaries embraced an "optimistic racial
egalitarianism" predicated upon the success of their program of "spiritual uplift." Along with a "practical knowledge of farming" and
"mechanical arts," Native Americans would be inculcated with a
"Christian character" and raised to the same cultural and spiritual level
as white Protestants. In pursuit of that goal, missionaries printed and
distributed Bibles, tracts, and other religious literature; taught hymns
and psalms; and offered a common education that was at once religious,
academic, and vocational.[90]

Patriotism no less than religious faith inspired the BFM missionaries.[91] Although acknowledging the mistreatment of Native Americans
by other whites, the missionaries "rarely found it difficult to harmo-
nize their own religious and cultural goals with the supposedly civilizing goals of their nation." By acclimating Native Americans to en-

croaching civilization, the missionaries felt, they were helping them to survive in the long run. In that sense, "doing the glorious work of the Lord and winning Indians to the enlightened lifestyle of middle-class Protestantism appeared quite consistent with doing the work of the United States."[92]

Not surprisingly, denominational triumphalism also figured in the calculations of some Presbyterians, who saw the mission as the vanguard of church expansion in competition with other denominations; the BFM itself was a product of heightened denominational self-awareness among Protestants. Nonetheless, spiritual dedication to Christianity was the primary motive not only for the BFM but also for most mainstream Protestant missionaries. They shared the belief that the impressive political institutions, science, and social and intellectual achievements of the West sprang from the civilizing influence of the gospel.[93]

In turning to the churches to revive its flagging Indian policy, the U.S. government exploited the Christian nationalism and republican political assumptions of the Protestant missionaries. Before the Civil War, the government subsidized Protestant missionary bodies, using them to civilize and pacify the tribes.[94] After the Civil War, the Grant administration pitted Catholic against Protestant, and Protestant denominations against one another, by doling out to the various churches the right to pick agents, teachers, and other staff on certain reservations. "It [costs] the government infinitely less," BFM secretary John C. Lowrie explained in 1868, to encourage education and agriculture for those under missionary care, "than to employ a military force for their restraint or punishment."[95] In addition, the government's systematic cooperation in their work further legitimated the goals of the missionaries.

If confidence in Protestant church and American state was the primary motive of the Protestant missionaries, virulent anti-Catholicism ran a strong second. The BFM saw itself as "locked in a battle with Rome for the souls of the heathen, and wrote with bitterness of their great rival."[96] The basic logic of the Protestant argument to the federal government was simple: Because Catholics are not true Americans, they are unable to prepare Native Americans for citizenship. The Protestant polemicist James M. King, for example, characterized Catholicism as "a rejected civilization" and reminded government officials as late as 1892 that "our civilization is not Latin, because God did not permit North America to be settled and controlled by that civilization. The Huguenot, the Hollander, and the Puritan created our civilization." Arguing against government support for Catholic missions, King charged that "much Roman Catholic teaching among the Indians does not prepare them for intelligent and loyal citizenship. The solution of the Indian problem consists in educating them for citizenship, as we educate all other races."[97]

Grant's peace policy featured a Board of Indian Commissioners established by Congress. Wealthy Protestants served on the board and monitored the government's procurement system, inviting churches to nominate Indian agents, to weed out dishonest or incompetent personnel, and to enhance the religious training of Native Americans.[98] The distribution of Indian agencies among the churches, announced in 1872, caused immediate dissatisfaction, with Catholics arguing with a good deal of justification that they had been slighted. The peace policy came at a time when Protestant missionary interest in Native Americans had been waning and Catholic activity in missions and schools was resurgent.[99] Protestants, facing a nationwide threat from growing "Romanism," saw the peace policy, a thoroughly Protestant endeavor in its origins, as a spectacular opportunity to regain lost ground. When the allotments were made, Catholics were shocked to receive only seven agencies, when on the basis of their previous missionary work they expected to receive thirty-eight.[100]

The Quakers and the Episcopalians, who had helped to originate the policy, were enthusiastic participants, and the Catholics made the best of what they felt was an unjust situation. By contrast the Methodists, who were favored in the distribution of the agencies, did the least. In the arguments, lobbying, and conflicts that followed the initial apportionment of agencies, interdenominational rivalry was often as strong a motivator as patriotism, religious nationalism, or simple compassion. "Examples of fights [among denominations] abound, and they are all disedifying if not scandalous," writes a historian of the policy. "If many [fights] can be explained by pettiness and denominational bias, the conflict between the Protestant mission groups and the Roman Catholics was nothing less than flagrant bigotry."[101]

Catholics, who had established a missionary presence among Native Americans in the sixteenth century, had the most to lose as a result of the government intervention, and they fought to protect their turf. In 1874 the Bureau of Catholic Indian Missions was formed to direct the work of the Catholic missions and lobby in Washington. The assignment of an agency to a particular religious group theoretically excluded other denominations from the reservation. Yet Catholics, invoking the American principle of religious liberty, insisted on the right to preach and teach on reservations officially assigned to Protestants. (Both sides, it should be noted, invoked religious liberty, but neither extended it to the Native Americans themselves.)[102] In 1881, signaling an apparent victory for the Catholics, Carl Schurz, the secretary of the interior, declared that reservations would be open to all religious denominations except where the presence of rival organizations would "be perilous to peace and order." On the reservations where Catholics and Protestants vied for influence, conflicts were numerous, resulting in "quite un-Christian feuds."[103]

The Indian schools were vehemently contested, for they were central to both the Catholic and Protestant missionary efforts.[104] In addition to government-run schools on reservations, the government funded "contract schools"—boarding schools as well as day schools—run by denominations. In 1883 Christian denominations were conducting twenty-two boarding schools and sixteen day schools with government aid in addition to those they conducted on their own. By 1887 contract schools, especially those maintained by Catholics, were receiving the lion's share of government aid. Officials of the Board of Indian Commissioners declared that its support of mission schools was entirely nonsectarian and refuted charges that Catholics had been unduly favored; after all, they noted, Catholics were committing more personnel and expending larger sums of money than other denominations in a push to accommodate more pupils under contract.

Despite these arguments, a Protestant-led campaign for a universal government "public" school system—a campaign inspired by the animus against contract schools—began in earnest after the 1887 passage of the Dawes Act.[105] Protestant reformers began to realize that neither the homestead allotments of the Dawes Act nor the granting of citizenship to the Indians would be sufficient to guarantee their attendance at schools. Of course, the drive for compulsory education did not logically entail or necessitate the closing of the Catholic mission schools, and Catholics reacted angrily to the administration of President Benjamin Harrison (1889–93) in its opposition to the contract school system. The Bureau of Catholic Indian Missions charged that Morgan, Harrison's commissioner of Indian affairs, was an aggressive nativist whose anti-Catholicism shaped Indian school policy. Equally offensive was the appointment of Daniel Dorchester, a Methodist minister and prominent anti-Catholic polemicist, as superintendent of Indian education.[106] The Catholic press, aided by Democrat-controlled newspapers, fought to prevent Senate confirmation of the two men.

Both had attacked the Catholic school system as un-American and unpatriotic. "Its crying defect," Dorchester wrote in *Romanism versus the Public School System,* "is that its teaching is not only un-American but anti-American, and will remove every one of its pupils, in their ideals, far from a proper mental condition for American citizenship, and enhance the already too difficult task of making them good citizens of a republic."[107] At an NEA meeting in 1888 Morgan accused Catholics of trying to destroy the public school system. The Catholic school system, he warned, "is a challenge to our Christianity, it is a challenge to our political life, it is a challenge to everything that we Americans cherish today."[108]

Morgan sought to advance the public school system by extending it comprehensively to Native American tribes. In his vision, students were to leave the Indian schools "speaking the same language, eager in the same pursuits of knowledge, loving the same institutions, loyal to the same flag, proud of the same history, and acknowledging the one God the maker of us all." Only public schools could effect this formation and transformation, for they were "the safeguard of liberty," the "nurseries of a genuine democracy," and the "training schools of character." "Nothing, perhaps, is so distinctly a product of the soil as is the American school system," Morgan wrote. "In these schools all speak a common language; race distinctions give way to national characteristics."[109] He called for a comprehensive, systematized, universal education: the common schools on the reservation, the agency boarding schools, and the national industrial schools were to follow a uniform course of study, similar methods of instruction, and standard textbooks in order to conform the Indian schools to the public school system of the states. Nonpartisan and nonsectarian, the schools were to be staffed by teachers chosen according to a rigorous professional standard and paid salaries comparable to those of public school teachers.

The Rev. Joseph A. Stephan, director of the Bureau of Catholic Indian Missions, had served as Catholic agent among the Sioux under Grant's peace policy and was a prominent enemy of the Harrison administration. Morgan's proposal was specious, Stephan charged, for the "nonsectarian" public schools were thoroughly shaped by prevailing Protestant assumptions. The Jesuit missionary L. B. Palladino also perceived a paradox in the Harrison administration's position on Indian schools. On the one hand, the government, at least since Grant's administration, had recognized the necessity of enlisting Christian churches in the cause of civilizing Native Americans. Now Harrison's administration was arguing for nonsectarian schools even while favoring the national Indian schools conducted by Protestants according to their denominational views.[110] In December 1893 Stephan bluntly charged that "the effort now being made to secularize, to 'non-sectarize' the Indian schools, is a dishonest, hypocritical one, whose sole aim and purpose it is to drive the Catholic Church out of the Indian educational and missionary field, in which it has gained glorious laurels, and to substitute for its influence and teachings the influence of other religious bodies."[111]

Catholics campaigned vigorously against Harrison in the election of 1892 and took credit for Grover Cleveland's victory. Nonetheless, support for public schools and opposition to the contract schools persisted; Protestants had completely withdrawn from the program rather than see Catholics advance their interests under its aegis. In 1896 Congress reduced funding for the contract school system drastically; in 1899 it completely terminated government support of the church-run schools for Native Americans. In the 1899 Appropriation Act, the partnership of church and government was officially dissolved, repudiated by both the U.S. Congress and the Protestant Mission Boards. The position represented by Thomas Jefferson Morgan, however, effectively won the day. Native Americans were to be educated in government national schools in order to become exemplary Americans in the Protestant tradition of the nation.[112]

In the long run, however, neither of the major Christian traditions was able to transcend the patronizing, colonizing attitude of its missionaries toward the various tribal cultures. Roman Catholics were no less Americanizing in their ambitions and efforts than were Protestants, although they did take a different approach to the process. Catholics certainly benefited from the lessons of the long history of involvement with the tribes. By the early nineteenth century some religious order missionaries had significantly refined their approach to indigenous culture, stressing elements of continuity between it and the historic Roman Catholic faith. Among the Nez Percés, for example, Catholic missionaries did not insist upon as radical a rejection of the past as did the agents of the BFM.[113]

Yet the story of the Nez Percés in the nineteenth century is a reminder that the Native Americans themselves were the real losers in the Catholic-Protestant competition. As a result of the competition between rival missionaries, who cared more about turf and creedal allegiance than about the integrity of the tribe itself, the Nez Percé tribe was racked by factionalism and disunity. A splintering of tribal customs and spiritual allegiance ensued. Thus an indigenous people's dignity and sense of self were casualties of the Christian missionary effort, for neither Catholic nor Protestant "educational" agencies were able to replace the tribe as the major formative agent in the spiritual identity of the Nez Percés.

The Ordeal of Civility and the Enclave Culture

From the end of the Civil War well into the 1920s, mainstream Protestant churches and mission boards, feeling the effects of cultural and religious differentiation, were actively competing, especially with Roman Catholics, for dominance in the mission and education fields. This was clearly part of a strategy to retain a cultural hegemony that was slipping away. The strategy was unsuccessful on its own terms, however, given the alacrity with which Catholics and Jews mended their fences, although the effectiveness of Protestant evangelical revivals in retaining immigrants and second- and third-generation Americans of Protestant descent meant that Protestants, like other competitors in the field, held their own. Their inflated mission statistics notwithstanding, Protestants did make modest inroads into Jewish and Catholic populations, but primarily their encroachments only mobilized the latter to more effective action. Because Catholics and Jews were already negotiating American citizenship and their religious role in a pluralist nation, however, the challenge posed by an aggressive evangelical Protestantism merely reinforced and perhaps accelerated enclave-building tendencies already present in these religious communities.

Christian missionaries of various denominations contended not only with each other, however, but also with a rhetoric of American inclusiveness based on the notion that full civil rights (for a select segment of the white male population, at least) inhered in unadorned humanity rather than in class, ethnic or national identity, or religious affiliation. To what extent did this rhetoric restrain missionaries who would equate American virtue with right religion? The historical evidence indicates a mixed answer to that question. The constitutional guarantee of religious liberty did not restrain missionaries from making triumphal claims to exclusive possession of universal truth or "the full Gospel." At times, however, competitors in the missionary field expressed respect for the right of people to hold contrary religious beliefs and seemed to counsel tolerance for deviation from evangelical norms of belief and conduct. Missionaries usually embraced some form of civility as a guiding norm, even if they often did so situationally, on strategic rather than patriotic grounds. Whatever their motivations, missionaries struggled with the tension between the American commitment to religious liberty on the one hand and creedal and confessional absolutism on the other. Some sought to overcome the tension or reduce it in various ways, whereas others simply tried to ignore the question and exploited the state's reluctance, on free-speech grounds, to restrict evangelization.

Mainstream Protestants who embraced civility, either pragmatically or essentially, had absorbed the implications of the fact that their faith community was but one among many. By the end of the nineteenth century it was becoming clear—to many missionaries, at least—that Protestantism as a core-culture was not immune from the trauma of modernization. Social theorists from Max Weber and Talcott Parsons to S. N. Eisenstadt and Peter Berger have described that trauma as involving a process of differentiation: "the differentiation of home from job, of political economy into politics and economy . . . of fact from value, of theory from praxis, differentiation of art from belief."[114] "Sundering cruelly what tradition had joined," writes John Murray Cuddihy, "modernization splits ownership from control, it separates church from state (the Catholic trauma), ethnicity from religion (the Jewish trauma). It produces the 'separated' or liberal state, a limited state that knows its place, differentiated from society. Differentiation slices through ancient primordial ties and identities, leaving crisis and 'wholeness-hunger' in its wake."[115]

Wholeness-hunger provided opportunities for missionaries, of course, as did the cleavage of church from state and religion from ethnos. Yet modernity also produced a countervailing force that could restrict or inhibit home missionaries or evangelical revivalists who would zealously exploit the sundering of "ancient primordial ties." For missionaries, this unavoidable and highly problematic product of modernity was "civic culture," the system of public rules and conventions that accompanied the process of social differentiation in an age of rapid industrialization and urbanization. The American values of religious liberty and tolerance undergirding this system ultimately produced a "divided mind," for they required religious groups "to try to be absolute in their convictions, but tolerant of other beliefs; strict in their internal discipline but accepting of a diversity outside it; evangelistic but not exclusivist; critical of other beliefs but ecumenical in their relations to other faiths."[116]

The problem of public behavior and decorum thus became strategic to the missionary enterprise. Describing the Jewish experience in the West at the end of the nineteenth century, Cuddihy notes that the modernization process, the civilizational process, and the assimilation process "were experienced as one." The experience exacted a heavy toll on traditional Jews, whose religious and civic life was experienced as one and undifferentiated, for "civility requires at a minimum, the bifurcation of private effect from public demeanor: intensity, fanaticism, inwardness, too much of anything, in fact, is unseemly."[117] The toll of civility could be heavy not only for immigrants but also for zealous religious missionaries trying to convert them from one "way of wholeness" to another.

Herein lay the crux of the challenge for the Protestant churches in their identification with the U.S. cultural mainstream. If the new Americans were to be socialized to a differentiated society that respects the principles of voluntarism, private initiative, and toleration, how to

retain "the old ascriptive cushions" of religion? That was a particularly vexing question for missionaries who sought conversions to a
different belief and behavioral system and wanted to separate the saved
from the unsaved, the born-again from the once-born, the American
citizen from the unwashed immigrant. Each day missionaries faced the
question of how the Protestant church was different from and prefer-
able to other "sects" or religious bodies. If the answer was that Protestantism is the American faith, then one must spell out the distinctive
religious content of that American faith. The noncoercive, nonascrip-
tive, voluntaristic aspect of that faith could not be ignored. Unlike
previous changes, the passage to modernity, Cuddihy argues, "cannot
be absorbed for the individual by the family, the church, a class, or an
economic or political interest. It is one that the individual must confront by making choices without dependence on a scripted guidance.
He is indeed forced to be free."[118]

One Protestant response to this dilemma was to model civil behavior for prospective converts. This modeling took the form of educational, social, and other charitable works, with an emphasis on personal
contact between missionaries and prospective converts (or "clients").
This shift of emphasis toward social work and personal example of
Christian virtue occurred within a larger context of growing bureau-
cratization and the professionalization of services, as the ethos of social work melded with the social gospel. It would be too much to suggest that missionaries of this type offered something for nothing, or that
the service came with no strings attached. But when relief work replaced
or displaced revival meetings, an important element of the motivation
for actual conversion was removed. If salvation came in the form of
schools, language centers, cultural programs, sports teams, and clin-
ics, it could be effectively filtered by the host religious community.

Thus the strategy of civic formation ironically undermined the conversion dynamic, for it led in many cases to a vigorous fortification of
the religious enclave from which the prospective converts were drawn.
A competition to nurture and provide the best for one's own people
ensued, with the prize often being the reestablishment and strengthening of the bonds of ethnicity and religion. Civic identity was not necessarily achieved at the expense of the religious message. Indeed, it
seems that the most successful missionaries, whether success is measured by sheer numbers of converts or by the creation of a new religious subculture, were those revivalists such as Dwight Moody and Billy
Sunday who privileged the religious content and interpreted the conventions of civility in its light while also doggedly resisting the polite
blandness that often undermined missionary efforts in a civil age. Evangelical preachers proclaiming the decidedly countercultural gospel of

dispensational premillennialism understood civility on strictly super-natural terms. And Catholic mission preachers, seeking a "second con-version" of lapsed Catholics with their own brand of hellfire and brim-stone preaching, could afford to offend their audiences. Not until they turned to non-Catholics did mission priests become relatively restrained and polite, according to the conventions of American civility. They were also much less successful in this venue.

Missionaries were naturally perceived as agents of change, as dis-rupters of the traditional order. The traditional order, such as it was, fought back. Resisting or transforming the conventions of civility proved to be a most resourceful response to the situation confronting missionaries of the mainstream. They liked to cultivate their mainstream image but could also turn it on its ear. Premillennialism was one of the devices for accomplishing both tasks.[119]

The ordeal of civility led to the strengthening of enclave cultures in turn-of-the-century America, in part because many missions produced two ironic results. First, they were far more successful in deepening the faith and commitment of the missionary band itself and their lapsed coreligionists than in winning new converts to the religion. Second, they sounded the alarm bell for the target group, leading that denomina-tion to redouble its efforts to meet the social and spiritual needs of its people. Part of the irony lay in the fact that the open-ended American experiment in pluralism and religious liberty produced, at least in the case of turn-of-the-century competition for souls, an inward-turning retrenchment rather than an ecumenical, public faith—a civic expres-sion of religion—to which the various denominations could contrib-ute without fear of diminishment.

Notes

1. "We grant . . . choice, but we also claim the right to bear witness to the conception which we believe to be the Gospel of the Grace of God." C. A. Brooks, *Through the Second Gate* (New York: n.p., 1922), 10–11.

2. Jonathan D. Sarna, "The American Jewish Response to Nineteenth-Century Christian Missions," *Journal of American History* 68 (June 1981): 47.

3. Frances Mary Riggs, "Attitudes of Missionary Sisters toward American Indian Acculturation," Ph.D. diss., Catholic University of America, 1967, 25.

4. Martin E. Marty, *Modern American Religion*, vol. 1: *The Irony of It All, 1893–1919* (Chicago: University of Chicago Press, 1986).

5. See Timothy P. Weber, *Living in the Shadow of the Second Coming: American Premillennialism, 1875–1982* (Chicago: University of Chicago Press, 1987).

6. Nathan Birnbaum, quoted in Emmanuel Sivan, "The Enclave Culture," in *Fundamentalisms Comprehended,* ed. Martin E. Marty and R. Scott Appleby (Chicago: University of Chicago Press, 1995), 16. Cultural theory holds that enclaves place special emphasis on the purity of the group, on reinventing tradition in such a way as to maintain strict boundaries between the elect and the reprobate, and on selectively imitating the enemy, who is perceived as skillfully in control of society's levers of power. Cultural theory is a hermeneutic device developed by the anthropologist Mary Douglas in her *Cultural Bias* (London: Royal Anthropological Institute, 1978); see also Mary Douglas, ed., *Essays in the Sociology of Perception* (Boston: Routledge and Kegan Paul, 1982); Mary Douglas and Aaron Wildavsky, *Risk and Culture* (Berkeley: University of California Press, 1982); Mary Douglas, *How Institutions Think* (Syracuse: Syracuse University Press, 1986); and Michael Thompson, Richard Ellis, and Aaron Wildavsky, *Cultural Theory* (Boulder: Westview Press, 1990).

7. Theodore Abel, *Protestant Home Missions to Catholic Immigrants* (New York: Institute of Social and Religious Research, 1933), 11–19.

8. *The Mormon Menace, Being the Confesstion of John Doyle Lee, Danite,* introduction by Alfred Henry Lewis (New York: Home Protection Publishing, 1905), viii.

9. *The Mormon Menace,* xi.

10. For an extended treatment of the Mormon theme, see Jan Shipps, "Making Saints in the Early Days and the Latter Days," presented to the Society for the Scientific Study of Religion, Salt Lake City, Oct. 27, 1989.

11. The full text of the memorial is found in Colman J. Barry, *The Catholic Church and German Americans* (Milwaukee: Bruce Publishing, 1953), appendix 4, 313–15. See the excerpts and commentary in *Documents of American Catholic History,* ed. John Tracy Ellis (Milwaukee: Bruce Publishing, 1956). Exaggerating numbers was not the sole province of the Catholics. Promoter Joseph McCabe of the Board of Home Missions of the Methodist Episcopal Church taunted Robert Ingersoll that, during the three decades after the Civil War, Methodists had gained 1,800,000 communicants. Church property had increased in value from $29 million to $160 million. Yet by 1899 the northern Methodist church reported a loss in membership. Marty, *The Irony of It All,* 157.

12. Most of the American hierarchy protested vigorously against the implication that they had neglected the spiritual welfare of immigrants and that there had been anywhere near the fantastic figure of ten million souls lost to the church in this country. Gerald O'Shaughnessy estimated that from 1881 to 1890 there was a total increase of 1,250,000 to the American Catholic population through immigration, a figure that included 119,000 from Canada, Mexico, and other non-European countries. Only seven hundred thousand Catholic immigrants came from the European countries whose delegates signed the Lucerne Memorial. See Gerald O'Shaughnessy, *Has the Immigrant Kept the Faith?* (New York: Macmillan, 1925), 165.

13. Barry, *The Catholic Church and German Americans,* 314.

14. Peter D'Agostino, "Italian Mission Clergy in the United States," unpublished paper, 3. For a full account, see Peter D'Agostino, "Missionaries in Babylon: The Adaptation of Italian Priests to Chicago's Church, 1870–1940," Ph.D. diss., University of Chicago, 1993. Giovanni Battista Scalabrini (1839–1905), Bishop of Piacenza, founded the Congregation of Missionaries of St. Charles Borromeo for work among Italian immigrants.

15. Jay P. Dolan, *The Immigrant Church: New York's Irish and German Catholics, 1815–1865* (Baltimore: Johns Hopkins University Press, 1975); John Joseph Parot, *Polish Catholics in Chicago, 1850–1920: A Religious History* (DeKalb: Northern Illinois University Press, 1981).

16. On this point, see the special issue of *U.S. Catholic Historian* (Summer 1993).

17. "The Secret Oath of the American Protective Association," in *Documents of American Catholic History*, ed. Ellis, 500.

18. Michael Williams, *The Shadow of the Pope* (New York: McGraw-Hill, 1932), 103–4. On the impact of the APA, see Arthur M. Schlesinger, "A Critical Period in American Religion, 1875–1900," *Proceedings of the Massachusetts Historical Society* 64 (1932): 546.

19. R. Scott Appleby, *Church and Age, Unite! The Modernist Impulse in American Catholicism* (Notre Dame: University of Notre Dame Press, 1992), 2–6.

20. O'Shaughnessy, *Has the Immigrant Kept the Faith?* 12.

21. Paul Robichaud, "Evangelizing America: Transformation in Paulist Missions," *U.S. Catholic Historian* 11 (Spring 1993): 61.

22. Isaac Hecker, *Questions of the Soul* (New York: D. Appleton, 1855), 166.

23. David O'Brien, *Isaac Hecker: An American Catholic* (New York: Paulist Press, 1992), 337.

24. Thomas Jonas, "The Divided Mind," Ph.D. diss., University of Chicago, 1980, 124. Hecker made very few converts during the course of his ministry, but the Paulists continued a yearly mission. The *Paulist Mission Chronicles* record the conversion of Protestants at the end of each mission account.

25. Jay P. Dolan, *Catholic Revivalism: The American Experience, 1830–1900* (Notre Dame: University of Notre Dame Press, 1986), xv–xvi.

26. Dolan, *Catholic Revivalism*, 11

27. Thomas E. Wangler, "The Birth of Americanism: 'Westward the Apocalyptic Candlestick,'" *Harvard Theological Review* 65 (1972): 415–36.

28. On the impact of his mission work in Nashville, see Michael B. McGarry, "Modernism in the United States," *Records of the Catholic Historical Society of Philadelphia* 90 (1979): 36. For a statement by Sullivan on the American ethos, see "'Protestantism and Catholicism in a New Age,' a Sermon Delivered by the Rev. William L. Sullivan at the First Congregational Church, All Souls, 6 April 1919," Archives of Harvard Divinity School; and William L. Sullivan, *Under Orders: The Autobiography of William L. Sullivan* (Boston: Beacon Press, 1929), 64–70, 90–95.

29. Sullivan, *Under Orders*, 66.

30. The Paulists lost five missionaries over the modernist crisis, and Hecker had been indirectly mentioned in Pope Leo's encyclical on Americanism. Hecker's close ally Alexander Doyle died in 1912, and the Catholic Missionary Union they had founded suffered administrative and financial problems after his death.

31. Marty, *The Irony of It All*, 25.

32. Sarna, "The American Jewish Response to Nineteenth-Century Christian Missions," 39.

33. Ibid., 42.

34. Paul R. Spickard, *Mixed Blood: Intermarriage and Ethnic Identity in Twentieth Century America* (Madison: University of Wisconsin Press, 1989), 171.

35. Spickard, *Mixed Blood*, 171, 187.

36. Jonathan D. Sarna, "The Impact of Nineteenth-Century Christian Missions on American Jews" in *Jewish Apostasy in the Modern World*, ed. Todd M. Endelman (New York: Holmes and Meier, 1987), 241–48.

37. A Williamsburg mission to the Jews called its journal *The Chosen People;* Arno Gaebelein chose the name "The Hope of Israel" for his mission; and the New Covenant Mission, Pittsburgh, called its journal *The Glory of Israel.*

38. Yaakov Ariel, "Evangelizing the Chosen People: Evangelical Missions to the Jews in America, 1880–1920," unpublished paper, 1993. Ariel's excellent work is part of his forthcoming study of Christian missions to American Jews.

39. William E. Blackstone, *The Millennium* (Chicago: Fleming H. Revell, 1904). Journals such as *Our Hope, The Jewish Era, Prayer and Work for Israel, The Chosen People, The Glory of Israel,* and *Immanuel's Witness* regularly published articles on Jewish religious themes, describing Jewish holidays, rites, and customs. See Arno C. Gaebelein, "Aspects of Jewish Power in the United States," *Our Hope* 29 (1922): 103.

40. Moses Rischin, *The Promised City: New York Jews, 1870–1914* (Cambridge: Harvard University Press, 1978), 199. See the mission journals such as *The Jewish Era, Immanuel's Witness,* and *The Glory of Israel.*

41. Ariel, "Evangelizing the Chosen People," 7.

42. "Notes from Our Mission," *Our Hope* 1 (1894): 24.

43. Louis Meyer, "Directory of Protestant Jewish Missionary Societies," *The Jewish Era* 23 (1913): 114–22. Missions to the Jews opened in New York City; Buffalo and Rochester, New York; Paterson, New Jersey; Philadelphia; Chicago; Boston; Minneapolis; Pittsburgh; St. Louis; Washington, D.C.; Baltimore; Cincinnati; Atlanta; Louisville; Memphis; Los Angeles; and San Francisco. A number of those cities had more than one such mission. New York had as many as ten, Philadelphia six, and Chicago five.

44. Leopold Cohn, *I Have Fought a Good Fight* (New York: American Board of Missions to the Jews, 1957), 106–16; Weber, *Living in the Shadow of the Second Coming*, 148.

45. Arno C. Gaebelein, "How the Hope of Israel Became Undenominational," *Our Hope* 4 (1897): 3–5.

46. Ariel, "Evangelizing the Chosen People," 11.

47. Ibid, 12. See, for example, Lewis A. Hart, *A Jewish Reply to Christian Evangelists* (New York: Bloch Publishing, 1906); Arthur U. Michelson, *From Judaism and Law to Christ and Grace* (Los Angeles: Jewish Hope Publishing House, 1934), 82–83; Louis Marshal, "On Christian Missions to the Jews," *American Hebrew* 125 (1929); and Stephen S. Wise, Introduction to Samuel Freuder, *My Return to Judaism* (New York: Bloch Publishing, 1924).

48. See, for example, A. Bernstein, *Some Jewish Witnesses for Christ* (London: Operative Jewish Christian Institution, 1909); Henry Einsprunch, *When Jews Face Christ* (Brooklyn: American Board of Missions to the Jews, 1939); and Louis Meyer, *Eminent Hebrew Christians of the Nineteenth Century* (New York: Edwin Mellen Press, 1982).

49. Arno C. Gaebelein, "Herman Warszwiak's Methods of Getting Crowds to Hear the Gospel," *Our Hope* 2 (1895): 2–5.

50. Ethical issues were discussed in missionary conferences. See, for example, Samuel Wilkinson, "The Moral Defensibility of some of the Methods Employed in Jewish Missions," *Yearbook of Evangelical Missions among the Jews,* 2 vols., ed. Herman L. Strack (Leipzig: J. C. Hinrich, 1906, 1913), 1:60–67.

51. Rischin, *The Promised City,* 199.

52. Ariel, "Evangelizing the Chosen People," 22.

53. By the beginning of the twentieth century, for example, there were 120 Jewish converts out of nearly 4,500 converts to Protestantism in America. *Immanuel's Witness* 3 (1901): 101. Other sources give smaller numbers of converts. See, for example, "The Sixth Annual Conference of the Chicago Hebrew Mission," *The Jewish Era* 12 (1903): 174.

54. See, for example, Arno Clemens Gaebelein, *Half a Century: The Autobiography of a Servant* (New York: Garland, 1988).

55. Robert I. Winer, *The Calling: The History of the Messianic Jewish Alliance of America, 1915–1990* (Wynnewood, Pa.: Messianic Jewish Alliance of America, 1990), 5–27.

56. Sarna, "The American Jewish Response to Nineteenth-Century Christian Missions," 48.

57. Ibid., 50.

58. *American Ecclesiastical Review* 1 (Feb. 1889): 43–48; English translation adapted from the New York *Freeman's Journal,* Jan. 5, 1889.

59. Antonio Mangano, *Religious Work among Italians in America: A Survey for the Home Missions Council* (Philadelphia: Board of Home Missions and Church Extension of the Methodist Episcopal Church, 1917), repr. as *Protestant Evangelism among Italians in America* (New York: Arno Press, 1975), 12.

60. Mangano, *Religious Work among Italians,* 13–14: "Out of the 600,000 Italian population of greater New York, the Roman Church by its own figures as far as I could obtain them, lays claim to only 180,000 including children as members of the Roman Catholic Italian churches, less than one-third the total Italian population."

61. Ibid., 10, 12.
62. Ibid., 8–9. The first mission for Italians in America was established in 1880 by the Rev. Antonio Arrighi under the auspices of the New York City Mission Society.
63. Ibid., 18.
64. Ibid., 26: "The Roman Catholic church realizes the value of environment and is busy establishing parochial schools to hold the Italian children to the church. Priests acknowledged to me that the leaders of the church are 'crazy to get the Italian children. They are going to make a place for themselves in this country.'"
65. Ibid., 30–31.
66. Abel, *Protestant Home Missions to Catholic Immigrants*, 105.
67. Ibid., viii, ix, x.
68. Ibid., 225: "Of the Protestant church's ministry to the foreign born, it must be recognized that the evidences of success are not numerous nor inpressive. . . . Many of our church leaders feel that the Protestant approach to population groups drawn from Catholic countries rests on no carefully-considred theory or policy and that in too many cases, the net result is to create friction between Catholic and Protestant churches without making a fundamental contribution to the religous lives of the people themselves. Indeed the question has been raised in high ecclesiastical circles whether Protestantism as such has any genius qualifying it for a ministry to Latin people. Whatever the answer may be, there will probably be general agreement that the present status of Protestant foreign work in our cities is far from satisfactory."
69. Ibid., 49–51.
70. Ibid, 51.
71. In *The Irony of It All*, 102, Marty quotes the *Alabama Baptist*, April 26, 1900, and cites the Southern Baptist Convention *Annual* of 1901.
72. Ibid., 103.
73. Stephen J. Ochs, *Desegregating the Altar: The Josephites and the Struggle for Black Priests, 1871–1960* (Baton Rouge: Louisiana State University Press, 1990), 52.
74. John Slattery, "Facts and Suggestions about the Colored People," *Catholic World* 41 (April 1885): 32–42.
75. Ochs, *Desegregating the Altar*, 67.
76. [Bishop Francis A. Janssens], "Colored Priests for Colored People," *St. Joseph's Advocate* 1 (April 1887): 229–31.
77. Ochs, *Desegregating the Altar*, 81–84.
78. John R. Slattery, "The Negroes and the Baptists," *Catholic World* 63 (May 1896): 265.
79. Slattery, "The Negroes and the Baptists," 266.
80. Ibid., 267, 268.
81. John R. Slattery, "A Catholic College for Negro Catechists," *Catholic World* 70 (Oct. 1899): 11–12.

82. In 1894 Slattery supervised the implementation of new regulations governing the training of blacks in the seminary. The regulations were clearly discriminatory, but Slattery defended them as necessary to appease bishops and other clergy who maintained that blacks were not capable of observing priestly celibacy. See Ochs, *Desegregating the Altar,* 92–93.

83. Slattery, "A Catholic College for Negro Catechists," 12.

84. Ochs, *Desegregating the Altar,* 109.

85. John R. Slattery, "How My Priesthood Dropped from Me," *Independent* 61 (July–Sept. 1906): 563–65.

86. John R. Slattery, "Native Clergy," *Catholic World* 52 (March 1891): 883–85; Jaime T. Phelps, "John R. Slattery's Missionary Strategies," *U.S. Catholic Historian* 7 (Spring–Summer 1988): 207.

87. Slattery, "How My Priesthood Dropped from Me," 565.

88. "For the BFM had more than strictly religious goals. Indians were to be stripped of their own life-styles, to be 'civilized' as well as Christianized, and to be transformed into upright and economically independent members of American society." Michael C. Coleman, *Presbyterian Missionary Attitudes toward American Indians, 1837–1893* (Jackson: University Press of Mississippi, 1985), 15–16.

89. R. Pierce Beaver, *Church, State, and the American Indians: Two-and-a-Half Centuries of Partnership in Missions between Protestant Churches and Government* (St. Louis: Concordia Publishing House, 1966), 177. In the early nineteenth century many Protestant missionaries served in nondenominational voluntary societies such as the American Board of Commissioners for Foreign Missions (ABCFM). By the 1830s the more conservative and denominationally conscious old school wing of the PCUSA believed that Presbyterian evangelical zeal should be channeled through church-controlled agencies.

90. Coleman, *Presbyterian Missionary Attitudes toward American Indians,* 20.

91. Ibid., 174ff. Coleman points out that the BFM was representative of mainline Protestant missionaries in general. "In their general attitudes toward the American Indians, and in the radical program they advocated for elevation of those heathens, the missionaries of the Presbyterian BFM shared in a consensus throughout the nineteenth century with members of other mission societies of the mainstream Protestant denominations and with 'friends of the Indians.' . . . All were moved by similar horror at the supposedly degraded ways of the heathen; and by a similar version of Protestant, civilized Indians capable, at some as yet unspecified date, of assimilation into citizenship of the United States." On their common goal, see Robert F. Berkhofer, Jr., *Salvation and the Savage: An Analysis of Protestant Missions and American Indian Response, 1787–1862* (New York: Atheneum, 1976), 15.

92. Coleman, *Presbyterian Missionary Attitudes toward American Indians,* 24.

93. Henry Warner Bowden, *American Indians and Christian Missions: Studies in Cultural Conflict* (Chicago: University of Chicago Press, 1981), 197.

94. The partnership with the government involved substantial financial aid. In *Church, State, and the American Indians,* Beaver observes, "It was the most potent stimulus of all to enlargement of Indian missions." As the secretary of the Board of the BFM said in 1858, "By uniting the agency of the Christian Church with the efforts of the Department of the Interior—Indian Affairs a great and united agency for good is completely secured" (174).

95. John C. Lowrie, *A Manual of the Foreign Missions of the Presbyterian Church in the United States of America* (1868), 37; see also George Hood, *Do Missions Pay? Or, the Commercial Value, Commercial Advantage, and the Success of Christian Missions* (New York: Mission House [BFM], 1872).

96. Coleman, *Presbyterian Missionary Attitudes toward American Indians,* 313. See also "The Pueblos of the Rio Grande Valley," in *Woman's Work for Woman* (1886), in which the anonymous author condemns the Roman Catholicism and syncretic religions of the Indians.

97. *Lake Mohonk Conference Proceedings, 1892,* 63–64, quoted in Francis Paul Prucha, *American Indian Policy in Crisis: Christian Reformers and the Indian, 1865–1900* (Norman: University of Oklahoma Press, 1976), 50–52. King read a paper entitled "Sectarian Contract Schools" in which he discussed the work of the National League for the Protection of American Institutions in fighting against the use of government funds by religious denominations.

98. The Board of Indian Commissioners was composed of prominent laymen from a variety of Protestant denominations: Quaker, Episcopalian, Presbyterian, Methodist, Baptist, and Congregational. Congress established the board in 1869 to exercise joint control with the secretary of the interior over the disbursement of funds appropriated for Indians. The board in turn appointed Quaker missionaries as government agents. Following the massacre of Piegan Indians by federal troops on January 23, 1870, Vincent Colyer, secretary of the board, suggested that the Quaker plan be extended to include other churches. President Grant approved the plan, and the government assigned seventy-three agencies to various churches. See Bowden, *American Indians and Christian Missions,* 191–92.

99. Peter J. Rahill, *Catholic Indian Missions and Grant's Peace Policy, 1870–1883* (Washington, D.C.: Catholic University of America Press, 1954).

100. The Methodists had fourteen agencies (54,473 Indians); the Orthodox Friends, ten (17,724); the Presbyterians, nine (38,069); the Episcopalians, eight (26,929); the Catholics, seven (17,856); the Hicksite Friends, six (6,598); the Baptists, five (40,800); the Reformed Dutch, five (8,118); the Congregationalists, three (14,476); the Christians, two (8,287); the Unitarians, two (3,800); the American Board of Commissioners for Foreign Missions, one (1,496); and the Lutherans, one (273). Catholics insisted that agencies, according to Grant's statement, should be assigned to churches that had missionaries at them in 1870 and to the one that had been there first. At other times Catholics argued that Indians themselves should be able to choose which denominations they wanted. A Baptist member of the Board of Indian Commis-

sioners proposed distribution according to denominational size because Baptists felt cheated in getting fewer than the Episcopalians and Presbyterians, who had fewer adherents. The Board of Indian Commissioners argued that no church had a right to any agency. What the government wanted from the churches was a total transformation of the agencies from political sinecures to missionary outposts. Prucha, *American Indian Policy in Crisis*, 50–52.

101. Beaver, *Church, State, and the American Indians*, 69.

102. Coleman, *Presbyterian Missionary Attitudes toward American Indians*, 58: "Quakers, Methodists, Episcopalians, and all the other Protestants fighting for the religious liberty of their own groups on the reservations, made no move to grant so much as a hearing to the Indian religions. The record of the Catholics was no better. They criticized Protestant bigotry and called for freedom of conscience, but that freedom did not extend to native religions, which were universally condemned. By religious freedom the missionaries meant liberty of action on the reservations for their own missionary activities."

103. Strong Catholic attacks on Grant's policy appeared in *Address of the Catholic Clergy of the Province of Oregon, to the Catholics of the United States, on President Grant's Indian Policy, in Its Bearings upon Catholic Interest at Large* (Portland, 1874); and *Catholic Grievances in Relation to the Administration of Indian Affairs; Being a Report Presented to the Catholic Young Men's National Union, at Its Annual Convention, Held in Boston, Massachusetts, May 19th and 11th, 1882* (Richmond, 1882).

104. See, for example, Richard Henry Pratt, *How to Deal with the Indians: The Potency of Environment* (Carlisle, 1903), 3.

105. The bulk of contract school funds went to Roman Catholics, which was intolerable to Morgan and the Protestant-oriented Indian reform groups. In 1889, they pointed out, $347,672 out of a total $530,905 was distributed to Catholic schools; the Presbyterians had only $41,825, a poor second. Prucha, *American Indian Policy in Crisis*, 304, 320. On the specifications of the Dawes Act, see W. J. Rorabaugh and Donald T. Critchlow, *America! A Concise History* (Belmont: Wadsworth, 1994), 320.

106. Morgan was, according to Coleman, "the first significant national figure in the history of American Indian education." *Presbyterian Missionary Attitudes toward American Indians*, 292. He exhibited a modern and aggressive Americanism, unquestioning belief in the public school system, and a professional Protestantism and anti-Catholicism. In 1869 he was ordained a Baptist minister and went to Baptist Union Theological Seminary in Chicago. See Thomas J. Morgan, *Roman Catholics and Indian Education* (Boston: American Citizen Co., 1893), 2.

107. Daniel Dorchester, *Romanism versus the Public School System* (New York: Phillips and Hunt, 1888), 185.

108. National Education Association, *Journal of Proceedings and Addresses* (Washington, D.C., 1888), 158.

109. Thomas Jefferson Morgan, *Studies in Pedagogy* (Boston: Silver, Burdette, 1888), 327–28, 348–50.

110. Thomas Jefferson Morgan, "Education for the Indians: Fancy and Reason on the Subject; Contract Schools and Non-Sectarianism in Indian Education" (pamphlet), University of Chicago Library.

111. *Annual Report of the Board of Indian Commissioners* (Washington, D.C.: Government Printing Office, 1893), 112–15.

112. Morgan became corresponding secretary of the Baptist Home Mission Society in 1893 and editor of the *Home Mission Monthly*. He continued his agitation for Indian education and his attacks against Catholicism. The growing American Protective Association that seized upon Catholic attacks on the Indian school system and the Catholic influence on the election of 1892 made the Morgan case one of its prime exhibits and eagerly welcomed him to its roster of speakers and writers.

113. Coleman, *Presbyterian Missionary Attitudes toward American Indians*, 315.

114. John Murray Cuddihy, *The Ordeal of Civility: Freud, Marx, Levi Strauss, and the Jewish Struggle with Modernity* (New York: Basic Books, 1974), 9.

115. Cuddihy, *Ordeal of Civility*, 10.

116. Jonas, "The Divided Mind," 2.

117. Cuddihy, *Ordeal of Civility*, 15.

118. Maurice Samuel, quoted in Cuddihy, *Ordeal of Civility*, 12.

119. William G. McLoughlin, *Revivals, Awakenings, and Reform: An Essay on Religion and Social Change in America, 1607–1977* (Chicago: University of Chicago Press, 1978), 145–50.

EIGHT

Education and Minority Religions

VIRGINIA LIESON BRERETON

Whenever and wherever I see one of these school houses in course of erection, I cannot help exclaiming there is going to be another of those temples of liberty, provided they are not polluted by sectarianism. In them the children of the high and low, rich and poor, Protestants, Catholics and Jews, mingle together, play together, and are taught that we are a free people, striving to elevate mankind, and to respect one another. In them we plant and foster the tree of civil and religious liberty.[1]

Despite the multitude of educators—family, religious institutions, peers, texts, clubs, and associations—public schools stand out, not least on a symbolic level, as the prime nurturers of American democracy, political and social equality, and morality, the very lifeblood of the American republic. That did not ensure harmonious support of them, though; on the contrary, their critical importance to the survival and well-being of the new nation made them institutions worth fighting over. Conflict became all the more inevitable when schooling in the late nineteenth century became compulsory and also increasingly important for national prosperity and individual economic and social mobility. Over the decades the sources of conflict have been many: the issue of location for a new school, school taxes, quality of learning and discipline, and accountability to rate-payers. But some of the fiercest and most constant battles have been over issues of religion, often entangled with issues of ethnicity and the retention of immigrant language and culture. Because religion involves the deepest issues of individual and group identity, and in an educational setting one person's religious neutrality amounts to another's apostasy, religious-educational conflicts have been among the most intractable.

Initially, it is difficult to consider afresh those religious struggles. Although a little exploration shows them to have been various and complex, in the historiography and in the public mind the contests have tended to collapse into simple plotlines, two in particular. The first relates how until recently there were two hostile sides to the school struggle—Protestant and Catholic. Catholics lost their mid-nineteenth-century bid for influence over public schools attended by their children and then went on to establish a separate system of parochial schools. Yet even though the Catholic hierarchy made the decision to establish a separate school system, they kept attempting forays—largely unsuccessful—into the public treasury to augment funding for that system.[2]

The second plot involves Jewish immigrants, public schools, and love at first sight. Jews flocked to the schools, performed as model pupils, and went on to use their educations to enter the professions out of all proportion to their numbers in the population. The more secular public education became in the late nineteenth and early twentieth centuries as a response to religious pluralism, the more pleased Jews were.[3]

The second story is accurate enough in its broad outlines, but its details merit closer examination. The first story likewise is true in its essential tale of Catholic-Protestant hostility and mistrust. But if we listen a little more carefully and a little more locally, we hear a number of other voices, and even the familiar, normally strident voices are sometimes modulated in interesting ways.

We also need to look beyond the two plotlines; additional, less familiar narratives deserve more attention than they have received. German and Scandinavian Lutherans often dissented from public schools and established parochial schools. Even when for one reason or another Lutheran groups did not set up parochial schools, they asserted their right to do so. The Missouri Synod Lutheran Church created a particularly successful system. Carl F. W. Walther, one of the most prominent leaders of the early Missourians, wrote, "May God preserve for our German Lutheran Church the gem of parochial schools! for upon it, humanly speaking, primarily depends the future of our Church in America."[4]

Lutherans frequently formed alliances with Catholics to fight legislation intended to weaken religious schools. In Wisconsin in 1890, for example, German Lutherans combined with Catholics to defeat Republican state legislators responsible for passage of the Bennett Law, a measure that threatened to circumscribe parochial school operations severely. Among other things, it defined English as the required language of all private as well as public school instruction and provided for local school boards to supervise private schools in their districts. The next year, with Democrats in control of the state legislature, the Bennett Law was repealed.[5] A similar scenario unfolded simultaneously in Illinois in the case of the Edwards Law, equally repugnant to parochial school proponents.[6]

In another series of narratives, Native American children and young people were variously encouraged, cajoled, and coerced into schools run by missionaries and later the federal government, at much peril to the traditional faith of their tribes. Pupils in these Indian schools and their parents were not always silent, submissive subjects, nor did teachers invariably succeed in acculturating students. On occasion these schools too became arenas of at least unspoken religious conflict. As schooling grew more secular in the late nineteenth century, evangelical Protestants began to dissent. Partly for practical reasons (they were unready financially and possibly psychologically to desert public schools), their earliest strategies for alternative education occurred on the post-elementary school level.[7]

In the early 1970s, telling the new narratives and modulating those more familiar would not have been possible. But thanks to the efforts of students of immigration (into Catholic and Jewish communities) and scholars of religious and ethnic minorities (especially Native American and conservative evangelical), it is now possible to glimpse more of the complexities contained in religious educational struggles.

Catholics and the "Protestant" Public Schools

There is little question that in the early nineteenth century most common schools were strongly Protestant in orientation and tone. Most public school students, teachers, and administrators were Protestant in background. Protestants congratulated themselves because as the century went on schools became generically Protestant rather than sectarian Protestant (that is, they taught a "general" Protestantism supposedly agreeable to all Protestants rather than an explicitly and contentious Presbyterian, Baptist, or Methodist perspective).[8] That claim, understandably, did not much impress Catholics. Moreover, it was usual for the Protestant version of the Bible, the King James Version, to be read aloud at the start of the school day. Protestants often could not understand why Catholics objected to the King James and why they saw its reading as an act that was far from religiously neutral. Prayers would be said and hymns sung that were Protestant in flavor. And not least, history and other texts contained pejorative allusions to Catholics, the chestnut among them being a description of the sixteenth-century Catholic practice of purchasing indulgences that so aroused the ire of Martin Luther.

Clearly, Catholics were often justified in seeing public schools as religiously alien territory. And undoubtedly their sense of alienation increased during the mid-1850s and early 1890s, periods of virulent nativist anti-Catholic activity. Accordingly, some famous battles transpired between Catholics and Protestants over the schools. Bishop John

Hughes's campaign for a share of the common school funds in New
York City in 1842 and 1843 is typical. Hughes did not succeed in ob-
taining the funds, but he did manage to bring about the demise of the
Public School Society, which was heavily Protestant, and thereby helped
the decades-long process of de-Protestantizing and secularizing New
York public schools.[9] The Cincinnati "Bible War" of 1869 was another battle royal. That year the Cincinnati School Board, made up of
Roman Catholics, German immigrant freethinkers, Unitarians, Jews,
and a few maverick evangelical Protestants, voted to exclude the Bible
and religious observances from the city's schools. The decision sparked
a nationwide debate. The Superior Court of Cincinnati reversed the
decision, but a few years later the school board was vindicated when
the Supreme Court of Ohio reinstated its original order.[10]

    As partisans saw matters, a great deal was at stake in these "wars."
Large numbers of Protestants considered schools as central to the creation and support of a homogeneous, moral, and politically enlightened
democracy. For many, morality, national unity, and democracy were virtually synonymous with Protestant Christianity. Catholics, of course, did
not see things that way, and the prospect of yielding the moral and religious formation of upcoming generations to Protestants was often un-
thinkable. Yet despite Catholic-Protestant hostility, and intense as it was
at times, the truth is that the picture was often more complicated than
the familiar one of two sides uncompromisingly arrayed against each
other. Throughout much of the nineteenth century, diverse voices, in
addition to those that clashed in anger, sometimes settled down to negotiation—and at times even spoke softly and ingratiatingly.

    Those diverse voices were above all local, a fact that has often been
ignored. Each place was different; even each neighborhood within large
cities or towns responded to its own conditions. Furthermore, situations could change over a decade or even within a year (as, for example, in the Lowell, Massachusetts, instance discussed later in this chapter). The bulk of educational funding came from town and village
sources, and therefore most policy decisions were made locally. Even
when policy came from state legislatures, local communities could often tacitly—or defiantly—decide to ignore it.

    Add to that the fact that during most of the nineteenth century there
were no neatly defined categories such as "public" or "private" and
the fact that a frequent designation for schools—"common"—did not
necessarily mean the same thing to everyone who used it. Especially in
rural areas, a number of educational arrangements were referred to as
"common" or "public," although they would not be so regarded now.
Often when a community contained a preponderance of Catholics—

especially Catholics of one ethnic group—common schools could appear quite parochial. Teachers might be Irish, for example, or German Catholic, sometimes even a priest or members of religious teaching orders, and paid either by parents or out of tax funds. The building might be owned by the town or by the Catholic Church. As for the curriculum, it might include religious teaching; certainly it would be penetrated throughout by a basically Catholic point of view.

Not just Catholics had public schools tailored especially to their immigrant cultures. In the Upper Midwest, concentrations of Scandinavians created schools that were in effect Norwegian or Swedish Lutheran but existed under public auspices.[11] Likewise, particularly in the early days of Mormon settlement in Utah, some common schools were inevitably quite Mormon in orientation. After the 1890 establishment of a formal public education system in Utah, school board elections were often fought over the question of whether Mormons or non-Mormons would attain a majority.[12]

Many arrangements were informal and might even have proved legally doubtful. In other cases the arrangements were more formal, although their implementers tended to remain flexible and accommodating in their attitudes. Some of these situations were celebrated: Lowell, Massachusetts, in 1835, Poughkeepsie, New York, in 1873, and Stillwater-Faribault, Minnesota, in 1892 and 1893. As the diversity in dates suggests, the experiments in compromise and accommodation were not limited to one part of the nineteenth century (although they had nearly ceased by 1898). But amicable arrangements likely became more difficult later in the century as common schooling became more systematized; the Catholic system expanded, antagonizing public school supporters; and Americans became more definite about what constituted a public school.

What made the arrangements possible—both formal and ad hoc—was the participation of leaders who were not always polarized in the ways history has recorded. On the Catholic side were lay people and clerics who had either been born in the United States or had lived there a long time. Many had themselves attended public schools. When they belonged to the same social class as Protestants in their area, they often maintained close contacts with those Protestants. Quite frequently, in fact, they felt more distance between themselves and newer Catholic immigrants than between themselves and Yankee Protestants. In other words, class affinities were sometimes more important than religious or ethnic ones. The same would be true among Jews in New York City. Uptown German Jews formed alliances with the WASPs who ran the school board and often felt alienated from newer, Eastern European Jews.

Donna Merwick and James Sanders have pointed out the fluidity in the Boston hierarchy before Cardinal O'Connell's arrival as head in 1908. Bishop John Fitzpatrick (1846–66) had graduated from Boston Latin School and had close friends among the Boston Brahmins; Bishop John Williams (1866–1907), a less outgoing personality, was a "native" Catholic. Among the diocesan priests, John Haskins was a graduate of Harvard University and a convert to Roman Catholicism from the Episcopal Church. Moreover, as Merwick indicates, until the late nineteenth century there existed a great intellectual diversity among priests of the Boston diocese, who, among other matters, held differing views of the "school question." Some ardently desired the creation of parochial schools, but many others were indifferent on the subject, actively preferred public schools, or simply were heartily sick of trying to raise funds to build Catholic schools in addition to church edifices.[13]

On the non-Catholic side, contrary to stereotype, was a wider variety of voices than the nativist Catholic-haters who equated "Protestant," "American," and "public education." There were also unbelievers, Unitarians, and other liberal religionists almost as alienated by the particular brand of Protestantism in the schools as were Catholics. (Some teamed with the Catholics in voting for the Cincinnati Bible ban). Even some Protestant evangelicals, fervent champions of common schools, were able to empathize with Catholics when they balked at reading the King James Version of the Bible and at hostile textbook references to their religion. Either from empathy or pragmatism these evangelicals realized that if all American children were to be attracted to the schools, some concessions and accommodations would have to be made to the sensibilities of Protestants who were not evangelicals. As one example of a group prepared to meet Catholics halfway, Geoffrey Blodgett has discussed the Democratic, muckraking Yankees of late-nineteenth-century Boston who made alliances with Irish Catholic politicians and were committed to an early form of cultural pluralism—not least of all in public schools.[14]

Not only were there potential bridges through personalities; historians such as Leslie Tentler have also taken note of the curricular convergences between public and parochial schools.[15] Despite their obvious and intentional differences, schools established by Catholics were to a great extent modeled on public ones, which were the predominant models, and parochial school students frequently continued their educations in public schools and therefore required a degree of curricular continuity. (Occasionally, public high schools would refuse to admit Catholic students unless they passed a qualifying examination.) Furthermore, as James Sanders has demonstrated, leaders of parochial school systems began to vie openly with public schools and were eager to have students take the same standard examination.[16] Preparing them for those tests was likely to promote educational similarities.

Catholics in Lowell

The situation in Lowell, Massachusetts, during the 1830s and 1840s allows a closer look at the dynamics and considerable complexities of accommodations. Fortunately, nineteenth-century Lowell has received a good deal of historians' attention, so it is possible to know about the social, religious, and cultural context in which school questions were worked out.[17]

The Irish were the only large Catholic group resident in Lowell until later in the century, and studying them has advantages. Inevitably, all ethnic Catholic groups struggled with public schools, but their struggles went considerably beyond the question of religion to embrace the issue of language. Most Catholic ethnics spoke a language of their own—German, Polish, French, or Italian—and were concerned that their children learn the language and that culture of which it was part. The survival of a language was often equated with the survival of Polish or German Catholicism, so immigrants greatly desired that whatever school their children attended teach that language.

The Irish case does not have that complication. Although some spoke Gaelic, by the time of Irish immigration it was a dwindling language even in Ireland, and the Irish had become English-speakers. Although Irish immigrants wished to preserve a distinct culture (which they vehemently distinguished from England's), language was no longer part of it, as was the case for German or Polish or French Catholics. Thus, Irish Catholics were primarily concerned with preserving their religion. The Irish are also interesting because, as Howard Weisz points out, their heaviest immigration—during the 1840s and 1850s—occurred just as the American public school system was being created and shaped.[18]

Initially, several favorable conditions helped foster educational compromise between Lowell's Catholics and Protestants. In the 1830s that city contained a core of long-settled and middle-class Irish Catholics. One leader, Hugh Commiskey, had been in the United States since 1790 and had settled in Lowell in 1828. He was friendly with Lowell's Yankee leaders, including the agents of the textile mills in the city. Every year, the Lowell Irish Benevolent Society, established in 1833, hosted a dinner at which Protestant leaders were the customary guests.

Catholic priests had not yet entered the parish school business; two short-lived attempts at parochial schools occurred in Lowell during the

1820s but failed for lack of resources and determination. Catholic clergy were busy raising funds to build churches and were not anxious to add parish schools to their tasks (nor were their parishioners eager to provide the funds for such schools). Fortunately, as far as they were concerned, they had no pressure from the hierarchy—what there existed of it—to provide parochial schools.

For their part, Yankee Protestants in Lowell were not eager to drive Catholics to the establishment of parochial schools. Besides their wish to gather all students into one system of schooling so a common culture could be created, they knew the community's resources would hardly permit establishing duplicate schools. The situation was ripe for negotiation, and a modus vivendi was worked out. Two special public schools were established, one in the basement of St. Patrick's Church in the Acre, an area of concentrated Irish residence, and the other in a new section of Irish settlement, Chapel Hill. The school board agreed to appoint Catholic teachers, ones approved by priests as well as the board. One priest was given the right to veto the use of texts he found offensive. These arrangements worked well for several years. In 1841 the Lowell School Committee furnished $500 to rent the basement of St. Patrick's Church, "in effect using public money to underwrite a portion of the parish debt."[19] By 1843 six "Catholic" public schools, one of them at a grammar level, existed. Lowell residents, both Catholic and Protestant, were proud of the arrangements; they "hailed the agreement as a noble experiment worthy of emulation throughout America."[20]

In the mid-1840s, however, the agreement broke down although it was never formally abrogated. Most scholars ascribe the breakdown to large-scale factors: social and economic changes in Lowell and in the wider religious and social climate of Massachusetts and the United States. The number of Irish Catholics increased rapidly in Lowell, and many newcomers were impoverished refugees from the potato famine of the late 1840s. Protestants grew alarmed about the numbers of incoming Irish and about the destitution of the immigrants. Meanwhile, Irish workers were replacing Yankee mill girls in textile mills, although they were not paid as much as native Americans and were treated with less respect. This transformation hurt Yankee-Irish relationships in two ways: It introduced a stronger note of economic competition than before and put Irish and Yankees in closer proximity, and it signaled the end of the idealistic days of the Lowell industrial experiment, of which citizens had been so proud. Added to all this ferment, and allied with it, was the rising tide of nativism, from which came the Know-Nothingism of the mid-1850s (the state of Massachusetts fell briefly into Know-Nothing hands in 1855). Thus, conditions that had fostered cooperation and good feeling had begun to deteriorate.

Perhaps more interesting are the smaller-scale reasons for the break-down in harmony, reasons that can be traced to the internal dynamics of the Irish community of Lowell. From the beginning, the community had proved vulnerable to factionalism—with immigrants from one part of Ireland often ranged against those from another. Early on, the Irish middle-class leadership strove to keep a lid on such conflicts. Then the middle-class Irish developed divisions exacerbated by a series of weak and sometimes troubled priests (who also fought among themselves). At length, Bishop Fitzgerald sent a cleric named James T. McDermott to Lowell to try to get a grip on the chaotic situation by settling the considerable parish debts and calming intra-communal tensions. A take-charge man by temperament, McDermott at first succeeded but then suddenly created a furor of his own in 1843 by demanding that the school board fire seven of Lowell's twelve Catholic teachers. He apparently resented the fact that when another parish had been created in Lowell those seven teachers had joined it in preference to his, suggesting that they were too independent for his taste. Presumably, his attempt to oust the teachers was part of a personal vendetta. When all but one refused to resign, Father McDermott instructed parents to keep their children home from school. After nearly three months of parental compliance, the boycott fell apart, but by that time the Lowell compromise was in tatters.

It was obvious that many Irish in Lowell and in Massachusetts were unhappy to see harmonious relations with Protestant school leaders break down. Some of McDermott's former supporters expressed anger with him for creating trouble, and Bishop Fitzpatrick even issued a rebuke. Eventually the fracas died down, but it is reasonable to suppose that non-Catholic educational leaders, in addition to responding to outside pressure, had lost some of their trust in local Irish religious leadership, in part because of McDermott's hotheaded actions. In any event, the number of Catholic teachers, even in "Irish" schools, diminished, and one school in the Irish area endured the ignominy of being named the Mann School, a good indication that non-Catholics were no longer as careful of Catholic sensibilities as they had once been. In 1848 and 1851, respectively, the brothers and priests John and Timothy O'Brien took up their duties in Lowell and were unswerving in their determination to create parochial schools. In 1852, accordingly, John O'Brien opened the Notre Dame Academy for Girls, much to the consternation of Lowell's public school leaders.

The Lowell example shows that accommodation was possible under a favorable set of circumstances: the presence of good will between Catholics and Protestants, usually greatly fostered by the existence of a middle-class Catholic leadership; residential concentration of a Catholic group, as in the case of the Irish who congregated in the Acre and Chapel Hill; and Catholic desire for assimilation and the perception of public schools as a route to that goal. In Lowell an "Irish" public school could be arranged with minimum impact on the rest of the population, and there was a basic fund of what was referred to as "liberal sentiment" in the community. For awhile, the Irish and non-Irish worked together peaceably.

Lowell in the late 1830s and early 1840s provides a useful counterpoint to a more dramatic incident in which mobs burned the convent in nearby Charlestown in 1834, the year before the Lowell compromise was worked out. Such agreements as were possible in Lowell arose from particular conditions at particular times in particular places, and they often broke down under the same sorts of particularities—in Lowell's case the personality and feuds of James McDermott, factors only loosely tied to the school issue itself. Of course, the accommodation might well have failed even without McDermott because larger social forces were astir, but the breakdown might have happened on a different, delayed, schedule and also with different results.

Lowell in 1843 was not unique in its educational harmony, and even situations remembered as those of Catholic-Protestant hostility appear more ambiguous when examined. Such an instance is the Eliot School case of 1859. The traditional account is simple: A Catholic schoolboy, Thomas Wall, attending one of Boston's public schools, refused to recite the Protestant version of the Ten Commandments at his teacher's request. Wall's refusal snowballed, apparently with the encouragement of the boy's priest, and other Catholic boys—possibly as many as three hundred—joined in protest. Wall, perceived as the ringleader, was finally beaten by the submaster, a Mr. Cook, so severely that his hands bled (Wall finally consented to say the Protestant version of the Ten Commandments). The other boys were suspended from school. Wall's parents took Cook to court, but authorities vindicated the schoolmaster.

What appears to be at first a case of Catholics arrayed against a Protestant school (with the Catholics losing before superior Protestant political power) is more complicated upon second examination. An important outcome of the case was that after waiting a decent interval—a few months—the school board ruled that no teacher would have the power to force children to read or recite anything antithetical to their beliefs and limited authority to eject students from school to the central board. In effect, the board censured the action of the Eliot School authorities and made repetition of such an occurrence less likely. Furthermore, it seems clear that the incident would not have happened at all but for a fluke that is difficult to explain; the principal of the Eliot School had in the past provided ways for Catholic children to avoid engaging in Protestant practices and recitations (it appears that he and the teachers looked the other way). Why he reversed himself on this occasion is a mystery; perhaps he had experienced pressure from someone on the governing board of the Eliot School. Finally, it is clear that various members of the Boston hierarchy, starting with Bishop Fitzpatrick, tried, successfully, to defuse the situation and kept the demonstrations from spreading to Catholic pupils in other Boston schools.[21]

After 1884, the year of the Third Plenary Conference in Baltimore, Catholic positions on schooling hardened considerably. The conference decreed that a parochial school be built in each parish, threatened to discipline priests and parishes that did not comply, and made it mandatory for parents to send their children to those schools. But even after the Baltimore conference, the major players, Catholic and Protestant, continued to find room for negotiating the school question. Many arrangements continued to be local to a family or a parish or a community or a city. Even after 1884, not all parish priests were enthusiastic about school-keeping; Boston, for instance, lagged behind in parochial school establishment. And where priests were zealous about parochial schools they sometimes encountered resistant parents. Such priests took the conference's decisions as tacit permission to punish parents who did not send children to existing Catholic schools, excommunicating them or withholding communion from them. Some parents fought back by appeal to the hierarchy, sometimes successfully. Many Catholic parents saw public schools as a route to social and economic mobility; they might compromise by sending their sons and daughters to parochial schools through the lower grades—typically until their first communion—and then transfer them to public schools for the upper grades. Catholic politicians tried to temporize. They could hardly afford to be seen as anything but friends of public schools, yet they could not ignore the teachings of their church, either. Public school leaders continued to want Catholic pupils and accordingly offered compromises, such as religious neutrality, that would make attendance possible and desirable.

Michael Perko, writing about a moment in Cincinnati when an arrangement mutually agreeable to Catholics and Protestants seemed possible, calls attention to the scenarios that might have been and asks whether the development of two parallel systems of education, one public and one parochial, was as preordained as it now appears.[22] On one hand, the question is moot; on the other hand, it encourages a harder look at situations that appear to contradict the dominant story.

In this regard it is useful to consider the Canadian situation. Owing to their particular historical circumstances, especially the compromises necessitated by confederation in 1867, Canadians arrived at different educational answers to problems of religious pluralism. Ontario, for instance, used tax funds to finance both its secular common schools and the schools of the Catholic minority (the "separate schools"). Ontario Catholics, if they wished, could elect to pay their education taxes to support Catholic schools. Quebec developed a system of publicly funded denominational schools. By turning to such arrangements, Canadians did not avert educational and religious rivalries and tensions among groups and within groups. They did, however, manage to settle on arrangements that can help others glimpse roads not taken.

Jews and the Public Schools

For decades, common wisdom has held that public schools were not an arena of conflict for Jews. These immigrants took to public schools with tremendous enthusiasm, and their children were successful students who used education to achieve rapid upward social and economic mobility. When Jews—parents and journalists—did raise alarms about schools it was often not so much the Christian or Protestant ethos that bothered them as physical conditions, especially those in ghetto schools: crowding, poor maintenance, and inadequate equipment. What seems to have exercised Jewish parents most were the repeated attempts of public school educators to track immigrant children, including theirs, into vocational education. This is how they interpreted the efforts to implement the Gary Plan in 1917, for instance, when they successfully teamed with other voters to defeat the reform mayor identified with that plan.[23]

Jews were, of course, sensitive to the persistent Protestantism of public schools and usually supported those who resorted to state legislatures, courts, and local school boards in the attempt to remove explicitly religious teaching from schools—prayers, reading the Bible, and singing hymns. In the nineteenth century, however, their dissatisfaction with "Protestant" common schools was usually muted; generally, Jews did not take the lead in political and court battles over religion in schools. They would do so in the later twentieth century. In general, the usual assumptions about Jews and their affinity for public education seem to hold up well. As long as public schools met a minimum standard in curriculums and physical plants, Jews were uniformly enthusiastic about them.

Nevertheless, scholarship has taught us to modify some assertions. First, the real love affair should be dated later in the nineteenth century. During the middle decades of that century Jews debated what kind of education was most appropriate for children— and public schools were far from a unanimous choice. Isaac Leeser, a prominent Philadephia Jewish leader, was a proponent of separate schools because he was afraid that public schools—"essentially Christian"—would draw Jewish children away from their faith: "They hear prayers recited in which the name of a mediator is invoked; they hear a book read as an authority equal if not superior to the received word of God; . . . we are in a great error if we suppose that Christian teachers do not endeavor to influence actively the sentiments of their Jewish pupils; there are some, at least, who take especial pains to warp the mind and to implant the peculiar tenets of Christianity clandestinely."[24] Around midcentury, a number of congregations and individuals established separate schools that taught both religious and secular subjects and provided alternatives to public schools. Even then, however, public schools had numerous champions in the Jewish community. Moreover, by the late 1860s and the 1870s most separate educational establishments had closed. By the time a new immigrant group of Eastern European Jews began their schooling in the 1880s, a majority of Jewish children attended public schools.

But even then the embrace of public schools by Eastern European immigrants does not seem to have been entirely voluntary. By the time they arrived, the already established Jews of German descent, almost without exception, urged public schooling upon the immigrants. Some of their concern was financial; if a separate system of schooling had been set up for or by the Eastern European immigrants, German Jews, possessors of the lion's share of communal resources, would have had to fund much of it. Part of their concern was also cultural. German Jews, worried and embarrassed by the ways of alien brothers and sisters in the faith, valued the conservative, assimilating powers of public schools. Thus, they became even firmer allies of public schools, and many filled prominent roles in the Jewish community and in public education.

In New York City, for instance, Julia Richman, Leon Goldrich, Edwin Goldwasser, and Felix Warburg crossed back and forth between positions as public school principals, superintendents, and school board members on the one hand and as directors of the YMHA or the Educational Alliance on the other. On occasion their support of public schools was coercive; in 1880 it was required that students had to be enrolled in public school in order to be accepted into the Hebrew Free School for supplementary religious education.

Another assumption that has been reexamined concerns whether Jewish immigrants found it relatively easy to transfer from traditional religious study to largely secular public school learning. Behind that assumption lies the premise that a good student is a good student whatever the place and the subject matter. Students of Jewish immigrant history, however, have contested the ease of transfer assumption and argued that the two kinds of learning were disparate. Mariam Slater, for instance, has pointed out that the expectations of Talmudic learning were quite different from those of Western learning: "Shtetl learning was ritualistic, scholastic, conservative and 'unrelated to technology, art or science.'" In contrast, Western learning is "pragmatic, humanistic, oriented to natural and social science, and innovative."[25]

Finally, the assumption that public schools facilitated Jewish social and economic mobility has also been reexamined. Sherry Gorelick has questioned the common expectation that New York City students who did well in elementary school usually graduated from high school, attended one of the city colleges free, and then made their way into the professions of law, medicine, or teaching at a minimum of personal or family expense. She argues that Jews achieved most of their mobility through success in business, a pursuit that did not, at the turn of the century, require advanced education. Painfully few Jewish sons and daughters made their way into the professions at this time, Gorelick notes, although those who did were highly visible and greatly celebrated inspirations to the rest. The testimony of at least one alumnus of public school education bears her out. Charlie Moses said, "Do you know what education really is? It's a way to get a responsible job at low pay. My friends who did not go to high school, the ones who went out to work, they have an economic life as good as mine. My contemporaries, whether they went to high school, college or not, their economic status has very little bearing on where they went to school."[26]

Yet scholarship, although qualifying Jewish romance with public schooling assumptions, has also amplified the reasons Jews had for embracing schooling. In Russia and Poland after 1887 formal quotas severely restricted the opportunities of Eastern European Jews for a secular education. Girls' access to schooling was particularly limited. Boys of elementary school age at least received religious education at the cheders, but girls were barred even there. What education they received came at home in their families. Thus, the American promise of free education open to all was for many Jewish parents and their daughters an extremely attractive one.[27] One immigrant girl commented, "My whole hope was coming to this country to get an education. I heard so much about America a free country for the Jews and you . . . didn't have to pay for schooling, so I came."[28]

Moreover, Jewish immigrants were eager to become Americans. For them more than for others who at least had hopes of returning to their homelands there was little thought of going back to Russia or Poland.

Arriving in the United States, they had cast their lot irrevocably with the new nation. They were eager to learn English and the basics of being an American citizen. Becoming an American was not easy and involved loss, but there was no real alternative. And for most Jews, as for many immigrants bent on assimilation, the route to becoming an American lay through public schools. Thus, most Jews had ample reason for embracing public schools, and anecdotal testimonies to this embrace are legion. Parents treated public school teachers as special beings and schools as "sacred citadels."[29] Max Weiner, a son of immigrant Jews in Chicago, explained, "Most of the parents had no education or very, very little. The teachers were looked up to as if they were God, and the fact that they were not Jewish had nothing to do with it. The teacher knew best."[30]

As suggested earlier, Jewish girls felt a special affinity for public schools, finding models and inspiration among female teachers, particularly, although not only, those who were Jewish. One female student recalled, "I loved my teachers. I loved them. . . . My teachers would give me books to read and take home. They were very, very good, very nice to me, and I remember them fondly for the rest of my life."[31] Another woman remembered a teacher named Elizabeth A. Bliss: "Nobody I knew was named Elizabeth; this you only read in books. We had kids named Jennie and Sarah and Beckie, Tillie—but *Elizabeth A. Bliss!* She lived in the suburbs, and she had a garden, and she came into the city in the springtime with an armful of peonies that to me was just beauty incarnate."[32] And it is true that some parents and children were so enamored of public education that they ignored or overlooked the heavily Christian bias of most teachers:

> The teacher was going to educate your child; therefore your child better obey the teacher. And whatever the teacher did was wonderful in the eyes of the parents. So the fact that your child was singing non-Jewish songs and celebrating the birth of Jesus and making Christmas decorations would never offend most people because this was like part of your education

> They didn't think, "This was something against the Jews." They thought, "This was the way a child was taught in schools."[33]

Statistics back up the impression of the near-universal approbation of public schools. In 1914 nearly all of the 275,000 Jewish children in New York City between six and fourteen were in public schools; fewer than a quarter of those children received any form of Jewish education.[34]

And yet it is important to recognize that the happy marriage between Jews and the schools was not without its conflicts and costs, the outcomes of which would become more apparent after World War II when

Jews embraced religious day schools in a way that would have been difficult to predict in 1915. In one sense, the schools did the job Jews expected of them only too well. Children became Americanized and moved ahead in society, but in the process there was danger that they would forget they were Jews. Several forms of supplementary Jewish education were provided, either congregational or communitywide, either after the regular school day or on weekends or both, but these forms were often vulnerable to criticism. Students were overtired at the end of a long public school day; there were not enough hours of instruction (or there were too many); older students dropped out after their bar or bat mitzvahs; and pedagogy was outmoded or boring. Early in the century, however, concerned educators and parents were optimistic enough to place their hopes in the possibilities of reform. Their response was rarely to establish alternatives to public schools but rather to strive to improve the quality of supplementary religious education.[35]

Despite their acceptance of public schools, Jews came into conflict with Christian teachers and administrators. They appear to have complained less of aspersions cast on Judaism than of obliviousness to Jewish concerns and sensitivities. A good deal of aggressive Christian teaching lingered in the supposedly "secular" New York City school system of the early twentieth century. Sometimes Jewish students chose the route of passive resistance mixed with ridicule. One recalled his response to Bible reading and prayers: "It made absolutely no impression on me. We used to do this in the auditorium. I remember the sound when the kids said 'forgive us our trespasses as we forgive those who trespass against us.' A thousand kids saying this sounded as if all the radiators were leading, pst, pst, pst."[36] Other students suffered more acutely from the insistence on Christian observances. The *Jewish Daily Forward,* a stout champion of public schooling, described how the observance of Christmas in public schools saddened and perplexed Jewish children:

> For Jewish children Christmas is a sad season. Their heads droop. As their friends rejoice they must remain blind to the store windows winking their lights at every passerby.
>
> In America, where the wall between Christian and Jew is not so high, the Jewish child is exposed to Christmas more than anywhere else. Children attend the same schools under the same teachers and sing the same carols. . . .
>
> If a child doesn't know why he's a Jew and not a Christian, at this time of year he feels like a blunderer in the wrong place, a stranger among friends with no world of his own. No spheres or spiritual firmament with stars and galaxies to light up his cosmic loneliness.

"Papa, what are we?"
"Jews."
"Why are we Jews?"
"Because we're not *goyim*."
"Why aren't we *goyim?*"
"Don't bother me."[37]

The *Forward*'s point was not that the schools were misguided in encouraging this confusion and alienation but rather that the father was remiss in not giving his son a stronger sense of what it meant to be a Jew. Although schools were blameless in some Jewish eyes, the fit between Jewish children and public schools was not always perfect. Occasionally, individual students would fight the pervasive Christian atmosphere:

> I have a very clear memory of one time that I got into trouble. I don't know if I was in fourth grade or fifth grade and we were singing the "Battle Hymn of the Republic," and I wasn't singing and the teacher asked why. "Well, I am Jewish, and 'he has seen the glory of the coming of the Lord' is about Jesus Christ, and I don't believe in Jesus Christ. I am Jewish, and I don't believe that he was a god."
>
> In those days, a great many of the teachers were Catholic, and so I was sent to the principal.

The principal was clearly sympathetic, "She took me on her knee and said, 'Don't mind her. Don't worry about her. Just go home and come to school tomorrow. I'll talk to the teacher. She'll understand that I'll have told you to come back to school.'" Here are signs of increasing secularization: The "Battle Hymn" was being sung, and although there is no indication that it would drop from the teacher's repertoire, at least Jewish students would not be forced to sing it if they had the courage not to conform.[38]

Other conflicts involved students, their parents, or both and stemmed from administrators' heavy-handedness or ignorance. Occasionally, students were penalized for their absences on Jewish holidays; it was not unusual for tests that could not be made up to be given on those days. Likewise, Jewish girls found themselves being forced to violate dietary laws in cooking classes by, for example, mixing meat and milk.

On at least one occasion the struggle against Christian influence in schools became not an individual but an organized group effort. On December 24, 1906, a day scheduled to be taken up with Christmas exercises in New York schools, Jewish parents in the city staged a boycott. The instigating factor in their protest was an address by the principal of P.S. 144 in Brownsville, Brooklyn, the previous year during a Christmas assembly. He had urged his audience of schoolchildren, many of whom were Jewish, to imitate Christ. Jewish parents, protesting the principal's remarks before the school board, had failed to get satisfaction, and the result was the Christmas 1906 boycott. The strike was effective on the Lower East Side, where one-third of the student body stayed home that day. Moreover, the action received sympathetic coverage in the non-Jewish press. The result of the protest was a decision by the board of education to forbid "the singing of hymns," "the reading from any distinctive religious treatise or book, other than the Bible," and the "assigning of essays upon any distinctive religious topic." Furthermore, the superintendent of schools was to "issue a circular annually cautioning the principals and staff in this respect (elimination of religious content in pre-winter vacation exercises)."[39]

Although American Jews at the turn of the century were happy with the schools (or managed to get action when they were not), all was not unbroken sweetness and light, even within the New York Jewish community. In 1908, for example, Lower East Side Jews presented several petitions to the board of education to request that the district's superintendent, Julia Richman, be removed from the Lower East Side. According to their complaints, Richman was "entirely out of sympathy with the needs of this part of the community" and "degraded and lowered parents in the eyes of their children, took advantage of every opportunity to suggest to the children that their parents were criminals" and had "placed herself in opposition to the residents." Louis Marshall, a major leader in the Jewish community, defended Richman, and the affair apparently blew over, but not without leaving its traces in the record.[40]

Schools for Native Americans

We are only beginning to recognize religious conflict in relation to schooling for Native Americans. The assumption has long been that young people simply went to the schools provided for them (nearly always by others, without consultation) and had their religion and culture drummed out of them. If they did not become acculturated to white society, they at least did not remain Native American. That some lingered in a sort of miserable limbo did not seem to trouble observers.[41]

It is certainly true that the civilizing attempts (and Christianizing attempts, often regarded as the same thing) were heavy-handed and often oppressive. Whether young Native Americans attended mission or federal schools (the categories were blurred until late in the period; missionary schools received government subsidies until 1897), they were typically forbidden to use tribal languages, wear customary dress, or follow native customs. They learned "white" subjects, although typically at a low academic level, without any admixture of Native learning. The ethos was Christian, even in the government schools. Some of this Christian influence was explicit. In Chiloco Indian School, Oklahoma, for example, a government boarding school established in 1884, a long grace was said before each meal, and at Riverside, another government boarding school, students were required to attend Sunday school.[42] Christianity was also implicit in the strenuous character building that virtually all the schools attempted. Students were trained to be industrious, courteous, prompt, and clean—all assumed to be Christian (and civilized) virtues.

Between 1890 and 1920 many educators of Native Americans preferred boarding schools, where students would be able to retain only minimal contact with their families.[43] Given this policy, off-reservation boarding schools were sometimes regarded as best because students could be removed particularly far from their families and be gathered from a number of different tribes. They would, therefore, find it more difficult to behave "clannishly." At Chilocco, one of the off-reservation schools, students received postage to write their parents or other kin only once a month, and even those letters were read by school personnel before they went out.

Nor did parents always exercise free choice in sending their children to school. At times they were threatened with loss of food rations if they refused to give up their children to the educators. Moreover, they were discouraged from visiting their children at school. When schools received subsidies on a per student basis, they were sometimes tempted into recruiting drives that came perilously close to kidnapping.

Without excusing what was done in the name of assimilation, efforts to do so seem not as successful as sometimes thought. There were few fights over education in the courts or legislatures, but much conflict took place on an individual and family level. Although often forbidden to use their tribal language in the Indian schools, children surreptitiously used it to talk with other children from their tribe. Despite discouragement children told traditional stories at night when they were alone about Coyote and Spider Woman. Children ignored or failed to understand Christian teachings or put Christianity and their own spiritual traditions together in syncretic fashion. It was not unusual for children to make fun of Christian teachings. One female informant, born in 1895, recalled, "The kids, we used to . . . when she tell us about how Jesus was born and we just laugh and act silly and our matron would say, 'Don't laugh.' Then we ask her, 'Did you see the baby?' You know, things like that . . . the older girls and us. At her questions like that. We just laugh about it. All the time we thought it was just silly for them not to go and see the baby when it was born because she said everybody went and see the baby."[44] Students snuck off to join annual buffalo hunts or tribal ceremonies. Those at home during vacations resumed the traditional dress and lifeways not allowed at school—and typically returned to school late. Sometimes they employed learning to their own purposes, for instance to record tribal traditions. Sometimes these attempts to negotiate between school demands and their desires would fail. It was common for Native American children to run away from school, and even though parents might return them there they did not necessarily punish them for their flight. While many Indian students "took the white road," many did not, either because they would not or simply could not. A Kiowa boy who was a boarding school student at the end of the century said, "It is hard to Indians to change. No matter how far in education he has, his Indian ideas stays with him."[45]

But the attempts to make Christians of Native American students failed not only because of the responses of the students but also because of a basic contradiction in the approach of the educators. Although their goal was acculturation, they set up schools separated from those for whites.[46] By so doing, and by mixing students from different tribes and providing English as a lingua franca, they inadvertently fostered pan-Indianism. In due time, at Wounded Knee and elsewhere, this foundation would bear fruit in the American Indian movement. In the meantime, it would ensure the preservation of native and syncretic religious practices—evidence that the most repressive educational practice can have oddly liberationist outcomes.

Conservative Protestants and the Public Schools

The increasing secularism in schools late in the nineteenth and early in the twentieth century, although not thorough enough for many Jews, was a matter of dismay for many Protestants. Their responses were perforce limited. They went to court (as in the Cincinnati case) to oppose attempts to dislodge the Bible and religious observances from the schools, and they sometimes appealed to legislatures and school boards to mandate Bible reading and the like, although not ultimately successfully. They did not in the late nineteenth century create alternative elementary schools, at least not in large numbers; the cost would have been prohibitive for what was only a nascent movement, especially in view of the fact that the criteria for primary education were becoming more rigorous and demanding. Probably they also did not yet fully realize how damaging the tides of religious pluralism would prove to be for their interests. How then were children raised conservatively "Christian" in the 1880s, 1890s, and the first two or three decades of the twentieth century?[47]

First it is useful to recognize that many conservative evangelicals would still have found public schools congenial. Chances are that early court decisions removing Protestant religious practices from public schools were often only symbolic. In areas where concentrations of conservative Protestants lived—the South, for example—it is likely that schools actually remained quite Protestant and therefore acceptable to conservative parents. Furthermore, children in places that had conservative Protestant subcultures were educated informally: within their families, in Sunday school, at revivals, and in YMCAs and YWCAs. Whatever unhappiness conservative Protestants may have felt about the increasing secularism of public schools did not translate into the establishment of separate day schools at the elementary or high school levels until late in the twentieth century.

Parents' and educators' consternation seemed reserved for schools of higher education.[48] Theological seminaries and colleges came under the earliest and most serious attacks for imperiling the faith of Christian sons and daughters, and alternative institutions of higher education were established long before the now-proliferating Christian day schools. Until the 1920s, however, the attack on higher education was muted. A few professors came under scrutiny, and some were dismissed for teaching evolution or higher critical views of the Bible. Others, such as Charles Briggs at Union Theological Seminary, New York, in the 1890s, underwent a heresy trial at the instigation of the Philadelphia Presbytery although he did not lose his position at Union.[49]

The more serious battles over higher education would await the 1920s, when some Protestant denominations would come into conflict over their church-sponsored seminaries and colleges and state legislatures would outlaw the teaching of evolution. Still, the foundations for a separate system of higher education were laid in the 1880s and 1890s when Bible schools, missionary training schools, and a handful of new liberal arts colleges were created or constituted as self-consciously religiously and culturally conservative. These included Moody Bible Institute in Chicago; Gordon Bible School (later Gordon College and Gordon-Conwell Theological Seminary) in Boston; the Missionary Training Institute (later Nyack College) in Nyack, New York; Wheaton College in Wheaton, Illinois; Houghton College in Houghton, New York; and Asbury College in Wilmore, Kentucky.

The purpose of these schools was not only to counter the loss of faith suffered by students in increasingly secular colleges and seminaries but also, more positively, to inspire zealous young people in practical ways not possible at other institutions of higher education and train them to be missionaries, evangelists, musicians, and Bible school teachers. Usually, Bible schools and missionary training schools, although considered "higher education," operated at roughly a secondary school level. Sometimes—especially in Pentecostal traditions—they were at an even lower level than high school, although students tended to be college age or even older. During the 1920s many such schools would become prime staging areas (the "West Point of Fundamentalism" in the case of Moody Bible Institute) for the struggle against modernism in education and the rest of American life.

Thus, schools were arenas of religious conflict—a wider variety of conflicts and more nuanced than has been recognized. We still deal with the legacy of the Manichaean battle between religious friends and foes of public education. To be freed from this dualistic thinking, it is necessary to be mindful of the complexity of the conflicts and the diversity of voices and narratives. Perhaps then we can examine present conflicts with more wisdom and see opportunities for compromise, informal arrangements, and local solutions.

Notes

1. Julius Freiberg, Jewish delegate to the Ohio State Constitutional Convention of 1874, quoted in Lloyd P. Gartner, "Temples of Liberty Unpolluted: American Jews and Public Schools, 1840–1875," in *A Bicentennial Festschrift for Jacob Rader Marcus*, ed. Bertram Wallace Korn (Waltham: American Jewish Historical Society, 1976), 180.

2. This plotline, of course, is told from the Protestant point of view; see, for example, Paul Blanshard, *American Freedom and Catholic Power* (Boston: Beacon Press, 1949). Some Catholic versions, in which public schools are regarded as Protestant dens of iniquity, are also unnuanced, however.

3. See, for example, Gartner, "Temples of Liberty."

4. E. Clifford Nelson, *The Lutherans in America* (Philadelphia: Fortress Press, 1975), 295.

5. For the Bennett Law, see Lloyd Jorgenson, *The State and the Non-Public School* (Columbia: University of Missouri Press, 1967), 187–201.

6. For the Edwards Law, see Jorgensen, *State*, 201–4.

7. A prominent racial minority—African Americans—is not dealt with in this chapter. It is not clear that they constituted a religious minority, first because they embraced a variety of types of Protestantism (as well as Catholicism) and, second, because the conflicts they had with missionaries and public school authorities usually had more to do with issues of racial oppression

than with religious issues. White educators tended to regard African Americans as more "Christian" and "civilized" than Native Americans. Thanks to slavery, they thought, blacks had benefited culturally and religiously from a longer history of close contact with whites than had Native Americans. For a comparison of white attitudes toward blacks and Native Americans, see David Wallace Adams, "Education in Hues: Red and Black at Hampton Institute, 1878–1893," *South Atlantic Quarterly* 76, no. 2 (1977): 159–76; and Donal F. Lindsey, *Indians at Hampton Institute, 1877–1923* (Urbana: University of Illinois Press, 1995).

8. To those of another era, the claim that schools were "unsectarian" in the way nineteenth-century Protestants meant seems unworthy of note, because the idea of a "Presbyterian" or "Methodist" public school seems bizarre. But in an age when denominational distinctions were more important and were hard-fought, the pan-Protestantism of public schools seemed a genuine advance for religious tolerance.

9. See Vincent P. Lannie, *Public Money and Parochial Education: Bishop Hughes, Governor Seward, and the New York School Controversy* (Cleveland: Press of Case Western University, 1968). For another controversy, see Vincent P. Lannie and Bernard C. Diethorn, "For the Honor and Glory of God: The Philadelphia Bible Riots of 1840," *History of Education Quarterly* 8 (Spring 1968): 44–106.

10. See, for example, John D. Minor et al., *The Bible in the Public Schools: Arguments before the Superior Court of Cincinnati in the Case of Minor v. Board of Cincinnati, 1870* . . . [1870] (New York: DaCapo, 1967). Robert Michaelsen, *Piety in the Public Schools* (New York: Macmillan, 1970), 90–111, contains an account of the "War."

11. Theodore C. Blegen, *Norwegian Migration to America* (Northfield: Norwegian-American Historical Association, 1940).

12. For Mormons, see Frederick Steward Buchanan, *Culture Clash and Accommodation: Public Schooling in Salt Lake City, 1890–1990* (San Francisco: Smith Research Associates, 1995), esp. chs. 1–3.

13. Donna Merwick, *Boston Priests, 1848–1910: A Study of Social and Intellectual Change* (Cambridge: Harvard University Press, 1973); James W. Sanders, "Boston Catholics and the School Question, 1825–1907," in *From Common School to Magnet School: Selected Essays in the History of Boston's Schools*, ed. James W. Fraser, Henry L. Allen, and Sam Barnes (Boston: Trustees of the Public Library of the City of Boston, 1979), 43–75.

14. Geoffrey Blodgett, "Yankee Leadership in a Divided City: Boston, 1860–1910," *Journal of Urban History* 8 (1981–83): 371–96.

15. Leslie Woodcock Tentler, *Seasons of Grace: A History of the Catholic Archdiocese of Detroit* (Detroit: Wayne State University Press, 1990), 84.

16. James W. Sanders, *The Education of an Urban Minority: Catholics in Chicago, 1833–1965* (New York: Oxford University Press, 1977), 134–35.

17. See Brian C. Mitchell, *The Paddy Camps: The Irish of Lowell, 1821–61* (Urbana: University of Illinois Press, 1988); Brian C. Mitchell, "Educating Irish Immigrants in Antebellum Lowell," *Historical Journal of Massachusetts*

11 (1983): 94–103; Brian C. Mitchell, "'They Do Not Differ Greatly': The Pattern of Community Development among the Irish in Late Nineteenth Century Lowell, Massachusetts," in *Building the American Catholic City: Parishes and Institutions,* ed. Brian C. Mitchell (New York: Garland, 1988), 88–108; Louis S. Walsh, "The Early Irish Catholic Schools of Lowell, Massachusetts, 1835–1852," *New England Catholic Historical Society Reports* (Boston: Thomas A. Whalen, 1901), 5–20; and Thomas Dublin, *Women at Work: The Transformation of Work and Community in Lowell, Massachusetts, 1826–1860* (New York: Columbia University Press, 1979).

18. Howard Ralph Weisz, *Irish-American and Italian-American Educational Views and Activities, 1870–1900: A Comparison* (New York: Arno Press, 1976), 13.

19. Mitchell, *Paddy Camps,* 62.

20. Mitchell, "Educating Irish Immigrants," 98.

21. For the Eliot School case, see Robert H. Lord, John E. Sexton, and Edward T. Harrington, *History of the Archdiocese of Boston* (Boston: Pilot Publishing, 1945), 2:587–601; see also the account in Jorgenson, *State and Non-Public School,* 90–93.

22. F. Michael Perko, *A Time to Favor Zion* (Chicago: Educational Studies Press, 1988).

23. See, for example, Lawrence A. Cremin, *American Education: The Metropolitan Experience, 1876–1980* (New York: Harper and Row, 1988), 236–37. For the Jewish educational experience in general, see Stephan F. Blumberg, *Going to America, Going to School: The Jewish Immigrant Public School Encounter in Turn-of-the-Century New York City* (New York: Praeger, 1986).

24. Gartner, "Temples of Liberty," 167.

25. Quoted in Sherry Gorelick, *City College and the Jewish Poor* (New Brunswick: Rutgers University Press, 1981), 133. No doubt the adjustment from one kind of learning to another was difficult for some immigrants and children of immigrants. But Slater may draw too stark a contrast between the two pedagogies. Learning in public schools, to judge from memoirs, may not have been as innovative or progressive as its press sometimes suggested; there seems to have been a good deal of reliance on memorization, rote learning, and old-fashioned discipline. Furthermore, learning in Eastern Europe had not been entirely dominated by traditional religious studies. Long before the large-scale emigration from Eastern Europe, the Enlightenment—the "Haskalah"—which stressed secular learning, instruction in the vernacular and in Hebrew (in preference to Yiddish), and training in agriculture and the crafts (versus commercial pursuits) had already made inroads into the hegemony of classical Talmudic learning. Thus, not all Eastern European Jews were strangers to secular learning.

26. Neil M. Cowan and Ruth Schwartz Cowan, *Our Parents' Lives: The Americanization of Eastern European Jews* (New York: Basic Books, 1989), 93–94. The nature of the tie between school and upward mobility continues to be a subject of contention; Thomas Kessner, for instance, argues that Jewish upward mobility was relatively rapid and attributes at least some of that

movement to Jewish attitudes toward schooling. Yet the realities of the connections between school and upward mobility are less important than the fact that most Jewish parents and children believed fervently in the connection and made their educational choices on that basis. Thomas Kessner, *The Golden Door: Italian and Jewish Immigrant Mobility in New York City, 1800–1915* (New York: Oxford University Press, 1977).

27. Susan A. Glenn, *Daughters of the Shtetl: Life and Labor in the Immigrant Generation* (Ithaca: Cornell University Press, 1990).

28. Glenn, *Daughters,* 47.

29. Kate Simon, *Bronx Primitive: Portraits in a Childhood* (New York: Harper and Row, 1983), 8.

30. Cowan and Cowan, *Our Parents' Lives,* 89.

31. Ibid., 98.

32. Ibid., 89.

33. Ibid.

34. Blumberg, *Going to America, Going to School,* 70.

35. The late nineteenth and early twentieth centuries were heady times for educational reform, with John Dewey and progressive education in their heyday. See Lawrence A. Cremin, *The Transformation of the School: Progressivism in American Education, 1876–1957* (New York: Vintage, 1961). In the Jewish community in particular, it was the era of the creation of bureaus of education. For the New York Jewish community's activities in educational reform, see Arthur Goren, *New York Jews and the Quest for Community: The Kehillah Experiment, 1908–1922* (New York: Columbia University Press, 1970); and Alexander Dushkin, *Living Bridge: Memoirs of an Educator* (Jerusalem: Keter, 1975).

36. Blumberg, *Going to America, Going to School,* 130.

37. Irving Howe and Kenneth Libo, *How We Lived: A Documentary History of Immigrant Jews in America, 1880–1930* (New York: Richard Marek, 1979), 200–201.

38. Cowan and Cowan, *Our Parents' Lives,* 102.

39. Leonard Bloom, "A Successful Jewish Boycott of the New York City Public Schools—Christmas 1906," *American Jewish History* 70, no. 2 (1980–81): 187–88.

40. See Selma Berrol, "When Uptown Met Downtown: Julia Richman's Work in the Jewish Community of New York, 1880–1912," *American Jewish Quarterly* 70, no. 1 (1980–81): 35–51.

41. The literature on Indian education is growing quite rich. See, for example, K. Tsianina Lomawaima, *They Called It Prairie Light: The Story of Chilocco Indian School* (Lincoln: University of Nebraska Press, 1994); Michael C. Coleman, *American Indian Children at School, 1850–1930* (Jackson: University Press of Mississippi, 1993); Robert F. Berkhofer, Jr. *Salvation and the Savage: An Analysis of Protestant Missions and American Indian Response, 1787–1862* (Lexington: University Press of Kentucky, 1965), ch. 2; Clara Sue Kidwell, *Choctaws and Missionaries in Mississippi, 1818–1918* (Norman: University of Oklahoma Press, 1995); and Sally J. McBeth, *Ethnic Identity and*

the Boarding School Experience of West-Central Oklahoma American Indians (Lanham: University Press of America, 1983).

42. McBeth, *Ethnic Identity*, 101.

43. These dates are considered the heyday of the Indian boarding school. See McBeth, *Ethnic Identity*, 76.

44. Ibid., 128–29.

45. Ibid., 73.

46. The positive interpretation is that white educators wanted to protect Indian children from the corruptions of the white world and from the ridicule of white children for students less "advanced" than themselves; the less positive explanation is the racism of the society (including many of the educators). Richard Henry Pratt, an advocate of schooling for Indians, tried to get some of his students admitted to white schools in the East; that is one of the reasons they ended up at Hampton Institute. See Lindsey, *Indians at Hampton*, 29.

47. For the background of Protestant evangelical education in the late nineteenth century, see Virginia Lieson Brereton, *Training God's Army: The American Bible School, 1880–1940* (Bloomington: Indiana University Press, 1990), especially chs. 1–3. See also William V. Trollinger, *God's Empire: William Bell Riley and Midwestern Fundamentalism* (Madison: University of Wisconsin Press, 1990).

48. This criticism of higher education for its godlessness and other moral and spiritual failings was hardly limited to conservative Protestants. Although the rise of the great research universities in the late nineteenth century was widely admired, it was also regarded with distrust by many religionists of all descriptions and also by cultural conservatives with no particular religious axes to grind.

49. Mark S. Massa, *Charles Augustus Briggs and the Crisis of Historical Criticism* (Minneapolis: Fortress Press, 1990). The classic text is Walter Metzger, *Academic Freedom in the Age of the University* (New York: Columbia University Press, 1961).

NINE

Minority-Majority Confrontations, Church-State Patterns, and the U.S. Supreme Court

ROBERT T. HANDY

The familiar uses of "church and state" terminology arose primarily with reference to European national states, many of which for centuries maintained a legally established and publicly supported church: Roman Catholic, Eastern Orthodox, or (after the Reformation) Protestant. Other organized religious movements were usually classed as illegal sects and were often persecuted by whatever church-state system was dominant in a given land. Such minorities could be forced to live an underground or marginal existence and could be driven into exile. As European nations founded colonies on other continents, efforts were regularly made to transplant a mother country's religious establishment to them.

In nine of the thirteen original English colonies that became the United States, established churches were founded in some form. In part because members of the growing number of churches, sects, and other religious movements also made their way into the colonies, often seeking places of refuge, establishments of religion were not popular among many settlers and were stubbornly resisted by others. As the practice of religious toleration spread in the later seventeenth and eighteenth centuries, such legal establishments became increasingly insecure. In the aftermath of the American Revolution they came to an end; the last one was voted out in Massachusetts in 1833. Since Article Six of the American Constitution of 1787 provided that "no religious Test shall ever be required as a qualification to any Office or public Trust under the United States," and the First Amendment in 1791 opened with the words "Congress shall make no law respecting an establishment of religion, or prohibiting the free exercise thereof," the historic, familiar words "church and state" came to refer to the interactions between "churches and states," or even more accurately still to the relations between the varieties and complexities of an increasingly pluralized religious life and the growing and later bewildering network of governmental agencies.

Because it was not until the 1940s that the Supreme Court began to apply the religion clauses of the First Amendment to the states, the latter's constitutions and laws often reflected more of the religious situation of their constituencies, which is why three New England states could retain their Congregational establishments of religion into the early nineteenth century. In many states certain attitudes and practices followed by the leading Protestant denominations were publicly favored in word and deed long after formal disestablishment had been accepted at national and state levels, persisting into (and beyond) the period of this chapter: 1865 to 1925. The Illinois Supreme Court stated in 1883, for example, "Although it is no part of the functions of our system of government to propagate religion, and to enforce its tenets, when the great body of the people are Christians, in fact or sentiment, our laws and institutions must necessarily be based upon and embody the teachings of the Redeemer of Mankind."[1]

Five years later, Philip Schaff, a prominent church historian, after declaring that the United States provided "the first example in history of a government deliberately depriving itself of all legislative control over religion" could also insist that "the separation of church and state as it exists in this country is not a separation of the nation from Christianity."[2] He used the term *Christianity*, but along with many others he emphasized Protestant Christianity primarily. By that date the rapidly growing Roman Catholic Church had become by far the largest single communion in the nation, with an estimated total of about eight million members. Collectively, however, the leading Protestant denominational families (Baptist, Congregational, Disciples of Christ, Episcopal, Lutheran, Methodist, Presbyterian, and Reformed) had an estimated membership of nearly seventeen million, approximately a quarter of the population at the time. Protestant church membership was then somewhat more narrowly defined than it later came to be, and the number of active constituents in most communions was generally considerably larger than the memberships.[3]

Most Protestants were convinced that they were the chief custodians of the cultural, moral, and religious life of the nation, and they were often so regarded. To be sure, the many differences among the various denominational families reflected their distinctive histories, theologies, and polities. Also most of them were internally divided, some sharply, along ethnic, racial, class, sectional, or theological lines. Although most denominations were growing, there were losses, too—to other traditions or to indifference. Yet the leading (and many of the smaller) Protestant communions shared certain common emphases. Despite variations in detail, they were Bible-centered, trinitarian, evangelical in theology, and missionary in emphasis. Shaped in part by the long and bitter struggle of the Reformation churches with the Roman Catholic Church, they were also anti-Catholic in varying degrees. Although they professed to believe strongly in religious freedom, the separation of church and state, and voluntaryism in religion, they also firmly believed that their country was in fact if not in law a Christian nation. They were committed to using their rights of free exercise to make it even more so (as they defined it), primarily through persuasion and influence—and by resisting those who saw the religious situation differently. Most Protestant bodies were sure that they were part of what later became referred to as the mainstream or mainline religious tradition in the culture, and they were generally so viewed by "minorities" (some sizable) outside the dominant Protestant perspective. Many local, state, and federal courts reflected the dominance of this mainstream religious position in their rulings.

State courts were responsible for interpreting their respective constitutions, but when the U.S. Supreme Court in 1892 declared that "this is a Christian nation," it illustrated how influential the mainstream still was in American life, even as the concept as then defined by many Protestants was being resisted. In a case in New York state, a circuit court decision was appealed to the Supreme Court, where it was determined that a congressional act prohibiting the importation of foreigners under contract or agreement to perform labor in the United States was not intended to prohibit a church from calling an English member of the clergy to serve as its rector. But Justice David J. Brewer, in stating the opinion of the Court, seized the opportunity to declare that the country was indeed a Christian one, adding at some length what were then conventional opinions on the matter. In so doing, he referred to many events, state constitutions ("organic utterances"), and court decisions, summing up by saying:

> If we pass beyond these matters to a view of American life as expressed by its laws, its business, its customs and its society, we find everywhere a clear recognition of the same truth. Among other matters note the following: The form of oath universally prevailing, concluding with an appeal to the Almighty; the custom of opening sessions of all deliberative bodies and most conventions with prayer; the prefatory words of all wills, "In the name of God, Amen;" the laws respecting the observance of the Sabbath, with the general cessation of all secular business, and the closing of courts, legislatures, and other similar public assemblies on that day; the churches and church organizations which abound

in every city, town and hamlet; the multitude of charitable organizations
existing everywhere under Christian auspices; the gigantic missionary
associations, with general support, and aiming to establish Christian
missions in every quarter of the globe. These, and many other matters
which might be noticed, add a volume of unofficial declarations to the
organic utterances that this is a Christian nation.[4]

Looking back, one can interpret this as in part an effort to rally divided Protestant forces in the face of a rising tide of minorities. But because Justice Brewer's opinion was not challenged, it became the unanimous judgment of the Court; it was a precedent to be cited often, as
when the Court in a 5 to 4 decision nearly forty years later affirmed,
"We are a Christian people."[5]

At the time of the 1892 decision the Court clearly reflected mainstream Protestant traditions; all of the justices were Protestants. Some
maintained active church connections. The chief justice was Melville
W. Fuller (1888–1910), a devout Episcopalian; among the associate
justices were John M. Harlan, a committed Presbyterian, and also
Stephen J. Field and his nephew David J. Brewer, both sons of Congregational ministers and former missionaries. Some of the other justices, for example, Henry Billings Brown and Samuel Blatchford, were
less directly identified with denominational traditions but represented
the Anglo-Saxon Protestant perspective. Since Roger B. Taney's term
as chief justice (1836–64) had ended, no Catholic was named to the
high court until 1894, when Edward D. White took his place on the
bench. He served as chief justice from 1910 to 1921.

The words of religious and judicial leaders could not, however, hide
the dilemma posed for Protestants in their quest for a more fully Christian America. How could that be done by a country in which the national constitutional provisions promised freedom for all in matters of
religion and forbade its government to institute religious tests for public
office? One of the most extensive efforts to face the dilemma and defend a widely accepted Protestant view was offered by a Presbyterian
minister, Isaac A. Cornelison, in 1895. He celebrated "the fact that we
have, in this country, a grand system of political institutions, entirely
separate from all ecclesiastical institutions." But along with most nineteenth-century Protestants, he believed that "the government of these
United States, was necessarily, rightfully, and lawfully Christian." His
way of dealing with the dilemma was to emphasize the rights of the
majority: "Christianity in a proper sense is the established religion of
this nation; established, not by statute law, it is true, but by a law equally
valid, the law in the nature of things, the law of necessity, which law
will remain in force so long as the great mass of the people are Chris-

tians."[6] Protestants generally understood themselves to be clearly in the majority, and so they were often seen by others.

Within some of the rapidly growing minority faiths, however, there arose increasing resistance to the announced goal of many mainstream religious leaders to make America a more fully "Christian" nation as they defined it. That effort fell under increasing attack from certain minorities, which sought a larger and more secure place for themselves and a larger role in American affairs. Their dissatisfaction with the way the relationships among religious bodies and the arms of government were being interpreted, and their awareness of the increasing tensions between the general Protestant consensus and their particular needs, led to efforts to redefine the situation.

Challenges to the generally accepted Protestant definition of church-state relations led to conflicts at local and state levels, often resulting in court cases, a number of which were appealed to and settled by the Supreme Court. Attention to some of the more important of these conflicts and accompanying cases are highlighted in what follows by reference to the resistance of four of the minority faiths, broadly defined, as they sought a larger freedom for themselves American culture: the Latter-day Saints (LDS), Roman Catholics, Jews, and African American Christians. Early in the process, what Jefferson had called "the wall of separation between church and state" was favorably cited by the Supreme Court and hence became an important legal precedent for later decisions. During the course of the struggles, the symbolic wall was heightened. But the fact that the free exercise of religion had limits, deeply rooted though it was in general public opinion, became especially clear to some of the minority faiths outside the Protestant mainstream.

A Challenge Denied: The Latter-day Saints

Fifteen years before Philip Schaff's *Church and State in the United States* appeared, Joseph P. Thompson, the retired pastor of New York's Broadway Tabernacle, wrote a book that had the same title. He dismissed Mormonism, then just over four decades old, as a doomed community. He was convinced that as it was being hemmed in "by a normal society" it would "die of inanition," for "public sentiment would leave the delusion to a natural death."[7] The practice of plural marriage (polygamy, or bigamy as it was often called) arose early in Mormon history, sanctioned by what the prophet Joseph Smith declared was a revelation from God but not written down until 1843, a year before Smith was murdered. It was not made public, however, until 1852, when a

Mormon general conference urged that Latter-day Saint males should, if possible, engage in plural marriage.

The practice was deeply offensive to most Americans reared in the Western moral code and directly contrary to the teachings and standards of most Christian bodies, which generally viewed the monogamous family as divinely established. When Brigham Young led the Latter-day Saints on their historic journey to a refuge in the Great Salt Lake Basin in Mexican territory, they seemed safely out of reach of American hostility. The Mexican war, however, soon changed that. In 1850 Congress organized what the Mormons called Deseret into Utah territory, with Young as governor. When he forced federal judges out for not following his leadership, U.S. military intervention brought only nominal submission.

Because the territory had no law against polygamy, Congress, responding to increasing popular pressure in 1862, passed the Morrill Anti-Bigamy Act. It not only made polygamy a felony in the territories, but it also dissolved the incorporation of the Church of Jesus Christ of Latter-day Saints as a charitable association and limited its property holdings to $50,000.[8] The act was largely ignored, for there was much resistance to it in Utah and national attention was then focused on the Civil War. But by the 1870s, when greater numbers of Gentiles entered Utah territory, opposition to the Mormons intensified and Congress passed the Poland Act in 1874, which extended direct federal control over most court cases in Utah. Contrary to Joseph Thompson's guess, the Latter-day Saints were continuing to thrive and grow, winning adherents at home and abroad. Believing that the Morrill Anti-Bigamy Act was unconstitutional, the church's leaders set up a test case in Utah territory. But to their consternation, George Reynolds was found guilty of polygamy in 1875 and sentenced to two years in prison at hard labor.

When Reynolds appealed to the Supreme Court the unanimous decision, delivered in January 1879 by Chief Justice Morrison R. Waite, denied the appeal. In giving the Court's reason for its judgment, Waite (an Episcopal vestryman) quoted a passage from Jefferson, enshrining it in a major decision that was to be cited frequently in various federal and state court decisions for many decades. In reply to an address to him by a committee of the Danbury Baptist Association in Connecticut, the president had taken the occasion to write on the first day of 1802 the words Waite now repeated in delivering the opinion of the Court: "Believing with you that religion is a matter which lies solely between man and his God; that he owes account to none other for his faith or his worship; that the legislative powers of the government reach actions only, and not opinions,—I contemplate with sovereign rever-ence that act of the whole American people which declared that their legislature should 'make no law respecting an establishment of religion or prohibiting the free exercise thereof,' thus building a wall of sepa-ration between church and State."[9]

So Jefferson's words played a prominent role in the Supreme Court's first encounter with the religion clauses of the First Amendment in the first major church-state confrontation to come before it. The Court thus opened a new era in the history of interrelationships between religious bodies and governments in America. Ironically, the metaphor of the wall, which later became so important to strict separationists, was high-lighted in a case in which Mormons expected that their freedom to believe in and practice their religion would be protected by that wall.

They found that hope sharply denied. Waite went on to say, elevat-ing the distinction between opinion and action into an important le-gal precedent, "Congress was deprived of all legislative power over mere opinion, but was left free to reach actions which were in viola-tion of social duties or subversive of good order." Insisting that polyg-amy "has always been odious among the northern and western nations of Europe," he called attention to a statute of James I that made the offense punishable in the civil courts with the death penalty, a statute adopted with modifications in all the colonies and then again in the state of Virginia in 1788. Waite's central point was put sharply:

> From that day to this we think it may safely be said there has never been a time in any State of the Union when polygamy has not been an offense against society, cognizable by the civil courts and punishable with more or less severity. In the face of all this evidence, it is impossible to believe that the constitutional guaranty of religious freedom was intended to prohibit legislation in respect to this most important feature of social life. Marriage, while from its very nature a sacred obligation, is nevertheless, in most civilized nations, a civil contract, and usually regulated by law.[10]

So the unanimous decision of the high court found that the statute under which Reynolds had been tried was constitutional and valid as prescribing a rule of action. Reynolds was forced to fill his prison term but became a hero among Mormons.

The Latter-day Saints remained unconvinced that their practice was unconstitutional and publicly defied the anti-polygamy laws. Thus was heightened the tension between the LDS Church and the federal gov-ernment in the early 1880s under a Republican administration in which Protestant influence was strong. A forceful critique of the Supreme Court's decision was issued by George Q. Cannon, Utah's delegate to Congress and also a high Mormon official. Congress responded to such resistance with the Edmunds Act (1882), which set longer prison terms and larger fines for persons convicted of the crime of polygamy and disqualified its practitioners from voting, holding public office, or serving as jurors on polygamy cases. The act provided the basis for what became known as the "raid," when federal marshals moved across Utah to arrest men involved in plural marriage, securing hundreds of convictions. Some prominent Latter-day Saints fled the country; others went into hiding. Then in 1889 and 1890 came a pair of decisions that caught the Mormons in a vise.

Federal authorities in Idaho territory, where the number of Latter-day Saints was increasing, had gone beyond the *Reynolds* distinction to bar from office-holding and voting not only those who practiced polygamy but also those who taught or encouraged it. An oath was required denying any such activities or membership in any organization supporting plural marriage. A district court found Samuel S. Davis, a Mormon who was monogamous (only a small minority of Mormons practiced plural marriage) and wanted to register to vote, guilty of conspiracy for violating the law, and he appealed to the Supreme Court. His counsel cited the Sixth Article of the Constitution and the First Amendment to no avail. Justice Stephen J. Field delivered the unanimous decision of the Court and affirmed the jurisdiction of the district court and its judgment, insisting that bigamy and polygamy are crimes by the laws of the United States and that few crimes are more pernicious. The free exercise of religion, he declared, must be subordinate to the criminal laws of the country. His opinion contained a crucial sentence: "Probably never before in the history of this country has it been seriously contended that the whole punitive power of the government for acts, recognized by the general consent of the Christian world in modern times as proper matters for prohibitory legislation, must be suspended in order that the tenets of a religious sect encouraging crime may be carried on without hindrance."[11] That the Court emphasized the sharp difference between "Christian" and "Mormon" was thus clearly put, with the latter deprived of what they believed to be their rights under the law.

The other major decision of 1890 covered two cases. Ever since 1862 Congress had been threatening to seize church property of the Mormons if they did not give up plural marriage. Amendments to the Edmunds Act (five years after its passage) disincorporated their church in Utah and appropriated church property, excepting that used for liturgical purposes. The church and a member of the prominent Romney family sued. The several matters were argued before the Supreme

Court early in 1889, but decision was postponed a year to increase pressure on Mormons to conform, to no avail. Again, the nub of the issue was the practice of polygamy, seen as "a blot on our civilization. The organization of a community for the spread and practice of polygamy is, in a measure, a return to barbarism," said Justice Joseph Bradley as he delivered the 7-to-2 majority opinion upholding the seizures. Bradley, who had been brought up in the Dutch Reformed tradition and was a firm exponent of the Protestant ethic, added that "it is contrary to the spirit of Christianity and of the civilization which Christianity has produced in the Western world."[12] A belief and practice that conflicted with a position deep-rooted in American culture and was a highly emotional issue for evangelical Protestants and others stood squarely in the way of the LDS future, and the powers of the federal government had been directed against a church put outside of "the spirit of Christianity" because of its distinctive practice.

Mormon leaders had been searching for a compromise, Kenneth D. Driggs has written, but that decision forced them "to realize that no compromise was possible. They had to elect between loyalty to their unique social, political, and economic customs and their very survival."[13] The head of the church was First President Wilford Woodruff, who was in a difficult spot. In 1888 he had affirmed that "the Lord never will give a revelation to abandon plural marriage" for "we cannot deny principle." But by 1890, as the federal government was closing in, he had to be concerned with what he defined as "the temporal salvation of the church."[14]

Looking at the situation from the outside, historians see Mormons as giving up on an important aspect of faith and practice in the face of the superior strength of the government acting through federal law in the interests of beliefs and behavior then prevailing in Western Christian civilization. But from the inside, as LDS historian Edward Lyman puts it, "Even if the church was figuratively backed to the wall and practical considerations demanded concessions, that does not necessarily deny the possibility of the divine inspiration Woodruff and his associates claimed as his ultimate motivation." By September 24 Woodruff believed he had received divine guidance, which he discussed with other LDS leaders and then issued the next day what came to be called the Woodruff manifesto. Countering charges that plural marriages continued to be contracted, he declared, "Inasmuch as laws have been enacted by Congress forbidding plural marriages, which laws have been pronounced constitutional by the court of last resort, I hereby declare my intention to submit to those laws, and to use my influence with members of the Church over which I preside to have them do like-wise."[15] On October 6 a general LDS conference unanimously accept-ed the manifesto.

The abrupt about-face in 1890 made it difficult for those involved in plural marriages. For the most part, families were left to handle the matter as best they could. On the one hand, they were urged to abide by covenants made; on the other, to obey the law of the land and in any case to show that the change had been sincerely accepted. Appar-ently, some simply remained quiet about continuing relationships, for governmental pressures eased as it became clear that no new plural marriages were officially being allowed. Amnesty was promised to those who had been indicted. Church property that had been confiscated was restored when it became evident it would not be used to favor the banned practice. As enforcement of measures was relaxed, the prac-tice of polygamy apparently continued quietly for a few years and was perpetuated by some splinter groups. It was not reinstated in the LDS Church, with its some two hundred thousand followers. The church gave up the distinctive practice that had set it against the society and government of which it was a part. Polygamy flew in the face of the Protestant mainstream, which strongly emphasized monogamy and was culturally dominant enough to suppress the Mormon challenge to it.

With their significant turn, Mormons began once again to prosper. They sought coveted statehood for Utah, for their numbers would then give them greater influence than they had under territorial status. As historians of the tradition have observed, they "adopted a 'line' con-sistent with the dominant policies of the nation" yet also "sought to preserve as many of their traditional goals as national sentiment would permit."[16] So the church turned away from its promotion of coopera-tive economic enterprises, gave up most of its businesses and the Utah political party it had controlled, and urged its members to join one of the major American parties. It was not until 1894 that Congress passed the Utah Enabling Act, and Grover Cleveland signed the proclamation admitting Utah as the forty-fifth state on January 4, 1896. To be sure, the political sailing was still not smooth because antagonisms and sus-picions continued. By the early twentieth century, however, it was clear that the Latter-day Saints had indeed come to terms with the demands of the majority; a religious minority had surrendered to the majority on a moral issue fought on legal grounds. In the struggle of many de-cades the importance of the Supreme Court in settling church-state is-sues that had arisen in territorial and state courts was significantly in-creased.

Catholic Educational Strategy and Mainstream Reaction

In referring to the admittedly approximate estimates of numerical size that are available, to list the Roman Catholic Church in America from 1865 to 1925 as a "minority" faith seems anomalous. It was by far the largest single communion in the country throughout the period and was outdistancing its Protestant rivals even as they were also steadily growing. Yet in a country in which Protestants, with all their divisions, were convinced that they were the effective majority in religious, cultural, and national life, a view often accepted by others, Catholics continued to be cast in a minority role and usually thought of themselves as such. In part, that was because they were increasingly a church of minorities. The estimated total Catholic population increased from about six million in 1880 to around sixteen million in 1915. Some ten sizable groups of immigrants from widely varying backgrounds made up the bulk of U.S. Catholics by the early twentieth century. In part, however, the "minority" role of Catholicism emerged because Protestant bodies maintained positions of power through long-familiar customs and institutional networks. Some of the latter (such as the Evangelical Alliance) cut across denominational lines and provided a measure of cohesiveness.

Many Protestant leaders saw the floods of immigrants, so many of them Catholics, as lower-class foreigners who were a threat to "Americanism" as they defined it. Anxious to preserve and increase their own influential role in national life, they continually reminded Catholics of their minority status, with varying degrees of vehemence. Even those trying to be evenhanded, as was Samuel Lane Loomis when he observed that "the religion of Rome is far better than none," could go on to provide a familiar list of criticisms of "Romanism," including such items as "it has kept the people from the Word of God . . . has lowered the tone of morality . . . has quenched free thought, stifled free speech, and threatens to throttle free government."[17] In the same year that Loomis wrote those words the American Protective Association was founded. It became the most conspicuous anti-Catholic group in the 1890s. Episodes of violence did not parallel those of the 1840s, but its attack was virulent enough.

Although Catholicism was under steady fire from the outside, from the inside it was confident and convinced of the truth and rightness of its theological and churchly traditions, stoutly defended through the centuries of controversy since the Reformation. It was also sure that Protestant opponents were wrong and that their denominations were in the process of further fragmentation and decay.[18] Hence it was not

only because of steadily increasing numbers that the power of Catholics in the society was growing but also because of their determination
to fulfill their mission in the United States as the church's leaders effectively developed their own network of burgeoning institutions to
help and guide their people. Catholic political strength mounted, especially as Irish-Catholic political strongholds developed in such cities as Boston, New York, Jersey City, Chicago, San Francisco, and
Kansas City.[19] Catholic prestige in the early twentieth century also increased as some well-known Catholics were named to high governmental office.

The two religious traditions, each compounds of persons and institutions of diverse backgrounds and histories and each exerting significant power in American life, tended to define themselves against each
other, often caricaturing their opponents in the process. The conflict
between the two religio-cultural movements showed up at various levels, conspicuously in tensions over what are conventionally called
church-state issues. Justin D. Fulton, head of an organization named
the Pauline Propaganda, was an extremist in his anti-Catholic views
yet expressed a fairly widespread Protestant perception of the political power of Rome, insisting that "seven millions of people are compelled to vote as the cardinal, archbishops, bishops and priests may
command."[20] That the American Catholic hierarchy had long accepted the patterns of the separation of church and state was usually ignored or taken as irrelevant. The cardinal in question, James Gibbons,
at the time of his investiture in Rome in 1887 proclaimed "with a deep
sense of pride and gratitude, . . . that I belong to a country where the
civil government holds over us the aegis of its protection without in-
terfering in the legitimate exercise of our sublime mission as ministers
of the Gospel of Jesus Christ."[21]

Yet it is was well known that various countries of Europe retained
special ties with the papacy. When Pope Leo XIII sent an encyclical letter
to American Catholics in 1835, *Longinqua oceani,* he gave due credit
to the reality that "the Church amongst you, unapposed by the Constitution and government of your nation, fettered by no hostile legislation, protected against violence by the common laws and impartial-
ity of the tribunals, is free to live and act without hindrance."
Nevertheless, he added, "She would bring forth more abundant fruits
if, in addition to liberty, she enjoyed the favor of the laws and the pa-
tronage of public authority."[22] The tension between Catholics and Protestants on church-state matters often spilled over into legislative battles and court cases at all levels of government—conspicuously on issues
relating to education.

The differing value systems of the two traditions were especially reflected in their visions of schools. Convinced that they represented the majority, and with few exceptions lacking the intent or resources to develop their own school systems when common schools would do, most Protestants were ardent supporters of public schools and expected them to continue to reflect a broadly "nonsectarian" Christian moral and religious position. But what to them was nonsectarian was visibly Protestant in tone to Catholics, who at great cost developed a parallel parochial system that combined basic education with distinctive religious emphases. But for various reasons not all Catholic parents were able to send their children to parochial schools, or they chose not to. Because local school boards controlled the educational patterns of public schools, tensions between the two somewhat different understandings of education often collided at board level, which in some cases led to local or state court cases. Some of these erupted when parochial schools, which were teaching secular as well as religious subjects, sought a fair share of public funds for their educational efforts.

One of the most important of the early cases to reach a state supreme court occurred when the Catholic members of the school board of Cincinnati tried in 1869 to bring the two systems together at public expense. During the course of infighting within the board, it was decided not only to rule out all religious books but also the reading of the Bible in public schools. A superior court injunction stopped the latter, but four years after the controversy had erupted Ohio's supreme court reversed the decision, thus leading to a stalemate that was to be repeated in variant forms in many localities. In the "Cincinnati Bible War" outcome, Catholics lost the bid for public support for their schools, but Protestants lost Bible reading in the common schools.[23]

There were many other such incidents. When Justice William J. Brennan reviewed many of the similar cases of the later nineteenth and earlier twentieth century in his concurring decision in the landmark *Abingdon v. Schempp* case in 1963, he concluded that in the majority of cases up to that time, where a local school board *required* religious exercises the courts did not enjoin them, but where local school officials *forbade* such practices the courts rarely overruled them.[24] Hence, an inconsistent pattern of stalemates spread because in some areas the Protestant flavor of the public schools was not significantly modified, whereas in others it was successfully challenged, often unintentionally leading to varying degrees of secularization in public school life.

Brennan reported that another trend began to show up as early as 1890, however, when some state courts began to challenge the appropriateness of state constitutional articles that differed significantly from the religion clauses of the First Amendment. The case that marked the change developed in the town of Edgertown, Wisconsin, when Judge John R. Bennett ruled in 1888 that the King James Version of the Bible, the one often used for Bible readings in public schools, was not a sectarian book. Appealed from a circuit to the state supreme court, that judgment was overruled in *State ex rel. Weiss v. School Board.* For the next forty years some states followed that lead and found such religious exercises in public schools unconstitutional. Thus some states adhered to a stricter definition of what was sectarian than others.[25]

Meanwhile, at the national legislative level, efforts were underway to prevent tax monies raised by any state or derived from any public funds or land for the support of public schools to fall under the control of any religious sect or sects. A measure to that effect introduced by James G. Blaine in 1876 passed in the House of Representatives but failed in the Senate, for there was strong opposition by many Catholics and those who wanted to leave such matters to the states. In the following decade Henry W. Blair, a senator from New Hampshire, tried five times to secure congressional legislation that would provide federal appropriations for state aid for public schools, but without success. Unless private schools could be included, it became evident that such measures could not pass. But those who advocated that all children be required to attend public school, as provided in a statute in Oregon, could not get their way, either. The Supreme Court's decision of 1925 in *Pierce v. Society of Sisters* said, "The fundamental theory of liberty upon which all governments of this Union repose excludes any general power of the State to standardize its children by forcing them to accept instruction from public teachers only. The child is not the mere creature of the State."[26] The stalemate continued throughout the period and well beyond.

A topic related to Catholic educational strategy in facing a Protestant majority is also relevant here. The exception to the policy of excluding denominationally controlled schools from assistance by public funds was an outgrowth of President Ulysses S. Grant's "peace policy" (1869–82), which gave power to thirteen denominations that cooperated with the government to control Indian agencies on reservations. The policy also greatly expanded the program of federal aid to missions and education among Native Americans. Because only seven of seventy-three agencies went to Catholics, interchurch hostility was increased. Yet when the program came to an end, funds for what were called contract schools operated by denominations were continued and expanded. The efficient Catholic Bureau for Indian Missions came to control almost two-thirds of those funds by 1890, while there was growing Protestant resistance to a program that was an exception to their general emphasis on no public funds for sectarian schools—and at a time when they were losing out. Five Protestant communions withdrew from the program in 1892, and the funds were reduced and then terminated by 1900.

Generalizing from this and other such incidents in speaking of growing church-state tensions, Robert H. Keller, Jr., observed a hundred years later that various denominations "suddenly became purist in reading the First Amendment" and "not until American Catholicism began to grow in size did 'strict separation' become a Protestant constitutional doctrine."[27] But a half-century before that, William Adams Brown, a Protestant theologian reflecting on Catholic-Protestant tensions in education, was bold enough to say that "the present situation is anomalous, and it is to be feared that Protestant opinion has taken its present shape rather as a counterpoise to Catholic theory than as a natural development of Protestant ideals."[28] The conceptual "wall of separation" was being heightened in part because of the mounting challenge of Catholicism to Protestant power in education.

Significantly, however, church-related charitable agencies concerned with the public good, guided by a Supreme Court decision of 1899, escaped the widespread stalemate. A taxpayer contended that congressional authorization for the expenditure of federal funds to build an isolation wing for Providence Hospital, owned and operated by the Sisters of Charity in Washington, D.C., was in violation of the establishment clause of the First Amendment. Joseph Bradfield secured an injunction halting that use of public money before the supreme court of the District but lost on appeal, and the matter was further appealed to the Supreme Court. Justice Rufus W. Peckham, deeply rooted in the Protestant tradition, delivered the unanimous opinion of the Court. The facts that the members of the hospital's corporation were members of an order of the Roman Catholic Church and that the hospital was conducted under church auspices were ruled as "wholly immaterial," for "whether the individuals who compose the corporation, under its charter, happen to be all Roman Catholics, or all Methodists, or Presbyterians, or members of any other religious organization, or of no organization at all, is not of the slightest consequence with reference to the law of its incorporation, nor can the individual beliefs upon religious matters of the various incorporators be inquired into."[29] The influence of any particular church might be powerful over the members of a nonsectarian and secular corporation, but the Court declared that to be not sufficient to convert it into a religious or sectarian body as long as it is conducted (as in this instance) for whatever sick persons as may place themselves under its care.

Bradfield v. Roberts had an important impact on later trends. As an early example, nearly a decade later the Supreme Court also permitted an exception in allowing grants for Catholic Indian schools that came out of trust and treaty funds, established when lands were bought from the Native Americans or were provided by treaty, if such funds were petitioned for. The Sioux did that, for a treaty of 1868 with them bound the United States to provide a school building and teacher for every thirty children. They petitioned for Catholic schools to continue, and the Court unanimously affirmed their right, citing the Bradfield case. Chief Justice Fuller delivered the opinion of the Court and declared that money from treaty funds belonged to the Native Americans and could be used for schools of their choice.[30]

Aside from that, however, the stalemate in the tensions and hostilities over public and private school systems long persisted, often complicated by increasing secularization in education for which those tensions were in part responsible. But charitable agencies devoted to the general public good were rarely caught in that stalemate. In 1988, J. Bruce Nichols called attention to the continuing significance of *Bradfield v. Roberts:* "Here was the beginning of legal reasoning on the role of religious welfare in modern society. Religiously based services were welcomed on the basis of their ability to provide a service with clear secular purpose."[31] Nichols focused largely on the cooperative practices of religion and government outside the United States, where domestic church-state laws have not often been directly applicable.

The Bradfield decision has also had continuing influence on American secular welfare services open to the general public by church-related institutions. The case advanced an important right for such efforts, particularly useful for minorities but not only for them. But the precedent did not provide a way to break through continuing sharp differences between public school systems favored by most Protestants (along with others) and most Catholics who were attached to parochial school systems for the education of their children.

The Jewish Struggle for Equality

By the time James Bryce made his often-quoted summary that in America "Christianity is in fact understood to be, though not the legally established religion, yet the national religion," the Jewish population was rapidly growing, largely through immigration from Eastern Europe.[32] Estimated at some two hundred thousand strong by 1865, sixty years later close to four million Jews lived in the United States. Before the Civil War, although not unaffected by the traditional anti-Semitism of many Christians, Jews were generally regarded as a tiny, peaceable minority entitled to a refuge in a freedom-loving land. By the latter part of the century, however, as their numbers rose dramatically, resistance to "foreigners" of many types, increased anti-Semitism, European trends, and church visions of a more Christian America provided a somewhat more hostile social environment. In that context, the various organizations of Judaism, along with communal agencies of the Jewish people, were deeply committed to the principle of religious liberty and the separation of church and state.

Searching for fuller civil and religious equality in a land that promised freedom, yet with many of their numbers trying to find ways of survival and security as a minority in a land that put both opportunities and barriers before them, Jews were often cautious as they moved toward what they were convinced were their legal rights and liberties. Reform Judaism, the most acculturated and Americanized part of Jewish religious life, took the lead in emphasizing the importance for Jews of the separation of church and state, pressing for the equality of the minority faith, and arguing for a secular although not a secularized America. Naomi Cohen has explained in detail how "Reformers shaped the response of the community on all significant church-state issues for fifty years after the Civil War," yet also noting that "Jewish opinion on matters of church-state separation and on defense strategy was never an unrelieved monolith."[33] Jewish concerns on matters related to the issues of church and state focussed largely in two areas: Sunday laws and public schools.

Most Protestant denominations wanted to maintain certain customs and laws relating to Sunday observance inherited from the legal traditions of colonial America. In the majority of the states in the later nineteenth century, laws restricting labor, manufacturing, selling, and public amusements on Sunday remained on the books but were enforced with varying degrees of strictness. They obviously were advantageous to church-going people, although increasingly they were defended on grounds that they benefited the welfare of the general populace. This was the line taken by Justice Stephen J. Field in presenting a Supreme Court decision on the matter in 1885: "Laws setting aside Sunday as a day of rest are upheld, not from any right of government for the promotion of religious observances, but from its right to protect all persons from the physical and moral debasement which comes from uninterrupted labor."[34] Of course this created difficulties for those who observed the seventh day of the week rather than the first as their Sabbath: a few small Protestant groups and especially Jews. Many were of strict Orthodox orientation, committed to abiding by traditional laws of Sabbath observance, as were most members of the developing Conservative movement. Many Reform Jews were somewhat more accommodationist in their Sabbath practices but were nevertheless concerned about the issue.

At a time when the wages of working people were low and the six-day week was standard, such laws handicapped observant Jews especially. More than twenty states had provisions for variously defined exemptions from Sunday law requirements, but at the same time there was sporadic resistance, often vociferous, to broadening such exemptions or making them easier for Jews to obtain. For recently arrived immigrants, often unacquainted with language, customs, and laws, it was especially difficult. In some cases, as in 1882 in New York City, the largest center of Jewish settlement in the United States, exemptions became harder to secure. Under the lash of intergroup tensions, police enforcement became more rigorous. By the turn of the century, Jewish leaders generally recognized that the Sunday laws, however inconsistently they were stated and enforced in various localities, were largely unassailable. Often reluctantly, as a matter of strategy, they tended to focus on seeking broader exemptions for their people rather than actively working for the elimination of Sunday laws, which might increase antagonisms and give anti-Semites more visible targets.[35]

On the educational front, the three main branches of Judaism lacked the numbers and resources to do what the Catholics were then busily doing: developing a network of schools. Although some Jewish day schools were founded, for the most part Jews became strong supporters of public education, needing its benefits even as they were troubled by the strong Protestant flavor of its school systems. They had many grievances: the reading of biblical passages (usually from the King James Version), prayer, Christian hymns, selections in books that from the Protestant perspective were defended as nonsectarian but were clearly not so viewed by Jews, and the penalization of Jewish students because of their absences on their holidays. Most were pleased with the Ohio Supreme Court's 1872 decision against Bible reading in public schools, *Board of Education v. Minor*, although the two Jews on that board had opposing viewpoints on the issue. But to try to mitigate or end such practices was not easy; the patterns found offensive varied according to decisions of local school boards, town ordinances, and state laws. Such changes as Jews generally sought came slowly. Although the decision led to countercrusades in many states, they generally welcomed

State ex rel. Weiss v. School Board by the Wisconsin Supreme Court in 1890, in which the Bible was judged to be a sectarian book.[36]

Although resisting linking public education with the concept of a Christian America, many Jews did not want to appear to be contributing to the secularization process—a delicate balance. But they did find it advantageous to seek allies wherever they could in the struggle, as prominent Jewish leaders worked with such liberal freethinking groups as the Free Religious Association and the National Liberal League. They often found the cause of the separation of church and state increasingly attractive.[37]

The Supreme Court's "this is a Christian nation" decision in 1892 was a setback for Jews, but they took little immediate public notice of it and chose to speak softly.[38] They did take alarm when the author of that decision, David J. Brewer, followed it up some thirteen years later with lectures further fleshing out his argument and then published them in book form. Particularly stinging was the implication that because Christianity "has been a potent and helpful factor in the development of our civilization, it is a patriot's duty to uphold it and extend its influence."[39] Jews were justifiably proud of their increasing role in American life and proven loyalty to the nation; they deeply resented having their patriotism questioned. Sharp criticisms of the book from Jewish perspectives appeared in many forms. The Reform movement's Central Conference of American Rabbis (CCAR) quickly created a Committee on Church and State and called for a campaign in support of separation. Focusing on the tense educational situation, for they saw devotional practices in public institutions as a manifestation of the "Christian state" idea, the committee produced and circulated widely a pamphlet, "Why the Bible Should Not Be Read in the Public Schools." Insisting that biblical readings could not be nonsectarian and impartial, the publication argued that their use led to other divisive practices, thus hindering the growth of democracy.

Looking back on the years around the turn of the century, Arthur Gilbert has recalled the cooperation between the "minority" traditions: "For many years Jews were able to count on Catholic support in their protests against religion—usually of Protestant form and substance—in the public schools; and Jews joined Protestants in opposing Catholic efforts to obtain financial aid for parochial schools."[40] But early in the new century in many localities Jewish protests mounted against religious exercises in schools. Although Catholics did not like the Protestant tone of many of those activities, they were in general terms Christian and a greater threat to Jews, who were rapidly increasing in numbers and gaining confidence in articulating their goals. "Where

Catholics had been in the forefront of the school fight in the nineteenth century," Naomi Cohen has concluded, "Jews now occupied that place."[41] Within the Jewish community, however, there was resistance to acting too forcefully lest further anti-Jewish sentiment be evoked. Moreover, there was little satisfaction among the devout in taking actions that increased secularist trends in public education. Yet as moves to require certain public school devotional exercises were being made in a number of states, and were successful in eleven, many Jews found it advisable to oppose such efforts.

Developments of major importance for the Jewish struggle for religious equality were emerging at the same time with the organization of major defense agencies outside the direct orbit of synagogal and rabbinic control. The first was the American Jewish Committee, formed in 1906. Led primarily by Jews who had earned a conspicuous place in American life, within a few years it became an acknowledged force in church-state matters. The Anti-Defamation League was founded seven years later, in general to fight against renewed waves of anti-Semitism. Among Jews rising to prominence was Louis D. Brandeis, in 1916 the first Jew to be appointed to the Supreme Court, although it took four months' struggle to secure Senate confirmation.

On specific issues of religion in public schools, for Jews as well as Catholics, stalemates continued, with the balance seemingly against those trying to eliminate religious practices that had a Protestant cast. In 1900 only Massachusetts had a law requiring morning prayer or Bible reading in schools, but by 1930 eleven states had passed laws making one or both such exercises obligatory. On the other hand, before 1900 only Wisconsin had banned Bible reading in the schools, but by 1930 five more states had done so.[42] It was not until the 1940s that radical changes in the church-state patterns shaped during the nineteenth century were made as minorities continued to grow in size and influence and the composition of the Supreme Court changed.

By 1925, however, the Jewish minority was approaching four million. Many Jews were finding themselves increasingly at home in America and had formed effective institutions of varying types to press for civil and religious equality in the life of the nation. Various tensions persisted, and continuing battles remained to be fought against assumptions and practices of the cultural and religious mainstream, more in some parts of the land than others. But Jews had gathered solid centers of strength, were gaining in self-assurance and wider acceptance helped by their remarkable increase in population, and had become a mounting force in American life.

African American Churches: Racial, Religious, and Governmental Hostilities

As in the case of most ethnic and religious minorities, by no means all blacks were members, active or nominal, of Christian or other faiths. But clearly the largest number of African Americans related to a specific religious tradition were associated with a range of Protestant denominational families, especially Baptist and Methodist. Although there were black members in many communions (including Catholic) that were predominantly white, after the Civil War the majority related to denominations under their own control. C. Eric Lincoln and Lawrence H. Mamiya, authors of a thoroughly researched study of the black church in the African American experience, have explained that "we use the term 'The Black Church' as do other scholars and much of the general public as a kind of sociological and theological shorthand reference to the pluralism of black Christian churches in the United States."[43] They focus on seven major large historic denominations—three Baptist, three Methodist, and one Pentecostal in background—all under black control and estimate that more than 80 percent of African American Christians are in those bodies.

Black denominations arose primarily because of the patterns of segregation in the nation and burgeoned rapidly after 1865. Benjamin E. Mays and Joseph W. Nicholson, authors of an influential study in the 1930s, summarized much history in a few words: "The Negro church began as a means of separating an unwanted racial group from common public worship; that is, it had a social and psychological origin." Although these communions were deeply committed to the Christian faith and influenced by the histories and polities of their denominational backgrounds, they also were conscious of standing up for the rights of the minority of which they were an important part, for "the church was the first community or public organization that the Negro actually owned and completely controlled."[44] Hence they prized freedom at congregational and denominational levels as communal, regional, and national bases from which to press for greater freedom in the white-dominated culture of which they were a part. They struggled to protect their liberty to worship and act as they chose.

In his magisterial, midcentury, three-volume study of American church-state patterns, Anson Phelps Stokes observed that in those matters "the Negro churches follow the pattern of the parent white denomination," and because "Baptists of course predominate" a strong tendency has been for black churches to emphasize the separation of church and state and protect the independence of local congregations.

"The churches of the Negro denominations," however, "are on the whole the more active and assertive in Church-State relations."[45] I understand this to refer primarily to their historic (and contemporary) abilities to include—indeed, to emphasize—relationships between religious movements and institutions (and governmental agencies and regulations), often through informal channels.

A look at certain court cases at local and state levels, some appealed to the Supreme Court, shows that they did not deal primarily with the religion clauses of the First Amendment but with civil rights as these affected the African American community. The importance of churches for the entire black community in these and other matters can hardly be minimized. Especially in the twentieth century, as much of the steadily growing black population shifted from a concentration in the rural South to the urban North, many black clergy saw the need for the creation of alternative organizations in the drive for fuller freedom and rights. Lincoln and Mamiya carefully note that "in spite of the proliferation of many of these groups in urban society, no black secular organization has been able to match the membership and resource commitment by black people to their churches." For them, the line between religious and secular agencies is not as sharp as in many other sectors in society, for "discussions about the Black Church and politics often miss the role of a believer's individual faith in nurturing and sustaining political activity over a long period of time."[46]

Despite this achievement, however, in the late nineteenth and early twentieth centuries African Americans lost heavily in their battle for a larger freedom and recognition of their human, civil, and voting rights. Their churches played direct and indirect roles of support and encouragement in a terrible time. But the tide ran against them. The story of Reconstruction, with its achievements (such as securing the franchise for many former slaves) and flaws, has been told many times. What it sought to do at its best was finally largely overcome by the southern drive for white supremacy, often ignored or supported by many northerners, including the majority of those in the white churches.

A federal civil rights act was finally passed in 1875 and prohibited racial discrimination in common carriers, licensed theaters, hotels, restaurants, juries, church institutions, and incorporated cemetery associations, although an effort to extend the act to the public schools was defeated.[47] But the Supreme Court did not let the act stand. In settling five cases brought before it at once in 1883 it struck down its major contentions, declaring that they were not authorized by the Thirteenth and Fourteenth Amendments and determining that, for the latter, "individual invasion of individual rights is not the subject matter of the amendment."[48] The one dissenter was a Virginian and a former slave-owner, Justice John Marshall Harlan, whose logical and impassioned dissent was longer than the decision of the Court. By emphasizing states' rights, the Court left the door wide open to state action, drastically limiting the right of newly freed persons to vote and clearly reflecting the majority mood of the time.

Mississippi paved the road to the victory of white supremacy by calling a constitutional convention in 1890 and imposing a poll tax and a reading test. The one black delegate pointed out to no avail that 123,000 blacks and only 11,000 whites were thereby disenfranchised. South Carolina followed suit in 1895; only two whites joined the six blacks who voted against the constitution that robbed African Americans of their votes. In state after state, the objections of African Americans were brushed aside.[49] Other evils followed in the wake of the exclusion of so many of one race from voting. "From 1890 to 1910 legislation was passed by all southern states which effectively disenfranchised African Americans," Lincoln and Mamiya observed, "and gave them license to lynchings and other forms of racial suppression."[50] In a cogent summary of analyses of voting patterns, Paul Kleppner, a historian, has referred to the disenfranchisement of blacks in the South in strong terms: "The demobilization that occurred in the post-1900 South was the largest, most extensive, and most enduring that this country has ever witnessed."[51]

As in the case of the Latter-day Saints, the court of last appeal was of no help in checking the monstrous tide. The trend toward stringent segregation was firmly upheld by the Supreme Court in its "separate but equal" decision, *Plessy v. Ferguson.* The decision ruled that required separate facilities for people of color did not imply that they were inferior and was consistent with the Fourteenth Amendment: "The object of the amendment was undoubtedly to enforce the absolute equality of the two races before the law, but in the nature of things it could not have been intended to abolish distinctions based upon color, or to enforce social, as distinguished from political, equality, or a commingling of the two races upon terms unsatisfactory to either." Again, the only dissenter was Harlan, one of the two southerners on the Court. In his lengthy dissent, he uttered a prophetic warning: "In my opinion, the judgment this day rendered will, in time, prove to be quite as pernicious as the decision made by this tribunal in the Dred Scott case."[52]

Other decisions soon drove further nails in equality's coffin. A case that arose in Alabama and reached the Supreme Court, for example, concerned Montgomery County, where it was reported that all white men who asked were readily registered but that no blacks were. Justice Oliver Wendell Holmes delivered the 5 to 3 opinion of the Court in _Giles v. Harris,_ declaring that "relief from a great political wrong, if done as alleged, by the people of a State and the State itself, must be given by them or by the legislative and political department of the government of the United States."[53] Churches were the main meeting places for blacks while the process of demobilization and the spread of anti- black Jim Crow legislation were at their peaks just before and during the Progressive Era. No wonder that "the ranks of the black churches, which constituted the sole place of sanctuary, expanded accordingly. Between 1890 and 1906, for example, the number of black Baptist ministers increased from 5,500 to over 17,000."[54] Important channels of information and encouragement were provided by black church presses, which also deepened a sense of unity among the people of an unjustly treated minority.

By the turn of the century, public opinion in the North had largely concluded that the racial problem was a southern one. With all too few exceptions, the nation's major white denominations offered little effective resistance to the passage of Jim Crow laws and the disenfranchising of southern African Americans. Ray Stannard Baker concluded in 1913 that "the North, wrongly or rightly, is today more than half convinced that the South is right in imposing some measure of limitation upon the franchise."[55] In his detailed study of the South's largest black denominational family in the late nineteenth century, James Melvin Washington based an important generalization on a vast range of evidence: _"The renewal of corporate self-confidence_ encouraged African-American Baptists to place more demands on their white friends. But their demands were usually carefully considered and quite moderate. In the age of Jim Crow, however, any request for a greater share of social power struck most white power brokers as unreasonable, if not absurd. There were few white Baptist leaders who were open enough to listen to black views, and moderate enough to share social power wherever possible."[56]

As in the case of schools, it took decades of struggle before many religiously inclined white people could see that separate but equal in a time of blatant racism was a contradiction in terms for churches as well as for other institutions and customs. Many advocates of the social gospel gave their attention to pressing matters of justice for working people in factories as they challenged the individualistic social ethics and the gospel of wealth, so popular at the time. Although church leaders in the North could be vehement in condemning lynching and criticizing the reduction of black rights, they were also often more influenced by racial stereotypes and attitudes than they recognized. In seeking evangelical Protestant unity, they tended to go along with southern white views of race, as illustrated by the founding of the Federal Council of Churches (FCC) in 1908.

Research, however, has shown that the social gospel had deeper concern for racial reform than has been generally remembered; the fact that the reforms its advocates sought were partial and slow in coming shows how powerful a force racism can be.[57] The FCC began to be more deeply aware of the problem during World War I, and following the race riots of 1919 in Chicago and elsewhere it finally created a permanent Commission on Church and Race. John F. Piper, Jr., has observed that "this marked the real start of the yet unfinished struggle by the united churches against racism in America."[58] But throughout the continuing struggle for justice it was the role of African Americans, aided and often led by their religious forces, that was at the heart of redefining relationships between a minority group and governmental agencies—and helping mainstream Protestantism recognize the evils of racism.

Conclusion

Much of the literature on the interrelations between religion and government in the United States, familiarly given the "church and state" label, has focused strongly on either the impact of the Constitution and its first ten amendments on shaping patterns of religious life in the early years of the nation or on the dramatic redefinitions of those patterns that began in the 1940s, when the Fourteenth Amendment was interpreted to apply the religion clauses of the First Amendment to the states—and by implication to all arms of government. Yet the period from 1865 to 1925, with its tensions and struggles between a Protestant mainstream and minority faiths, was also one in which the religious map was being redrawn. What has happened as trends in local, state, and federal court decisions changed since 1940 cannot be fully understood apart from the history that has been briefly summarized in this chapter.

Symbolically, the "this is a Christian nation" Supreme Court decision of 1892 represented an effort to perpetuate the nineteenth-century tradition that the country was indeed Christian, widely interpreted in Protestant terms. All members of the Court were then Protestants, some conspicuously so. In a series of decisions the power of government had been given Supreme Court backing to force one minority religion to give up a practice important to it. In another set of state and national legislative and court actions, the largest of the "minority" faiths was denied financial support for its educational system, even

though it provided a great deal of "secular" education in its extensive
school system. The courts generally backed the continuation of Sunday laws, although that disadvantaged those who observed Saturday
as their holy day. Exemptions from such laws were given with varying
degrees of difficulty, often grudgingly. A racial minority made the most
of the opportunity to exercise its religious traditions freely, even as its
civil and voting rights were sharply denied, in many instances with the
support of state and federal courts.

The Supreme Court itself, however, was slowly changing, in part
because of the pressure of minorities. Two years after the 1892 decision, a Catholic, Edward D. White, was named to the Court for the
first time in three decades and later became chief justice. The secularization process about which so much has been written was illustrated
in the lineup of the Court when Oliver Wendell Holmes, who proved
to be an agnostic concerning God and a skeptic with regard to revealed
religion, was named to the bench in 1902, to serve for three decades.
Then, in 1916 Louis Brandeis became the first Jew to become a member of the high court. The stalemate between public and parochial
education continued throughout the period, but the right of state governments to require attendance of all children at public schools was
decisively denied in 1925.

The demographic and cultural changes going on throughout the
period and influencing certain legislative and legal actions did not,
however, markedly affect prevailing public opinion on matters of
church and state. Historians have noted that by 1940 a number of those
of Protestant background on the Court were quite nominal in their ties
with whatever church connections they may have retained.[59] Yet the
concept of mainstream and minorities in religion was slow to fade or
be sharply challenged. A few prominent Protestants began to be aware
of the need for fresh understandings in view of changing realities. In
1937 Samuel McCrea Cavert, general secretary of the Federal Council
of Churches, remarked that "we can no longer discuss the relation of
Church and State, even in America, on the basis of the old assumptions
which have held the field down to our own day."[60]

Soon the long series of Supreme Court decisions that reshaped
church-state understandings had begun, as illustrated in cases that recognized certain rights of minorities; for example, *Everson* (providing
for public funding of the transportation of children to both public and
private schools) and *McCollum* (holding as unconstitutional religious
instruction in public schools).[61] In 1954 African American churches
along with some formally secular associations were instrumental in
outlawing school segregation with the Supreme Court's decision in

Brown v. Board of Education, a conspicuous example of how a minority faith was influential in changing national policy on a major issue and at the same time helping reshape the views of many in the Protestant mainstream.[62]

It was not until 1955, however, that public awareness of the larger setting for many of the significant changes was sharply increased with the publication of Will Herberg's *Protestant, Catholic, Jew.* Herberg called attention to what had been developing since colonial times but was much accelerated after the Civil War: the steadily increasing pluriformity of religion. He declared that "Protestantism today no longer regards itself either as a religious movement sweeping the continent or as a national church representing the religious life of the people; Protestantism regards itself today as one of the three religious communities in which twentieth century America had come to be divided."[63] In reality, the situation was much more complex, for many more than three communities were involved. But the fact that the book caused such a stir and has been so often quoted shows how important changes during the period considered in this volume were for an understanding of religion and its interrelationships with governmental agencies during the last half of the twentieth century.

Notes

1. As quoted by Morton Borden, *Jews, Turks, and Infidels* (Chapel Hill: University of North Carolina Press, 1984), 126.

2. Philip Schaff, *Church and State in the United States* (New York: G. P. Putnam's Sons, 1888), 20–21, 53.

3. For estimates on the size of American religious bodies, from which these gross numbers are drawn, see Edwin Scott Gaustad, *Historical Atlas of Religion in America,* rev. ed. (New York: Harper and Row, 1976). Gaustad's prefaces explain the deceptions and difficulties of making such estimates. Bases for counting change over time; some bodies tend to count only communicants, other all baptized members, and still others seem to include total constituencies.

4. *Church of the Holy Trinity v. United States,* 143 U.S. 457 (1892) at 471.

5. *United States v. Macintosh,* 283 U.S. 605 (1931) at 625.

6. Isaac A. Cornelison, *The Relation of Religion to Civil Government in the United States of America: A State without a Church, but Not without a Religion* (New York: G. P. Putnam's Sons, 1895, repr. New York: Da Capo Press, 1970), vi, 341, 362.

7. Joseph P. Thompson, *Church and State in the United States* (Boston: James R. Osgood, 1873), 141.

8. Various Mormon sects arose from time to time, some of them gathered in the Reorganized Church or Latter Day Saints (RLDS, 1860), but this chapter deals with the oldest and largest body centered in Salt Lake City that was so deeply involved in highly publicized church-state issues. For fuller treatments of the historical background of the struggles, see Jan Shipps's chapter in this volume and Shipps, *Mormonism: The Story of a New Religious Tradition* (Urbana: University of Illinois Press, 1985).

9. *Reynolds v. United States*, 93 U.S. 145 (1879), at 164. Significant parts of this and some other related decisions that follow have been reprinted with commentary by John T. Noonan. Jr., *The Believer and the Powers That Are: Cases, History, and Other Data Bearing on the Relation of Religion and Government* (New York: Macmillan, 1987), 194–207.

10. *Reynolds v. United States*, at 165.

11. *Davis v. Beason*, 133 U.S. 333 (1890), at 343.

12. *The Late Corporation of the Church of Jesus Christ of Latter-day Saints v. United States, Romney v. United States*, 136 U.S. 1 (1890), at 49.

13. Kenneth David Driggs, "The Mormon Church-State Confrontation in Nineteenth-Century, America," *Journal of Church and State* 30 (1988): 287.

14. As quoted by Edward Leo Lyman, *Political Deliverance: The Mormon Quest for Utah Statehood* (Urbana: University of Illinois Press, 1986), 106, 135. See also Edwin B. Firmage and Richard C. Mangrum, *Zion in the Courts: A Legal History of the Church of Jesus Christ of Latter-day Saints* (Urbana: University of Illinois Press, 1988).

15. Lyman, *Political Deliverance*, 136, quotation on 296. The significance of the manifesto is carefully discussed in chapter 3 of this volume.

16. Leonard J. Arrington and Davis Bitton, *The Mormon Experience: A History of the Latter-day Saints* (New York: Knopf, 1979), 243.

17. Samuel Lane Loomis, *Modern Cities and Their Religious Problems* (New York: Baker and Taylor, 1887), 87–88.

18. See Jay P. Dolan, "Catholic Attitudes toward Protestants," in *Uncivil Religion: Interreligious Hostility in America,* ed. Robert N. Bellah and Frederick E. Greenspahn (New York: Crossroad, 1987), 72–85; see also chapter 2 of this volume.

19. James Hennesey, *American Catholics: A History of the Roman Catholic Community in the United States* (New York: Oxford University Press, 1981), 208.

20. Justin D. Fulton *The Fight with Rome* (Marlboro, Mass.: Pratt Brothers, 1889, repr. New York: Arno Press, 1977), 2.

21. As reprinted in John Tracy Ellis, ed., *Documents of American Catholic History,* 4th ed. (Wilmington: Michael Glazier, 1987), 2:42.

22. Ellis, ed., *Documents of American Catholic History,* 502.

23. *Board of Education v. Minor,* 23 Ohio 211 (1872).

24. *Abington School District v. Schempp,* 374 U.S. 203 (1963), at 230–304; see esp. 275.

25. *Abington School District,* 275–77. The full name of the important state case in 1890, which built on the 1872 *Minor* decision in Ohio, was *State of*

Wisconsin, ex rel. Frederick Weiss, et al. v. District School Board of School-District No. 8 of the City of Edgerton, 76 Wisc. 177, 44 N.W. 967 (1890). See John O. Geiger, "The Edgerton Bible Case: Humphrey Desmond's Political Education of Wisconsin Catholics," *Journal of Church and State* 20 (1978): 13–28.

26. *Pierce v. Society of Sisters,* 268 U.S. 510 (1925), at 535. In *American Catholics,* 248, Hennesey has said that *"Pierce* has been hailed as a Magna Carta for Catholic education in the United States."

27. Robert H. Keller, Jr., *American Protestantism and United States Indian Policy, 1869–1882* (Lincoln: University of Nebraska Press, 1983), 208, 214. Keller discusses the peace policy in full; see also Francis Paul Prucha, *American Indian Policy in Crisis: Christian Reformers and the Indian, 1865–1900* (Norman: University of Oklahoma Press, 1976). Background information on this complex topic can be found in the relevant sections of chapters 7 and 8 in this volume.

28. William Adams Brown, *Church and State in Contemporary America* (New York: Charles Scribner's Sons, 1938), 120.

29. *Bradfield v. Roberts,* 175 U.S. 291 (1899) at 298.

30. *Quick Bear v. Leupp,* 210 U.S. 50 (1908). The case is discussed with extensive excerpts by Noonan, *The Believer and the Powers That Are,* 214–17.

31. J. Bruce Nichols, *The Uneasy Alliance: Religion, Refugee Work, and U.S. Foreign Policy* (New York: Oxford University Press, 1988), 28.

32. James Bryce, *The American Commonwealth,* 2d ed. (London: Macmillan, 1891), 2:576–77.

33. Naomi W. Cohen *Jews in Christian America: The Pursuit of Religious Equality* (New York: Oxford University Press, 1992), 93–122, quotations on 75 and 101. Relevant to this whole section is an important doctoral dissertation by Shlomith Yahalom, *American Judaism and the Question of Separation between Church and State* (Jerusalem: Hebrew University, 1981). See also chapter 8 in this volume for a discussion on Jews and the public schools.

34. *Soon Hing v. Crowley,* 113 U.S. 703 (1885), at 710.

35. Cohen, *Jews in Christian America,* 72–79, 109–15.

36. Ibid., 83–85, 103–4; see also note 25 of this essay.

37. Jonathan D. Sarna, "Christian America or Secular America? The Church-State Dilemma of American Jews," in *Jews in Unsecular America,* ed. Richard John Neuhaus (Grand Rapids: Eerdmans, 1987), 15–17.

38. Naomi W. Cohen, *Encounter with Emancipation: The German Jews in the United States, 1830–1914* (Philadelphia: Jewish Publication Society, 1984), 98–99.

39. David J. Brewer *The United States a Christian Nation* (Philadelphia: John C. Winston, 1905), 65.

40. Arthur Gilbert, "Jewish Commitments in Relations of Church and State," in *Church-State Relations in Ecumenical Perspective,* ed. Elwyn A. Smith (Pittsburgh: Duquesne University Press, 1966), 58.

41. Cohen, *Jews in Christian America,* 106.

42. Lloyd P. Jorgenson, *The State and the Non-Public School, 1825–1925* (Columbia: University of Missouri Press, 1987), 135.

43. C. Eric Lincoln and Lawrence H. Mamiya, *The Black Church in the African American Experience* (Durham: Duke University Press, 1990), 1; see also chapter 5 of this volume.

44. Benjamin E. Mays and Joseph W. Nicholson *The Negro's Church* (New York: Institute of Social and Religious Research, 1933), 37, 279.

45. Anson Phelps Stokes, *Church and State in the United States*, 3 vols. (New York: Harper and Brothers, 1950), 3:540.

46. Lincoln and Mamiya, *The Black Church*, 232.

47. H. Shelton Smith, *In His Image, But . . . : Racism in Southern Religion, 1780–1910* (Durham: Duke University Press, 1972), 255.

48. *Civil Rights Cases*, 109 U.S. 3 (1883), at 11.

49. John Hope Franklin, *From Slavery to Freedom: A History of Negro Americans,* 3d ed. (New York: Vintage Books, 1969), 339–41.

50. Lincoln and Mamiya, *The Black Church*, 28.

51. Paul Kleppner, *Continuity and Change in Electoral Politics, 1893–1928* (New York: Greenwood Press, 1987), 165.

52. *Plessy v. Ferguson*, 163 U.S. 537 (1896), at 544, 559. Justice Henry Billings Brown delivered the opinion of the Court; Brewer did not hear the argument or participate in the decision. The Scott decision, *Dred Scott v. Sandford*, 60 U.S. (19 How.) 393 (1857), denied that a descendant of a slave could ever be a citizen and rejected the power of Congress to exclude slavery from the territories.

53. *Giles v. Harris*, 189 U.S. 475 (1903), at 488.

54. Lincoln and Mamiya, *The Black Church*, 28.

55. Ray Stannard Baker, "Problems in Citizenship," *Annals of the American Academy of Political and Social Science* 49 (Sept. 1913): 100.

56. James Melvin Washington, *Frustrated Fellowship: The Black Baptist Quest for Social Power* (Macon: Mercer University Press, 1986), 159.

57. Ronald C. White, Jr., *Liberty and Justice for All: Racial Reform and the Social Gospel (1877–1925)* (San Francisco: Harper and Row, 1990); Ralph E. Luker, *The Social Gospel in Black and White: American Racial Reform, 1885–1912* (Chapel Hill: University of North Carolina Press, 1991).

58. John F. Piper, Jr., *The American Churches in World War I* (Athens: Ohio University Press, 1985), 173.

59. Noonan, *The Believer and the Powers That Are*, 238–39.

60. Samuel McCrea Cavert, "Points of Tension between Church and State in America Today," in Henry Pitney Van Dusen, Robert Lowrey Calhoun, and Joseph Perkins Chamberlin, *Church and State in the Modern World* (New York: Harper and Brothers, 1937), 191.

61. *Everson v. Board of Education of the Township of Ewing*, 330 U.S. 1 (1947); *McCollum v. Board of Education*, 333 U.S. 203 (1948).

62. *Brown v. Board of Education*, 347 U.S. 483 (1954).

63. Will Herberg, *Protestant, Catholic, Jew: An Essay in American Religious Sociology* (Garden City: Doubleday, 1955), 139–40.

TEN

"God's Right Arm"? Minority Faiths and Protestant Visions of America

JAMES H. MOORHEAD

As minority faiths strove to understand the meaning of America and their place in it during the late nineteenth and early twentieth centuries, mainstream Protestantism inevitably cast its shadow over their endeavors. Protestants claimed to hold a controlling interest in the definition of American identity, and by reason of numbers and position in seats of cultural and political prestige they could not be ignored. Yet the Protestant recension of the American dream was not simply an alien vision against which minority faiths defined their own. A curious combination of parochial and cosmopolitan impulses, Protestant notions of national identity offered numerous points of contact with—as well as divergence from—the aspirations of minorities. In this ambiguous situation, ideas originally derived from Protestantism could be at least partly detached from their origins and function as a kind of civil religion or common American faith that minority faiths might turn to their own uses. Thus minority faiths and the Protestant mainstream engaged in a complex pattern of contests and negotiations as together they redefined American identity. The writings of two major Protestant spokesmen in the late nineteenth century help to frame the dynamics of this process.[1]

In his best-selling *Our Country* (1885), the Rev. Josiah Strong declared: "America is to become God's right arm in his battle with the world's ignorance and oppression and sin." Three years later, near the close of his massive *Christianity in the United States,* Daniel Dorchester pictured divine providence brooding "over the boundless fields of this country" in order to lead all humanity to a better future. Dorchester and Strong expressed the conventional Protestant faith that the United States occupied a unique, divinely appointed role as redeemer nation. Yet that common faith was far from monolithic; it was a collection of diverse, sometimes conflicting, ideas and impulses.[2]

American Protestants envisioned a national destiny at once cosmopolitan and tribal. Tribalism was readily apparent in an era witness-

ing the enactment of Jim Crow laws, the formation of nativist organizations such as the American Protective Association, the resurgence of
the Ku Klux Klan after 1915, and the triumph of pseudoscientific notions of Anglo-Saxon superiority. In an often-cited passage Strong reflected that ethnocentrism. Rejoicing that God had made the Protestant Anglo-Saxons "the die with which to stamp the peoples of the
earth" and that God had made America the "principal seat" of this
power, Strong asked, "Is there any reasonable doubt that this race . . . is
destined to dispossess many weaker races, assimilate others, and mold
the remainder, until, in a very real sense, it has Anglo-Saxonized mankind?" Dorchester cast the history of America as a drama in which God
had reserved America for settlement by Protestants of Anglo-Saxon
stock, and from these people had come most of that which was good
and worthy in the United States.[3]

Yet despite the fact that both men believed that English-speaking
Protestants held proprietary rights over the nation's destiny, neither was
as narrowly parochial as some of their comments would suggest. His
assertions of Protestant and Anglo-Saxon superiority notwithstanding,
Strong also allowed that the "mixed origin" of its people would
strengthen America, and Dorchester averred that "the composite character of our population, in which so many bloods mingle, will be the
means of building up a superior type." Moreover, both men believed
that the calling of America was to promote liberty, justice, moral uplift, and material progress for all people. Protestant and Anglo-Saxon
hegemony in the United States was important because it served universal aims. "Our plea," said Strong "is not America for America's sake;
but America for the world's sake." What John Higham has written of
the ideology of Anglo-Saxonism in the late nineteenth century applies
equally well to Protestant visions of the nation: They "kept parochial
and cosmopolitan ideals revolving in a single orbit."[4]

Protestant conceptions of American destiny also vacillated between
self-congratulation and self-criticism. While celebrating American democracy and material progress, Dorchester and Strong worried about
the implications of these values. They extolled democracy but warned
that democracy unchecked by moral restraint would descend into anarchy. They rejoiced in material progress but cautioned against materialism. Because America was a set of principles to be realized more than
a finished product, loyal Americans could never rest content. In the
spirit of the Puritan jeremiad, they needed to engage in ceaseless self-
criticism and repentance as a means of corporate rededication to America's destiny.[5]

The equivocal character of the Protestant notion of America evoked a corresponding ambivalence among minority faiths. Eager to be insiders, they often responded enthusiastically to the rhetoric of freedom, justice, democracy, and progress for all. These ideals assured them that they, too, participated in the promise and mission of America. But because the dominant white Protestant culture claimed special trusteeship over that destiny and often overlaid it with notions of Anglo-Saxon superiority, those ideals also had an alien ring. To endorse uncritically the prevailing Protestant vision of America was at one level to accept the preeminence of white Protestants and acknowledge one's status as a second-class citizen. Minority faiths would have faced a simpler dilemma had the regnant nationalism been an unambiguous tribalism rooted in blood and place. Then the choice would have been clear: resistance or surrender. Because myths about America were more indeterminate, however, they created an ideological arena in which both minority faiths and the Protestant mainstream could find partial agreement and frequent conflict. Indeed, minority faiths, in contesting prevailing Protestant views of the nation, might claim that they were the true Americans, uttering a prophetic jeremiad calling the country back to its true destiny. Thus the meaning of America remained subject to continuous renegotiation, as together minority faiths and the Protestant mainstream haggled over questions of national identity.

According to many Protestant leaders, Roman Catholicism was an inveterate enemy of American institutions. That suspicion, rooted in hatreds as old as the Reformation, also had nineteenth-century sources. Especially under Pius IX, the Vatican issued pronouncements condemning the separation of church and state, democracy, and religious toleration. Although these statements were directed chiefly at anticlerical forms of liberalism and nationalism in Europe, they were interpreted by some to suggest that the spirit of Catholicism was perhaps too authoritarian to fit into the democratic ethos of America. Moreover, a flood of Catholic immigration, beginning in earnest after the Irish famine of the 1840s, gave the American Catholic Church a distinctly foreign tinge. Because many of these newcomers huddled in burgeoning cities that became symbols of disorder, and because most were working-class folk generally voting Democratic at a time when Protestants outside the South generally identified the Republican Party and middle-class mores with godly Americanism, Catholicism readily appeared alien and threatening. Thus Josiah Strong lamented the absolutism of Roman Catholicism and warned of the danger posed by its urban

masses "led to the polls like so many sheep" by "petty political popes."
"How grievously," added Dorchester, "have morals been debauched,
pauperism, insanity and crime augmented, and moral progress retarded by these exotic masses!"[6]

Many Catholics were at pains to demonstrate that their coreligionists, far from being "exotic masses" or docile sheep, firmly defended
basic American values. Cardinal James Gibbons, occupant of the
archepiscopal see of Baltimore, gloried in America's heritage of religious
and civil liberty: "But, thank God, we live in a country where liberty
of conscience is respected, and where the civil constitution holds over
us the aegis of her protection, without intermeddling with ecclesiastical affairs. From my heart, I say: America, with all thy faults, I love
thee still. Perhaps at this moment there is no nation on the face of the
earth where the Church is less trammelled, and where she has more
liberty to carry out her sublime destiny, than in these United States."
The assertion that democracy provided the conditions in which the
Christian church could flourish echoed Protestants' contentions, as did
Gibbons's insistence that the Gospel in turn nourished democracy. But
unlike Protestants, he made the Catholic tradition the ultimate origin
of American liberty. Citing ancient precedents, he reminded his readers that the Magna Charta, "the corner-stone of constitutional government," was framed by the Archbishop of Canterbury and Catholic laity;
that Maryland, under Catholic aegis, was "the cradle of [American]
civil and religious liberty"; and that the American Revolution counted among its honored heroes Catholics such as Charles Carroll, Tadeusz
Kosciuszko, the Marquis de Lafayette, and Kazimierz Pulaski. By asserting the central role of Catholicism in the creation of American democracy, Gibbons thereby staked out Catholics' claim to contemporary participation in it.[7]

Archbishop John Ireland of St. Paul offered yet more extravagant
praise of America—"the providential nation." "Even as I believe that
God rules over men and nations, so do I believe that a divine mission
has been assigned to the Republic of the United States. That mission is
to prepare the world, by example and moral influence, for the universal reign of human liberty and human rights. America does not live for
herself alone; the destinies of humanity are in her keeping." In company with Gibbons, he tried to rework the national myth in order to place
Catholicism at its center. Contrary to Protestants' boasts, their faith had
impeded the realization of liberty. In place of principles favorable to
liberty, Protestants turned to "private judgment." Private judgment in
turn bred anarchy and anarchy "political despotism." "If," he concluded, "in later times liberty has asserted itself in Protestant lands, it has

but recovered by its own energies . . . , and to-day wherever it thrives, its strength comes to it from the principles proclaimed and defended by the Catholic Church during the whole course of the Christian era."[8]

In 1889 Father Anton Walburg, a Cincinnati pastor, offered a very different assessment of America and the church's place in it. The prevailing Anglo-Saxon culture was "the bulwark of Protestantism and the mainstay of the enemies of the faith." Characterized by a hypocritical and callous materialism, that culture was "impervious to the spirit and the doctrines of the Catholic religion." Perhaps a Redemptorist priest most succinctly stated that attitude when he greeted a newcomer to the United States with the words "you are here in Sodom and Gomorrah."[9]

These contrasting readings of America translated into different policies. Conservatives generally called for education in parochial schools, maintenance of immigrants' language and customs, the exclusion of the faithful from secret societies, and minimal contact with Protestants. In short, they sought to create a safe haven in which Catholics might be free of the contagion of American life. They wished, in Walburg's words, to prevent "our simple, straight-forward, honest Germans and Irish [from plunging] into this whirlpool of American life . . . , where their consciences will be stifled, their better sentiments trampled under foot." By contrast, "Americanizers" such as Ireland, although favoring parochial education, were willing to strike compromises with the public school system. They wanted Catholics to give up their native languages in favor of the tongue and ways of America. They adopted a relaxed posture toward secret societies and gladly interacted with Protestants on public occasions. By these policies, American Catholics could shed their image as foreigners and win acceptance from society at large. In headier moments, some implied that this new Catholicism in the United States would renovate the church in the Old World. In the midst of war with Spain, Denis O'Connell wrote to Ireland: "When Spain is swept of[f] the seas much of the meanness and narrowness of old Europe goes with it to be replaced by the freedom and openness of America." O'Connell urged the archbishop to press on with his policies and "force upon the Curia . . . the great triumph of Americanism."[10]

As O'Connell's remarks suggested, differing visions of America also implied differing understandings of Catholicism. For conservatives, the Catholic faith was an immutable deposit of truth protected by the magisterium of the institutional church. "Catholic principles," wrote Salvatore Brandi, an Italian Jesuit who had taught for some years in the United States, "do not change: not because time goes by, not because one changes nationality, not because of new discoveries, not for reasons of utility. They are always those which Christ taught, which the Church has proclaimed." The Americanizers, however, believed that the church could and should change with the currents of history. "Church and age!" John Ireland declared. "They pulsate alike: the God of nature works in one, the God of supernatural revelation works in the other—in both the self-same God."[11]

It was not that liberal Catholics saw themselves as ardent patriots while conservatives did not. The difference was more subtle. Liberals viewed their American identities as a vital part of their Catholicism. Conservatives, equally loyal and patriotic, regarded these identities as separate. "Being Catholic," as Jay Dolan has written, "had nothing to do with being American." New York's conservative Archbishop Michael Corrigan gave succinct expression to this division of allegiances: "We also are Americans as much as any one else. Yes, we are, and we glory in it . . . ; but in the matter of religion, doctrine, discipline, morals and Christian perfection, we glory in thoroughly following the Holy See."[12]

Pope Leo XIII reinforced the latter style of Catholicism when he issued *Testem benevolentiae* in 1899. The encyclical condemned a collection of ideas the pope termed "Americanism," which included the belief that the church should adapt itself to the spirit of the age and that Catholicism in American should be "different from that which is in the rest of the world." Leo made clear that the condemnation did not extend to American Catholics' legitimate pride in the United States, nor did he assert that the offensive doctrine was being taught. He noted merely that certain Europeans had made the charge and expressed confidence that "our Venerable Brethren the bishops of America would be the first to repudiate and condemn it." Because of its studied ambiguity, *Testem* offered something to American liberals and conservatives alike. The latter greeted it as a vindication of their position; the former, taking refuge in the fact that Leo had left the actual existence of the heresy uncertain, replied with Gibbons that Americanism as defined by the pope "has nothing in common with the views, aspirations, doctrine and conduct of Americans." Although no one was condemned or deposed, *Testem* put the church on notice that the ethos of American culture could be brought to the altar only with great caution, if at all. Leo's successor, Pius X, further discouraged the alignment of the church with the spirit of the age when he condemned theological modernism in 1907.[13]

The Americanist controversy contributed to the triumph of what Robert Curran has called a bifurcated or compartmentalized American Catholicism. As their hearty support of America's war with Catholic Spain in 1898 and of the American participation in World War I indicated, Catholics took second place to none in their loyalty to the nation. But after 1899 the easy consonance that "Americanizers" such as Gibbons and Ireland had felt between Catholic ideals and the American polity was problematic. Leo XIII had made it more difficult to assert that loyalty to American political values and allegiance to an hierarchical, authoritarian church meshed in a single rationale. To a considerable degree, Catholics lived in two separate worlds that would not have theoretical integration until much later in the writings of John Courtney Murray, a Jesuit, and in the liberalizing decisions of the Second Vatican Council. Yet in this interim, bifurcated Catholicism continued to produce, as it had in Michael Corrigan, an ardent loyalty to the United States. In fact, at the moment when numerous Protestant thinkers began to succumb to disillusionment following World War I, many Catholics espoused myths of American exceptionalism and innocence. The intellectual isolation of Catholics rendered them relatively immune to this loss of confidence, and they, more than their Protestant counterparts, could affirm an optimistic vision of America hauntingly like that of Daniel Dorchester and Josiah Strong.[14]

Many African Americans had long questioned the notion that the United States had an exemplary mission to the world. The horrors of slavery and racism led them to invert the prevailing myth of the Redeemer Nation. David Walker, a free black, in his *Appeal to the Colored Citizens of the World* (1829) insisted that America, far from being a new Israel, was a counterpart to ancient Egypt, holding in bondage God's African Israel. Slaves reiterated the same point when they sang, "Go down, Moses, way down in Egypt land, / Tell ole Pharaoh to let my people go." Antebellum black nationalists, calling for emigration and repatriation to Africa, implicitly preached a similar message. Rejection of the American mission, however, was not the only alternative. Blacks could appeal to the American promise of liberty for all and assert that the problem was not the national myth but rather the failure of whites to live up to it. By this reading, America might yet become the Redeemer Nation. As the Civil War drew to a close, many African Americans had devoutly hoped the United States was about to fulfill its true destiny. Speaking before the House of Representatives in 1865, the Rev. Henry Highland Garnett expressed their hopes. With slavery destroyed, "The nation has begun its exodus from worse than Egyptian bondage" and might now "give to the world the form of a model Republic."[15]

The years after the Civil War gave the lie to Garnett's hopes. Northerners soon wearied of the effort to assure civil rights, and the rising

tide of Anglo-Saxonism made them increasingly sympathetic to Southern racists. As federal troops were withdrawn from the South, the
Reconstruction state governments fell to white "Redeemers," and
blacks descended into new forms of bondage. Stripped of voting rights,
subject to newly created systems of segregation, terrorized by the burning crosses and lynch law of the Ku Klux Klan and similar groups,
African Americans entered a period often called the nadir. In response
to this oppression, some African Americans called upon their fellows
to emigrate to Africa and leave forever a corrupt nation in which they
could have no part. Henry McNeal Turner, a fiery bishop of the African Methodist Episcopal Church, strongly supported emigration and
contended that the mistreatment of his race "absolves the negro's allegiance to the general government, makes the American flag to him a
rag of contempt, instead of a symbol of liberty."[16]

Although emigration won the support of only a minority of blacks,
many religious leaders did speak of an African, not an American, mission to the world. Often expressed practically through missionary work
in Africa rather than speculatively, this idea of mission also had its
theoreticians. In 1884 James Theodore Holly, an African American
serving as Episcopal bishop of Haiti, argued that God carried out human redemption through different ethnic groups descended from the
sons of Noah: Shem, Japheth, and Ham. God first used Shem's offspring, the Jews, to record his word in scripture and then raised up the
Christian church, largely from among the European posterity of
Japheth, to spread that word throughout the world. But the Japhetic
people could not bring the divine plan to completion, for these
"warlike . . . nations shall be overthrown at the battle of Armageddon."
To the African progeny of Ham belonged the honor of actually establishing God's reign on earth. "The African race," he explained, "has
been the servant of servants to their brethren of the other races during
all the long and dreary ages of the Hebrew and Christian dispensa-
tions." Although African meekness under suffering was by no means
a major theme in Holly's work, the motif enabled him to make a another, very different point: African Americans would enjoy "the noblest
place of service in the coming kingdom."[17]

AME minister Theophilus Gould Steward expected a similarly grand
role for Africans. In *The End of the World* (1888), Steward controverted
Josiah Strong's assertion that Anglo-Saxons would usher in the kingdom of God on earth. "The sin of the age," he insisted, "has been in
associating Saxonism with Christianity, if not in placing it above Christianity. Saxonism must utterly and signally fail, in order that Christ may
be all in all." Steward anticipated that the Western nations would be

scattered in a destructive war, Africans would then speedily convert to a Christianity liberated "from the dominance of the principle of clan," and the "excluded darker races" would be the chief instruments in the establishment of the millennial order. Then would come to pass the prophecy of Psalm 68:31: "Princes shall come out of Egypt and Ethiopia shall soon stretch out her hands unto God."[18]

Despite their dissent from the white Protestant vision of America, Holly and Steward were still deeply informed by it. Like most black nationalists of the nineteenth century, they understood their mission to fellow blacks—whether in the United States, Africa, or the Caribbean—to be one of uplift. Uplift was essential because at present, as Holly put it, the "race is under a dark and heavy cloud of spiritual ignorance." Holly decried "the servile character of the free colored people of the United States" and recognized that his beloved Haiti was woefully backward in many respects. He remained optimistic for his people because they were learning "the arts, sciences, and genius of modern civilization" from "this hardy and enterprising Anglo-American race." The logic of his argument—degraded people of color needing uplift and uplift defined by the example of the English-speaking people—indicated that Holly was not completely free of the mythological world inhabited by Strong and Dorchester. Notwithstanding his faith that Canaan's children would displace Japheth's offspring in the millennium, Holly implicitly allowed that Canaan could rise only as he was willing to follow the example of Japheth. Steward manifested a similar ambivalence. In order for the "excluded darker races" to fulfill their eschatological destiny, the Christian nations of Europe and America had to be shattered. Yet he served with pride as a military chaplain during the Spanish-American War and subsequently in the Philippines. Returning from the Pacific in 1902, he reflected on "the opportunities into which . . . [blacks] have been thrown" in America. They had been *"pitched* into a civilization stimulating to the highest development." Several years later he declared that the American flag "stands as the symbol of our liberty, . . . the banner of hope and the flag of the free."[19]

Even allegedly more secular black leaders reflected similar ambivalence, and they often did so in religious overtones. Frederick Douglass, the patriarch among African American leaders until his death in 1895, had consistently supported with equal ardor the ideals of his nation and the longings of his people for freedom. Because white America refused to grant equality, Douglass felt intense stress between his loyalties. For him as for so many others, the Civil War temporarily merged these allegiances. "This was a moment," David Blight has written, "when Afro-Americans might wrest a new definition out of the terrible duality of their lives. America's first principles might be appealed to, not only to free the slaves but to save the nation. Both causes possessed a sacred quality, and they might be mingled in one holy war." As the nation retreated from its promise of liberty to the captives during Reconstruction, Douglass thundered desperate jeremiads, calling white Americans to remember the meaning of their dreadful conflict. Through remembrance and repentance, he hoped to reunite black aspirations and American identity at a time when they were in danger of sundering.[20]

Booker T. Washington, who achieved prominence as a leader about the time of Douglass's death, revealed the same divided loyalties but resolved them in differing ways. While Douglass vigorously denounced racism, segregation, and the denial of civil rights, Washington accommodated to these realities and urged blacks to concentrate upon industrial education, self-discipline, and hard work. Thus African Americans would advance economically, attain the respect of whites, and by their success attain indirectly social and political equality. "When a black man," Washington said in a succinct summary of his philosophy, "is the largest taxpayer in a community, his neighbors will not object very long to his voting and having his vote honestly counted."[21]

Although Washington emphasized America's special place in the world, he hinted that blacks, too, had a separate and unique destiny without which the nation could not fulfill its mission. Comparing his people to God's elect nation in the Old Testament, he argued "that the very qualities which make the Negro different from the peoples by whom he is surrounded will enable him, in the fullness of time, to make a peculiar contribution to the nation of which he forms a part." Blacks fulfilled that role as servants whose suffering was analogous to that of Jesus. "If the Negro who has been oppressed, ostracized, denied rights in a Christian land, can help you, North and South, to rise, can be the medium of your rising to these sublime heights of unselfishness and self-forgetfulness, who may say that the Negro, this new citizen, will not see in it a recompense for all that he has suffered and will have performed a mission that will be placed beside that of the lowly Nazarene?" Such words undoubtedly comforted racists that African Americans would not challenge white hegemony, but Washington's lines also contained a barb. "There is no power that can separate our destiny," he said of whites and blacks immediately before his soothing remarks. The message was subtle but clear: Only insofar as whites accepted the unique contributions of African Americans could the destiny of the entire nation be fulfilled. In the peroration to his famous address to the Atlanta Exposition in 1895, he declared that only as "racial animosities" were blotted out would "our beloved South [become] a new heaven and a new earth." Blacks, although submissive to whites, still held the key to the success of the American mission.[22]

Washington's accommodationist leadership was, of course, rejected by many leaders. The exposés of lynching by Ida Wells Barnett, the blunt attacks on racism by the young intellectual W. E. B. Du Bois, the short-lived Niagara movement, and the creation of the NAACP signaled that many African Americans wished to return to the tradition of David Walker and Frederick Douglass—a tradition that denounced injustice and demanded equal treatment for blacks. This return to militancy intensified the ambivalence that African Americans felt about their American identity. Du Bois, in *The Souls of Black Folk* (1903), provided the classic expression of the dilemma: "One ever feels his two-ness,—an American, a Negro; two souls, two thoughts, two unreconciled strivings; two warring ideals in one dark body, whose dogged strength alone keeps it from being torn asunder."[23]

When America went to war in 1898 and again in 1917, most black leaders offered at least lukewarm and sometimes enthusiastic support, believing that displays of valor on the battlefield would prove African American patriotism and promote the inclusion of blacks within the national dream. Thus Du Bois declared in 1917: "This is a much our country as yours, and as much the world's as ours. We Americans, black and white, are the servants of all mankind and ministering to a greater, fairer Heaven." But he added a proviso: "Let us be true to our mission. No land that loves to lynch 'niggers' can lead the hosts of Almighty God." Even amid the fervor of flag-waving, the "two unreconciled strivings" were only provisionally and partly harmonized.[24]

Indeed, signs already abounded that many blacks could no longer keep the "two warring ideals . . . from being torn asunder." Among the masses of blacks beginning to flood into northern cities, new religious prophets proclaimed a more radical separation from whites and their visions of national destiny. In 1914, Timothy Noble—soon styling himself Noble Drew Ali—organized the Moorish Science League and called upon blacks to find their identity apart from the religion of whites. In 1916 Marcus Garvey, a Jamaican, arrived in New York City and shortly founded the Universal Negro Improvement Association. UNIA, replete with the trappings of a black civil religion, aimed at pan-African unity and the creation of a separate nation for blacks. "White and black will learn to respect each other," Garvey explained in 1924, "when they cease to be active competitors in the same countries. . . . Let them have countries of their own, wherein to aspire and climb without rancor. . . . We want an atmosphere all our own. We would like to govern and rule ourselves and not be encumbered and restrained." UNIA won the support of numerous black ministers and the sympathy of hundreds of thousands of other African Americans. Despite Garvey's imprisonment for mail fraud and despite the breakup of his movement in the 1920s, the widespread appeal of his message testified that many blacks continued to have difficulty in seeing themselves in the prevailing myth of America.[25]

At the time Strong and Dorchester were penning their hymns to American nationalism, the intellectual leadership of American Jewry was in the hands of people supremely confident of the compatibility of their faith and their Americanism. They were Reform Jews who had found in America their land of promise. Initially born in Germany as a response to the opportunities posed by the Enlightenment and Emancipation, Reform sought to purge the religion of many of its cultic practices and ethnic trappings—a project derived from the conviction that Judaism was a rational, progressive, and cosmopolitan faith. Reform dramatically altered the messianic hope of Judaism. No longer looking for a restoration of their national homeland, Reform Jews saw the mission of Israel as the universal one of holding up before all peoples the banner of monotheistic religion. Reform enjoyed limited success in Europe, but in America it prospered, especially among the German Jews who had immigrated to the United States before the 1880s. Part of the zeal of American Jewry for Reform derived, in Michael Meyer's words, from the fact that "in America Reform Jews could feel that their own concept of mission might be woven into a larger still inchoate national purpose." Thus "the people chosen of old would play their role as part of a people chosen of new."[26]

To be sure, many in the movement wished to retain their German culture and language, and that issue sparked debates analogous to arguments within Catholicism. But on the whole, Reform Judaism pressed toward full amalgamation into American life. Isaac Mayer Wise, rabbi and founder of Hebrew Union College in Cincinnati, expressed the trend dramatically. "With us," he declared in 1874, "Judaism is nothing outlandish; it is no exotic curiosity; it is neither German, French, nor Polish: it is American, and fully so, in language, spirit and form."[27]

The Pittsburgh Platform, drafted by nineteen rabbis in 1885, provides the classic expression of this outlook. Although the statement affirmed the necessity of maintaining "historical identity with our great past" and asserted that Judaism offered "the highest conception" of God, it nevertheless stressed what Judaism had in common with other religions and with the spirit of the age. "Christianity and Islam being daughter religions of Judaism, we appreciate their mission to aid in the spreading of monotheistic and moral truth. We acknowledge that the spirit of broad humanity of our age is our ally in the fulfilment of our mission." The task of Judaism, in short, was a universal one, and the rabbis were eager to remove any taint of particularity from it. "We consider ourselves no longer a nation but a religious community, and therefore expect neither a return to Palestine, . . . nor the restoration of any of the laws concerning the Jewish state." For the traditional expectation of a messiah who would restore the fortunes of the Jewish people, they substituted a messianic age that would bring "the reign of truth and righteousness among men." The rabbis did not, of course, wish Judaism as a distinct entity to disappear, and they insisted that it had a unique role to play in world history, but that role subserved universal rather than parochial ends.[28]

This emphasis upon the cosmopolitan destiny of Judaism enabled Reform rabbis to affirm simultaneously the universal elements in American nationalism and claim them as their own. Emil G. Hirsch, a Chicago rabbi who exercised great influence in Reform circles, declared that the United States was "the practical expression and activization of . . . fundamental conceptions of Judaism." Both rested on the assumption that before God all people were free and equal. Thus he insisted that the mission of Judaism could find its fullest expression within the American republic. "We feel," he exulted, "that if anywhere on God's footstool our Messianic vision will be made real, it is in this land where a new humanity seems destined to arise." Thus "we can sing with all others, 'My country tis of thee! sweet land of liberty, Of thee I sing; Land where *my* fathers died, land of *our* Pilgrims' pride.'" Just as John Ireland and James Gibbons tried to claim that the founders of America built upon Catholic principles, Hirsch made the same assertion on behalf of Judaism. "In the "May-flower" *our* Bible crossed the Atlantic," he claimed. The powerful role of the Pentateuch in the consciousness of the Puritan founders made them "more Hebraic" than many Jews themselves. In fact, "Puritan Hebrewism alone enabled the pilgrims to exercise dominion over the wilds of their new home." Thus Hirsch pushed on to a straightforward conclusion: "Clinging to his Judaism, the Jew will be a more strenuous, a more loyal, a more enthusiastic American."[29]

Yet even as Hirsch, Wise, and other Reform advocates confidently wrote their manifestos, an upsurge of new immigration was changing the character of American Jewry. In the wake of the Russian pogroms following the assassination of Czar Alexander II in 1881, a massive trek brought nearly two million additional Jews to the United States by World War I. For these Eastern Ashkenazic Jews, "clinging to . . . Ju-

daism" meant something very different than it did to the drafters of
the Pittsburgh Platform. It did not connote what that document had
called "a progressive religion, ever striving to be in accord with the
postulates of reason"—a religion prepared to jettison ancient customs
and regulations "such as are not adapted to the views and habits of
modern civilization." Reform made sense to a people who had experienced Emancipation and the possibility of inclusion in the larger society. It had little relevance to Eastern European Jews who had not enjoyed these prospects. Having lived in self-contained small towns
(shtetls) or in cities such as Warsaw, where for the most part they constituted a desperately poor proletariat, they perceived Judaism as the
total way of life associated with these communities. To alter those folk-
ways was to surrender one's identity as a Jew. Abraham Cahan, in his
novel *The Rise of David Levinsky* (1917), has his immigrant protagonist observe:

> The orthodox Jewish faith, as it is followed in the old Ghetto towns of
> Russian or Austria, has still to learn the art of trimming its sails to suit
> new winds. . . . It is absolutely inflexible. If you are a Jew of the type to
> which I belonged when I came to New York and you attempt to bend
> your religion to the spirit of your new surroundings, it breaks. It falls to
> pieces. The very clothes I wore and the very food I ate had a fatal effect
> on my religious habits. A whole book could be written on the influence
> of a starched collar and a necktie on a man who was brought up as I
> was.

Indeed, for Levinsky the act of shaving his beard became a "heinous
sin" leading to the unraveling of his identity.[30]

In one sense, Cahan's portrait was overdrawn. Eastern European
Jews were neither as uniformly observant nor as inflexible as he implied. Even before its transplanting in America, the culture of Eastern
Jewry was variegated and in ferment. Socialism, Zionism, and anar-
chism—although the dreams of a minority—flourished alongside religious orthodoxy. Among a few creative literary figures, *Yiddishkeit*
flowered. A celebration of the Yiddish language and culture, *Yiddishkeit* embodied a deep appreciation for traditional Judaism and also
exhibited something of a secular spirit as it struggled to probe and
communicate the total cultural experience of the Jewish people. While
the Eastern Askenazi brought a fresh infusion of traditional Judaism
to America, they also imported the creative chaos of these new movements. Yet whether as rigorously observant Jews, Zionists, or socialists, the new immigrants had a distinct sense of themselves as a people
apart from the rest of America. Differentiated by language, culture, and
(initially) poverty, they knew themselves to be, in a common phrase of

the early twentieth century, "hyphenated Americans"—a people constituted by dual loyalties.[31]

But still they wished to share the destiny of America, a destiny that would give the freedom and opportunity to live a normal life to all people. Many immigrant memoirs testify to the extent to which the traditional messianic hope was invested in the United States. For example, Mary Antin, years after emigrating from Russia, remembered a poignant seder in the old country: "Passover was celebrated in tears that year. In the story of Exodus we would have read a chapter of current history, only for us there were no deliverers and no promised land. But what said some of us at the end of the long service? Not 'May we be next year in Jerusalem,' but 'Next year—in America!' So there was our promised land." Similarly, in 1917 Marcus Ravage remembered reading Rumanian newspapers "filled with . . . eulogies of the land of our aspirations [America], which for some reason or other was continually referred to as Jerusalem." Although the Eastern Askenazi loved the particularities of their own cultures too ardently to accept Reform Judaism's facile elision of the Jew into the American, many of them were no less convinced that the United States offered redemption.[32]

Even the particularities of Jewish experience could be made to subserve American identity. Zionism provides a case in point. Initially opposed by most American Jews, especially the Reform community, Zionism appeared to its critics to be a retrograde movement that would prevent assimilation into American life and arouse fears that Jews' allegiance was divided. The eminent lawyer Louis Brandeis played a major role in overcoming these objections. In 1915 he contended that dual loyalties were pernicious only if they were incompatible. If similar, two allegiances were mutually supportive, and both Zionism and Americanism derived from identical commitments: democracy and social justice. "Zionism," he wrote, "is the Pilgrims' inspiration and impulse over again." Although some Zionists objected to his deracination of the movement from *Yiddishkeit*, Brandeis succeeded in making it more widely acceptable, both within the Jewish community and without. "Every American Jew who aids in advancing the Jewish settlement of Palestine," he summarized, "will be a better man and a better American for doing so."[33]

Perhaps the particularities of the Jewish experience served to affirm American destiny most subtly—and powerfully—through the promotion of mass consumption. Part of America's mission, it was long assumed, lay in giving all people a chance to attain material comfort. To be sure, religious leaders—whether Protestant, Catholic, or Jewish—warned that abundance without the savor of religion would destroy the nation. Josiah Strong wrote a majority opinion for most faiths when he declared, "The means of self-gratification should not outgrow the power of self-control." Yet he also rejoiced in the advance of civilization, adding, "And what is the process of civilizing but *the creating of more and higher wants?*" Indeed, the decades following the Civil War witnessed the creation of many "more and higher wants" as a burgeoning economy enlisted the wiles of advertising agencies to sell its goods. As never before, the acquisition and display of consumer goods became a way of affirming the promise of America and one's place in it. Jews, eager to express aspirations denied in Eastern Europe, quickly saw the possibilities. They realized, Andrew Heinze has observed, "that Americans sought in the world of consumption, a parity with each other." Thus they purchased clothes and pianos for the parlor, they took vacations in the Catskills, and thereby marked themselves as full participants in the American Dream. Yet if the culture of consumption tended at one level to make the Jew less distinguishable from Gentile Americans, it simultaneously heightened his or her Jewish identity. For consumption was also used to enhance distinctly Jewish holidays, such as Hanukkah.[34]

This two-sidedness—consumption as an act of assimilating and of maintaining one's Jewishness—was perhaps best illustrated in that remarkable band of Jewish pioneers who did so much to shape the mass consumption of entertainment through the motion picture industry. Of movie moguls such as Samuel Goldwyn, Louis B. Mayer, and Adolf Zukor, Irving Howe has perceptively written, "It was something of a miracle and something of a joke. They had come from the Ukraine and Poland and Austria-Hungary; they still spoke with Yiddish accents; but it was they, more than anyone else, who reached the fantasies of America, indeed of the entire world—a universalism of taste which shaped the century and which they could shrewdly exploit because they innocently shared it."[35]

By the early 1920s most American Jews felt a powerful identification with the American promise. They fought loyally in the nation's wars and affirmed, whether metaphorically or literally, that America would be the new heaven and new earth where all people might enjoy equal liberty and a chance for prosperity. They decisively rejected, however, the extreme Americanizing posture that had characterized Reform Judaism during the 1880s. They did not feel the need to cast off their Jewish cultural heritage in order to be American. Even Reform was backtracking to this position. In 1922 Isaac Berkson summed up the meaning of these developments for the understanding of American identity: "The idea that the predominating stock of the inhabitants of the United States is Anglo-Saxon is a myth. The composite American is a multiform hyphenate." In short, many Jewish thinkers had taken the universalistic elements in the version of American identity offered by the Protestant mainstream and had made them into a charter for a more thoroughly pluralistic nation in which no group, religious or ethnic, could claim preeminence.[36]

At its outset, Mormonism exhibited in a heightened form the typical Protestant confidence in American destiny. America was both the beginning and the end of God's plan. The Garden of Eden had been located in Jackson County, Missouri, and when in 1830 God decided to restore the church through his prophet Joseph Smith and bring his purpose to eschatological fulfillment, he chose the continent where time had begun. America, the Book of Mormon made clear, was "a land . . . choice above all others." Mormons ardently professed republican sentiments and saw God's hand in the Constitution. As they endured hostility and persecution in Missouri and Illinois during the 1830s and 1840s, Mormons continued to profess that they were upholding the national identity against those who would destroy republican values.[37]

Yet early Mormons could not unambiguously affirm the United States as an elect nation, for it was their own community that formed the chosen people. The Latter-day Saints pointedly testified to this fact by calling non-Mormons "Gentiles." Unlike most Protestant Christians who awaited a spiritual kingdom and lived dispersed among other religious bodies, the Saints gathered as a separate people and sought to build a political millennial order over which they would exercise control. After assassins murdered Smith and Mormons began their trek to the Great Basin, the sense of separate destiny deepened, and many Saints shared the disgust of Brigham Young: "I never intend to winter in the United States [again] . . . we don't owe this country a single Sermon." Certainly they did not, Young suggested, owe anything to a country "as corrupt as Hell." Mormon identification with ancient Israel deepened during the great migration westward. Just as the Hebrews had marched through the Red Sea, the fleeing Saints walked across the frozen Mississippi River. Once in the Great Basin, they sought to erect their own protected domain. They quickly petitioned Congress for statehood, not because they wished to fuse with the rest of the American people but because they wanted to protect their distinctiveness under the mantle of states' rights. In 1852 Mormon singularity became even more apparent when the church publicly avowed what it had been practicing in secret for a decade: celestial marriage, or polygamy.[38]

By the 1880s it was clear that other Americans were not willing to leave Mormons undisturbed in their Rocky Mountain enclave. Protestant ministers kept up a drumbeat of criticism of the church for its practice of polygamy and for its endeavor, in Josiah Strong's words, to set up "a temporal kingdom." As early as 1862 Congress made bigamy a crime. Despite the feebleness of enforcement during the Civil War and early Reconstruction, the federal government had begun to move against Mormons in earnest by the end of the 1870s. The Supreme Court in 1879 ruled that polygamous marriages did not enjoy the protection of the "free exercise" clause of the First Amendment. In the following decade Congress passed laws subjecting polygamists to imprisonment and disfranchisement and threatening the Church of Latter-day Saints with the loss of its property. By 1887 the federal government had jailed more than two hundred Mormons and driven many more into hiding.[39]

In 1890, to protect the temporal interests of the church, President Wilford Woodruff issued his famous manifesto, indicating his intention to abide by federal anti-bigamy laws and urging his coreligionists to do the same. The church's concession prepared the way for the achievement of the Mormons' long-sought goal—statehood—in 1896. Ironically, in gaining that end Mormonism had to surrender a distinctive institution that statehood had supposedly been designed to protect. The abandonment of plural marriage was symptomatic of a wider series of changes. The hierarchy of the Latter-day Saints, although still active behind the scenes, gave up efforts to exercise direct control of public life in Utah. The effort to set economic policy largely collapsed under the pressures of a market economy. The People's Party, the political arm of Mormonism, was forced to disband in the 1890s. To ensure that not all Mormons flocked to one political party, church leaders went into the wards (the individual congregations) and assigned people to Democratic or Republican affiliation. Thus the Mormon move into the American system, although occurring under duress, nevertheless proceeded in a deliberate fashion.[40]

With these changes, the Latter-day Saints shifted toward a new understanding of themselves as a chosen people. In 1889, Edward Tullidge, a dissident Mormon, accurately summarized the direction in which the church was begrudgingly moving. "The idea never was," he insisted, "that this Latter-day Israel was to be as a kingdom within a kingdom. It never was marked down in the divine programme that this Zion of America was in any sense a foreign power (even of divine cast) to be formed within the native galaxy of the American Republic—a kingdom of God whose destiny it was to supersede and obliterate the present United States." Instead, the Mormon Zion's purpose was "to give a more glorious destiny to the American nation itself." As history, Tullidge's analysis was false, but as an indication of the path Mormonism was tracking his statement was accurate.[41]

Mormons found occasion to seal their patriotism in war. When the bombardment of Fort Sumter rent the Union in 1861, Mormon loyalty to the nation had been lukewarm at best. The Saints regarded that struggle as a judgment upon the nation for its mistreatment of Joseph Smith, and many suggested that the destruction of the United States would enable the Saints to reclaim their Zion in Missouri. Mormons exhibited an entirely different attitude to the conflict with Spain in 1898. Although not among the jingoists clamoring for war—a hesitation shared by many religious bodies—they enthusiastically supported the struggle once it had come. Utah filled its quota of volunteers more swiftly than most states, and Mormons soon fell in with the spirit of expansionism. One Mormon newspaper argued that the United States was fulfilling the prophecy in Daniel 2 wherein a stone smashes an image representing the kingdoms of this world and then grows to fill the world. Traditionally, Mormons had understood the stone to be the Mormon community itself, but the newspaper averred in June 1898 that it was the United States that, by its intervention in Cuba, had "struck the image of the Old World imperialism on its feet of iron and clay and shattered it to the four winds." Two months later the newspaper, echoing prevailing notions of Anglo-Saxon mission, spoke of the English-speaking peoples' global mission of "dragging from the dark recesses of ignorance and superstition millions of human beings and placing them within the benevolent power of human progress." As the United States first avoided and then plunged into another war in 1917, the Latter-day Saints again mirrored the shifting attitudes of the nation. At first supportive of American neutrality in the struggle between the Central Powers and the Allies, the Mormon community—despite President Joseph F. Smith's tepid endorsement of the declaration of war—championed the struggle with ardor. Mormon leaders urged the purchase of Liberty Bonds, Utahans volunteered for military service in large numbers, and the rhetoric of Latter-day Saints echoed the millennial visions of the nation's Protestant president, who saw the conflict as "the war to end all wars."[42]

By World War I, Mormonism had lost its status as a "near nation." Although not understanding themselves as merely one denomination among others, the Latter-day Saints had largely abandoned the effort to be an autonomous community. The idea of a kingdom of God in America remained deeply embedded in Mormon consciousness, but that hope increasingly resided in the nation at large. Moreover, the end of polygamy and the cessation of Mormon efforts to control tightly the economic and political life of Utah removed the practices that had set the Saints at variance with their neighbors. The traits that remained—emphasis upon hard work, self-improvement, material progress, and the family—made Mormons appear to be the quintessential stereotype of the solid citizen. These qualities, coupled with the abiding faith that the United States was indeed "a land . . . choice above all others," pointed the way toward the Mormon espousal in the twentieth century of conservative versions of American exceptionalism, versions that echoed more than a few of the ideals of mainstream Protestants in the 1800s.

In his provocative study of the origins of modern nationalism, Benedict Anderson argues that all national identities are the creation of imagination. Strangers who do not know one another believe and act as if they were members of a single intimate community. White Protestants offered a powerful mythology to create such an imagined community in the United States: God had providentially reserved a land of bounty where men and women might enjoy liberty and prosperity, exhibit the viability of democracy, and serve as an example to all humankind. Although frequently cloaked in Protestant language and overlaid with notions of Anglo-Saxon superiority, the underlying symbols of national identity were too protean to submit to the control of a single religious tradition. As David Howard-Pitney has observed, "On one level, 'America' refers to a particular society and polity; on another, it represents a mythical space of unlimited human potential. It is the setting in which humanity's dreams can and will be finally realized." Thus all the minority faiths surveyed in this chapter found creative ways of using that symbolism to affirm their own visions of American destiny—visions in which they as much as mainstream Protestants defined the meaning of America.[43]

To make this observation is not to suggest that all minority faiths engaged in a uniform process of Americanization. Each tradition tracked a different course—and often multiple courses—in its effort to come to terms with prevailing Protestant visions of the United States. Some Catholics attempted to recast the Protestant myth of national origins to place themselves near its center and stressed the congruence of Catholic values and American life. Others no less ardent in their love of the notion bifurcated Catholicism from Americanism, and it was this position that gained strength after Pope Leo's actions of 1899. In a strategy bearing some similarity to that of the Catholic liberals, many

Reform Jews asserted the Hebraic roots of American ideals and simultaneously sought to demonstrate that Judaism, purged of the taint of exotic particularities, was fully harmonious with prevailing American ideals. Yet as the Eastern Ashkenazic immigrants arrived in great numbers and as *Yiddishkeit* and the beginnings of Zionism stirred American Jewry, many sought another path than that of nineteenth-century Reform and argued that the very universality of American ideals permitted ethnic and religious particularities to flourish without in one whit detracting from loyalty to American ideals. To be an American was, in Isaac Berkson's phrase, to be "a multiform hyphenate." Some African Americans, flirting with various forms of black nationalism amid a rising tide of lynching and segregation, came close to a complete repudiation of mainstream understanding of America, but even in that community clever inversions of prevalent myths such as America as New Israel or as harbinger of the kingdom of God kept most African Americans in creative conversation with the mainstream. For Mormons, the change of attitude toward the meaning of America was dramatic. Hounded out of Missouri and Illinois before the Civil War and locked in a battle for survival in the 1870s and 1880s as the federal government sought to exterminate the faith's most distinctive institution, polygamy, the Mormon community appeared to be on the verge of losing any connection to a nation that was, in Brigham Young's words, "as corrupt as hell." At the end of the day, however, the desire to attain, via statehood for Utah, a limited sphere of autonomy prompted Mormons to abandon polygamy, and the way was clear for at least a partial identification of America itself (not merely the LDS) with the coming kingdom of God.

These various responses attested the extraordinary capacity of minority faiths to resist, adapt, and redefine prevailing mainstream Protestant notions of the meaning of America, and they also posed an implicit question: Could those Protestant ideas still be said to prevail by the 1920s? The French observer André Siegfried asked in 1927, "Will America remain Protestant and Anglo-Saxon?" Much Protestant activism in what John Higham has called the "Tribal Twenties" sought to assure an affirmative reply to the question. The enactment of immigration restriction legislation in 1924, the "hooded Americanism" of the revived Ku Klux Klan, the vicious anti-Semitism of the widely disseminated (and spurious) *Protocols of the Elders of Zion,* the vigorous defense of the amendment banning the sale and manufacture of alcoholic beverages, the attacks on the presidential candidacy of Al Smith because he was a "wet" on Prohibition and a Catholic in religion—all of these and similar endeavors demonstrated the visceral desire of many white Protestants to retain hegemony over the symbols defining America. Yet the ferocity of these responses signified weakness more than strength. Protestantism was enduring the pains of what Robert Handy has called "the second disestablishment," the Protestant loss of a commanding role in American culture.[44]

The loss was, of course, far from absolute, but it was still real. Protestants themselves contributed to that end by the internecine wars they fought during the fundamentalist-modernist controversy of the 1920s, a story beyond the scope of this discussion. But the point is that the minority faiths themselves played no small part in the weakening of white Protestant hegemony. Their creativity in adapting and reinterpreting the symbols of American destiny broadened the framework of discourse within which citizens explained national identity. That discourse still had room for much religious language, but Protestants could no longer presume that the right to moderate the conversation was theirs. Indeed, as Jonathan Sarna remarks in the introduction to this volume, the conversation about the meaning of America was already moving toward the broader, more pluralistic conception of American identity that Will Herberg would encapsulate in the title of his 1955 book, *Protestant, Catholic, Jew.* Nor would the conversation end with Herberg. A subsequent and even deeper pluralism has renewed, in what some choose to call "culture wars," the debate about the meaning of America.[45]

Notes

1. For a provocative and somewhat different account the relationship between the so-called mainstream and minority faiths, see R. Laurence Moore, *Religious Outsiders and the Making of Americans* (New York: Oxford University Press, 1986). The ambiguities of Protestant visions of America are treated at greater length in James H. Moorhead, "The American Israel: Protestant Tribalism and Universal Mission," in *Many Are Chosen: Divine Election and Western Nationalism*, ed. William R. Hutchison and Hartmut Lehmann (Minneapolis: Fortress Press, 1994), 145–66.

2. Josiah Strong, *Our Country: Its Possible Future and Its Present Crisis*, ed. Jurgen Herbst (New York: Baker and Taylor, 1885, repr. Cambridge: Harvard University Press, 1963), 253; Daniel Dorchester, *Christianity in the United States: From the First Settlement down to the Present Time* (New York: Phillips and Hunt, 1888), 779. For further information on American Protestants' views of American destiny, see Conrad Cherry, ed., *God's New Israel: Religious Interpretations of American Destiny* (Englewood Cliffs: Prentice-Hall, 1971); Winthrop S. Hudson, ed., *Nationalism and Religion in America: Con-*

cepts of American Identity and Mission (New York: Harper and Row, 1970); Robert T. Handy, *Undermined Establishment: Church-State Relations in America, 1880–1920* (Princeton: Princeton University Press, 1991); and John Edwin Smylie, "Protestant Clergymen and America's World Role, 1865–1900: A Study of Christianity, Nationality, and International Relations," Th.D. diss., Princeton Theological Seminary, 1959. For my interpretation of religious notions of American mission over the span of American history, see James H. Moorhead, "Theological Interpretations and Critiques of American Society and Culture," *Encyclopedia of the American Religious Experience: Studies of Traditions and Movements*, 3 vols. (New York: Charles Scribner's Sons, 1988), 1:101–15.

   3. John Higham, *Strangers in the Land: Patterns of American Nativism, 1860–1925*, 2d ed. (New York: Atheneum, 1971); David H. Bennett, *The Party of Fear: From Nativist Movements to the New Right in American History* (Chapel Hill: University of North Carolina Press, 1988) 183–237; Strong, *Our Country*, 205, 206; Dorchester, *Christianity in the United States*, 23–43 and passim.

   4. Strong, *Our Country*, 210; Dorchester, *Christianity in the United States*, 778; Higham, *Strangers in the Land*, 33. While Strong undeniably exhibited ethnocentrism in *Our Country*, he vigorously opposed the exploitation of Chinese and Africans by Western powers, stoutly championed the rights of black Americans, and progressively became an internationalist, stressing the interdependence of all people. See, for example, Wendy J. Deichmann, "Josiah Strong: Practical Theologian and Social Crusader for a Global Kingdom," Ph.D. diss., Drew University, 1991; Ralph E. Luker, *The Social Gospel in Black and White: American Racial Reform, 1885–1912* (Chapel Hill: University of North Carolina Press, 1991), esp. 268–75; Dorothea R. Muller, "Josiah Strong and American Nationalism: A Reevaluation," *Journal of American History* 53 (Dec. 1966): 487–503; and Ronald C. White, Jr., *Liberty and Justice for All: Racial Reform and the Social Gospel* (New York: Harper and Row, 1990), 18–20.

   5. Strong, *Our Country*, 102, 155, 163–64, 210; Dorchester, *Christianity in the United States*, 767–68, 778–79. On the influence of the jeremiad, see Sacvan Bercovitch, *The American Jeremiad* (Madison: University of Wisconsin Press, 1978).

   6. Strong, *Our Country*, 75; Dorchester, *Christianity in the United States*, 764; James Hennesey, *American Catholics: A History of the Roman Catholic Community in the United States* (New York: Oxford University Press, 1981), 116–220; Robert P. Swierenga, "Ethnoreligious Political Behavior in the Mid-Nineteenth Century: Voting, Values, Cultures," in *Religion and American Politics*, ed. Mark A. Noll (New York: Oxford University Press, 1990), 146–71.

   7. James Gibbons, *The Faith of Our Fathers: Being a Plain Exposition and Vindication of the Church Founded by Our Lord Jesus Christ*, enlarged ed. (Baltimore: John Murphy, 1895), 271, 275, 281.

   8. John Ireland, *The Church and Modern Society*, 2 vols. (New York: D. H. McBride, 1903), 1:59, 192; see also Marvin R. O'Connell, *John Ireland*

and the American Catholic Church (St. Paul: Minnesota Historical Society, 1988).

9. Anton H. Walburg, *The Question of Nationality in Relation to the Catholic Church in the United States* (1889) quoted in *American Catholic Thought on Social Questions,* ed. Aaron I. Abell (Indianapolis: Bobbs-Merrill, 1968), 43; Robert D. Cross, *The Emergence of Liberal Catholicism in America* (Cambridge: Harvard University Press, 1958), 24.

10. Abell, *American Catholic Thought,* 43; O'Connell, *John Ireland,* 455. On the division between Americanists and conservatives, see Cross, *The Emergence of Liberal Catholicism;* Robert Emmett Curran, *Michael Augustine Corrigan and the Shaping of Conservative Catholicism in America, 1878–1902* (New York: Arno Press, 1978); Philip Gleason, *The Conservative Reformers: German American Catholics and the Social Order* (Notre Dame: University of Notre Dame Press, 1968); Thomas T. McAvoy, *The Great Crisis in American Catholic History, 1895–1900* (Chicago: Henry Regnery, 1957).

11. John Louis Ciani, "Across a Wide Ocean: Salvatore Maria Brandi, S.J., and the *Civilta Cattolica,* from Americanism to Modernism, 1891–1914," Ph.D. diss., University of Virginia, 1992, 335; Ireland, *The Church and Modern Society,* 1:115.

12. Jay P. Dolan, *The American Catholic Experience: A History from Colonial Times to the Present* (Garden City: Doubleday, 1985), 311; Curran, *Michael Augustine Corrigan,* 499.

13. John Tracy Ellis, ed., *Documents of American Catholic History* (Milwaukee: Bruce Publishing, 1956), 553–65; Cross, *Emergence of Liberal Catholicism,* 182–224.

14. Curran, *Michael Augustine Corrigan,* 505–15; Dorothy Dohen, *Nationalism and American Catholicism* (New York: Sheed and Ward, 1967), 134–62; William M. Halsey, *The Survival of Innocence: Catholicism in an Era of Disillusionment, 1920–1940* (Notre Dame: University of Notre Dame Press, 1980); John Courtney Murray, *We Hold These Truths: Catholic Reflections on the American Proposition* (New York: Sheed and Ward, 1960).

15. Garnett quoted in Earl Ofari, *"Let Your Motto Be Resistance": The Life and Thought of Henry Highland Garnett* (Boston: Beacon Press, 1972), 201, 203. On these issues, see David Howard-Pitney, *The Afro-American Jeremiad: Appeals for Justice in America* (Philadelphia: Temple University Press, 1990), esp. 3–16; Wilson Jeremiah Moses, *The Golden Age of Black Nationalism, 1850–1925* (Camden: Archon, 1978); Albert J. Raboteau, *Slave Religion* (New York: Oxford University Press, 1978); Albert J. Raboteau, "'Ethiopia Shall Soon Stretch Forth Her Hands': Black Destiny in Nineteenth-Century America," University Lecture in Religion, Arizona State University, January 1983.

16. Turner is quoted in William E. Montgomery, *Under Their Own Vine and Fig Tree: The African American Church in the South, 1865–1900* (Baton Rouge: Louisiana State University Press, 1993), 204. See the remainder of the book for an overview of the African American experience in the postbellum South.

17. James Theodore Holly, "The Ethnological Development of the Divine Plan of Human Redemption," *AME Church Review* 1 (Oct. 1884): 79–

85. Holly's career is examined in David M. Dean, *Defender of the Race: James Theodore Holly, Black Nationalist Bishop* (Boston: Lambeth Press, 1979). On the missionary movement, see Sylvia M. Jacobs, ed., *Black Americans and the Missionary Movement in Africa* (Westport: Greenwood Press, 1982). For a more detailed analysis of millennial motifs, see Timothy E. Fulop, "'The Future Golden Day of the Race': Millennialism and Black Americans in the Nadir, 1877–1901," *Harvard Theological Review* 84, no. 1 (1991): 75–99.

18. Theophilus Gould Steward, *The End of the World; or, Clearing the Way for the Fullness of the Gentiles* (Philadelphia: A.M.E. Book Rooms, 1888), 122, 123–24, 135; see also William Seraile, *Voice of Dissent: Theophilus Gould Steward (1843–1924) and Black America* (Brooklyn: Carlson Publishing, 1991).

19. Holly is quoted in J. Carleton Hayden, "James Theodore Holly (1829–1911), First Afro-American Episcopal Bishop: His Legacy to Us Today," in *Black Apostles: Afro-American Clergy Confront the Twentieth Century*, ed. Randall K. Burkett and Richard Newman (Boston: G. K. Hall, 1978), 131, 133; and in *African-American Social and Political Thought, 1850–1920*, ed. Howard Brotz (New York: Basic Books, 1966), 169. Steward is quoted in Seraile, *Voice of Dissent*, 145, 155.

20. David W. Blight, *Frederick Douglass' Civil War: Keeping Faith in Jubilee* (Baton Rouge: Louisiana State University Press, 1989), 119, 219–39.

21. Booker T. Washington, "Address Delivered at Hampton Institute," Nov. 18, 1895, in *African-American Social and Political Thought*, ed. Brotz, 372.

22. The quotations are drawn from Washington's "Atlanta Exposition Address" (1895), "Our New Citizen" (1896), and "On Making Our Race Life Count in the Life of the Nation" (1906), as quoted in *African-American Social and Political Thought*, ed. Brotz, 359, 361, 380.

23. W. E. B. Du Bois, *The Souls of Black Folk* (Chicago: A. C. McClurg, 1903), 17. For information on this era, see August Meier, *Negro Thought in America, 1880–1915: Racial Ideologies in the Age of Booker T. Washington* (Ann Arbor: University of Michigan Press, 1963).

24. Quoted in Howard-Pitney, *Afro-American Jeremiad*, 105.

25. Garvey quoted in *African-American Social and Political Thought*, ed. Brotz, 576. See also Randall K. Burkett, *Garveyism as a Religious Movement: The Institutionalization of a Black Civil Religion* (Metuchen: Scarecrow Press, 1978); and Moses, *Golden Age of Black Nationalism*, 251–71.

26. Michael A. Meyer, *Response to Modernity: A History of the Reform Movement in Judaism* (New York: Oxford University Press, 1988), 227. See also Naomi W. Cohen, *Encounter with Emancipation: The German Jews in the United States, 1830–1914* (Philadelphia: Jewish Publication Society of America, 1984).

27. Sefton D. Temkin, *Isaac Mayer Wise: Shaping American Judaism* (New York: Oxford University Press, 1992), 266.

28. The Pittsburgh Platform as reproduced in Nathan Glazer, *American Judaism* (Chicago: University of Chicago Press, 1957), 151–52.

29. Emil G. Hirsch, "The Concordance of Judaism and Americanism," in Emil G. Hirsch, *Twenty Discourses* (New York: Bloch Publishing, [1906]), 8, 10, 15, 19, 20.

30. Abraham Cahan, *The Rise of David Levinsky*, introduction by John Higham (New York: Harper and Brothers, 1917, repr. New York: Harper and Row, 1960), 110, 111. On the Eastern European Jewish immigration, see Irving Howe, *World of Our Fathers: The Journey of the East European Jews to America and the Life They Found and Made* (New York: Simon and Schuster, 1976); and Moses Rischin, *The Promised City: New York's Jews, 1870–1914* (Cambridge: Harvard University Press, 1962).

31. Howe, *World of Our Fathers*, 417–59; Rischin, *Promised City*, 38–47, 115–220.

32. Mary Antin, *The Promised Land* (Boston: Houghton Mifflin, 1912), 141; Marcus Ravage, *An American in the Making: The Life Story of an Immigrant* (New York: Harper and Brothers, 1917), 42. For calling my attention to these citations, I am grateful to Diane Winston, "'A Place of Deliverance': Secular Millennialism among Eastern European Jewish Immigrants in the Nineteenth Century," Ph.D. seminar paper, Princeton Theological Seminary, 1993.

33. Melvin I. Urofsky, "Zionism: An American Experience," in *The American Jewish Experience*, ed. Jonathan D. Sarna (New York: Holmes and Meier, 1986), 211–21; quotations from Brandeis are on 216. See also Naomi Cohen, *American Jews and the Zionist Idea* (New York: Ktav Publishing House, 1975); and Stuart Knee, *The Concept of Zionist Dissent in the American Mind, 1917–1941* (New York: R. Speller, 1979).

34. Strong, *Our Country*, 26, 164, emphasis in the original; Andrew Heinze, *Adapting to Abundance: Jewish Immigrants, Mass Consumption, and the Search for American Identity* (New York: Columbia University Press, 1990), 6. For a thoughtful account of the implications of mass consumption for American culture as a whole, see Alan Trachtenberg, *The Incorporation of America: Culture and Society in the Gilded Age* (New York: Hill and Wang, 1982), 130–39; and T. J. Jackson Lears, *Fables of Abundance: A Cultural History of Advertising in America* (New York: Basic Books, 1994). The role of the Protestant mainstream in promoting consumerism as part of the national identity is suggestively probed in William Leach, *Land of Desire: Merchants, Power, and the Rise of a New American Culture* (New York: Pantheon Books, 1993), esp. 191–224; and in Leigh Eric Schmidt, *Consumer Rites: The Buying and Selling of American Holidays* (Princeton: Princeton University Press, 1995). See also the discussion of "the other Protestant ethic" in Colin T. Campbell, *The Romantic Ethic and the Spirit of Modern Consumerism* (New York: Basil Blackwell, 1987), 99–137.

35. Howe, *World of Our Fathers*, 165–66.

36. Isaac B. Berkson, *Theories of Americanization* (1920), quoted in *Nationalism and Religion*, ed. Hudson, 129.

37. Book of Mormon, I Nephi 13:30. For a perceptive account of early Mormonism as a claimant to the nation's republican tradition, see Kenneth

H. Winn, *Exiles in a Land of Liberty: Mormons in America, 1830–1846* (Chapel Hill: University of North Carolina Press, 1989). See also Leonard J. Arrington and Davis Bitton, *The Mormon Experience: A History of the Latter-day Saints* (New York: Alfred A. Knopf, 1979), 3–43; and Jan Shipps, *Mormonism: The Story of a New Religious Tradition* (Urbana: University of Illinois Press, 1985).

38. Young as quoted in Winn, *Exiles in a Land of Liberty,* 236; Arrington and Bitton, *Mormon Experience,* 83–184; Eugene E. Campbell, *Establishing Zion: The Mormon Church in the American West, 1847–1869* (Salt Lake City: Signature Books, 1988); Klaus J. Hansen, *Mormonism and the American Experience* (Chicago: University of Chicago Press, 1981), 113–46; Marvin S. Hill, *Quest for Refuge: The Mormon Flight from American Pluralism* (Salt Lake City: Signature Books, 1989); Shipps, *Mormonism,* 82.

39. Strong, *Our Country,* 109; Arrington and Bitton, *Mormon Experience,* 160–84; Edward Leo Lyman, *Political Deliverance: The Mormon Quest for Utah Statehood* (Urbana: University of Illinois Press, 1986), 7–123.

40. Lyman, *Political Deliverance,* 124–290; Thomas G. Alexander, *Mormonism in Transition: A History of the Latter-day Saints, 1890–1930* (Urbana: University of Illinois Press, 1986).

41. Tullidge is quoted in Klaus J. Hansen, *Quest for Empire: The Political Kingdom of God and the Council of Fifty in Mormon History* (East Lansing: Michigan State University Press, 1967, repr. Lincoln: University of Nebraska Press, 1974), 182–83.

42. For the quotations and the information regarding the Mormon response to American wars, I am indebted to Ronald W. Walker, "Sheaves, Bucklers, and the State: Mormon Leaders Respond to the Dilemmas of War," in *The New Mormon History: Revisionist Essays on the Past,* ed. D. Michael Quinn (Salt Lake City: Signature Books, 1992), 267–301.

43. Benedict Anderson, *Imagined Communities: Reflections on the Origin and Spread of Nationalism* (London: Verso, 1983), 31; Howard-Pitney, *Afro-American Jeremiad,* 5.

44. André Siegfried, *America Comes of Age* (1927), quoted in Martin E. Marty, *Modern American Religion,* vol. 2: *The Noise of Conflict, 1919–1941* (Chicago: University of Chicago Press, 1991), 63; David M. Chalmers, *Hooded Americanism: The History of the Ku Klux Klan,* 3d ed. (Durham: Duke University Press, 1987), esp. 28–38; Higham, *Strangers in the Land,* 264–99; Robert T. Handy, *A Christian America: Protestant Hopes and Historical Realities,* 2d ed. (New York: Oxford University Press, 1984), 159–84.

45. Will Herberg, *Protestant-Catholic-Jew: An Essay in American Religious Sociology* (Garden City: Doubleday, 1955); James Davison Hunter, *Culture War: The Struggle to Define America* (New York: Basic Books, 1991); see also Robert Wuthnow, *The Restructuring of American Religion: Society and Faith since World War II* (Princeton: Princeton University Press, 1988).

Contributors

R. SCOTT APPLEBY is associate professor of history and director of the Cushwa Center for the Study of American Catholicism at the University of Notre Dame. He is the author or coauthor of four books, including *The Ambivalence of the Sacred: Religion, Conflict, and Reconciliation*. With Martin E. Marty, he coedited the five volumes of the Fundamentalism Project.

JAMES D. BRATT is professor of history at Calvin College, Grand Rapids, Michigan, and a specialist in American religious history. He has written extensively on the history and culture of Dutch American communities in the Midwest, notably *Dutch Calvinism in Modern America: A History of a Conservative Subculture* (1984).

VIRGINIA LIESON BRERETON teaches at Tufts University and has written *Training God's Army: The American Bible School, 1880–1940* (1990) and *From Sin to Salvation: Stories of Women's Conversions, 1800 to the Present* (1991).

JAY P. DOLAN is professor of history at the University of Notre Dame. A historian of American religion, especially American Catholicism, his best known book is *The American Catholic Experience: A History from Colonial Times to the Present*. Most recently, he was the general editor of a three-volume work, *The Notre Dame History of Hispanic Catholics*.

ROBERT T. HANDY is Henry Sloane Coffin Professor Emeritus of Church History at Union Theological Seminary in New York. Since his formal retirement in 1986 he has served as a visiting scholar at Princeton University and adjunct professor at Drew University. In addition to articles, his most recent book is *Undermined Establishment: Church-State Relations in America, 1880–1920* (1991).

BENNY KRAUT is professor and director of Judaic studies at the University of Cincinnati. The former book review editor of *American Jewish History,* he is the author of *From Reform Judaism to Ethical Culture: The Religious Evolution of Felix Adler* (1979), *German-Jewish Orthodoxy in an Immigrant Synagogue* (1988), and major essays on Jewish-Christian relations in the United States.

JAMES H. MOORHEAD is the Mary McIntosh Bridge Professor of American Church History at Princeton Theological Seminary and the author of *American Apocalypse: Yankee Protestants in the Civil War, 1861–1869* (1978). He is completing a study of American Protestant ideas of the Kingdom of God in the late nineteenth and early twentieth centuries.

MARK NOLL is McManis Professor of Christian Thought at Wheaton College. He is the author of *Princeton and the Republic, 1768–1822* (1989) and *A History of Christianity in the United States and Canada* (1992).

JONATHAN D. SARNA is the Joseph H. and Belle R. Braun Professor of American Jewish History at Brandeis University. Among his publications are *The Jews of Boston,* with Ellen Smith (1995); *Religion and State in the American Jewish Experience,* with David G. Dalin (1997); and *The American Jewish Experience* (second edition, 1997).

JAN SHIPPS is professor emeritus of history and religious studies at Indiana University–Purdue University at Indianapolis. The author of *Mormonism: The Story of a New Religious Tradition* (1985), she is also the senior editor of *The Journals of William E. McLellin* (1994). She is working on a history of the Latter-day Saints since World War II.

DAVID W. WILLS is the Winthrop H. Smith '16 Professor of American History and American Studies (Religion and Black Studies) at Amherst College. He is coediting, with Albert J. Raboteau, a multivolume documentary history of African American religion.

Index

Abbelen, Peter, 237
Abbot, Lyman, 41
Abel, Theodore, 253, 274n68
Abingdon v. Schempp (1963), 317
Accommodation, 2, 5; Catholic, 61–63, 65–66; in public schools, 283–89
Acculturation: Catholic debates on, 66–71; Jewish, 15–16, 47; Jewish civic, 22–25; of Jewish nationalism, 35–39; Jewish social, 25–27, 53n33; Jewish religious, 27–35
Act Concerning Religion (Maryland 1649), 61
Adams, Henry, 41
Adams, John Quincy, 89
Adaptation, selective, 5
Adler, Felix, 24, 52n19
Adler, Samuel, 28
African American religion, 4, 187n114; biblicism of, 210–12; and biracial revivalism, 162, 184n83; "Church patriotism" in, 152; church-state separation supported by, 325–26; cultural and religious alienation of, 138, 174n6; denominations of, 149, 177n37, 178n40, 325; Garvey movement in, 170–72, 187n108, 187n109, 345–46; Islamicizing movements in, 170; and Kansas settlements, 145–48, 165, 176n26; optimism of, 140; separationist, 170, 345; triumphalism in, 342–43. *See also* African Methodist Episcopal Church; Black Baptists; Emigrationism, African; Exodus piety
African Americans: ambivalence toward America among, 343–44; civil rights struggles of, 326–29; education of, 300n7; Kansas settlements, 145–48, 165, 176n26; Northeastern and Mid-

western migration of, 168–70, 186n99; political subordination of, 139–40; Protestant-Catholic competition for, 255–59; in the South, 138–39, 174n7; special destiny of, 342–43, 344; Western migration of, 165–66, 167–68, 172–73, 184n90
African Methodist Episcopal Church, 149, 177n37; Astwood's race-neutral proposal for, 154–55; attempted mergers with other black Methodists, 163; emigrationism in, 149–50, 157–59, 180n49; exodus from St. George's Church, 150–53, 179n44, 180n49; formation of, 154, 180n50; historical memory of promoted, 153–54; missionary activities of, 157, 159; Payne's reform proposals for, 155–59, 181n60; Turner's influence on, 158–59
African Methodist Episcopal Zion Church, 149, 163, 177n37
Agudat ha-Rabbanim, 34, 35, 55n49, 56n54
Ahlstrom, Sydney, 2
Albanese, Catherine, 3
Alexander, S. D., 144
Ali, Noble Drew, 170, 345
Allen, Richard, 151–55, 180n49, 180n50
Amana Society, 208–9
American Baptist Home Mission Society, 160, 162, 233, 247
American Baptist Publication Society, 160, 161, 162, 212
American Bible Society (ABS), 194
American Bible Union, 205
American Colonization Society, 141–44, 159, 167, 186n96

50; anti-Reform stance of, 31–32; German Jews' conflicts with, 21–22, 50*n*12; Protestant disdain for, 41–42; public schooling urged upon, 291–92, 302*n*25; Yiddish culture of, 35, 348
Eddy, Mary Baker, 209
Edmunds Act (1882), 97, 312
Edmunds-Tucker Act (1887), 97, 100, 101*n*1
Einhorn, David, 28, 34, 245
Eisenstadt, S. N., 267
Eliot School case (1859), 288–89
Elliott, Walter, 243
Emigrationism, African, 140–45, 164, 166–67, 172, 175*n*11, 175*n*20, 341–42; African Methodist Episcopal, 149–50, 157–59; black Baptist, 160–62, 183*n*76; in Garveyism, 171–72, 187*n*109. *See also* Liberia
Enclaves: cultural, 8, 270*n*6; Catholic, 240; Mormon, 85, 88, 100–101; of Protestant immigrants, 6–7; strengthened by countermissionary activity, 235, 266, 269
English Revised Version of the New Testament, 194–95, 196
Entire sanctification, 208
Evangelical Protestants: biblicism of, 197; biracial revivalism, 162, 184*n*83; missionary drives of, 232–33, 246–50; response to Mormons, 94–95, 99–100
Evolutionary theory, 71, 75; in biblical criticism, 193
Exodus piety, 7, 138, 141, 174*n*6, 186*n*101; African emigrationist, 142–45, 157–59, 160–62, 164, 166–67, 172, 183*n*76, 341–42; in the AME Church exodus from St. George's, 150–53, 179*n*44; in AME independence, 154–55; in the "black Jewish" tradition, 168, 170; in the Garvey movement, 170–72, 187*n*109; in Islamicist movements, 170; in the settlement of Kansas, 146–48; in the settlement of Oklahoma, 165–66, 167, 168; in Western migration, 172–73, 184*n*90

Faunce, W. H. P., 41
Feldman, Egal, 51*n*14

Felsenthal, Bernhard, 28, 36
Field, Justice Stephen J., 308, 312, 321
Finke, Roger, 104*n*18
Fishberg, Maurice, 24
Fitzpatrick, Bishop John, 284, 287
Flaget, Benedict, 65
Fleischer, Rabbi Charles, 24, 52*n*19
Flipper, Joseph S., 182*n*71
Foote, Julia A. J., 216–17
Frank, Leo, 47
Fraternal organizations: African American, 168, 185*n*92; Jewish, 27, 43
Free African Society, 180*n*49
Free Religious Association, 41, 42
Freedmen's Emigrant Aid Society, 143
Friedlander, Israel, 15, 32, 33, 37, 38, 51*n*18, 55*n*47
Fuller, Justice Melville W., 308, 320
Fulop, Timothy E., 230*n*100
Fulton, Justin D., 316
Funk, John, 117

Gaebelein, Arno, 247, 248, 272*n*37
Gaines, Bishop W. J., 218
Garnett, Rev. Henry Highland, 341
Garvey, Marcus Mosiah, 170–72, 187*n*108, 187*n*109, 345–46
Gary Plan (1917), 290
Gaston, Benjamin, 160
Gaustad, Edwin Scott, 331*n*3
Genovese, Eugene D., 219, 231*n*103
Gerber, David A., 176*n*25
Gibbons, Cardinal James (archbishop of Baltimore): American values defended by, 238, 338; Catholic use of the Bible defended by, 205–6; on church-state separation, 316; and missions to African Americans, 256; in the modernism debates, 72
Gideons, 195
Gilbert, Arthur, 323
Gladden, Washington, 41
Godbey, W. B., 208
Goldrich, Leon, 291
Goldstein, Rabbi Herbert, 33
Goldwasser, Edwin, 291
Goodspeed, Edgar J., 219
Gorelick, Sherry, 292
Gottheil, Richard, 36
Grabau, Johannes A. A., 120, 122

Willowski, Rabbi Jacob David, 1–2, 34
Wilson, Woodrow, 194
Wise, Rabbi Isaac M.: Americanism of,
5 1*n*16, 138, 346; on Bible reading in
public schools, 199–200; countermis-
sionary activity of, 232, 248, 249; and
the problem of intermarriage, 245;
Reform Judaism influenced by, 28, 29
Wise, Rabbi Stephen S., 36
Wolf, Simon, 45
The Woman's Bible, 212, 215, 216
Women reformers: biblicism of, 210–16,
229*n*79
Woodruff Manifesto, 81–82, 98, 99,
101*n*1, 101*n*2, 313–14, 352
Woodworth-Etter, Maria, 162
World Parliament of Religions, 41
World War I: attacks on Protestant im-
migrants during, 110–11, 112; Mis-

souri Synod Lutherans' counteroffensive on, 123–24; Mormon patriotism
during, 353
Wright, Richard R., 178*n*42

Yamma, Bristol, 141
Yeocum, Rev. W. H., 150–51, 152
Yeshiva University, 31
Yiddish, 33–34, 35, 348
Young, Brigham, 91, 93, 236, 310, 351
Young Israel synagogue movement, 33

Zahm, John, 75
Zangwill, Israel, 38
Zhitlovsky, Chaim, 38–39
Zionism: Americanization of, 36–37,
349; cultural, 37–38; in premillennial
theology, 246–47; Reform Jews' de-
nunciation of, 30